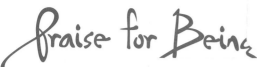
Praise for Being

"I think this text is theoretically sound, useful, non-patronizing, and resourceful. Kudos to Elbow and Belanoff."

B. Cole Bennett, Abilene Christian University

"This text makes me want to teach 101 again! It makes me want to write *with* my students."

Cheryl L. Johnson, University of Idaho

"Overall, the book makes a great attempt to give students' writing back to them—a noble goal."

Jacqueline Rhodes, California State University—San Bernardino

"I doubt if anyone can speak more confidently and effectively than Elbow and Belanoff when it comes to matters of voice. [. . .] Elbow and Belanoff seem to have culled the best material from their years of classroom experience and present it here in a text that will please students and instructors alike."

Alison Russell, Xavier University

"I loved the chapter on research, as well as the chapter on interviewing as part of the research process. [. . .] The section on analyzing on-line sources (and the class activity that goes with this section) was superb."

Michelle Toby, Pasadena City College

"The research section was one of my favorites. I liked the frank and casual approach to explaining to students the value of research and how the authors really de-mystified the whole process."

Julie Abraham, South Dakota State University

"I find the research coverage to be excellent, one of the best I've seen."

Lawrence Rodgers, Kansas State University

"The language is extremely accessible—friendly without being patronizing."

Martha Marinara, University of Central Florida

"[*Being a Writer*] is a pleasure to read."

Alison Russell, Xavier University

"I especially liked the frank, casual, and friendly, almost conversational tone of the explanatory and theoretical sections. [. . .] I enjoyed reading almost every word, and I think most students would, too."

Julie Abraham, South Dakota State University

"The book has an especially good tone—conversational, warm, and helpful, but not condescending."

Sally Crisp, University of Arkansas at Little Rock

"A resounding Yes! in terms of trying it."

Michelle Toby, Pasadena City College

"I loved this book. I would adopt it for my class in a heartbeat."

B. Cole Bennett, Abilene Christian University

i

Being a Writer

Being a Writer

A Community of Writers Revisited

Peter Elbow

University of
Massachusetts at
Amherst

Pat Belanoff

State University of
New York at
Stony Brook

Mc Graw Hill

Boston   Burr Ridge, IL   Dubuque, IA   Madison, WI   New York
San Francisco   St. Louis   Bangkok   Bogotá   Caracas   Kuala Lumpur
Lisbon   London   Madrid   Mexico City   Milan   Montreal   New Delhi
Santiago   Seoul   Singapore   Sydney   Taipei   Toronto

McGraw-Hill Higher Education

*A Division of The **McGraw-Hill** Companies*

BEING A WRITER: A COMMUNITY OF WRITERS REVISITED

Published by McGraw-Hill, a business unit of The McGraw-Hill Companies, 1221 Avenue of the Americas, New York, NY, 10020. Copyright © 2003, by The McGraw-Hill Companies, Inc. All rights reserved. No part of this publication may be reproduced or distributed in any form or by any means, or stored in a database or retrieval system, without the prior written consent of The McGraw-Hill Companies, Inc., including, but not limited to, in any network or other electronic storage or transmission, or broadcast for distance learning. Some ancillaries, including electronic and print components, may not be available to customers outside the United States.

This book is printed on acid-free paper.

1 2 3 4 5 6 7 8 9 0 DOC/DOC 0 9 8 7 6 5 4 3 2

ISBN 0-07-237873-5

Publisher: *Steve Debow*
Executive editor: *Lisa Moore*
Senior developmental editor: *Alexis Walker*
Senior marketing manager: *David S. Patterson*
Senior media producer: *Todd Vaccaro*
Project manager: *Christina Thornton-Villagomez*
Production supervisor: *Carol A. Bielski*
Cover design: *Mary E. Kazak*
Photo research coordinator: *Jeremy Cheshareck*
Photo researcher: *David Tietz*
Interior design: *Maureen McCutcheon*
Typeface: *10/12 Garamond*
Compositor: *ElectraGraphics, Inc.*
Printer: *R. R. Donnelley and Sons Company*

Library of Congress Cataloging-in-Publication Data

Elbow, Peter.
    Being a writer: a community of writers revisited/Peter Elbow, Pat Belanoff.
      p. cm.
    Includes index.
    ISBN 0-07-237873-5 (alk. paper)
    1. English language—Rhetoric. 2. Report writing. I. Belanoff, Pat. II. Title.
  PE1408 .E378 2003
  808'.042—dc21

                                                                        2002021279

www.mhhe.com

About the Authors

Peter Elbow

Peter Elbow is emeritus professor of English at the University of Massachusetts at Amherst where he directed the Writing Program. Before writing *A Community of Writers* and *Being a Writer,* he wrote two other books about writing: *Writing without Teachers* and *Writing with Power: Techniques for Mastering the Writing Process.* He is the author of a book of essays about learning and teaching, *Embracing Contraries.* In addition, he wrote *What Is English?,* which explores current issues in the profession of English, *Oppositions in Chaucer,* and numerous essays about writing and teaching. His most recent book is *Everyone Can Write: Essays toward a Hopeful Theory of Writing and Teaching Writing.*

He has taught at the Massachusetts Institute of Technology, Franconia College, Evergreen State College, and the State University of New York at Stony Brook—where for five years he directed the Writing Program. He served for four years on the Executive Council of the Modern Language Association and was a member of the Executive Committee of the Conference on College Composition and Communication. He has given talks and workshops at many colleges and universities.

He attended Williams College and Harvard University and has an MA from Exeter College, Oxford University, and a PhD from Brandeis University.

Pat Belanoff

Pat Belanoff is associate professor of English at the State University of New York at Stony Brook. She has been both president of the SUNY Council on Writing and a member of the College Steering Committee of NCTE. Pat is a coauthor (with Betsy Rorschach and Mia Oberlink) of *The Right Handbook,* now in its second edition. She has also coedited (with Marcia Dickson) *Portfolios: Process and Product* and (with Peter Elbow and Sheryl Fontaine) *Nothing Begins With an N: New Investigations of Freewriting.* Pat has a doctorate in medieval literature from New York University and continues to teach and publish in this area too.

Brief Contents

Contents

PART II   Revising

Sharing and Responding

To the Student

This book has two main messages: Writing is hard. Writing is easy.

It's no secret that writing is hard—or at least that writing *well* is hard. Still, it's useful to explore the nature of that difficulty.

Imagine you are having a relaxed, interesting conversation with your best friend. You're in a comfortable room where you both feel right at home. You are both talking with great pleasure. You find you have lots to say because you like talking to this person who likes you and is interested in what you have to say.

Then someone else comes into the room and starts listening to the conversation. A friend. But quickly you feel that something is peculiar because this friend doesn't say anything, doesn't join in, only listens. It makes you feel a little funny, but you keep up your talking.

Then more people start coming in. Some of them are strangers and they don't say anything either: They just listen.

Then someone pulls out a tape recorder and starts recording what you say.

Finally your friend, even though she won't join in the conversation, starts quizzing you as you are talking and asks:

- "Are you really sure that what you are saying is interesting?"
- "Are you sure that what you are saying is right?"
- "Are you sure you understand what you are saying?"

And she doesn't just ask questions, she gives "helpful suggestions":

- "Make sure that what you say is well organized."
- "Think carefully about who is listening. Are you speaking in a way that suits these listeners?"
- "Watch your language; don't make any mistakes in grammar; don't sound dumb."

This is an allegory of writing. In writing, you must keep on putting out words, but no one answers or responds. You are putting out words for an audience but you don't know how they are reacting. You may know who the intended reader is (often someone who will *grade* your writing), but you don't really know who else *might* read it—who might find it lying around. You are trying to get your thinking right, your organization right, and your language right—all at the same time. And there are spelling and punctuation to worry about too.

No wonder writing is hard.

But we have another message: Writing is easy. Writing is easier than talking because it's safer than talking. For you can "say" something on paper and no one has to see it. If you've ever blurted out something wrong to the wrong person and wanted to bite your tongue off as soon as the words came out of your mouth, you know that you can never undo what you've spoken. But in writing you can blurt out anything and see what it looks like on paper and no one ever needs to see it. Even you don't ever have to see it again. Writing is safer than talking.

Writing lets you "talk" about any topic at all, even if you don't know anyone who is interested enough to listen. And there are certain things it's hard to talk about with anyone. Writing lets you "talk" to anyone—"tell them" anything—and you can decide later whether to show it to them.

People expect you to make sense when you talk; otherwise, they'll stop listening or think you're odd. But you don't have to make any sense when you write. You can go on and on forever when you write; you can't do that in speech because people will stop listening after a while no matter how much they like you.

Admittedly, in describing how easy writing is, we're talking about writing in itself, not about *good* writing. It gets harder when "good" enters the picture or when you're writing for a tough reader, particularly a tough reader who will judge the writing.

But even when your goal is to produce good writing for a harsh judge, you can *start out* this way, just writing for yourself. Afterward, it's not so hard to revise it and *make* it good. When you do all that easy writing, surprising amounts of it are already pretty good. Those parts that are *potentially* good but badly written are not so hard to fix up once you've got them down in one form or another. And the parts that are bad or useless are easy to drop. *What's hardest about writing is simply unnecessary: trying to get it right the first time.*

Behind what we've just said is the fact that writing requires two mental abilities that are so different that they usually conflict with each other: the ability to *create* an abundance of words and ideas; and the ability to *criticize* and discard words and ideas. To write well we need to be both generative and cutthroat. You probably know how frustrating it is trying to use both "muscles" at once: trying to come up with as many words and ideas as possible, while trying at the same time to make sure that none of them is wrong or weak. It's like trying to pat your head while you rub your belly. We get stuck. But we can get unstuck if we separate the two mental processes: We can think of more words and ideas if we hold off all criticism (as in brainstorming); and we can be more critical and tough-minded if we have already piled up more words and ideas than we need.

In short, even though writing gets most of us into the pickle of trying to use two muscles that work against each other, it is writing that creates the ideal conditions for using those muscles one at a time.

About the Structure of this Book

Workshops

The workshops make up the main part of the book. They contain the activities and main writing assignments (one major assignment per workshop). Each workshop has a different focus and offers a different kind of learning experience. We believe that most of the learning will come from these workshop activities and assignments, not from any ideas or information we give. Twelve workshops are too many for one semester, but you might want to try your hand informally at those workshops your teacher leaves out.

Some of the workshops ask you to write something that builds upon what you wrote for an earlier one, but all the workshops can stand on their own. Whatever sequence of workshops your teacher uses, *make sure* to keep all your writing for your portfolio and for possible later use.

At the end of most workshops, we have included a section titled "Ruminations and Theory." In these sections we share some of the ideas that interest us most about writing, thinking, and language. We hope you'll join us as we explore. But we have no doubt that the main way you learn is by doing the workshop's activities, not by reading theory. We won't feel bad if you skip them.

Sharing and Responding

In 56 pages near the end of this book, we've explained all the good methods we know for getting feedback from classmates on your writing. It's easy to jump to this final section because all the pages have shaded edges. The ability to give responses to your classmates' writing and to get their responses to your own writing may be the most important thing you learn from this book. You can use these feedback techniques in pairs or in small groups. You can use them for all writing tasks, in school and out. We have a separate introduction to that section. ("Sharing and Responding" is also available separately, in print and online.)

Prologue and Appendix

The prologue is a "Writing Skills Questionnaire" that can help you learn much more from our book. Even if your teacher does not ask you to fill it out, you will find it useful. The appendix, "Writing under Pressure," is a series of pointers on handling essay exams and other kinds of stress situations.

We would like feedback on our book. Please tell us which parts work well for you and which parts don't. If you can tell us why, that's even better. Which aspects of your writing change and which aspects seem unchanged? In our workshops we're trying to issue invitations, not orders, but that's not easy in a school setting. We welcome your feedback about all this as well as about individual workshops and assignments. Maybe someday we'll revise this book, but our main feeling now is one we're sure you often feel about a writing task: relief at calling it done—at least for now.

Peter Elbow
Pat Belanoff

To the Instructor

The book you are holding is a condensed revision of the third edition of *A Community of Writers*. We have put this book together for first-year college students in a one-semester writing course.* We've made our book as practical as we can, with lots of hands-on workshop activities. But we don't hide our interest in theory; our book reflects much recent scholarship in composition. And we push students to become thoughtful about their writing process through regular entries in a writing-process diary.

This book is much like its parent, *A Community of Writers*. It teaches writing through a series of active experiential workshops rather than through discursive instruction. But we've eliminated almost all readings because we recognize that many teachers like to provide their own readings and some programs require students to use a separate reader of some kind. We've added to each workshop a mini-exercise called "Writing as Play." Too often a writing class is all work and no play; play is good for its own sake, but it can also be a good teacher. We've also cut a few workshops, used a new sequence, and made many smaller revisions throughout.

In using this book, teachers face hard questions: How long shall I spend on each workshop? Which workshops shall I use? What order shall I choose? In response we have bad news and good news. The bad news is that we have never been able to figure out the right sequence. The good news is that even though we're never satisfied when we teach the first year writing course (the hardest teaching there is), we can't think of many wrong answers to those questions. That is, what strikes us as most important in teaching writing is not the choice of activities or how long to spend on them, but whether the activities are *good* ones and are used with an active *workshop* approach, and whether these activities are used with the right *spirit:* humane, respectful, and writerly. Still, we are willing to offer some concrete advice.

---

*This book will also be useful for high school seniors or college sophomores or juniors—for we haven't much differentiated our audience in terms of age or skill level. The core of our book is a series of writing activities that we have found appropriate whether we're working with young children or college faculty.

1. *How long to spend on each workshop?* Each workshop consists of a set of activities designed to illustrate and teach an important dimension of writing; each has a main assignment and subsidiary exercises. When faced with lots of wonderful things to do, haste is a danger. You can spend as little as a week on a few workshops that you don't want to emphasize too much, but we find it a killing schedule to reduce very many to a week.

2. *Which workshops to use and in what order?* As you see from the brief table of contents, we have divided the workshops in this brief edition into three sections: (1) Creativity and the Writing Process; (2) Revising; and (3) Important Intellectual and Academic Tasks.

   We suggest that you choose a few workshops from each category. If you are teaching a regular one-semester writing course and have twelve to fourteen weeks, here is our advice: from the first section, choose the first workshop and two others; from the second section, choose two of the three workshops; and from the third section, choose the last workshop and two others. This makes eight workshops. You might choose nine workshops if you are impatient for more and are efficient at management. Choose seven if you want to make sure you don't feel rushed (particularly if your semester is shorter).

   If you happen to be teaching a first-semester course that will be followed by a second semester that emphasizes argument, persuasion, and academic research, you might choose fewer workshops from the third section. If you feel your students are already skilled and experienced writers, you might be tempted to choose fewer from the first section; however, we discourage this. We keep finding that even the most skilled writers (including teachers) benefit from exploring the complex and generative processes at the heart of writing.

3. *Which workshops in particular?* This is a personal choice, and we don't think there are wrong answers. But if we had to choose a likely default sequence of eight workshops, here's what we come up with (this week!): Workshops 1, 3, 4, 5, 7, 8, 9, 12.

We've tried above all to make a book that is *writerly*. The basic principle that guided us as we wrote and revised and attended to feedback is that we all learn writing best by writing: writing a great deal, in various modes, to various audiences, and with ample feedback (but not too much) from diverse readers. This book is not a handbook that lays out rules of grammar or guidelines for good usage—nor even principles of good writing. It is a book of writing activities.

Our *prologue* offers a skills questionnaire that we've found crucial for helping our students learn better. It's best to ask students to fill this out at the beginning of the semester, again in the middle, and finally at the end. They should refer to it when completing their portfolios, as it will provide some personal history for them to contemplate.

Our *appendix*, "Writing under Pressure," offers students practical advice on handling in-class exams and other kinds of writing in conditions of stress.

About "Sharing and Responding"

As you can easily see from the way "Sharing and Responding" stands out at the end of the book, it is not like a workshop that you cover at a certain point in the semester. Instead, it is meant to be used with *every* workshop and indeed with any writing situation you set up for students.

"Sharing and Responding," is an unusual feature we're particularly proud of: a series of graduated activities designed to help students learn to respond usefully to each other's writing. ("Sharing and Responding" is also available separately in print and online.) We've met many teachers who say, "Peer feedback doesn't work." We're convinced, from our own experience, that it *does*. We believe it's a matter of giving students more guidance; that's what this final section of our book aims to do.

When Peter Elbow published *Writing without Teachers* in 1973, peer response groups were little known, and the idea of students working by themselves in groups to give feedback to each other's writing tended to be dismissed as "the blind leading the blind." Since that time, however, peer response has come to be accepted by most writing teachers and scholars in composition as useful and important to the teaching of writing. Yet even now, few textbooks give specific and detailed help to students for engaging in this complex activity. And students sometimes think of peer feedback as merely an idiosyncratic, experimental activity that their particular teacher happens to like.

We've learned that teachers with the widest range of diverse styles and approaches to the teaching of writing often want their students to learn to use peer response. But many teachers have learned that it's no good saying blithely, "Okay, now get into groups and give feedback to each other." Trying it this way—without preparation and sustained help—has led many teachers to declare, "I tried peer response groups and they just don't work!"

We've written the "Sharing and Responding" section to remedy this problem. Students can give each other remarkably useful and productive feedback on their writing if they are given substantive help and instruction. And they usually take the process more seriously and do a better job when they see this help laid out carefully in a published book, not just in *ad hoc* teacher handouts and oral instructions.

In this section of our text, then, we have gathered together a full and detailed sequence of activities and techniques for students to use in sharing their writing with each other and giving and receiving useful feedback. We start with plain sharing—no response at all—and then work through a developing sequence for helping students respond to each other's writing. These techniques build gradually from safety and simplicity to greater risk and complexity. We urge you to lead students through the sequence in the order we present it. Even so, students need to understand that any one of the "Sharing and Responding" sections can be usefully applied to any assignment— though, as you'll see in the workshops themselves, we do make suggestions about which type of feedback might be most helpful for a particular assignment.

The ultimate goal for peer responding is for the *writer* to be in control of the process: The writer, not the reader, should decide what kind of responses he or she needs for a given draft. But it's no good telling someone, "Ask for whatever kind of feedback you want," if that person doesn't know many options. Thus, we urge you to take at least half the term to help students *try out* all these techniques for responding to each other's writing.

When we use these techniques for peer responding, we sometimes ask students to work in pairs, sometimes in small groups. We sometimes change groups during the semester; often we stick with stable pairs or groups so that students can build up safety by coming to trust each other. We sometimes try for both goals by keeping permanent pairs throughout the semester and periodically shifting the *pairings* of pairs to make new groups of four.

Please note. Before sending students into pairs or groups to learn a new kind of response technique, it's *crucial* to illustrate and practice it in the whole class on one or two sample texts.

Acknowledgments

We are grateful for help in what (like most writing and revising tasks) has proved to be a bigger job than we expected. We thank our numerous friends and colleagues who tried out early drafts and used the first three editions of *A Community of Writers,* and we thank the students in their classes and in our own. These students and teachers have given us many good comments that have guided us during this rewriting. As always, we thank the students who have taught us and allowed us to use their work. We thank Lisa Moore, our editor, for all her wise help and encouragement. We thank the McGraw-Hill production staff for their talent and professionalism. But we feel a special debt of gratitude to Alexis Walker, development editor, for her amazingly hard work, deft skill, and discerning taste in seeing the whole process through to completion. We feel lucky to have had the chance to work with her. We greatly appreciate the helpful and detailed feedback we received from many reviewers: Richard L. Larson, Carol Singley, Michael Steinberg, John Trimbur, Maureen Hoag, Susan Kirschner, Jane Terry Lee, Ben W. McClelland, M. Terry Mitze, Betty P. Pytlik, Nancy L. Schultz, and Pia S. Walters, Nancy S. Thompson, John M. Clark, Veronica M. Keane, Mara Holt, Patricia H. Perry, Yeno Matuka, Richard C. Wing, Diane Dowdey, Karen S. Uehling, George P. E. Meese, Lindal Buchanan, Julie Bergan Abraham, Kelly Bradbury-Veldhuisen, Stephanie G. Walker, Alison Russell, Dana Morgan, Jan Hoegh, Lucinda Coombs, Gwynda Casey, B. Cole Bennett, Jacqueline Rhodes, William Johnson, Judith G. Gardner, Lawrence Rodgers, Martha Marinara, Sally Crisp, Paul Almonte, James Kastely, Michelle Toby, Heidemarie Z. Weidner, Cheryl L. Johnson, and Lisa J. McClure. Barbara Jones of Sam Houston State University shared with us a journal of her class's experience with the text across an entire semester; many thanks to her and to her students. Joan Mullin of the University of Toledo offered many valuable insights, particularly concerning the approach to visual literacy. Justin Brent of the State University of New York at Stony Brook contributed an excellent review of the text and some of the material on the Web in Workshop 11. We extend our sincerest thanks for his fruitful collaboration.

We also thank Doris Alkon, Paul Connolly, Gene Doty, Abigail Elbow, Cami Elbow, Claire Frost, Laurie Kutchins, Glen Klopfenstein, Irene Papoulis, Marlene Perl, Pat Perry, Debrah Raschke, Valerie Reimers, Barbara Rhodes, John Wright, and Frances Zak.

Peter Elbow
Pat Belanoff

Prologue: Writing Skills Questionnaire

To help you get more out of our text and take more control over your own learning, we've made a list of specific writing skills we are attempting to teach. If you fill out the questionnaire, you will notice better what you are learning and not learning—and you will thereby help us do a better job of teaching you. You will benefit *most* from this questionnaire if you fill it out three times—at the beginning, middle, and end of the course. This will help you monitor and control your learning more closely.

You'll see below a series of questions for you to answer—questions that will help you see more clearly what you can do well and what is still hard for you. In short, these questions take the large and multidimensional ability to write well and break it down into its many dimensions. Answer each question by putting a letter in the appropriate column to the left of the question.

Use the letter **Y** for **YES**, the letter **N** for **NO**, the letter **S** for **SORT OF**, and a question mark **?** for **I DON'T KNOW**.

Beginning	Middle	End	
			Attitudes toward Writing
___	___	___	Do you enjoy writing?
___	___	___	In general, do you trust yourself as a person who can find good words and ideas and perceptions?
___	___	___	Do you think of yourself as a writer?
			Generating
___		___	Can you freewrite—that is, can you put down your words and thoughts as they come to you and put your whole attention on those words and thoughts and not on questions of whether they are alright?
___		___	Can you use private freewriting to figure out what you think or feel about something or figure out what you ought to do?

Beginning	Middle	End

On a topic that *doesn't* much interest you (perhaps an assigned topic), can you nevertheless generate lots of ideas and words fairly quickly and freely—not be stuck?

Can you come up with ideas or insights you'd not thought of before?

Revising

Can you read through a rough messy draft and find a main point or something to build on?

Can you revise in the literal sense: "re-see"—to rethink and change your mind about major things you have said? That is, can you find a *new* shape or focus in a piece of your writing that you had already shaped or focused?

Can you adjust something you've written to fit the needs of particular readers?

Can you find problems in your reasoning or logic and straighten them out?

Can you revise your sentences so they are clear to readers on a first reading?

Can you make your sentences lively? Can you give them a human voice?

Copyediting

Can you get rid of most mistakes in grammar, spelling, and punctuation—enough so that most readers are not put off?

Can you get rid of virtually *all* such mistakes—so that even picky readers are not put off?

Feedback

Can you enjoy sharing with friends a draft of what you've written?

Can you read out loud to listeners a draft of your writing in such a way that you really "give" it—so that you don't mumble or hold back?

Can you openly listen to the reactions of a reader to your writing and *try* to see it as she sees it, even if you think her reactions are all wrong?

Beginning	Middle	End

Can you give noncritical feedback—telling the writer what you like and summarizing or reflecting what you hear the words saying?

Can you give movies of your mind as a reader—a clear story of what was happening in your mind as you were reading someone's writing?

Can you give criterion-based feedback—telling the writer how the draft matches up against the most common criteria of good writing?

Collaboration

Can you work on a task collaboratively with a partner or a small group: pitch in, share the work, help the group cooperate, keep the group on the task?

Awareness and Control of Writing Process

Can you give a detailed story of what was going on when you were writing—a story of your thoughts and feelings and a story of what was happening in the writing itself?

Can you notice problems or "stuck points" in your writing process and begin to figure out what the causes are?

Can you vary the way you go about writing—depending on your analysis of your writing process, or depending on the topic, audience, and type of writing?

Creativity and the Writing Process

PART I

Discovering Yourself as a Writer

An Introduction to the Variety of Writing Processes

Essential Premises

Everyone can learn to become comfortable putting words and thoughts down on paper. Writing doesn't have to be a struggle.

There is no one thing, "writing." Your experience will vary with your situation—especially depending on topic, audience, and kind of writing. It helps to learn different "writing gears."

You can improve your writing best by learning to notice and reflect on how you usually write.

Main Assignment Preview

We have three related goals for this workshop.

1. First, we will show you how to get words and thoughts on paper quickly, easily, and productively—helping you realize that there are always plenty more where they came from. In this way we can help you build a foundation of confidence in the face of a blank page—confidence you can draw on later when writing tasks get harder. Our emphasis here is on *generating* words and ideas.

2. Second, we will introduce you to a wide variety of *kinds* of writing—to show you that there is no one thing, "writing," but rather different kinds of writing for different situations.

3. Third, we will use short pieces of writing to help you become more conscious of what you are doing as you write so that you can take more control of your own writing process.

The heart of this workshop is a series of short writing tasks that involve different writing processes. Some of the pieces will be for others to read and some only for yourself; some pieces will have a specified topic and some will not. Your teacher will probably ask you to do some of this writing in class and some of it at home. By trying out different kinds of writing and reflecting on what is happening each time, you will get over something that causes many people trouble: the tendency to use just one "writing gear" for every writing task.

Your *main assignment* is to create a collage of good passages so as to build a kind of portrait of yourself as a writer at this point. This will be a piece of finished writing that you can share with others and with your teachers. We won't do much with revising in this workshop, but we'll show you how to use a kind of cut-and-paste revising process that is ideal for making a collage.

A Spectrum of Writing Tasks

Activity One: Freewriting

Freewriting means writing privately and writing without stopping. Take 10 minutes now and just write whatever words come to your mind; or write about whatever you want to explore at this moment.

Don't worry about whether your writing is any good or even whether it makes sense. Don't worry about spelling or grammar. If you can't think of the word you want, just put down a squiggle. Keep on writing and see what comes. If you run out of something to say, just write "I have nothing to say"—or write about how you feel at the moment—or keep repeating the last word or the last sentence. Or write swear words. More will come.

Exploring the Writing Process
On Scribbling

There seems to be a sort of fatality in my mind leading me to put at first my statement and proposition in a wrong or awkward form. Formerly I used to think about my sentences before writing them down; but for several years I have found that it saves time to scribble in a vile hand whole pages as quickly as I possibly can, contracting half the words; and then correct deliberately. Sentences thus scribbled down are often better ones than I could have written deliberately.

Charles Darwin

Don't worry about trying to write fast and capture *everything* that comes to mind. The main thing in freewriting is trusting yourself and trusting your words: take a spirit of adventure. The no stopping doesn't mean you have to hurry or be tense. You can write slowly and take time to breathe and keep your hand or arm from tensing up. Since you don't have to worry about whether there are any mistakes or whether someone else might like or dislike what you write, try to pour your full attention onto the feelings and thoughts in your mind.

Invite risks. Remember, freewriting is private.

Activity Two: Focused Freewriting

This is writing where you pour words down on paper quickly without planning or worrying about quality, but you stay on one subject. Here's an example of freewriting on the topic of "laughter" by Cristy Cornell, a student:

> It's a relief to laugh. It takes every part of my body. I like the rush of endorphins or whatever scientists call them. It reduces everyone to a level playing field, a common ground. It's hard to lie I think when you laugh it puts you in touch with something. I don't know what. I think I missed the point of this exercise, what kind of stuff

---

Writing as Play Freewriting, Bad Writing, Garbage

One of the reasons freewriting can be helpful is that it lets you ignore questions of quality—ignore any worries about right/wrong, good/bad. As you freewrite, it's important to give yourself permission to write "badly" or even to write "garbage."

Try the following exercise. Do a piece of private, nonstop freewriting in which you *try* to make everything as bad as possible. What do you think is bad writing? What have you been told is really awful? Grammatical mistakes? Misspellings? Awkward sentences? Big words? Small words? Bad words? Generalizations? Bad feelings? Experiment with whatever kinds of badness come to mind—and see if you can get as much of it as possible into a piece of nonstop private writing.

Before you throw this writing away, check it out. We've discovered that many features of writing that students think of as bad are actually good. For example, many students have been warned away from using a strong or personal or loud voice, but these features are often found in excellent writing. You'll certainly get some good insights about what your mind has come to think of as "bad."

was supposed to be on this list anyway? I saw a thing/show on tv about these british twins who laughed all the time it was really weird. But I started laughing just hearing them laugh. One put a bright colored hat on her head & the other laughed they went around in circles in those revolving doorways they got in banks and they roared like it was the funniest thing they ever heard. It reduced tension for sure. Maybe that's why you laugh when you're nervous. I wonder if anyone's written a poem about laughter. So do I bring a story or poem to this literary round table thing or do I just show up w/some story about my lost passion—how I wanted to be Marie Curie & still wish I had a scientific mind or that I stopped playing the sax because I hated my band director? So, anyway LAUGHTER. Ha Ha Hee Hee. I like how Joey always puts Ha Ha and Hee Hee in his emails. I can hear him laughing that way. Anyway, jokes. I never get them. I think it's in the timing. I have none of that. But laughing. I laughed so hard at a Mark Halliday reading that tears ran down my face. And Brigit Pegan Kelly read with the speed of a freight train. What is this all about anyway? I don't know. I hate questions like these. Laughing. What's it all about? It's about letting go of something. It's a knot unknotting like something unraveling. It's in my lungs I think. It goes with those words a little maybe it's a letting go or a breathing out it's a build up and release. Maybe that's my word? Release? Release in the lungs? Sure. Okay. My feeling is of letting go, or release is that even a feeling? I feel released? No. I'm doing the releasing so that's not right. Is it maybe in the belly? Or maybe inbetween? In the shoulder muscles? Try lungs. I think it's there and so it's a pull in and it's a letting go its putting that breath out there & seeing where it goes or maybe watching what it takes out of the body with it. Yeah, it's in the lungs. Okay that's right. But feeling? I guess release. That's not the right word but it's the best I can think of. Release a letting go, a sending forth into the air it's about making a noise too and you need lungs to do that.

Focused freewriting is especially useful for the hardest thing about writing: *getting started*. Try 10 minutes of focused freewriting on one of these topics:

- Write about a time when writing went particularly well or badly. What was the topic and who was the audience? Try to tell in detail how you went about writing and what happened. What can you learn from this example?
- Write about someone who was important to your writing: a teacher or someone else who was helpful or harmful.

Remember, this is still private writing.

Activity Three: Clustering or Mapping

Try a cluster diagram on one of these topics:
* What does writing mean to you?
* What is a writer?
* Do you think of yourself as a writer?

Put the word "writing" or "writer" in the middle of a sheet of paper, then jot down all around it the words and concepts that you associate with writing. The ones that seem most central you can write closest to your central word; if they seem less important, write them farther away. Try to keep related ones more or less together; you can also draw connecting lines between words that seem related. (See Figure 1 for an example of someone's cluster diagram on the topic "reading.")

A cluster diagram is thus a "map" of how concepts and ideas and feelings live in your head. Such diagrams are a good means for quickly getting down lots of possible subtopics and connections, and also for giving a quick overview of a large conceptual territory. (You might think of traditional outlines as a more orderly form of clustering or mapping. For more about using outlines, see the Appendix about writing under pressure.)

Activity Four: Invisible Writing

We think you'll find it helpful to try something surprising: to write in such a way that you can't even see the words you are writing. It's easy to do this if you write on a computer: Just turn down the screen so it doesn't show your writing at all. (If you don't have access to a computer, you can skip this—though in fact, you can do invisible writing by using two sheets of paper and carbon paper and a spent ballpoint pen.)

Take 10 minutes now and give this technique a try. Possible topic for invisible writing:
* Write about the *physical conditions* for your writing. Where and when do you like to write? What implements do you use and

Exploring the Writing Process
The More, the More

"The more you have thought and written on a given theme, the more you can still write. Thought breeds thought. It grows under your hands."

Henry David Thoreau

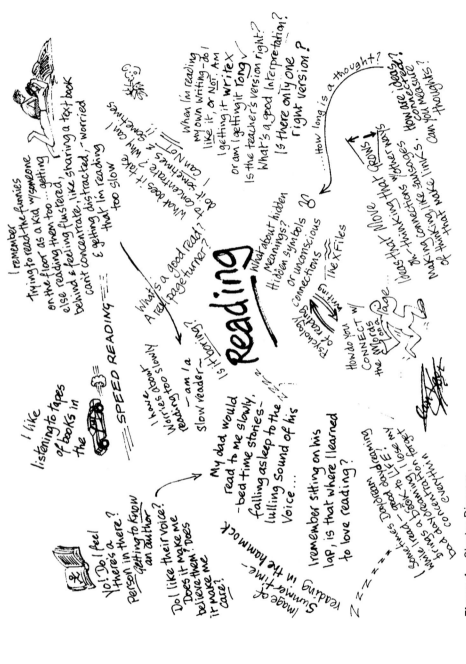

Figure 1 Cluster Diagram

why: pen, pencil, typewriter, computer? What kind of pad or paper? Do you need silence and solitude or do you prefer to have music on or other people around?

Most people get used to invisible writing before too long, and then they find it surprisingly useful. Invisible writing helps you write *more* because you can't pause or you'll lose track of what you're saying. More important, invisible writing increases your *concentration*. It does wonders if you are tired or if your mind is wandering. It's great for getting going on a piece of writing you don't want to do. It forces you to focus better on your thoughts—on the emerging meaning in your head. Invisible writing makes most people realize how often they get distracted from their topics in their regular writing: either because something else is on their minds or because they stop too often and look back at what they have already written.

Activity Five: Public Freewriting

Try using your "freewriting muscle" or "freewriting gear" to produce something that's not private but rather is for sharing with others (in this case with your classmates). It is not for evaluation, but only for the sake of communicating with them. Because it is public writing, you may want to pause and think and perhaps change some things as you go. It's fine to take a moment at the end to look over what you've written and see whether you want to cross out or change anything. But the idea is to share your thinking-on-the-run—not to produce something careful.

Try writing informally on one of the following topics:

- Write a short introduction of yourself to others in your class. What would you like them to know? You don't have to tell more than you feel comfortable telling.
- Introduce yourself as a writer. What are your strengths as a writer and learner? What are you proud of? What do you most want to learn? What do you need from others in the class to do your best as a student and writer? What can you contribute to a learning community?

Now read your short piece out loud to a partner, to a small group, or to the whole class. *Please* read slowly and distinctly. Don't sabotage your words by mumbling or reading too quickly. The sharing will help everyone in the class learn more about the writing process and about each other.

Activity Six: Process Writing

Process writing explores what happens when you write. What usually works best is simply to tell the story of what actually went on as you were writing—in your thoughts, your feelings, and on the page. Write with as much detail and honesty as you can. The goal is not to judge yourself or prove anything or reach big conclusions; you are just trying to *notice what happened* in a spirit of calm, benign acceptance.

Try it now. Write for 10 minutes about what was going on as you wrote one of the preceding pieces. Look for the details or specifics of what you did and what happened—and also how you felt.

If you do process writing regularly (and we will try to twist your arm to make that happen!), you will reach plenty of interesting conclusions; you don't have to *try* for them. But if you are like most people, you'll have to put some effort into remembering some of the details: the steps you went through and the feelings and thoughts that went on in your head. Notice how this student used the form of a story to remember details of what was happening:

> First I thought of my brother and the words tumbled onto the paper as fast as I could write. Time went by faster than I expected. I was pleased because I came up with some memories and thoughts that were new to me—though the memories made me sad. Then when I wrote about my mother, I began to feel mixed up and I slowed down and I couldn't figure out what I wanted to say. I knew what I felt about my brother. I wasn't sure of my feelings when I came to my mother. I stopped for a long time and walked around feeling stuck. Then . . . [and so on]

Sometimes process writing is easier if you do it after two writing sessions—especially two sessions on the same piece—and compare what happened. Remember that process writing is not only about the act of writing itself, but also about *everything* that goes into the writing: finding thoughts about your topic before you sit down to write, talks with others, feedback, daydreaming, false starts, and so on.

You'll see many pieces of process writing scattered throughout this book in shaded boxes. Some are written by students, some by published writers, and some by us. We've put in lots of process writing because we're fascinated by the enormous variation in what happens when people write—differences between people and even between what happens to the same person on different occasions. We want to give you lots of short but useful examples of people reflecting on what happened when they wrote. We speak more about process writing at the end of this workshop in the Exploring Theory section.*

---

*In scientific or technical fields, the term *process writing* is often used quite differently—namely, to refer to writing that describes some particular and often technical process (for example, how to analyze blood samples in a lab or how to construct a piece of equipment).

Activity Seven: Letter

Letters are partly public and partly private. That is, they go to a reader, but usually only to one or two readers. Of course there are open letters or "letters to the editor," but those feel different from most other letters precisely because they are so much more public. Letters to friends and family are often informal and casual. Sometimes we don't even look them over before mailing them. If you are anything like we are, you often send very quick and casual e-mail letters. But letters can be just as formal as any writing if they are intended for strangers or for business purposes. Still, even in the most formal letter, we usually write directly *to* the receiver—addressing her* in the second person—which is not so common in many other kinds of writing.

Try writing a letter to your teacher introducing yourself. Say as much or as little as you want at this point. We suggest that you talk about your goals, hopes, and needs for this class: what you want to get out of it, what you can contribute, what you hope will not happen, and what makes you nervous or anxious about the class.

This is not writing for a grade; it is writing to communicate. We teachers can teach better if we know more about our students and what they want and need from the course.

Activity Eight: Collaborative Writing

Much of the world's writing is done collaboratively. We collaborated to write this book. Probably most writing in business and government and research is done collaboratively. There is often a collaborative element even in individual writing (for example, when you use an idea you learned from someone else, or when your ideas change as a result of discussing them with others or getting feedback). Collaboration is more companionable, but it can also be more complicated because you have to work things out together.

Try working with one or two others to produce a few paragraphs on one of these topics:

- What are some of the most helpful and least helpful things that teachers have done in assisting you with your writing?
- What makes a good teacher of writing?

---

*Sometimes we refer to persons in general as *she* or *her*, and sometimes as *he* or *him*. We have definite reasons for this policy. First, we want to avoid the sexism of referring to all persons with masculine words; there's no doubt that the gender of pronouns has an effect on readers. But second, we want to avoid the awkwardness of phrases like "he or she" and the vagueness of always going to the plural "they" and "them." The singular pronoun tends to convey a more concrete meaning and thus more force. We'd actually like readers to *see* people when we talk about "she" or "he." Sometimes they'll see female persons and sometimes male persons.

Collaboration can be a great pleasure but it can also be difficult. We treat it at length in Workshop 4 and give lots of suggestions. For the short piece needed here, what's probably easiest is to talk together till you pretty well agree on your main thought. Then one person can write a very *rough* version; the other person can write a revision; and one of you can go on to final polishing and copyediting after discussing the revision.

Activity Nine: Evaluated Writing

Many students have never written except for a teacher, and the teacher has always noted mistakes or given some sort of evaluative comment or even a grade. Have you, like many students, fallen into assuming that writing *means* writing for evaluation? We will try to convince you that this is a pretty crippling way to think about writing. Of course much of your school writing will be evaluated by your teacher, but this text will encourage you to do a great deal of writing that will not be evaluated—some private, some just for classmates or friends, and some of it even for your teacher to read and not evaluate. Did you notice that none of the writing we've asked you to do so far was intended for evaluation?

But try now to write something that is intended for your teacher to evaluate in some way. Possible topics:

- Write a short summary of one of the sections of "Ruminations and Theory" in this workshop (pages 20–24), or a summary of something else your teacher may suggest. This is a test of careful reading as well as careful writing.
- Describe the differences between speaking and writing.

Activity Ten: Revising

Try revising one of the shorter pieces you have written so far.

For now we won't talk about techniques for revising (as we will in some later workshops). Pick a short piece that interests you but doesn't satisfy you. Don't just change a word here and there; wade in and make substantive changes—changes even in what you actually said. Experiment.

Notice that "revising" doesn't necessarily mean making something better: It means making it different. You won't learn the difficult skill of making things better unless you are adventuresome about making them *different*—perhaps even worse.

Activity Eleven: Cover Letter

When a writer sends his manuscript to a publisher or magazine or editor, he always includes a letter introducing it. Almost any teacher, scholar, fiction writer, or poet who reads something to an audience *says* something before she starts to read in order to create some link between herself and her audience. We find that cover letters can serve as this kind of link too.

Many teachers ask for cover letters with all major assignments. We do. We find we can give much more useful feedback if our students tell us a bit about what was going on for them as they wrote (giving us some process writing), and then answer questions like these:

- What was your main point and goal in this paper? What effect were you trying to achieve?
- What do you see as the strengths of the paper, and what would you try to do if you were to revise it some more?
- What didn't you manage to include? Are there other thoughts you'd like to share?
- What feedback or reactions did you get at various times in this paper, and how did you make use of them, if at all?

And most important of all:

- What kind of feedback or response would you like from your reader?

Here's an example of a cover letter written by one of the students we've worked with:

> I had a very good idea of what I wanted to write about the song I picked. This is one of my favorite songs. I like it because of the meaning it has and because of its great rhythm. In starting to write this, the inflow of information just flooded the paper. I kept putting down the things that I felt were trying to be said. After I analyzed almost every detail and every line of the song, I began to question where this song is leading and what he is really trying to say. I began with the idea that this song was about suicide in general and in the end I ended up contradicting that idea and finding a new meaning to the song. I was very surprised at finding this new meaning just from this analysis. I now listen to the song in a different light.
>
> I have to credit a friend of mine who brought out the idea of the threat of nuclear war as the major idea in the song. If he didn't point it out to me, then I really wouldn't have been so interested in trying to find out the deeper meanings of this song.
>
> Please tell me which points are strongest and clearest and which ones don't work for you. Where it doesn't work, is it the point itself or the writing that doesn't work? I feel kind of unsure about the structure. Any suggestions?

When you turn in your main assignment for this workshop, write a cover letter to go with it.

MAIN ASSIGNMENT
A Collage about You as a Writer and How You Write

A "collage" in the original sense, as coined by artists, is a picture produced not by painting or drawing but by gluing actual objects on the canvas—objects such as theater tickets, bits of colored paper, cloth, cardboard, or metal. (The word *collage* comes from the French word for glue. See p. 15 for an interesting contemporary visual collage.) A *written* collage consists of separate, disconnected bits of writing rather than one continuous piece. Usually there are spaces or asterisks at the "joints" between the pieces of writing.

A collage can serve as a "quick-and-dirty" way to produce a finished piece of writing. That is, you can simply pick out the passages you like best and put them together in whatever order strikes you as most interesting. It is traditional in collages to organize the bits intuitively.

In effect, a collage allows you simply to *skip* what are often the hardest parts of the writing process: revising weak passages (you just throw them away); getting the whole piece unified (all the bits are *related,* but there may not be an exact center); figuring out the best order (you settle for a sequence that seems fun or interesting); and making transitions between sections (there are none). And yet the finished collage is often effective and satisfying.

Since the collage you are to produce is a portrait of yourself and your experiences in writing, think of your teacher and your classmates as your audience for this assignment: You are introducing that side of yourself to these relative strangers and also helping them learn about how writing is for different people. But think also of *yourself* as your audience: You will manage to tell things about yourself that you didn't know before.

Here are the simple steps you need to follow in making your collage:

1. Look through all the pieces you have written so far and choose the pieces—or *passages*—you like best for giving a picture of how you write.

2. Write some more short bits about you and your writing. What you have already written will lead you to other possibilities: incidents, memories, pieces you liked or hated.

3. Spread them out on a table or on the floor so you can see them all.

Kurt Schwitters, "One Morning" (1997).
The term "collage" usually refers to visual art, as in this interesting modern example.

4. Arrange them in what seems the best order. Feel free to do the choosing and arranging by instinct or intuition.

5. You might now see the need to write one or two more sections. Perhaps other experiences or thoughts come to mind—perhaps an opening or closing piece, but not a traditional "introduction" or "conclusion."

6. Next, revise it all, but in a minimal and purely "negative" way. That is, don't rewrite, except for tiny changes (unless there's some particular section you really want to rework). Just *leave out* words, phrases, sentences, or passages that don't work.

7. Copyedit your collage carefully and type it so that it looks its best when your friends and classmates see it. You may need help with copyediting from a classmate, family member, or roommate. You can return the favor by carefully proofreading something of theirs, since most of us have an easier time seeing mistakes or usage problems in someone else's writing than in our own.

Here's an example of a collage entitled "Myself as a Writer: School versus Personal Writing" created by Tara O'Brien, a student:

> Ever since I learned to write, I've just written what I think the teachers want to read. When they give the assignment, I write for the grade I want to get. I've always known that I don't want a career in the field, so why should I put any extra effort into my papers? Only my teachers read the work, so I didn't even have to impress my classmates.

> Impressing classmates, however, should be somewhat of a goal. I wonder why teachers don't encourage students to express themselves. Most of the time, kids write thinking that only the teacher will read it. If they were taught at an early age that sharing is the best way to become a better writer, not many grownups would have a problem doing so. I was hardly ever given the opportunity to exchange work with my classmates. I truly believe that if I was, I'd be more open about doing it now. I'm always scared that others will think my writing is dumb or that it doesn't make sense. I might have had a totally different opinion if I had felt comfortable since I was younger.

> I don't mind reading my work aloud in small groups because I know everyone else has to do it, too. In tenth grade my teacher, Mr. Macdonald, assigned us a term paper on the topic of our choice. It was easy to get an A because he basically only cared about mechanics and grammar. In eleventh grade my two least favorite teachers were Mrs. Loiter and Ms. O'Brien. Mrs. Loiter was rude and snobby, and you could easily tell who her favorites were (one of whom I was not!). She thought the world of creative writers and totally disregarded the pathetic rest of us. Ms. O'Brien's

class required 15-page term papers on the most boring topics possible. If they were half a page shorter than the required length, the grade would definitely show it. Why do teachers use these methods? Writing should be a comfortable exercise, and it makes me mad to know that some people make it so uncomfortable.

I can write pretty well when I'm given a topic, but I have the hardest time thinking of one on my own. Sometimes I have trouble with introductions and conclusions in essays or papers. I think writing long reports is extremely boring, plus I can never put thoughts into logical order. I am usually grammar-conscious, though, and I used to be a spelling bee champ! The one thing I'd really like to change about my writing is my tendency to procrastinate. I terribly dislike deadlines, even though I understand the need for them.

I love journal writing. It's so helpful for anyone with a problem. Writing down my confusing and angry feelings allows me to deal with them much more easily. I can solve and understand my problems better when I see them down on paper. When I know a teacher will be checking up on my journal writing, I keep up with it much more. It seems like every time I try to do it on my own, I get out of the habit after a little while because I start writing pages at a time. It gets tiring!

Back in junior high, all of the girls used to write each other notes. I have all of them saved in a few shoe boxes in my closet. Ever since then, I've always liked sending and receiving letters. I'm meticulous about sending thank-you and birthday cards (go ahead—call up my relatives!). I don't know how I became like this—my parents are terrible about keeping in touch with people. My mother always asks me, "How do you do it? Really, what's your secret?" No matter how hard I try, she doesn't get it. My boyfriend and I always trade greeting cards. Whenever we fight, writing helps us communicate better. We can understand each other's points of view, even though it's not guaranteed we agree! I think people take writing, as opposed to speaking, more seriously. Sometimes we just blurt out things without thinking previously. But usually when we write, we put a lot of thought into our words. Letters are like conversations that we can keep forever. We may not remember phone calls, but we can always look back on letters and reminisce.

Maybe as I grow older, I'll mature as a writer. I can see somewhat of a difference in my style over the years, and hopefully this difference will expand. Writing for school, as opposed to writing on my own, brings out another side of me. It's as if my mind goes into auto-pilot! I have been trying to let go of some of my inhibitions when it comes to papers and essays. I do realize that it makes reading much more interesting if the material is personal. For now, though, I'm happy with my cards and letters!

Suggestions for Collaboration

The collage form is natural for collaboration. You can take passages from each of several writers and decide collaboratively on which pieces to choose and what order to put them in. You then have a group collage. It is not necessary to look for agreement: Your collaborative collage will probably be even stronger if it shows sharp contrasts between different people's experiences and feelings and conclusions. It becomes a kind of dialogue or conversation, not a monologue. More about this in Workshop 4.

Sharing and Responding

We are not suggesting feedback or revising for this first workshop, but sharing is definitely in order: reading your piece to listeners for the sake of communication and enjoyment, not for reactions. You have probably already shared some of the short pieces. It will be a pleasure now to share the whole collage. You will get the most benefit and enjoyment from reading it out loud, perhaps in small groups. But remember, no feedback at this point, just communication and enjoyment. Please read what we say about sharing in the "Sharing and Responding" section at the end of this book.

If you are not used to reading things out loud to others, you may find it embarrassing or difficult. Timidity and fear get in the way. The trick is to read it as though you really *mean* it, as though you *respect* your own words, as though you want to *give* the words to your listeners. Listeners are not supposed to give feedback, but they should stop you and tell you if they can't hear you well. Listen to your voice and enjoy it. If you learn to read your writing out loud so others *get it,* you will see a powerful improvement in your writing. It can also be useful and enjoyable to trade papers and have people read each other's papers out loud.

Exploring the Writing Process
On the Differences between Freewriting and Public Writing

My freewriting is less presentable in handwriting than the public writing. My freewriting is a bit more imaginative than the public writing. The public writing seems more formal than the personal writing done in the freewriting exercise. I tried to cut down the sentences in my public writing to a shorter type rather than the possible run ons in the long sentences found most presently in the freewriting exercise. I seem to be preoccupied with the fact that I have problems with writing. This is reflected in my public writing. I am not at ease with writing publicly and tend to be very formal toward the audience or the reader. New or more complex words tend to pop into my head easier than when I am intent on trying to deal with grammatical problems in my writing. I do understand that shorter and briefer sentences are the best but I like to make my sentences a little more extravagant.

Student

If your collage is a collaborative one, it is fun and helpful to have the different authors each read their bits. Listeners will enjoy hearing the movement back and forth among the different voices.

Process Journal and Cover Letter

We ask you to keep a process journal for this course. It might be a whole notebook, a section of a larger notebook, a folder where you keep separate pieces of process writing, or a file on your computer. We make regular process writing a requirement in our courses.

The best time to do process writing is right after you have been writing. The goal is to find out what really happened—the facts of what occurred on that particular occasion. Don't struggle for conclusions; trust that they'll come.

We spoke earlier of doing process writing in the form of a *story* of your writing session. Another good approach is to plunge into an exploration of what was most difficult or frustrating for you in that session. Explore what happened: What led to this difficulty? How did you deal with it? Tell everything you can. Interesting insights often come. In short, you can use process writing as a way to get some understanding of what is difficult for you in your writing. As you explore difficulties or frustrations over a number of sessions, you will begin to figure out some ways to avoid them or work around them.

In each workshop we'll give you a few questions to help you remember and notice your writing process. If you can remember what is useful and interesting without our questions, feel free to ignore them (unless your teacher asks you to answer specific ones). Here are some possible process writing questions for this workshop:

- What did you notice about trying to write without stopping when you freewrote?
- Did you notice any difference between writing privately and writing for an audience? Were there differences in writing to different audiences?
- Sharing: What was it like reading your words to others? listening to theirs? having your collage distributed?

For your cover letter, it's good to include some or all of your process writing. But don't forget to answer some cover letter questions. Here are the main ones: What is your main point and what effect are you trying to have on readers? What do you feel works best in your paper and where are you unsatisfied? What changes did you make on the basis of any feedback? And most important: What feedback do you want now from a reader? But your teacher may ask you particular cover letter questions that pertain to this assignment.

RUMINATIONS AND THEORY
Freewriting and Process Writing

Why We Think Freewriting Is Important

Why should freewriting be so helpful if it is so easy and invites such carelessness in writing and thinking? And why does it also invite some of our best writing and thinking?

First, let's look at why it's easy—in comparison with the difficulty of regular writing:

- Writing is usually judged or even graded, but freewriting is not.
- Writing usually means thinking about spelling and grammar, but in freewriting you can put all that out of mind.
- Writing is supposed to make sense, but freewriting can be incoherent or nonsensical.
- Writing is supposed to stay on one topic and be organized, but freewriting can jump all over the place.
- Writing is usually for an audience, but freewriting is private. Thus, freewriting is even *safer* than speaking, since we almost never speak except when someone's listening.

- Writing is usually supposed to be more important and dignified and "better" than speech. ("Why take the time to write something out unless you are going to try to get it right?") But freewriting is an invitation to let words be less important and less careful than speech—and to see what you can learn from them.

Thus, freewriting removes all the difficulties of regular writing. But in one sense, freewriting is *more demanding* than regular writing. It insists on the hardest thing of all: writing without stopping. But it makes that demand in a context of high safety. Thus, freewriting gets you going, gets you rolling. The hardest thing about writing is to make yourself keep putting words down on paper, and that's just what freewriting makes happen.

In addition, even though freewriting allows you to be careless or relaxed, it almost always heightens your thinking. That is, freewriting allows you to stop thinking about the *medium* of writing—about spelling and grammar, forming letters with your hand, choosing words, and being concerned with quality. It makes writing as easy as speaking. And therefore it helps you to devote *all your attention* to what you are trying to say. You need no longer be distracted by the process of writing.

Careful writing requires you to take the chaos inside your head and turn it into coherence on paper. But this is too hard for most of us to do in one step. Freewriting provides a helpful middle step: getting the chaos in your head on paper. It's not so hard to improve once it's down on paper. What's hard about writing comes from trying to *improve* what's in your head *while* you are in the act of writing it down. With freewriting you get two steps to produce coherence instead of struggling to produce it all in one step.

Thus, freewriting is full of "wrong words." Putting down the *wrong* word often leads you to the right word ("I dislike him. No, it's not that I dislike him, it's that I'm always uncomfortable around him.") For some mysterious reason, it usually helps to write down that wrong word rather than stop writing and search mentally for a better one. Freewriting makes you write it down. You get to notice that it's not quite right, yet still write it down. Then when you come back, you can usually find a much better word.

Despite all this freedom and all these wrong words, we have virtually never seen a passage of freewriting that we couldn't understand easily, while we've seen many passages of careful writing that we couldn't make head or tail of. And most passages of freewriting have voice, energy, and life.

It's not that freewriting is always *good*. Far from it. But interestingly enough, it's easier to tighten and clarify bad freewriting than bad careful writing. Try it. Find a long stretch of bad freewriting and also a piece of careful writing that you struggled over but that is still weak or problematic. Now try to clean up both passages. You'll discover that the careless writing is easier to fix. The careful writing, on the other hand, is sort of delicately glued together and therefore hard to reglue.

Sometimes a skilled student objects, "But freewriting is for blocked beginners, and I'm a fluent, skilled writer already." It's true that freewriting is good for unskilled students, but we find that *skilled, experienced* writers and teachers get even more out of freewriting. It's an exercise whose payoff increases with the expertise of the writer.

In case you think that only loose, artistic spirits advocate freewriting, notice the following passage from the official United States Coast Guard writing guide for officers: "Instead of staring at a blank piece of paper, let your mind run freely. Jot down your ideas in sentence form or as an outline without regard to order, grammar, punctuation, or syntax. Keep writing as long as the ideas keep coming."*

You can't predict how freewriting will work for you. Some people start off with coherent freewriting, but as they use it, they gradually drift into freewriting that's more jumpy and surprising. Some people start off jumpy. We've discovered that better writers seem to allow more shifts and jumps into their freewriting—and more talking to themselves. They trust themselves enough to follow their minds where they lead. We sense that people go through stages: perhaps a stage where you write only, "Nothing today, nothing, nothing," over and over—or some other kind of refusal to make meaning. It is important to give yourself permission for this and not measure freewriting by the *quality* of what you turn out. We sense that freewriting "works" in an underground way to help what the writer needs to work on, but obviously that's a statement of faith. (We first heard of freewriting from an important pioneer teacher of writing, Ken Macrorie. We've listed a couple of good books by him in the Works Cited section at the end of this book. We've also cited a book of essays about freewriting, edited by Belanoff, Elbow, and Fontaine.)

Why We Think Process Journals Are Important

Writing usually seems a mystery: Sometimes you slave over something and it comes out awful, and sometimes you dash something off and it comes out good. But of course, dashing everything off won't solve all your writing problems either. Thus, it is common to feel frustrated

---

*John V. Noel and James Stavridis, *Division Officer's Guide* (Annapolis, MD: Naval Institute Press, 1989), p. 265. Our thanks to Barbara Barata, a teacher at the Coast Guard Academy, for showing us this passage.

and even helpless about writing. Frequent process writing can help you understand your mental processes better and give you more power and control over yourself as a writer. You can figure out what specific procedures work for you, under what kinds of conditions, and for what kinds of tasks—and what kinds of procedures undermine your thinking or tend to get you stuck.

If someone asks you out of the blue to explain how you *usually* write, you are very apt to say things that are actually false. For example, you might say, "It always helps me to write an outline first." But what about that assignment when you didn't have time and produced a well-organized piece without an outline? Or that time when you got stuck trying to keep to an outline, which you eventually abandoned anyway? "Words always come slowly and with effort. Writing always discourages me." Yet what about that time when a whole train of thought bubbled up into your mind as you were writing, and you felt confident as you were writing? How could you make that happen more often?

People's memories play tricks on them, and they succumb to thinking there is one neat pattern to their writing. But if you do regular process writing, you'll discover that the truth is more complicated, and usually much more interesting. And more useful.

Still, it feels odd to some students to write about their writing. It makes them feel self-conscious. "It's hard enough to think about *what* I'm writing without also trying to think about *how* I'm writing." It often confuses people to try to analyze their tennis stroke as they are trying to hit the ball. But process writing doesn't ask you to watch yourself writing *while* you write, only to think back afterward to what happened.

A sports metaphor is instructive here. In every sport, serious players and coaches make videotapes of the games and later watch the tapes carefully to reflect on matters of technique they didn't have time to reflect on during the game. Teachers and psychiatrists watch tapes of themselves on the job to see what worked and didn't work. Process writing is a matter of "looking" back at your memory tapes and writing about what you see.

The coauthor of this book, Peter Elbow, became interested in writing because he went through a long period of writer's block. He had to quit graduate school because he couldn't write his papers. The way he got himself going again (five years later) was by doing process writing about almost every writing session—and discovering what was getting in his way. This process writing grew into Elbow's first book, *Writing without Teachers*. But neither of us thought about using this kind of writing as a teaching tool until we learned about it from Sondra Perl in the New York City Writing Project.

Psychologists use the term "metacognition" for thinking about thinking, which is what you do in process writing. Metacognition gives you more power over your future learning and over yourself. The most important writing you do in this course may be your process writing. It's simple. Just tell what happened. Yet because it consists of self-reflective thinking, it is also the most cognitively sophisticated writing, and it has the biggest payoff for learning.

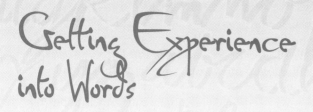

Getting Experience into Words

Image and Story

Your poetry issues of its own accord when you and the object become one.
Bashō

Essential Premises

The best way to make your words powerful—to make readers *experience* the meanings in your words—is to make sure that *you* actually experience what your words are about. Finding nice words is all very well, but actually experiencing your meanings—seeing, hearing, and feeling what you are writing about—will carry you further. It takes extra energy and concentration.

A good way to write a story is to let it grow out of a strongly experienced image.

Main Assignment Preview

Our goal in this workshop is to help you make readers *experience* what you are writing about, not just understand it. We're after words that don't just *describe* the tree outside the window but make your reader *see* it—and hear it and smell it. This means using words that somehow carry some of the life or energy of that tree. This is a somewhat mystical way of putting things, but in fact it's not so hard to get this valuable quality into your writing if you take the right approach.

The basic process here—getting experience into words—applies to all kinds of writing, including essays. But it is easier to learn how to do it with descriptive and narrative writing. That is, it's easier to learn how to get visual and sensory experience into words, and know when you have succeeded, than to get cognitive or intellectual experience into words. When you learn the process we're teaching in this workshop, you'll be able to apply it to essays.

The crux is this: If you want to get your reader to experience something, *you* must experience it. If you want your reader to see something, then put all your effort into *seeing it.* For your reader to hear or smell something, you must hear or smell it. Put all your effort into, as it were, having a vision. Don't worry about words; worry about seeing. When you can finally see, hear, and smell things, just open your mouth or start the pen moving and let the words take care of themselves. They may not yet be elegant or well-organized words, but don't worry about that. You can take care of that problem later. If you are actually seeing and hearing what you are talking or writing about, your words will have some of that special juice that gives your experience to the reader. If you don't see what you are describing, you may find very nice words but they are less apt to make the reader see what you are talking about.

The point of this workshop is *real* description: transporting the thing itself inside readers' minds. Sometimes readers say, "She's so good at describing things; she told me about 15 things in the scene." But those 15 items were often just mentioned or verbally described, not really conveyed into the reader's head.

Exploring the Writing Process
On the Aim of Writing

My task which I am trying to achieve is, by the power of the written word to make you hear, to make you feel—it is, before all, to make you *see.* That—and no more, and it is everything. If I succeed, you shall find there according to your deserts: encouragement, consolation, fear, charm—all you demand—and, perhaps, also that glimpse of truth for which you have forgotten to ask . . .

To arrest, for the space of a breath, the hands busy about the work of the earth, and compel men entranced by the sight of distant goals to glance for a moment at the surrounding vision of form and colour, of sunshine and shadows; to make them pause for a look, for a sigh, for a smile—such is the aim, difficult and evanescent, and reserved only for a few to achieve. But sometimes, by the deserving and the fortunate, even that task is accomplished. And when it is accomplished—behold!—all the truth of life is there: a moment of vision, a sigh, a smile—and the return to an eternal rest.

Joseph Conrad

Your *main assignment* for this workshop will be to develop an image into a story. Your teacher will let you know whether you should save this piece for revision later in the semester or do an extensive revision immediately.

Developing Images

This section of the workshop consists of a sequence of focused activities designed to help you get more life and experience into your words. Most of the activities involve speaking rather than writing. We suggest even using your hands and gesturing. The goal is not "acting" or "illustrating" things for an audience but rather getting as much as possible of your self invested in the words you use. This is practice in *giving* words.

You can do these activities in pairs or small groups, but your teacher may well have you do some of them all together with the whole class.

It will be hard to fit all of the activities into one session unless you have a long period of time. Thus you may spread them over two sessions. If you do that, be sure to do at least a bit of writing at the end of the first session—writing about whatever image you are currently working on. Don't hold off writing till the end of the second session.

Activity One: Letting Words Grow Out of Seeing

Think of some small object—for now something simple that you know well. For example, you might think of your favorite mug or coffee cup on the kitchen counter. The goal is to describe your mug in spoken words so as to make your listeners *see* it.

What's important here is to take your time and not utter a word until *after* you close your eyes and put all your effort into *seeing* that mug on the counter. Don't try to see the whole kitchen or even the entire crowded counter. Focus all your energy on seeing that mug—hallucinating, if you will. Take your time. Don't worry about words or about classmates listening. The important thing is to wait with your eyes closed until you can really see what you are going to describe. When you are finally having that actual experience inside your head, open your mouth and say what you are seeing, letting the words take care of themselves.

Invite yourself to make some gesture or body movement as you speak. The goal is not so much to act out or illustrate what you are saying (though that's fine too) as to get so involved in your seeing and saying that you just invite some movement to flow naturally. Perhaps you'll find yourself pushing your arm or fist away as a kind of emphasis for certain words; perhaps you'll make a slow gradual movement of your arms as you are speaking. See what your limbs or body "want" to do with your speaking. Standing up will make natural movement easier. Of course you may feel shy or self-conscious about this. If it bothers you too much, you may need to skip this gestural part of the activity. But the truth is that body movement invites language with more presence and involvement.

Perhaps your speech is halting and full of pauses as you struggle to see and hear inside your head—not "literary" or even grammatical. Perhaps you wander around in your description, changing focus as you pause. Perhaps you talk about the mug, then about the flower pattern, then the light on the surface, then the crumbs on the counter, the half-eaten bit of toast right next to the mug. There's nothing wrong with this: It often results from the effort to see. But now pause a moment and look for the center of gravity, the most important point in your scene, and give your description again, trying to get it whole and into one piece of energy. For example, you might end up with

> I see my favorite mug. It's white with a twining pattern of blue flowers. Kind of oriental pattern. Narrow, small mug, but thick sides. I look inside. Dull gleam on the side of it from the fluorescent light. A few sips of cold black coffee left.

Listeners should just listen. No response. This is their chance to enjoy and to get better at listening. Then the next person gets a turn to describe her object. Make sure she too takes plenty of time to *see* it before talking.

This procedure should take just a few minutes for each person; a minute or so for remembering or finding an object, a minute or so for going inside your head and trying to really see it, and less than a minute for saying what you see. Short descriptions are fine, no more than four or five sentences. Here are a few guidelines:

- *No people or big scenes.* People are too big and complicated to describe at this point. (But you might describe the *hand* holding the mug.) For now, keep to more or less one object with no more than those few things that are near the mug or interact with it, such as a spoon standing in the mug, or the page of newspaper underneath the mug.
- *Go easy on feelings.* The goal for this exercise is to present the mug, not your feelings about it. By all means, *feel* your feelings about the mug and the scene; that will help you. But don't describe your feelings—describe what you *see* (and hear and smell).
- *No stories.* Again, it's tempting to tell the story of who gave you

the mug and how you once knocked it off the counter and slopped coffee all over the linoleum. Of course these memories are part of the mug for you, but skip them for now.

A story is tempting because it's the most captivating form of discourse. Everyone feels the basic tug of plot: "and next . . . and next . . . and next." But for this exercise, we are pushing away stories in order to concentrate on the central task of really seeing—not settling for the easy momentum of "and then this happened . . . and then . . . and then." In effect, this exercise asks you to take a snapshot and stick to one instant of time—to tell what could fit in only one still photograph. It's fine to describe the one instant of spilled coffee on the floor with mug fragments scattered around, but only that single snapshot/instant. In a little while we'll get to stories or moving pictures.

Activity Two: Can Listeners See It?

After everyone has had one turn at presenting a small image, go around again presenting new images, using the same procedures. This time let listeners give a tiny bit of feedback after each telling: Have them tell you which bits or details, if any, they could see (or hear, smell, taste, feel). This is a difficult test. Don't despair if listeners can't really see *anything* of what you describe. It happens frequently. Words that carry real experience are rare. Don't give up; don't assume you are incapable. Everyone is capable of seeing what's in their mind and describing it so that others will see it too. But it's a slippery skill. And some listeners are harder to reach than others. Try to notice which details did get through.

Exploring the Writing Process
On Focus

The problem with having listeners see it is that some people have no "pictures" in their head. My fiancé, for example, has difficulty imagining anything. It doesn't mean it's a bad description; he just can't engage his imagination at will. Perhaps I need to spend more time forming a "focus," before writing or speaking. Did you know it's harder to imagine one particular small thing than it is to picture an entire beach scene? It seemed *too* focused for me.

Danielle

But if they can't see or hear what you describe, don't think of it as a problem of words—wrong words or lack of words; work on *experiencing* your object more fully or more intensely. You may have interesting ideas or words about your object; you may have strong feelings about it. But if listeners aren't seeing it, you may not be *really* seeing it either.

Activity Three: Letting Listeners Give an Impetus

Now give listeners a bigger role. Get them to ask you about details you may not have thought of. For example:
- Tell me about the handle on the mug.
- Tell me about the surface of the counter.

Invite listeners to introduce other senses:
- What do you hear?
- What does the surface of the mug *feel* like?
- What do you smell?

Don't think up or make up answers to these questions. Look and see what the *real* answer is. That is, if you don't see the handle or feel the surface, close your eyes and pause till you do. Wait for answers to come. Keep the image in mind, look at it inside your head, and make *it* give you the new answers.

Activity Four: Letting an Image Move toward a Story

Now invite the germ of a story or narrative by having a listener ask you, "What happens next?" But don't move too fast. Your story will be better if you don't try to *tell a story,* but just try to *enrich an image.* Above all, avoid the temptation to jump into a long story, especially a corny story. "And then a hand drops a poison tablet into the mug!" No. The point is to let the next event be small and real—generated by the image rather than imposed by you on the image. Put the image in charge. This is practice in standing out of the way, not steering but letting the image steer: letting details and events be generated *by reality,* not imposed by a creator.

So when someone asks you, "What happens next?" your job is easy. Just close your eyes, go back inside your head, and look at the mug and *wait.* Wait to see what does happen next. Don't be in a hurry. Some events may come to your mind that are too made up. You'll usually be able to tell that they are manipulations of your mind, not products of the mug itself. They'll be too contrived or phony. Let them go. Wait for the event that really happens or really wants to happen. Perhaps it will just be

The rock song on the radio ends and a man's voice—fake-cheerful —announces the time, "It's 8:47 now, folks."

For your listeners, the question is always, "Do you believe it? Did it really happen, or was it just made up?" Again it is a matter of *experiencing*—applied this time to an event, not just an image: Did you give the *experience* of the event to the listeners?

Activity Five: From Talking to Writing

So far, this has been mostly talking, but it's crucial to *start* a piece of writing right away when all this experiencing is still alive in your head—when you have been exercising your skill at internal seeing. You need at least 15 minutes for this writing, more if possible. (Your teacher may take charge of the timing.)

It might seem most natural to write from your own image. And that is all right. But we suggest choosing someone else's image. Choose an image that somehow feels interesting to you, that somehow intrigues you or resonates or feels perplexing. It's better if you don't even know why the image or description feels right or clicks for you. Writing from someone else's image often liberates your imagination. It gives you practice in relinquishing control and letting the image generate material. It's not *your* image and so you'll have less need to own it or control it, and you'll have fewer preconceptions about it.

If you have more than one session, it can be helpful to start the later sessions by hearing each other's rough exploratory writing based on images from the previous session. It needn't take much time if you

---

Writing as Play   Extending the Story through Collaboration

Now your group or pair is ready to try collaborating to develop one image and help it grow into a story.
- One person starts by suggesting a time of day.
- The next person provides an image occurring at that time of day.
- The next person adds a *detail,* but from a different sense (sound, smell, feel).
- The following person tells what happens next.
- Another person gives another detail or tells what happens next.

And so on, as far as you want to carry it. Make your own variations. This sequence of tasks works with a small group or even a pair: Simply go around and around the circle or take turns.

Remember all the things you just worked on: Concentrate on *having* an experience, not on finding words; wait and look; let your image be in charge—don't impose on the image. If you collaborate, you'll all have to hold the same image in mind even as it develops. In a sense you are working on a collaborative hallucination.

quickly read in pairs or small groups. No need for response. Listen for how the images you heard in the previous session have been enriched and transformed in the writing. (We are grateful for having learned about these seeing activities from John Schultz's work, listed in the "Works Cited" section at the end of this book.)

Here's an example of the image writing that one student, Mitchell Shack, generated from a spoken image he came up with using the activities in this workshop:

> My image of an ice-cream man starts as I hear the ice-cream bells ringing the next block away. As he comes closer, he puts on his blinking red lights and his sign, Watch-children, comes out on the driver's side of the truck. I go around the opposite side and find a window about 3 feet square. Around the outside of the window are pictures of bomb-pops, snow-cones, chocolate bar pops, ice-cream cones, shakes, hot fudge sundaes and a bunch of other treats. Next to each of these items is the price, usually about 20 or 30 cents higher than the same item bought in the supermarket. There is a little ledge where the ice-cream man puts down the various

Exploring the Writing Process
On Letting Words Grow Out of Seeing

I didn't even want to do this exercise but felt I had to. Yoon's image seemed Asian, although I think I changed it as I wrote. I saw the road going down into the woods and I knew at some level that it was only one fork of the road because I seemed to be standing just before the break— but I saw that road more and more, twisting and winding (it was dust-colored) into the trees and forest surrounding it and disappearing into the dark.

But then the leader suggested looking at different parts of the image. I did. And there was the other fork going up a sloping grass-covered hillside toward an open blue sky. That open blue beckoning sky was there all along.

I was floored by what such a simple game led me to. I certainly won't listen when someone says it's stupid. Is it possible my resistance led me into the forest and obscured the blue sky—and when I stopped resisting I saw the blue sky? It was even a different bodily sensation. The tension left my bones and muscles. Wow!

Pat Belanoff

items and counts the pennies, dimes, and nickels the children give him. He places the change in a chrome change dispenser he wears on his waist. Inside the truck I see a metal freezer—actually it looks sort of like a refrigerator placed on its back. On shelves over the freezer are boxes of gum, candy, baseball cards and other sweets. The outside of the truck is mostly white, except for the area I mentioned earlier around the window. The shape of the truck reminds me of a modified bread delivery truck. Next to the window is a little cutout where there lies a garbage can on the other side so the kids can dispose of the wrappers. Towards the front of the truck on the passenger's side is a door similar to the kind you find on a school bus. Looking into the truck from the doorway, you can see the driver's seat—it's worn in with a jacket hanging over the chair. There's a big steering wheel and a little metal fan aimed at the seat. There are great big rear view mirrors outside of the window next to the seat and door. Above the front windshield are the big letters spelling ICE CREAM, and next to it is the infamous bell the kids can hear for five blocks away.

Here is Mitchell's process writing on how he worked to bring the image to life:

I had to think of vivid images of what I see when I think of the ice-cream man. Since there was no ice-cream truck in front of me, I had to rely totally on the images I had from my memory. Since it had been a while since my last encounter with an ice-cream truck, I had trouble remembering some of the details. I found that I could remember more when I closed my eyes and concentrated on what I saw when I looked at the ice-cream man. As I started writing down the major things, more detail popped into my head. I kept on remembering more things as I kept thinking and my picture in my mind became much more vivid. I could remember myself studying the pictures of the various ice-cream cones and figuring out what I could get with the money I had. I remember racing into the house when I heard the bells and running upstairs to get the money.

I tried to remember the most minute details like getting Italian ices with the little wooden spoon and turning over the Italian ice to get to the bottom which was the best part. It almost seemed as if the ice-cream truck was there—too bad, I was getting hungry and would have loved a hot fudge sundae. Anyway, by creating this image in my mind, all the details and little things I forgot over the years came back to me as clear as ever.

Later on in this workshop, you'll see how Mitchell Shack developed his image into a full-fledged story.

MAIN ASSIGNMENT
From Image to Story

Take an image and use it as a germ in order to write a draft of your own story. You may want to base your story on one of your own images (as Mitchell Shack did), or you might find it fruitful to build on someone else's image. In fact, you may want to start fresh on some new image since this is your chance to do some of what we tried to stop you from doing during the exercises: to describe a person, a large scene, or your feelings.

But as you do this more ambitious writing, make sure to rely on the central process we've been emphasizing in this workshop. Don't search out words and make up stories; instead get yourself to have experiences. When you feel stymied, stop, close your eyes, look inside, listen. Go through this root experience again and again, as often as you need to. It is a foundation for good writing, writing that conveys an experience to readers. If this process sounds odd to you, think of the word *imagination.* We are simply asking you to use a mental ability that is *basic in every human mind*—that ability we all call on every night when we dream—the ability to use an *image* as the basis for *creation.*

"Oh, dear, I don't write stories. I don't know how." Many people feel this way—and critics have written lots of fancy theory about different kinds of stories or narrative. But we all naturally tell stories every day in the midst of our conversations. ("You know what happened when I was standing in line to pay for my hamburger?") There's no need to be complicated about the story-making process for this assignment. (Later on, if you wish, you can make a special study of "narrative.")

The simplest method creates one of the most powerful effects—and it's the method you just used in the "Writing as Play" exercise: "Here's an image. Then this happened. And then this happened. And then this. And then . . ." and so on till you reach a sense of ending. You'll see that Mitchell Shack went in the opposite direction and used his image as an ending or climax. His image led him to think of a series of events that led up to it. Either method leads to a sequence of events that is chronological—the sequence follows time.

But from books and movies, we're all familiar with *nonchronological* sequences, the most common being "flashback": Start with the ending but then "flash" back to the beginning and work your way forward. There's also a tradition of starting in the *middle* and then moving back to the beginning (the *Iliad* and *Odyssey* begin *in medias res*—"in the middle of things"). You will sometimes find yourself slowing down time or speeding up and skipping across hours or years; you'll find yourself zooming in to a close-up view of tiny details or panning out to a large wide-lens view. But if you just trust your imagination—your image and your ability to look inside—these choices will happen by themselves. Afterward, when you get around to revising, you might want to make some conscious changes and move things around in time—or change some camera angles.

It's important to realize that the events in your story don't have to be vivid or earthshaking—"special." In fact, when stories don't work well, it's usually because the writer tried too hard for special or striking events. Such stories suffer because the writer didn't rely on *imagination*—didn't just close her eyes and look inside to see what "did" happen—that is, what is *likely* to happen—what the scene *calls for.* If you really use your imagination, you are liable to come up with very ordinary events—but they are most likely to work on readers— to give them an experience. The person with the mug on the kitchen counter might just suddenly notice a song on the radio that he likes; it might bring back a particular memory; he might decide to have a second cup of coffee, and then decide not to go to his job that morning, and then walk out the door into the sunlight—and that's the end of the story. Your only job is to go there and see and hear what's happening, and take your reader with you.

Don't worry if this approach leads you to write down words that seem jumbled or awkward—not as polished as the writing you usually do. Trust the words that come. You can take time later, when you revise, to clean them up—to cut, rearrange, and add. This way, you'll be working with language that has more life in it.

When you write your story, you may have the impulse to make it "say" something to the reader, or to send a message or a deep meaning. Let us warn you against this impulse. If you start out with a meaning or a moral in mind, the story often comes across as heavy-handed or preachy. Almost always you do best to concentrate on what might be called "letting the story tell itself," or "letting the meaning take care of itself." You always have chances later, during revising, to spell out meanings more clearly—or, better yet, to help the events *imply* the meaning more clearly. Have faith in the materials you choose, in your vision, and in the power of the story once you set it loose. In fact, it's not even necessary that *you* know what the story means. If you have a strong urge to tell a story, fictional or real, that shows that it means something to you, and often that meaning will be more powerful if you leave it unstated.

Here's the story Mitchell Shack developed from the image writing.

An Ice-Cream Man   *Mitchell Shack*

It was a scorching hot day in the middle of July, almost 100 degrees out-side. I was playing football with a bunch of kids from my neighborhood. We were playing ball for almost an hour and I had worked up a good sweat. My throat was dry and I was in desperate need of an ice-cold glass of iced tea. We went into a huddle and I started daydreaming about jumping into a cold pool. The score was tied at 21 apiece and we all agreed that the next team that scores would win the game. We were about 15 yards out from the end zone (actually the area between my friend's mailbox and the pine tree across the street). Our team discussed our options and decided we were going to play on fourth down instead of kicking.

We lined up at the line of scrimmage and I was ready to start the down when I heard a faint sound. It sounded like a mixture between the fire bells in school and the bell I used to ring on my tricycle. I stepped back to throw the ball when I heard the noise again. This time it clicked in my head that what I was hearing was the ice-cream man the next block away. I dropped the ball and announced, "I forfeit! The ice-cream man is coming." I reached into my pockets in search of a few coins, but to my dismay they were empty. "Darn," I thought to myself, "I must have left my money in my pants in my room." I started to run toward my house and looked back to see my friends doing the same. The long game and the excessive heat seemed to have little effect on me, for I was running as fast as I ever had. I turned the corner and started running down my block. I could see my house at the end, and it seemed as if I was never going to reach it. I ran and ran and then sprinted up the driveway. I reached out for the doorknob to open the door and tried to turn it, but it didn't budge an inch. I started banging on my door and ringing the doorbell, hoping my mom would hear.

My mom came to the door and I was halfway up the stairs before she had a chance to yell at me for almost breaking down the door. I ran into my room in search of my pants containing my allowance money. I checked my floor, under my bed, my closet, my hamper, and behind my dresser, but the pants were nowhere to be found. "Mom! Mom! Where are my pants?" I screamed down to her. "I just took the laundry from your room—check the laundry basket," she replied. So downstairs I ran and grabbed the basket from atop the washing machine. I dumped the laundry on the floor and searched for my pants. I threw socks and shirts all over the place before I found what I was looking for. I reached into my pockets, grabbed the change, and flew out the door. Again I ran down the block, huffing and puff-ing all the way. I turned onto the street where I was playing and saw the truck in the distance. "Oh no, I better hurry—I think he's getting ready to leave," I thought to myself. The truck from far away looked like an old bread truck, but it would not have mattered one bit if it looked like a garbage truck, just as long as it sold ice cream.

I started getting close to it, when the red blinking sign WATCH—CHILDREN went on and the truck began to move. "Stop! Stop!" I yelled as

An Ice-Cream Man   *continued*

I ran holding up both my hands. I put on my afterburners and ran in hot pursuit of that beat-up white truck. "Stop! Stop!" I continued to scream, but it had no effect and the truck kept on driving. I ran past my friends who were hysterically laughing as they watched me run while they unwrapped the ice cream they had just bought. The ice-cream truck stopped at a stop sign then turned the corner without noticing me at all. I figured I had better take a short cut so I ran through my friend's backyard, hopped a fence and sprinted through a little patch of woods. I noticed that I had ripped the pocket of my pants, probably while climbing over the fence. I was too concerned about intercepting the ice-cream truck to worry about my pants and I came out of the woods and ran in the middle of the street so I could flag down the truck. I held out both hands and screamed, "Stop!" as I saw the truck approaching, but I noticed something looked different. The truck came to an abrupt halt and I ran alongside it. I looked up but instead of a window, I found a sign reading "Bob's Bread Delivery Service." "Oh no, I stopped the wrong truck," I thought to myself as the driver stepped out and asked me what was wrong. "Oh, nothing. Forget it," I said to the driver, "I just thought you were the ice-cream man." He started laughing and pulled away. I felt like an idiot and just sat there on the curb and tried to catch my breath.

I figured I had better get home and clean up the mess I made out of the laundry. I walked about two blocks, when I turned the corner and saw the ice-cream truck on the side of the road. I couldn't believe my eyes. I thought he was gone for good. I ran alongside the truck and knocked on the closed window. I looked at the pictures next to the window and wanted to buy everything he had. The man came to the window and said. "I'm sorry—we're closed. I'm just packing up a few things before I go home." "Oh please," I pleaded with him. "I ran two blocks home, my house was locked. I couldn't find my pants, I wrecked my mom's laundry, I chased after you another three blocks, ran through my friend's woods and ripped my pants, stopped the wrong truck and when I finally catch up with you, you tell me you're closed!" "You did all that just to buy an ice-cream cone— I think we can make an exception," he said as he smiled at me. I said I wanted a hot fudge sundae and he turned around and started to make it.

I watched him as he was making it, and my mouth watered just looking at all the ice cream, lollipops, bubble gum, chocolate bars, Italian ices, and other candy I saw inside the truck. He reached into the freezer to scoop out some ice cream and I started counting my change as I placed the coins on the little ledge outside of the window. He finished making the sundae and handed it to me along with a plastic spoon. I went to hand him my money when he said, "Forget about the money. This treat is on me." "Thanks a lot! Thank you, thank you very much!" I blurted out. He closed the window and drove off. I just sat there eating my ice cream, watching the truck fade away into the distance. I was the happiest kid alive.

Suggestions for Collaboration

A group or pair of you who collaborated on an image and the germ of a story might want to continue together and write a story collaboratively. In collaborating, you can divide the task by *sections,* where each of you writes a different part of the story. Or you can divide the task by *stages,* where one person starts by doing a rough draft, and each succeeding person takes the draft through the next stage. (We've used both of these techniques in collaborating on this book.) If you collaborate, you may have to give special attention to the problem of making the writing consistent, especially if different members write different sections.

Sharing and Responding

Feedback should focus on the main thing we are working on in this workshop—namely, the ability to make readers and listeners *experience* what you're describing. "Summary and Sayback" will be helpful (in "Sharing and Responding" at the end of this book), but perhaps the following pointed questions will also help:

- Which parts do you see most? Tell me in your own words what you see.
- Where do you feel the most energy, voice, and life in my story?
- Are there places where you feel me trying to take the image where it doesn't want to go?
- What does the story mean to you?

Exploring the Writing Process
On Writing from Memory

I began writing about a woman whom I remember from my early childhood and soon realized that I really wanted to write about my grandmother. I was remembering her in the detail it takes to make a reader see a character, and it was a very pleasant experience. She hadn't been that clear to me in years. Even if the piece goes nowhere else, the writing of it was a pleasurable reliving of a long buried time of my life. It was important that I cared for the character I was writing about.

Jo Ferrell

After you've gotten feedback on your draft, your teacher may ask you to revise it immediately. Or she may ask you to set it aside for revision later.

Process Journal and Cover Letter

The mental process we emphasize in this workshop may be new and difficult for you. But it's a vital process for all writing and thus useful to reflect on.

- Was it hard for you to see your object and stay focused on it? Could you get the *seeing* or *experience* to lead to words, instead of your having to look for words? What helped?
- Could you let the image lead to a story instead of your having to make up a story? What helped?
- Were these processes easier in speaking or writing?
- Did you know the meaning the story had for you from the start, or did it sneak up on you—or are you still not sure?

For your cover letter, it's good to include some or all of your process writing. But don't forget to answer some cover letter questions. Here are the main ones: What is your main point and what effect are you trying to have on readers? What do you feel works best in your paper and where are you unsatisfied? What changes did you make on the basis of any feedback? And most important: What feedback do you want now from a reader? But your teacher may ask you particular cover letter questions that pertain to this assignment.

RUMINATIONS AND THEORY
Writing and Getting Carried Away

Have you sometimes had the experience of getting excited with what you are writing, getting carried away, and feeling very pleased with your words? But then later discovering that the writing you produced in that excitement was terrible? Or at least discovering that others thought your writing was terrible? We've certainly had this experience ourselves.

Being carried away can lead to writing that is jumbled or disorganized. The excitement we feel in writing removes all sense of perspective and control and produces a mess—a rich mess, perhaps, but still a mess. "What is your point?" "No focus here!" "Sloppy!" are some comments that you might have gotten. Because of this experience, some people try to *avoid* getting carried away. And some teachers warn against it. They conclude that you should write only when you are cool and in control. "Exercise careful *craft* at all times." And yet in this workshop we seem to be advocating getting carried away. When we suggest that you move your hands or body or give a gesture, we are trying to help you get further *into* your vision and thus, in a sense, to get carried away.

But you don't have to make an either/or choice between being excited and being cool. You can be excited or caught up in your meaning when you are writing *drafts*—and we think you should. Then when you *revise,* you can be coolly controlled and tough. Each of these opposite frames of mind helps enhance the other. That is, if you know you will be tough and controlled as you revise, you'll feel safer about letting yourself get carried away at the earlier stages. And if you've let yourself get carried away as you generate a draft, you'll feel tougher about revising, more willing to wield the knife. So the control problem is solvable if you allow one period for being excited and another period for being cool.

But there is another problem with being carried away. You can get so caught up with your *feelings* that you lose sight of what you are writing about—lose sight of the coffee mug, when the whole point is to see the mug even better. We're not trying to argue against having feelings as you write; we're not trying to insist on the idea of the artist as coolly detached and paring his fingernails as he looks down on life from a distance. (James Joyce uses this image for the artist in *Portrait of the Artist as a Young Man.* Wordsworth similarly advises recollecting emotion *in tranquillity.*) But you can use your strong feelings to carry you *to* the coffee mug or to the ideas in your essay—to help you see the images and experience the ideas more vividly. If you only get carried away to your *feelings* about the image or idea, readers will get very little. Here's how the Japanese poet Bashō put this idea (in the passage from which we took our opening epigraph):

> Go to the pine if you want to learn about the pine, or to the bamboo if you want to learn about the bamboo. And in doing so, you must leave your subjective preoccupation with yourself. Otherwise you impose yourself on the object and do not learn. Your poetry issues of its own accord when you and the object have become one. . . . (Bashō, quoted in Balaban 33)

Once you get clear about what "being carried away" means— being carried into greater contact with what you are writing about— it makes writing much easier and more enjoyable. We suspect that few writers would continue writing unless they learned to experience the excitement of genuine contact. This is the excitement of inspiration, which means literally "a breathing into." In your process writing, you might notice the occasions when you feel the excitement of making some kind of contact with what you are trying to describe.

Jonathan Swift, the author of *Gulliver's Travels,* said that good writing is nothing but finding the right words and putting them in the right places. In a sense, of course, he's right; and this is a fine way to describe good *revising*. But for *producing* or *generating* good writing, you'll find it helpful to think of writing as the other way around (as Bashō does). Don't seek words or worry about where to put them. Put all your energy into becoming one with what you are writing about. You can learn this ability most easily with descriptive and narrative writing, but then you can learn to apply it to essay writing.

It is a relief to take this approach to writing. It means that you don't need a fancy vocabulary or syntactic complexity to write well. Plenty of good words and good syntax will come of their own accord. Writing turns out to be a richer and more interesting experience this way, because it isn't so much a struggle to find good words as it is a struggle to have or relive or enter into experiences. Interestingly enough, some experienced and skilled writers have a harder time taking this approach. They try too hard to find fancy words and elegant phrasing as they write. They forget to put their effort into experiencing what they are writing about. As we read their writing, we are more aware of their impressive words than of the meaning or experience of what they are saying.

Moving from Private Writing to Public Writing

Exploring the Relationship between Content and Genre

Essential Premises

It is usually easier to find words for our thoughts and feelings if we write words that are not for the eyes of others. Sometimes we are more eloquent when we're not worrying about readers. After we write privately, we can look back over what we've written and use parts of it for *public writing*—pieces meant for the eyes of others.

It's not hard to take rough exploratory writing and use it as the germ for different pieces in different genres. For example, we can easily use the same raw ingredients for making a story, an analytic essay, or a persuasive essay.

Main Assignment Preview

This workshop will help you start from the safety of private writing so as to allow maximum freedom, creativity, and exploration; and then work with what you have produced in private to build it more carefully into the kind of finished product you want—or that some audience wants. In the first section of this workshop, we will invite you to do lots of private writing. In the second section, we will show you how to *mine* or *raid* this private writing for various public purposes.

Your *main assignment* will be to explore various possibilities that are latent in your private writing; then decide on one kind of public essay you could create; and then create it.

Section I: Private Writing

You may be someone who can write everything you need by sitting down and writing it right. Fine. But we suspect that you will learn to produce richer and more interesting writing if you try out one or both of the following techniques: Sondra Perl's "Composing Guidelines" and the "Open-Ended Writing Process." Both are somewhat structured methods, but after you have tried them out, you can adjust them to your own needs.

Activity One: Sondra Perl's Composing Guidelines

Your teacher may ask you to guide yourself through Perl's guidelines by reading them to yourself as you engage in writing at your own speed. In this case, we urge you to follow them with full concentration, making sure to spend enough time to get rolling at the various stages of writing. On the other hand, your teacher may read out loud from the guidelines to lead the whole class through an extended session of writing. Some students feel distracted by having to proceed at the same pace as everyone else, but we have found some of our own best writing sessions occur when someone leads us through the guidelines with a group. It keeps you going. (See the box on page 50 with Pat Belanoff's process writing when she was led through the Perl guidelines.) However you are introduced to the guidelines, under-

Exploring the Writing Process
On Writing for One's Eyes Only

I got out this diary, & read as one always does read one's own writing, with a kind of guilty intensity. I confess that the rough & random style of it, often so ungrammatical, & crying for a word altered, afflicted me somewhat. I am trying to tell whichever self it is that reads this hereafter that I can write very much better; & take no time over this; & forbid her to let the eye of man behold it. . . . But what is more to the point is my belief that the habit of writing thus for my own eye only is good practise. It loosens the ligaments. Never mind the misses & the stumbles. Going at such a pace as I do I must make the most direct & instant shots at my object, & thus have to lay hands on words, choose them, & shoot them with no more pause than is needed to put my pen in the ink. I believe that during the past year I can trace some increase of ease in my professional writing which I attribute to my casual half hours after tea.

Virginia Woolf

stand that the goal is to teach you a process you can use and fiddle with on your own.

Remember that this is private writing. Write with the understanding that this is not to be shown to anyone. You may end up with passages you want to share, but that's a decision to be made by you later.*

1. Find a way to get comfortable. Shake out your hands. Take some slow, deep breaths and settle into your chair. Close your eyes if you'd like to. Relax. Find a way to be quietly and comfortably aware of your inner state. Try to let go of any tension by slow breathing.

2. Ask yourself, "What's going on with me right now? Is there anything in the way of my writing today?" When you hear yourself answering, take a minute to jot down a list of any distractions or impediments that come to mind. If there are noises or other distractions, notice them, and then bring your attention back to yourself.

3. Now ask yourself, "What's on my mind? Of all the things I know about, what might I like to write about now?" When you hear yourself answering, jot down what comes. Maybe you'll get only one or two things; maybe a list. If you feel totally blocked, you may write down "Nothing." Even this can be taken further by asking yourself, "What is this 'Nothing' all about?"

4. Ask yourself, "Now that I have one idea—or many—is there anything I've left out, any other piece I'm overlooking, maybe even a word I like, something else I might want to write about sometime that I can add to this list?" Add anything that comes to mind.

5. Whether you have one definite idea or a whole list of things, look over what you have and ask, "What here draws my attention right now? What could I begin to write about, even if I'm not certain where it will lead?" Take the idea, word, or item and put it at the top of a new page. (Save the list for another time.)

6. Now—taking a deep breath and settling comfortably into your chair—ask yourself, "What are all the things I know about this topic and all the associations I have with it? What can I say about it now?" Write down everything you can in response to these questions. Write as much as you can using the "freewriting muscle" you've been developing. Perhaps it will be one connected

---

*We thank Perl for permission to copy these guidelines. We have made tiny modifications. Sondra Perl is a Professor of English at Herbert H. Lehman College and founder of the New York City Writing Project.

sequence of thoughts; perhaps it will be separate, disconnected bits. Keep going.

7. Now having written for a good while, interrupt yourself, set aside all the writing you've done, and take a fresh look at this topic or issue. Grab hold of the whole topic—not the bits and pieces—and ask yourself, "What makes this topic interesting to me? What's important about this that I haven't said yet? What's the heart of this issue for me?" Wait quietly for a word, image, or phrase to arise from your inner and nonverbal *feeling* of the topic—your "felt sense" of the topic. Write whatever comes. (For more on "felt sense," see the "Ruminations and Theory" section at the end of this workshop.)

8. Take this word, image, or phrase, and use it to explore further. Ask yourself, "What's this all about?" As you write, let the felt sense deepen. Where do you feel that felt sense? Where in your body does it seem centered? Ask yourself, "Is this right? Am I getting closer? Am I saying it?" If not, ask yourself, "What is wrong or missing?" and keep writing. See if you can feel when you're on the right track. See if you can feel the shift or click inside when you get close: "Oh yes, this says it."

9. If you're at a dead end, you can ask yourself, "What makes this topic hard for me?" Again pause and see if a word, image, or phrase comes to you that captures this difficulty in a fresh way—and if it will lead you to some more writing.

10. When you find yourself stopping, ask, "What's missing? What hasn't yet gotten down on paper?" and again look to your felt sense for a word or an image. Write what comes to mind.

11. When again you find yourself stopping, ask yourself, "Where is this leading? What's the point I'm trying to make?" Again write down whatever comes to mind.

12. Once you feel you're near or at the end, ask yourself, "Does this feel complete?" Look to your felt sense, your gut reaction, even to your body, for the answer. Again write down whatever answer comes to you. If the answer is "No," pause and ask yourself, "What's missing?" and continue writing.

How and Why the Guidelines Work. When the guidelines help us write, it's because they help us focus our attention better and keep checking back and forth between the words we are writing and the felt meanings inside (the "felt sense") that are so often the source for our words.

There's nothing sacred about the exact format or wording of the guidelines. They aren't meant to be a straitjacket. To help you adapt them to your own style and temperament, here is a short list of the four most productive moments in the process. After you try out the complete set, you can use these as an abbreviated version of the guidelines:

- Relax, stretch, clear your mind, try to attend quietly to what's inside—and note any distractions or feelings that may be preventing you from writing. Invite yourself to be aware of your body and your physical surroundings.
- Start with a list of things you could write about. Often we can't find what we really want to write about until the third or fourth item—or not until that subtle after-question, "Is there something I have forgotten?"
- As you are writing, periodically pause and look to that felt sense somewhere inside you—that feeling, image, or word that somehow represents what you are trying to get at—and ask whether your writing is really getting at it. This comparing or checking back ("Is this it?") will often lead to a productive "shift" in your mind ("Oh, now I see what it is I want to say").
- Finally, toward the end, ask, "What's this all about? Where does this writing seem to be trying to go?" And especially ask, "What's missing? What haven't I written about?"

An example. Here is what Peter Elbow wrote using the Perl guidelines.

I'm sitting here writing with my pen. About writing with a word processor. Seems odd. I normally write <u>on</u> my WP, but today I'm in a workshop with other teachers and we have a chance to write together about whatever we need to write.

The two main skills in writing are <u>making a mess</u> and cleaning up the mess.

That is, it's hard to write well unless we are inventive and fecund—open to lots of words and ideas. That means being open and accepting to the words and ideas which come. Not being too quick to reject and say no. When we do that, we make a mess. We write down (or at least consider) too much. ~~We~~ Too many words; we start down too many paths. Branching and complex. We need that mess.

Yet in order to write well we also need to do just the opposite: we need to ~~say no and~~ be skeptical and rejecting—to throw away or change everything that's not the best; to reject what <u>looks</u> or <u>sounds</u> nice but isn't really, in the end, up to snuff.

It turns out that the WP is ideal for both these mental oper-ations. ~~It helps~~

It ~~helps in make~~ makes it easier than with pen and paper to make <u>more</u> of a mess. We can throw down everything to the screen easily in more [I skipped a few blank lines; I think I assumed I'd come back and say more.]

Yet it also makes it easier than with pen and paper to clean up that mess. It's so easy to throw away what's discarded, fix words and spellings—and come up with neat copy.

Indeed, I would say that the main <u>psychological</u> danger in writing with a WP is that its fixing and cleaning up is so easy—indeed so fun—that it's tempting to stop every time you mistype or misspell a word or change your mind about a word and go back and fix it.

Learn to block that impulse. Learn to sustain your generating. Learn to keep on writing—as though it were pen and ink or typewriter and it were too hard to make a change. Otherwise you will distract yourself from your generating. Learn, in short, to <u>make</u> a mess.

You can let yourself write notes to yourself in your text when you're not sure. Instead of stopping and scratching your head and thinking when you become puzzled, you can <u>keep on</u> writing about your puzzlement. (Because it's so easy to erase them later.) I tend to put these remarks in CAPS—or indent them 5 spaces [in a block that's all indented]. So I can see later that they're not part of the text.

Why that's useful. When you keep writing

But—edit on screen/paper.

~~Start anywhere—cause you can move it around~~

WHAT'S IT ALL ABOUT?

    —new power

    —new relationship to words

    —addiction

    —my duty

    —new horizons

WHERE DO YOU FEEL IT?

    I feel it in my upper stomach.

    WHAT'S THE PHRASE?

    <u>new power</u>

    <u>It's scary: but it leads to addiction. It can change your rela-tionship to writing.</u>

    <u>click</u> [I felt a click here; a shift of felt sense. Asking myself what it's about, what's the phrase, and where I feel it—these acts

led me closer to what seemed interesting and important. Leading to what follows.]

<u>Screen is something half way between mind and paper.</u>

Mind is a mess: paper is supposed to be neat. When I'm writing on screen, it feels like it's sort of—half—still in my mind. It's a second mind. It's ~~not~~ still partly <u>in</u> me.

Like my mind I can't look at all of it at once, I can only put my attention on one bit at a time. I don't yet have complete detachment from it till I print it out.

It gives me a second mind.

WHAT'S LEFT OUT?

Techniques.

—How to adopt right attitude.

—Not be scared. You can't hurt the machine.

—You <u>can</u> get into trouble by losing text if you aren't careful to back up—but don't be worried.

—Writing as play.

WHAT DO I LOVE ABOUT IT?

—That it lets me get so much down.

—When I have a new idea, I just start writing it (using a carriage return to start a new line). I don't have to worry about putting it in the right order. I can jump back from idea to idea.

—<u>Because</u> you know you can correct, you have <u>permission</u> to write a messier way.

—You can start anywhere, in the middle, add late idea—cause you can move things around.

—It's so easy to revise. I suddenly see a new idea or new arrangement after I'm almost done—and I can wade in and do it—and print out clean copy.

—I can experiment. Leave one version as it is. <u>Copy.</u> Start revising but leave the old one. In case I lose good aspects of the old one in the revising process.

—I can print out 3–4 copies—at middle stage—and give 'em to someone else. And they'll be neat and easy to read.

—Spelling and grammar checker. Handwriting and spelling have always been superficials of writing, but they've influenced readers more than anything else. Form of snobbery. If your spelling and handwriting and grammar are bad, I won't take you seriously. Now anyone can turn out professional copy.

WHAT'S HARD/DON'T LIKE

Another mind. Sometimes I make such a mess that I feel in a swamp. Too many options. Once I remember feeling. "Oh, I wish I were writing in ink on expensive velum so that I would just choose

a word and be done. Not feel like I have to keep revising and changing. I want something <u>final</u> (I must find that process piece I wrote
when I was in that situation).

Sometimes I try to revise too much on screen. Too much
chaos in the mind.

It's an enharmonic, changeable medium: it's a mind or it's
paper—and it moves back and forth. If on screen, it's fluid—it's
my mind; if I print it out, it stops being fluid and changing and I
get it still and quiet where I can deal with it. I can take a mind
scan.

Need it.

One can move back and forth.

It's like a brain photograph.

Exploring the Writing Process
On Writing When Using Perl Guidelines

Didn't write what I intended to write—intended to be pragmatic—write out what I *needed* to write out. But someway the other topic forced itself on me and became too exciting to ignore. Topic appeared on paper when I searched my head for something I really wanted to write about. Found all the prompts helpful except one.

The nonhelpful one was, "Use image, idea, phrase, and keep trying to get it right"—because it felt right to me already. The spot when I started on metaphor and metonomy. Don't know why I got on that. Doesn't connect in very well—and yet I know there's a connection, and I guess I saw it as relevant. But I did drop it when Peter said, "Where is this going?"

While writing, I found pleasant revealings coming forth and thought, "Gee! These are good ideas!" Thought of typing it up and giving copies to Peter and Don for comment—not sure I was thinking of them as audiences. Didn't really feel I was writing for them as I wrote—they came to mind because I know they have thoughts on these subjects. I'd like them both to think I'm on to something good—but I'm really wanting this idea worked out for myself. Believe they could help me do that.

I did have some feeling of going around in circles, not putting things together into one Bingo result—but I do think there's stuff there to explore. I'm glad I wrote this.

Pat Belanoff

Activity Two: Trying the Open-Ended Writing Process

The open-ended process is another way to encourage exploratory, private writing. Where the Perl guidelines help you find words for what is sort of in your mind but not in words, the open-ended process pushes you to figure out entirely new thoughts and ideas that are as yet nowhere near your mind.

The open-ended process consists of a simple movement back and forth between two basic activities: freewriting and summing up.

1. *Start by freewriting.* (Or start by listing things you might write about and then start freewriting.) Simply explore whatever topics emerge for you while you're doing this unfocused freewriting.

2. *Pause and sum up.* After 10 or 15 minutes of freewriting, stop and take a deep breath, stretch, look around, then look back or think over what you've written. Then write down a sentence, phrase, or image to summarize the most interesting or important thing you find in your freewriting. Look for a center of gravity: that piece of your writing that seems to pull on you most strongly. It doesn't have to be the main thing in your freewriting. You might focus on some small detail from your freewriting if that's what tugs on you now. You might even write down a thought that didn't occur in your freewriting but occurs to you now as you pause. The point of these summings-up is to provide a springboard for your next piece of freewriting, your next dive into language.

3. *Freewrite again.* As you write, learn to keep on writing even if you don't know where you are going. Learn to ride waves of writing for longer and longer periods of time. When words start to run out after only five minutes, force yourself to keep going. Remember, you don't have to stay on the same subject. Write "What else could I write about?" and "What else?" and keep on writing to see what comes. The goal is to lose yourself in language, to lose perspective.

4. *Stop again to sum up.* Keep following this back-and-forth chain of freewriting and summing up wherever it leads you. To get the real benefit from the process, you need to follow through at least three cycles: three freewrites and three summings-up. More is better.

How and Why the Open-Ended Process Works.   The open-ended process gets its power from alternating two contrary uses of the mind or two opposed ways of producing language. During the freewriting you are immersed in your words: Your head is down and you are scooting along in an underbrush of language; you tend to be working more in words than in thoughts. Indeed the goal is to get lost in the words and not worry about the thoughts or where they are going.

When you pause and sum up, you extricate yourself from the underbrush of words and, as it were, climb up a tall tree to see where you have gotten yourself; you seek perspective and detachment. In this process you are trying to work more in thoughts than in words. (This is another way to consult felt sense.) These summing-up sentences or phrases help keep your freewriting productive. For if you do nothing but freewrite for hours and never stop to climb a tree, you sometimes just go in circles.

As you move back and forth between the two activities, sometimes your writing will change: in subject, in mode, or in style. For example, you might have been writing about an event that happened to you; but now your pausing and summing up lead you to focus your writing on the person who was involved in that event. Let these changes occur. Perhaps you've been writing to yourself, and now you realize you want to write to someone else—a letter, perhaps. You may want to write a poem, prayer, or dialogue. The open-ended writing can lead you closer to what you were trying to get at from the beginning; but sometimes it takes you further afield to something surprising.

Your teacher may well introduce the open-ended process in class. Sitting and writing privately in a public group might seem odd at first, but we want you to practice this new procedure once with some direction. Otherwise you tend to drift into your usual writing habits. The goal is to learn a *new* writing process so that you can then use it flexibly by yourself.

An example. Here is the private, open-ended writing done in class (on a computer) by Melissa Fogel, a student:*

> Alienation . . . like being alone, like feeling shut out, with no friends, no one to turn to. then there is a light, somewhere down that halll, of someone who feels the same someone who shares in the utter feeling of alone. shes warm and kind and she knows how to feel.
>
> • • •
>
> I called, he was warm and sharing the way he said I love you last night was with care, like he was beginning to know what it means to say those words, to say them and to mean them. sometimes I feel like I don't have a problem sometimes I feel like my only friend is the city we live in the city of angels lonely as I am together we cry. so becky banged andy. so I have Jeff. I cant wait fgor the dream sequence its so beautiful and lovely, lovely what a

---

* She wrote this privately but at the end of the semester volunteered it to us as a sample of private writing.

cheesy word, its white and red and everything is like the dawn, foggy yet glissening. I cant wait, only a couple of more days. The times I feel alone, are sometimes truthful other times they are brought on by my own anxieties, and that scares me more than being alone. Today is blue and blue, ironic I wear those colors right now. The banquet is tonight. and that horrible horrible neophite ceremony. Why scare others. I don't want others to feel the fear I experience so often. Expose them to sunshine, not thunder storms. The rain was coming down hard, and the crash of thunder was so monstrous, I thought I would hide my head under the pillow. I remember the raccoon, it just jumped right out at me. Initiation is a time to reflect on the meaning of Kappa, it is a time to recognize all the good of sisterhood, I look forward to experiencing the other side of the beauty. Oh joy another hour and a half.

• • •

Who am I? Where do I go from here?

• • •

I am Melissa the great the wonderful, with a face of anger, sometimes happiness, I guess it depends on the mood my life has. The tone of the day almost like writing, whats the tone melissa, why I do not know, the tone today is fun, happy, get it done, eat and merry, be loyal to kappa. Its blue day for gods sake, your favorite color in the world, Jeff's too. Is he far away thinking of me now. I am so shungry right now I wish I had finished that slim fast shake, since we will be here for the entire time. now that I am totally off track. I wonder if I am the only sophomore that is taking this class. Good thing I took, that horrible typing class in the eleventh grade. Well lets try to get deeper . . . If I stay and let myself be subject to the life I create for myself, I accept without hesitation or sigh that life, the one where I stay in Mass. and live on expressing myself through friends and family, that family I call Kappa. If I go I delete that, its just not worth it today anyway, tomorrow ask me again. When I think about jeff he scares me, not because he scares me physically, not even him. Its the idea of having a boyfriend again that scares me. falling in love again means sacrificing my feelings for another, it means taking the risk of somehow being left, being alone again and learning to cope all over again. Danny left me high and dry, now I cant stand him, but I'm over him. gone. Jeff is the sweetest, he's everything a girl could ask for and the physical is slowly slipping into place, which might be better for me, who knows. All I know right now is that I miss him, miss him to death.

• • •

Our hearts meet somewhere along a sea of lonliness, somewhere among the vast mountains of trust. Then my hand grabs
his, and we walk the path I call life.

• • •

And so this class drags on. . and on. . Maybe if I try to save
her I can. No she is brain washed, lost in the crowd of men who
want to take her away from our family. for so long it was tight, together we shared not always with words but with actions and he
the masked ass of the century destroyed that closeness in one
fell swoop. She is only a child looking for some attention, he could
see that in her lost eyes of a sea of blue. See that she was crying out of the term middle, he seized her while she cried, and gave
her a shoulder to lean on, why did she fall. Because we all looked
away for a split second and she was gone. Now we all pay. . . I just
want her to be happy. She wont with him, even though he was there
when we were busy, he is a do nothing a go nowhere. and she lives
with that, nothing else. Can I stop and help you little girl. Do you
need my shoulder to cry on, I won't hurt you in the end, I am sister I will not leave. I am sister, trust me please. My little brat from
behind, catch up come play in the yard with us, no I want to swing,
swing in the rain. It feels good on my tongue. But it is not safe little girl, don't you see it's not safe. She falls quick, hard under the
swing set, we don't see her. Wait I see her. She lies in a pool of mud
and blood. Someone help her she is falling. Now she is falling again
into another pool of mud and blood. This time the consequences
more than a couple of stitches. but wait do you remember sister?
The stitces did not hurt the little girl, she asked for a piece of
gum, maybe there is hope, maybe she will survive with a smile left
on her time beaten face. Maybe she will live and live long with the
family, the ones who forgive and forget, nomatter what you do or
say, or who you go out with.

• • •

So I am alone and afraid of feeling alone. Should I go and do
something about this, or work through it, like so many other times,
by myself. I also look forward to the end of this week with all the
beauty it possesses. The song the laughter and the fun at the end
of it all. I am also fearing the closeness I have with Jeff. It scares
me, to think I fall again. Then there is my sister, Will she be o.k. boy
you have a lot to think about!!!!

Fogel wrote a cover letter describing her experience with the
open-ended process, which we reprint below. (An essay she developed from it can be found on pages 66–68.)

Process Letter

Dear Peter,

I have participated in this exercise before. The amount of freedom is so amazing. The feeling of writing whatever your mind may find deep within its core allows the writer to express herself without any fear of denial. I do believe some of our writing in this fine University of ours is extremely narrow and limited. One has guidelines and rules and finds oneself lacking creativity. This type of writing had me smiling again, with my fingers typing away, yearning for more and more. However, because I am so used to being confined in my writing, my thoughts did not wander as much as they used to. I found myself staying on one topic very diligently. With more practice I could probably find creative aspects of writing lurking behind the closed doorway.

I found that a bunch of my underlying fears of whatever seemed deep in my thoughts, would surface, no matter how hard I tried to retain them. Maybe this sort of writing is a release from the everyday tensions. It did remind me of diary writing: the kind of writing that enables you to let go of your anxieties and fears, to come up with solutions to the problems you write about.

The honesty of my writing today was present. There was a lack of superficial qualities in my writing. I wasn't putting up a front for a professor, or running for a thesaurus to help improve my wording. I was me, a horrible speller and a not-so-great writer. I was creative and I enjoyed the writing experience.

My heart and soul was in this writing today, something I haven't felt in years!!!

Sincerely,
Melissa Fogel

Process Questions about Private Writing

- What did you notice when you did private writing for this workshop?
- Is private writing familiar to you, or something new? Sometimes, when people haven't done much private writing, they keep thinking about readers even when the writing isn't meant for those readers. Did this happen to you?
- What did you notice using the Perl guidelines?
- Did it make sense to you to pause and look for your felt sense of inner meaning or intention—and try to compare that to what you'd written? Did that process lead you anywhere?

- What did you notice using the open-ended process? What kind of path did it lead you on—staying in one area or moving far afield?
- If you did some of this private writing outside of class, did that make a notable difference?
- Did this private writing tell you anything about how you usually write?

Section II: Using Your Private Writing to Create a Piece of Public Writing

In this part of the workshop, we will ask you to use your *private, exploratory* writing as seeds or raw material for a piece of *public* writing. We'll ask you to do a number of 10- or 15-minute sketches to try out different *genres*. Genres are kinds of writing—for example, description, narration, dialogue, or essay. We want to show you that there are many different possibilities lurking in any piece of rough exploratory writing.

You'll get a feeling here for how you can steer a piece of rough, unformed private writing into whatever kind or genre of final product that you want. In the process, you will come away with a better understanding of the tricky relationship between form and content. Sometimes you will feel yourself (putting it crudely) pouring existing ideas or content into new containers, and sometimes you will feel that the containers are helping you think of new ideas. That is, sometimes the exercises will lead you to revise or shape your private writing to fit different genres. But sometimes the process of thinking in terms of a genre will make you think of new content or ideas that weren't even in your private writing.

Step One: Looking Back over Your Private Writing

Some theorists think that we haven't, in a sense, finished expressing any thought until we finally make it public. We disagree. It's perfectly natural to express some thoughts and feelings and keep them to ourselves. We often need privacy in order to explore our thoughts or feelings without having to consider what others might think about them. You may well not want to share much of what you got on paper in your private writing.

But of course we often do want to communicate to others what is inside our heads. If we've written our thoughts and feelings down on paper, occasionally we can simply hand it over unchanged to readers. But private writing often needs to be revised in order to communicate its sense to others.

The first step is to look back over your private writing just to get it fresh in mind. As you look back, you're likely to have mixed feelings about it. You may feel good about how much you wrote, or about how diverse it is, or about how you were able to record your thinking and feeling in a way you'd never done before. As you read it over, part of it will probably "click" with the felt sense of it still in your head, and the match will feel gratifying to you. Or perhaps you'll be pleased because this private, exploratory writing is not very much of a mess at all: Some of it may well be clear, shaped, and strong.

But you may hate what you wrote: "Yuk. What a mess! What drivel my mind is full of." This reaction often occurs when people first try out private exploratory writing. It's important to remember that you weren't trying to produce good, well-organized writing; you were trying to give yourself the safety to produce, as it were, an accurate brain X-ray or mind-dump. Minds are messy.

If your private writing seems to be a disorganized mess, it shows that you let your writing record the many diverse side paths that every mind inevitably considers. If you read through that mess in the proper spirit, you will find *more* possible topics and potential trains of

Exploring the Writing Process
On Sharing, Privacy, Safety

I want to thank you for emphasizing safety around sharing our writing—for your invitation to keep our writing private when we need to do so. You gave us permission to share or not share, whichever we were most comfortable doing. I have, however, come to realize that there are some powerful sociopolitical factors that complicate the issue of safety for me. I realized that as a member of a minority group, the line between safety and self-respecting survival is frequently blurred. The oppressive powers that foster one's feelings of being unsafe count on fearful silence as a means to continue the oppression. To create a place for myself at the table, I sometimes find that the need to make myself purposely *unsafe* is more important than my instinctive and sensible need to be safe. And thus, I sometimes give myself voice and demand that society acknowledge my existence—I become visible in a world which might otherwise choose to ignore me.

Susan Luppino,
in a letter to Peter Elbow
after a workshop

thought for writing than if you had written something careful and well organized.*

Your private writing may well contain

- *Contradictions.* You might have thought or felt X at one point, but then later on you wandered into thinking or feeling Not-X. If you are going to engage in good thinking, you need contradiction; you need to wrestle with both sides or get both sides to

---

*Our minds are not just messy; they often contain thoughts and feelings we don't like. Your writing might seem to be in a rut, grinding over unpleasant feelings in a tiresome or depressing way. Some people who are not used to private exploratory writing say, "How depressing" or "How childish" or "How irrational." But remember, if this material came out on paper, it must have been in your head. You can't get rid of it just by not writing it down. Everyone obsesses sometimes. Writing it down can in fact help you "put it down" so you can let go of it, not think about it, not carry it around anymore in your head. (If it really bothers you or gets in the way of functioning well, you might want to talk about it to someone you trust or to a counselor.)

Writing down thoughts or feelings you don't like can also give you *perspectives* on them. For example, if we find angry or unfair or even violent feelings inside us, we can explore and figure out what events or situations led to those feelings. There's no blame in *having* bad feelings—they are inevitable. There's only blame in acting badly. If you explore how certain events or situations led to your feelings, and how you deal with those feelings (and how other people deal with them), you will have material for excellent stories and analytic essays.

Exploring the Writing Process
On Writing as Release

I find it is so much easier to say something to a person when, instead of saying it face-to-face, I am able to write the message down. In fact I tried that system just today. I had a problem with my friend, but when I tried to speak to him about it, I just could not find the words, even though I knew exactly what I wanted to say. I complained about the situation to another friend who gave me the suggestion that I write a letter. Even if I didn't give it to him, I would at least have my thoughts expressed on paper. I tried the advice and, believe it or not, it worked. I believe that I got everything down that I wanted to say, completely and honestly. When I didn't have to look at his face and know that he was listening to me at that very moment, I felt so free at the thought of expressing my emotions. I did end up giving the letter to him, but that's another story.

Katie Houston

wrestle with each other. In this way you'll come up with new thinking, not just a restatement of your old thoughts.

- *Changes of topic and digressions.* Your writing might have been going in one direction but suddenly veered off or changed direction completely. There's cognitive power in this jumpy diversity: There are seeds for different pieces of writing. But even more interesting than that, there are important unstated insights contained in every jump or digression. Look closely at each jump or shift. Pause and ask yourself, "How did my mind make that jump? What is the connection?" Even if there doesn't *seem* to be any connection (say you jumped from radios to swimming), there was always something in your mind that served as a bridge between radios and swimming. Noticing that bridge will throw some light on both of them. The mind is incapable of pure randomness.

Step Two: Trying Out Genres

A genre is a widely recognized form of writing. Some genres are large, inclusive, and loosely defined—for example, poetry and prose. Some genres are smaller and less inclusive, such as essay and fiction. Then there are even smaller, more specific genres—which are the ones we will ask you to try out in this workshop: (1) description or portrait, (2) narrative or story, (3) dialogue, (4) persuasive essay, (5) expository essay, (6) satire or parody, (7) meditation or personal essay, and (8) poetry (we leave this one broad). We could add "letter" to this list, but we assume that most of you probably explored letters in the first workshop.

You may not have time to try out all these genres. Your teacher will give you direction about how many and perhaps which ones to try. As you try them out, notice when you find yourself pouring existing ideas or content into various containers and when the containers make you think of new ideas.

1. Description or Portrait.   If your private writing already contains a very full description or portrait, you might skip this exercise. In effect, your private writing already led you to the genre of description or portrait. Just take a moment more to write about what changes you would consider, if any, to focus the description and make your piece public: Would you shape it any differently? What would be the center? Are there any changes in style or approach you would want to make?

But if your private writing doesn't have much description, read through it or think back over it and try to find a *scene,* an *object,* or a *person* that could be important to you. Perhaps you'll only be able to find the *germ* or seed of a scene, object, or person. Do 8 to 10 minutes of descriptive writing. First, close your eyes and try to experience your subject using your eyes, ears, nose, and touch. Then go on to describe it in writing.

Obviously you can't complete a large scene in this short time. But take a minute or two at the end to make a note to yourself about how you'd go on to shape it or organize it if you were to finish it. These are just sketches. The goal is simply to get a start—to test how fruitful it might be to write a longer piece of public writing in this genre of description.

Melissa Fogel discovered that her private, open-ended writing led her finally to an image of her sister swinging on a swing and then falling off—and indeed this image became the germ of her revised public piece of writing.

Peter Elbow tried out a fast sketch of an image of himself at the computer:

> His shoulders began to hunch more as he got more frustrated with the computer. He was sitting forward on his chair, his eyes as though pulled into the screen. Periodically he would stop, lean back, try to take a deep breath and relax, but then as he struggled more, he would hunch again and you could see his muscles gradually become tense. On one side of the computer were papers and notes he was trying to write from. On the other side and on the floor around him were the computer manuals—propped open to various pages with random objects: books, pencils, boxes of floppy disks. Behind him a window showed clear, bright blue sky, but he was oblivious to it. At this point, he didn't even live in the same universe with that blue sky.

2. Narrative or Story.   Where are the potential stories in what you wrote? Look for crucial events, moments, turning points. These points might even be in what you not wrote, but only implied. For example, perhaps your writing is nothing but your feelings about a certain person or your thoughts about a certain issue. But there *are* various stories you could find or make that would relate to that person or issue. Choose one and start at an important moment in that story—not necessarily the beginning—and just write for 8 to 10 minutes to get the feel for how you might write a story. This may lead you to new material or new insights.

If your private writing is already mostly story or has an extended narrative in it, just take a couple of moments and jot down what shaping and adjusting you'd do to make it a public piece. Would you heighten or play with the plot? the mood? the narrator or that narrator's point of view?

Melissa Fogel tried using her private writing for narrative:

Once upon a time, in a fast-paced city of lights, action, and turmoil, there lived a family. This family wasn't an average family. For in the big city it is hard to find average families. This family, like every other family in the big city, had problems. These problems had nothing to do with money or violence, like most in the city. This family struggled with emotional stress that revolved around one of the family members, the middle child. This middle child was a beautiful girl, for she had eyes the color of the sky and skin that only a china doll could retain. She had long brown locks of curls, and in the sun you could see the gold highlights glowing. She had unique style and sensitivity, and she would share the world with you if she could. There were other children in the family, an older sister and two younger brothers. They all went about their own lives, sometimes fighting, like normal adolescents. But under the surface fights about clothes and the car, they shared a love and respect that isn't easy to come by in the big city. One day the middle child announced that she had a new love. Everyone was happy for the girl. They knew this boy was a very lucky person. But as time went on, problems with this boy began to appear. Changes in the middle child began to take place, changes that no one could understand, not even the sister and brothers that loved her more than the world itself.

3. Dialogue.   You may not think of yourself as a dialogue writer, but there may already be *germs* of dialogue in your private writing: places where you said "No" or "But wait a minute" or "I agree" or "Here's one thing for sure." In passages like that, you are really speaking to another voice—even if that other voice is just another feeling or opinion in your own head. You will find even more passages that *imply* a dialogue, such as if you wrote about someone who disagrees with you. And if you wrote, "Then we got into a fight" or "She asked him out for a date," you can break that kind of thing out into an actual dialogue or conversation of what they said to each other.

Take 8 to 10 minutes and start a dialogue, perhaps with that person you disagree with, perhaps between two conflicting feelings. Perhaps there are two people in your private writing who had an interchange or who disagree with each other; get them talking. But it's not necessary that people disagree. If they simply have different temperaments, any dialogue they have will be fruitful. Start the conversation and just see where it goes.

Don't forget that you can easily write productive dialogues with objects or ideas: with a house, a book, a place, a piece of clothing. You can have a fruitful dialogue with anything that is important to you in your exploratory writing. The trick is simply to have one member of the dialogue say something to start off. As little as "Hello" or

"What was it like being the house we've all lived in, and seeing and hearing everything we've all said to each other?" Just see what answer comes; let the conversation proceed. Get your pen moving and the dialogue will unfold and create new material and new ideas that are not part of your original exploratory writing. The dialogue may affect or even change the views or feelings you had when doing your exploratory writing.

When Peter Elbow looked back over his private Perl writing (printed on pages 47–50 above), he realized that he could start a dialogue between himself and the computer.

Peter: Why do you always give me such trouble? Why do you so often mess me up or not do what I want you to do? I paid a lot of money for you. I got instructions. Most of all, why won't you talk to me when I need you?

Computer: Actually, I talk to you quite often.

Peter: Yes, you send me messages—"bad command," "insert target disk in Drive B"—worse yet, "FATAL ERROR"— but when I'm really in trouble, you just sit there silent and refuse to do what I want you to do.

Computer: Unfortunately it's you who gives me trouble: You refuse to do what's needed. But I don't hold it against you. I just wait for you to catch on. I do everything you ask me to—no matter how many times you ask me to do it; I never forget anything; I'm never bored or impatient. There's only a problem when you don't know my language or you ask me to do something that is impossible. I'm not programmed to know your language perfectly. It's your job to learn mine. As soon as you speak meaningfully to me, I'll speak meaningfully to you.

Peter: Don't take that superior tone with me! "I never make a mistake. I never make a mistake." Why do you keep saying that to me?

Computer: I didn't say that; I never have. But in fact I never do make a mistake. In our dealings, I'm sorry to say that it's only you who makes mistakes.

Peter: SEE! I won't put up with this arrogance. (Wait a minute; let me get ahold of myself. It's only a machine. Calm myself.) OK, I'll be more reasonable with you. I admit it. Of course I make mistakes. But I'm doing the best I can. I try to do things right; and when something doesn't work, I look at the manual; I go over my steps one at a time and try it again and again. But still it doesn't work. Sometimes I get so mad I want to hurl you across

	the room. And you just sit there silent, superior, condescending.
Computer:	*But that's it, don't you see? You are so irrational. Why do you give me the same order again and again when you see it's not working? And then you get so angry because you're doing something irrational.*
Peter:	*But I can't help it.*
Computer:	*Yes, that's what perplexes me. Why do I bring out irrationality in you? I've been watching you these months. I've never seen you as furious and fuming—as close to violence—with anyone else as with me. Not with your wife or children or students or co-workers. What do I do that brings out your irrationality?*
Peter:	*That's a good question.*

4. Persuasive Essay.   What are some of the important opinions or beliefs in your exploratory writing? What if you tried to persuade people to agree with you? Are there certain people you particularly want to persuade? You'll find that the genre of persuasive essay—the process of trying to persuade someone—will often bring up reasons or arguments that you didn't think of earlier when you were just expressing or exploring your opinion for yourself.

Take 8 or 10 minutes now and start the germ of a persuasive essay, beginning perhaps with summing up your point as briefly as possible. Before you stop, jot down quickly as many reasons as you can think of that you might use; and try to sketch out a possible organization for the essay. If what you wrote privately was already more or less in a persuasive mode (or if a big chunk of it was), just write for a few moments about how you would shape it or make it stronger. (Workshop 9 deals more fully with persuasion.)

Melissa Fogel tried using her private writing for a persuasive essay:

I of all people know what it's like to use a boyfriend for a sense of security and escape. I also know what the consequences are for doing such a thing. Relationships these days are under tremendous stress. The problems one of us decides to take on become a problem for the couple. Sometimes even the smallest problems cause the largest rifts between two people. However to stay involved with someone because it is the easiest thing to do, or because of the fear of being on your own, produces a strain no other problem can compare to. When hiding behind someone, you can lose a sense of identity and pride. You can become so wrapped up in the lie that you can't see the truth, even when people are trying to tell you so. The lie can fester and create long-term disaster.

After a while, you can't see the trouble brewing. This trouble can come in all forms. It can cause fighting between those who are trying to make you see the truth, it can hurt the people that care about you, and most of all it can hurt you. You may give up on yourself—decide that you're not good enough for others. You may stop caring for your health and your appearance. You may even lose the qualities you had when you began the relationship. Sometimes when you're unsure if you are falling into this trap, you should break off the relationship for a while and try to regain your life and self once again. You may find that liking you is more important than whether or not someone else likes you.

5. Expository Essay.   What's the most interesting question, issue, or concept in your exploratory writing? Most people think of an essay as explaining something that they understand. But if you want the most interesting essay—and want to have the most interesting time writing it—don't look for answers or conclusions or explanations; look for questions or perplexity. What do you need to understand better? You'll discover that you can produce good writing even though you don't yet really understand the issue you are trying to write about. Remember that many good published essays don't give solutions: They clarify or analyze a question so that others can understand it better and go to work on it.

So sniff out the issue of greatest interest to you and take 8 to 10 minutes to start exploring it. You can think of what you are writing as an example of the general form known as *expository essay:* an essay that explains something or figures out a problem. But there are also different subgenres that represent different ways of explaining or figuring out the problem—each of which could give a slightly different shape to your writing:

- *Analysis.* Perhaps your private writing talks about lots of things that are all connected to an incident or related to a topic or feeling, but it's not clear how it all adds up or what the main point is. The basic question is the one that lies behind all thinking and writing: "What sense can I make of this tangled pile of data?" Analysis means untangling a tangle.
- *Definition.* Perhaps your private writing leads to some complex or slippery *concept* you want to figure out (e.g., selfishness). The clearest and most down-to-earth kind of defining is "ostensive" defining—that is, pointing or giving examples. (X and Y are examples of selfishness. Z looks like selfishness but it is not, and here's why.) This is really the same approach used in zoological definition: Genus tells how something is like its cousins; species tells how it differs from its cousins. Thus the essay of definition is closely related to the next subgenre.

- *Compare–contrast.* It's often hard to define or analyze one thing by itself. It's much easier when you can compare it to others—continually holding them up against each other to find similarities and differences. This gives mental leverage. In your private writing, you can probably find two or more people, places, or ideas that invite comparison.
- *Process essay.* In scientific or technical writing, a process essay explains how to do something (e.g., how to perform a certain experiment or how to make water from hydrogen and oxygen). But process essays are not limited to these disciplines. You can write about the steps you go through, for example, to cook a particular meal or prepare a garden plot in the spring—or to do something less concrete such as convincing a parent or teacher of something. Your private writing probably contains at least the germ of some process that you could explain in a process essay.
- *Research essay.* Does your private writing suggest some areas you'd like to study more? You can now write out some of the questions you would pursue. You can take up the issue again in Workshops 10 and 11 about research essays.
- *Five-paragraph essay.* This is a school-invented genre, and unfortunately, it is the only genre that some students are taught. The first paragraph introduces the thesis, the three "body paragraphs" each give a reason and an example, and the last paragraph gives a conclusion that restates the thesis. The five-paragraph essay limits thinking because it is so rigid in form. But it is a handy formula to use in certain conditions where you don't have time to think through or explain any complexities. It can be a particularly handy genre for short, timed exams: "In 20 minutes, explain what is distinctive or powerful about such and such a novel or poem."

Select one or more of these essay subgenres and write for at least 10 minutes on each one you pick.

6. Satire or Parody. There might well be germs of satire or parody in your private writing: moments where you make fun of something or someone. If not, what could your private exploratory writing lead you to make fun of? A person you'd like to show as silly? An opinion or view that needs puncturing? Yourself when you realize you did something silly? A situation or scene that is on the brink of the ridiculous (e.g., people who show off)?

The essence of satire is to exaggerate or distort. Thus you could satirize someone in your exploratory writing (or yourself) by simply describing but exaggerating certain traits. Or you could put down the thoughts and feelings that run through the person's head (a monologue) but overdo it—carry the thoughts and feelings beyond the plausible, exaggerate the manner of talking. Or you can make fun of an opinion or view by stating it or even arguing for it, but pushing it a bit too far. Or you could create a tone or voice that is off: Be highly dignified about something trivial, or very flippant about something serious.

Peter Elbow tried writing a kind of parody or satire and started off like this:

> He gradually began to get good at using his computer. What a relief. No more error messages. He learned all kinds of shortcuts and "macros." He began to impress his friends and colleagues with all kinds of fancy formatting. After a while, though, his friends started to notice subtle changes. At first they were impressed. He didn't make all those careless mistakes he used to make, slips of the tongue, forgettings, mixing up one name with another. He began to be more precise, But that was when they began to wonder: "Peter never used to be precise." Then they noticed that he no longer seemed so creative and independent. He did everything well—but only if it was clearly explained to him. It was when someone noticed a slight *monotone* quality to his way of speaking that they turned to each other with fear in their eyes: "Do you think the computer could have gotten into him?" And then they noticed a frightening gleam in Peter's eye. . . .

Writing as Play   Cut-and-Paste Poetry

Young children seem to be naturally drawn to poetry, but most people become somewhat intimidated by it as they grow older and hear all the talk about the complexity of great poetry. We know that some of you have continued to write poetry since childhood, or have perhaps come back to it. We will attempt no formal definition of poetry here; we'll just say that for us, poetry is utterance where the language is special or the voice particularly matters; it is language one wants to savor. We find that most people can write poetry with a little encouragement if they know they don't have to show it to anyone else. We also believe that the very process of writing poetry brings us to a richer understanding of the potential in all language—including even the language of formal essays.

As you read back over your private writing, you may find language that already seems somehow resonant—words that feel right on your tongue or phrases that recur in your ear. Perhaps you can shape some of this into poetry. Remember that poetry does not have to rhyme or even have a formal design; much modern poetry has neither. You may find that you can create poetry out of some of your private writing with minimal changes. Or you may want to extract some passages—lines and phrases—and build a poem from them.

Writing as Play   Cut-and-Paste Poetry *continued*

It turns out that there is an easy or "cheating" way to make poetry—to create language with more weight or voice with more resonance. Choose a piece you've written that you sense has some good ingredients. Freewriting is fine. Now go back through it and look for phrases and lines that sound resonant or catch your eye. Just pull them out; use them to make a kind of "found" poem. (That term is most often used for poems that poets make out of words they find written by others; but you can make a found poem from your own words.)

Peter created a found poem out of his messy Perl process freewriting (printed earlier in this workshop). He copied out phrases that felt most interesting to him and chose from them, rearranging them to make what follows. Not a great work of art, but fun to create:

Brain Photograph

Too many words
too many paths
mind is a mess
paper is neat

stop
go back and fix it
block that impulse
make a mess, keep on writing

new power
upper stomach
hand
a second mind
addiction
another mind
half in my mind
mind scan

it's still in me
jump back
I won't take you

I wish I were writing in ink on expensive vellum
I want something final

7. Meditation or Personal Essay.   These are particularly interesting public forms because they often function as a somewhat *private genre turned public:* an invitation to others to overhear the inner speech we have with ourselves. It might well be that a portion of your private exploratory writing could be turned into a meditation or personal essay without having to make many changes at all.

Melissa Fogel's private writing was already meditative and personal. By focusing on one topic, she made a meditative personal essay, which is reprinted below:

Be Brave Sweet Sister   *Melissa Fogel*

My sister Jennifer and I were the closest two sisters could be. We were not abnormal, we had our fights, yet they were fights you'd have with any life-long roommate. All of my childhood memories are filled with her face. Her baby blue eyes, her long curly brown hair and of course her chubby little cheeks. Our days were spent torturing our little brother, playing dress up with mom's clothes, climbing trees, sledding down the back of our yard, riding bikes until we couldn't walk, or just singing along to the radio in our make-believe band. I die a little each time I think that the laughter left our family, or my sweet little sister has vanished from my life.

Jennifer has been dating a man our family has trouble relating to. Although she would love to blame it on the color of his skin, this is far from the truth. My family has trouble relating to his ten-year leap over her age, his twenty-two arrests, and his three times in jail serving longer than six months. Take all the legal problems away and my family will not relinquish their problem with this man. My sister is young, beautiful, and intelligent; however she has very little self-esteem, and seems to let herself get lost in the crowd. The man she dates does not help in this situation; he only lets her hide under his arms. Jennifer needs someone to motivate her in school and life—to show the world that she is an incredible woman with enormous gifts to give. He just hides her, and feeds her fear.

The days without her now are almost empty, almost depressing. She and I fight on the subject whenever one of us can muster up the energy. Some days I want to reach for her thin little neck and start strangling. For the path down this lifetime she has chosen will only break the rope that ties our hearts together. The anger I feel rises inside of me until I can hardly see straight. My nails bury themselves into my skin and tears cascade down the pale cheeks of my pain-ridden face. I can see the anger in Jennifer as well. Her blue eyes become black and there is no reflection of the sister she once loved staring back at her. I am the enemy, with a black heart and red horns that stick strangely towards the sky. Our clashes have become so ugly, that I began to fear seeing her in the halls of the house—the same halls we used to bang into while playing a fast-paced game of tag. Now these halls are empty, lonely, and ugly.

The pain of losing her is harder to describe than the anger. The pain gnaws on the inside of my heart, making it slowly bleed to death into a sea some call the soul. I have painful reminders of what our relationship used to be like in the back of my mind trying to break free and huddle over the mess we have now. My days at home are so dark. The rooms seem so cloudy, even when the sun peers through the hazy windows. The cloud

Be Brave Sweet Sister   *continued*

seems to follow me into every sphere of my life, hanging over my head and gliding along the paths I choose to follow. It shadows my every move and makes others aware through the ugly darkness that covers my face. It seems as if this cloud will never let me free, until I confront the pain that steals my body from a happier existence.

That is where the fear becomes effervescent in the scope of my life. This confrontation that seems inevitable pulls at my sleeve as a nagging child does to her mother. In every scenario I play on the record player of my mind, Jennifer either wins the war, or drives off for good. I can't lose her entirely, I would die without my sister. Yet I can't see her with someone who does not bring out the Jennifer I know and love. I fear the loneliness I will experience without her. I fear the pain she will have to endure in a life under his wing, and I fear the guilt that will creep into my heart if I make her leave him for a life of loneliness.

I remember one rainy afternoon. Despite the warnings we heard from our parents, my sister, brother and I went out to play. We ran over to our neighbor John's house, because he had the coolest swing set. It was wet and I had a really eerie feeling about the day. My sister ran over to the swing set to a bench where four people could sit and began to swing really high. She called me over but I couldn't do it; I didn't feel right about it. So I called her over to come play with me. To no avail: She wouldn't stop swinging. About ten minutes later I heard a scream. I ran over to find my little sister underneath that swing lying in a pool of blood. She was crying. The rest is memory to the adults, because they took over from there. Jennifer was rushed to the hospital, where she was given fifteen stitches in the top of her head. I remember waiting by the window, so scared I would never see her again. She came home with a goofy story about how she was very brave, didn't cry and asked the doctor for gum while he was sewing her up.

The story seems ironic to me now. I'm calling out to my sister, for I have this awful feeling about this boyfriend of hers. Yet she doesn't hear me; she keeps on swinging. I keep calling; she keeps swinging. I want her to come home and every day I wait for her to come back to her big sister. Maybe one day she will come home with a new story of how she let him go, was very brave, didn't even cry and asked for a piece of gum.

MAIN ASSIGNMENT
Developing Your Sketch into a Full Draft

For your main assignment, take one of the quick sketches you have made and develop it into a full draft. Perhaps your teacher will direct you to use a particular genre. (You could also develop two sketches into two drafts so that you can compare more fully the effects of varying the genre. If you do two drafts, they will probably be rougher.)

The simplest way to choose which sketch to work on is to think back and decide which one brought you a "click"—a feeling, even if faint, that tells you that this is an interesting direction (or "container") in which to develop some of your private writing.

After you choose a sketch—that is, choose a genre—look back over all your private writing and take a few quick notes on what you want to include in your first draft. Sometimes you need to do a genuine rewriting: The private writing puts you in a position where you can now start fresh on what you want to say. But don't change more than is necessary. You may find long stretches of your private writing that need only small cuts and adjustments to make them usable for a draft. Inexperienced writers sometimes write lively and interesting rough private writing, but in revision they throw away or ruin the most lively, perky, and individual language and the most adventuresome, powerful thinking and instead go for what sounds safe and "nice" and conventional. So don't be timid. Look for words and passages where you sense energy and juice and life.

Once you have a draft of your major assignment for this workshop, your teacher will either give you an opportunity for more feedback and revision or ask you to set it aside to work on later—perhaps for another workshop in this book.

Suggestions for Collaboration

Full collaboration is probably harder here than in many other workshops, since you are starting from private writing that is liable to be quite personal. Still, some of you might find that you have similar themes, issues, or even stories in your private writing and would like to write something together. If so, you are in a good position to write a collaborative collage. See Workshop 4 for how to produce together a collage that explores a theme or issue in a rich and interesting way.

Sharing and Responding

Since you and your classmates are likely to end up with a wide range of diverse kinds of writing in different genres, there are no common feedback questions to suggest. It is probably most appropriate to use one of the first four methods for feedback described in "Sharing and Responding": plain sharing; pointing and center of gravity; summary and sayback; or what is almost said.

It might also be useful to get movies of the readers' minds to find out what is going on moment by moment as people read or listen to your work (this technique is also in "Sharing and Responding" at the end of this book). For this kind of feedback, it helps to interrupt your reading three or four times (or make them pause as they are reading), and have them tell you what is going on in their minds at that moment.

Process Journal and Cover Letter

- How did you feel looking back over your private writing? Encouraged, discouraged, bothered? Why?
- What was it like moving from private to public? Did it make a big difference in how you wrote?
- What was it like doing all those short sketches or trial starts? Could you get yourself to jump in and do one burst of writing and then move on to another? If you found it hard, what would it take to become more comfortable with it?
- How did you decide which genre or audience to use?

For your cover letter, it's good to include some or all of your process writing. But don't forget to answer some cover letter questions. Here are the main ones: What is your main point and what effect are you trying to have on readers? What do you feel works best in your paper and where are you unsatisfied? What changes did you make on the basis of any feedback? And most important: What feedback do you want now from a reader? But your teacher may ask you particular cover letter questions that pertain to this assignment.

RUMINATIONS AND THEORY
Are Genres Form or Content?

Do you usually start writing by thinking mainly about what you want to say or about how you want to say it? That is, are you thinking about content or form?

Starting with Content

In this textbook we often suggest doing freewriting or exploratory writing without worrying about organization. "Invite chaos," we say; "worry later about organization or form." In making this suggestion we might seem to be making an interesting (and arguable) theoretical assumption: that first you create content (pure content-without-form, as it were) and then you give it form..

Even though *Genesis* tells us that God took this approach when He created the heavens and the earth (starting out with "formless matter"), it is only one approach to creation. Yet the approach is remarkably helpful to many people in their writing. Whether skilled or unskilled, many people find it a relief when they allow themselves to produce "raw content-without-form." They find it enabling to turn out pages and pages of writing without worrying about whether it's organized or fits a certain form.

In this workshop we highlighted this one-sided approach. We asked you to produce, as it were, gallons of formless content, and then we asked you to pour those gallons into various bottles or forms.

Let us now turn around and look at the other way of talking about form and content in the process of creation. In the first place, strictly speaking, all writing has form: There's no such thing as content-without-form. All that private writing you did has *some* form. Perhaps the form is mixed or messy, but that's form too. Besides, what looks messy at first glance is often quite patterned. What you wrote may have a large coherent pattern that is obscured by local clutter, digressions, and interruptions.

For example, if you look carefully at your seemingly chaotic private, exploratory writing, you may see that it is shaped by a single narrative flow—or even by an interesting flashback narrative pattern. Or perhaps your exploratory writing has a three-step pattern: (1) event; (2) reactions to the event; and (3) reflective thoughts about that event and your reactions. Or maybe you'll find the opposite pattern: a movement from reflective thoughts back to the events behind those thoughts. The point is that if you manage to record what's going on in your mind, you are almost certainly recording patterns. Our minds operate by patterns even when we are confused. The human mind is incapable of pure randomness or chaos. Therefore, when you look at your private exploratory writing, don't just accept the chaos as useful and valid (which it is); keep an eye out also for the *order* hiding behind the seeming chaos.

This realization leads to a very practical consequence: There are always organizations and genres already lurking in your seemingly messy exploratory writing—organizations and genres that you can discover and prune into shape (like recovering a shapely tree that has become overgrown). Just because you weren't aware of writing within a particular genre doesn't mean that you wrote genreless material. When you organize your chaotic private writing, you probably don't have to create organization from scratch; you can clarify the latent organization that's already there. Or more likely you can choose and develop one of the two or three overlapping organizations that are operating, like overlapping wave patterns caused by two or three pebbles dropped in a pond.

In sum, there's no such thing as "starting with content only"; you can't have *any* of content that is not fully formed. But it's useful to *pretend* to start with content only; that is, you can put all your attention on following a train of words or thoughts where they lead and totally ignore consideration of form.

Starting with Form

But it's just as valid to take the opposite approach; it's possible to pretend to start with form only. That is, it can be helpful to start with an organization or genre and look to content afterward. For a genre isn't just a mold to pour unformed raw writing into—or a sewing pattern to lay on top of whole cloth to show us where to cut. A genre can serve as a way to *generate* or invent content. Choosing a genre will make you think of words and ideas that you might not think of otherwise. For example, if you decide to use narrative as a form, you will not just arrange your material in terms of time; you will almost certainly think of new events—connecting or even causal events—that you had forgotten. If you are vacillating between a persuasive and an analytic essay, the persuasive genre will cause you to think of reasons and arguments; the analytic genre will cause you to think of hypotheses and causal relationships.

It's perfectly normal to start by choosing a genre. For example, we sometimes decide to write a letter to someone when we're not yet sure what we'll say. Or we may decide to write an essay with a certain organization (for example, a point-by-point refutation of someone else's view), and that organization will help us to think of points. Or someone may choose a genre for us: "Write a persuasive essay on any topic." In loop writing (next workshop), we ask you to start with minigenres (portrait, narrative, letter, and so forth). In this workshop, however, we asked you to think about these genres or types only after you have done lots of writing.

Because language is inherently both form and content, we can never really have pure content or pure form. It is only our consciousness that tends, at any given moment, to emphasize one more than the other. If we use process writing to study our mind's work when we write, we will gradually learn when it's helpful for us to put more attention on form as we write, and when it's helpful to put more attention on content. In this way we can take better control of our writing process.

Writing as a Social and Collaborative Process:

Using Dialogue, Loop Writing, and the Collage

Essential Premises

Dialogue. If you want to enrich your thinking about any topic, and get more invested and involved in it, bring others into the process. When others come at the same topic, they don't just add to the thinking, they multiply the thinking through the interaction of ideas. Writing a dialogue is a helpful introduction to collaborative writing. But you can also write a productive dialogue by yourself.

Loop writing. If you come at the same topic from different angles and use different writing structures or genres, you will find a much wider variety of ideas and even points of view.

Collage. If you use a collage structure, you can communicate more richness and complexity in a piece of writing—even contradiction—and still give readers a sense that the piece hangs together.

All three methods are playful. Using a spirit of play in your writing is one of the best ways to make writing more satisfying for you and more effective for readers.

Main Assignment Preview

Students often experience two problems in dealing with school writing assignments: not being interested in the topic ("boorrrring") and not having enough to say. The activities in this workshop—collaborative writing, dialogue, and loop writing—are powerful ways to overcome these problems. All three techniques are most useful if you want to find more thoughts and insights about your topic, or if you feel bored and unconnected to what you have to write about. They are less useful if you already know what you want to say or are in a hurry for a final draft. As creative, generative processes, they tend to make a mess. If it is not feasible for you to work with others, you also can use these techniques by yourself.

There are two "warm-up" activities for this workshop, in addition to the main assignment. The first activity is to write a dialogue with a partner. The second is to explore the loop writing process with others in your class.

The main assignment is to write a collage with one or more partners. (Other options: a solo collage; a collaborative essay; a solo essay.)

Activity One: Write a Dialogue

The dialogue is a venerable form of writing. Plato wrote famous dialogues that recount philosophical conversations between Socrates and some of his contemporaries. But Plato wrote *both* voices in these dialogues (though he is said to have based them on real conversations). We're asking for something more genuinely collaborative from you and your partner: a dialogue in which each of you writes one voice. Your dialogue can be as short or as long and ambitious as you want to make it. Either way, it will serve as a warm-up for the main assignment.

Here's what we suggest. With a partner, decide on a topic or issue that you are both interested in—one you would like to explore through "talking on paper." Perhaps your teacher will suggest a topic. If you have a choice, it's best to choose an issue or topic that you'd like to understand better. One suggestion is to write about your past collaborative or cooperative experiences working with others: on collaborative projects or on a team, or with friends or family members.

Starting the Dialogue

Writing a dialogue may sound difficult, but you won't have trouble if you realize you are just having a conversation in writing. Every conversation is really a form of collaboration. Have you ever had an e-mail exchange that went back and forth three or four times? That's a written dialogue. Online "chat rooms" are buzzing with written dialogues. We are all practiced at simply replying to what someone says and carrying on with an exploration of a topic through talk—or even through writing or e-mail.

After you have chosen your topic, one of you simply starts. Think about how actual conversations start. Someone just says something. Often the starting point is a little story. "I liked social studies group reports. We got together at someone's house and had a lot of fun while we were getting the work done. It was more fun and less lonely." Or "When I was a kid, I always had to do the dishes with my brother and sister. We could never divide up the jobs evenly. We spent more time fighting than doing the dishes. Why did we do this night after night? You'd think we'd have figured out some system." But sometimes dialogues start with the simplest germ: "Hi. What do you think about collaborating?" Or "I hate collaborating." (Remember that what you write here is only a rough draft. Before you show it to anyone, you will have a chance to delete and add and change things.)

After one person writes the opening remark, the sheet of paper goes to the other person and she writes her reply: whatever the opening remark leads her to say. With a computer, you can take turns at the keyboard. If you have networked computers, you can each sit at your own terminal and write the dialogue online. *E-mail* provides an ideal and natural way to write a dialogue.

It's all right to let the written conversation wander around a bit, much as spoken conversations do. Sometimes one person says, "Yes, I agree." The other can reply, "What makes you agree? How would you describe your experience?" And in conversations we often say, "No, I disagree" and then tell why. This works well in writing too; then the two of you can go on to have a written argument. Sometimes there's a kind of pause, when a thread of thought has come to an end, and it's up to the next person to start off a new thread; for example, "Well, I can't think of anything more to say about this point. But here's another point I'd like to discuss."

You can go on this way anywhere from 3 to 23 pages, depending on how much time you have and how long a piece your teacher asks for. Some of the Socratic dialogues are more than 50 pages long; in fact, Plato's *Republic* is a long book in the form of a dialogue. If you are going to revise your dialogue, make sure you write more in your first draft than you need for your final version. If your teacher asks for a three-page dialogue, try to start off with five or six pages.

Here's another way to produce a dialogue on paper: Start by talking. Simply discuss a topic with your partner, but take notes as you go along to record the most interesting points and issues that came up. Then reconstruct the best parts of your conversation on paper. (This may be what Plato did with the Socratic dialogues.)

Revising the Dialogue

Look over what you have and decide together how to make a finished product. Remember that dialogues are naturally informal and conversational in tone, as you'll see from the mother–daughter dialogue printed on pages 78–81. There's no conflict between an informal tone and careful philosophic thinking. What you want to end up with is a conversation in writing that throws light on an issue and is also interesting to read because it captures in writing the liveliness and voice of conversation. Your conversation might record a disagreement, even a fight, or you might trade your thoughts and ideas and not disagree at all. There is a whole range of possibilities—the full range of ways that people talk to each other in conversation. Conversations and dialogues are particularly satisfying if you can zero in on an issue or a question that you disagree about or want to understand better. The conversation helps you figure things out.

Your teacher might ask you to revise your rough draft carefully and extensively to get it as good as you can make it; she may ask you just to clean it up quickly for sharing and then go on; or she might even ask you to treat it as an exercise and leave it unchanged—as a private conversation between the two of you.

If you revise, whether quickly or carefully, you'll want to consider these questions:

- What are the most interesting parts?
- What is the focus, the emphasis? Have you figured anything out or reached a conclusion? You may have to write a bit more to give focus or closure.
- Which parts will you rearrange or discard?

It's interesting to share dialogues, whether for feedback or only for learning. It's particularly interesting to read them aloud (each person taking one voice) for other pairs or perhaps for the whole class. Reading aloud helps you notice where you've managed to get your written language to sound natural and where it comes out stilted or awkward.

Finally, take a moment to notice the nature of the collaboration you've engaged in. You produced a genuinely collaborative piece of writing, yet you avoided most of the difficulties of collaboration—that is, you collaborated to agree on a topic and on which parts of the dialogue to cut and keep and what to add or change. But you didn't have to agree on any ideas or write sentences together or find a common voice or style. And you probably produced a lively, useful, and interesting piece of writing. (If not, try to see now what got in the way and how to do it better next time.)

For an example of a published dialogue, see the newspaper piece reprinted here. A mother and daughter discuss the comparative influence of parents and peers on young people. (This dialogue was first published in *The Guardian,* one of England's premier newspapers.)

Who Influences Children More, Their Parents or Their Peers?   *Bel Mooney and Kitty Dimbleby*

Dear Kitty,
Being a parent, as I've often told you, is very difficult, so there has to be something in it for us, apart from love. Why look after you for 18 years, and put your welfare before most other things? Because I made you and I want

Who Influences Children More, Their Parents or Their Peers? *continued*

to go on "making" you. Is it an ego-trip to say my two children are the best things I've ever produced and—yes—I do take some credit (with your Dad) for the kind of people you are.

You can see why it's hard for me to take a new American theory that it isn't us poor old parents, but the peer group which has the most influence on teenagers like you. Judith Rich Harris has just published a book called *The Nurture Assumption,* which says goodbye Freud, goodbye guilt—if your kids turn out bad, you can say it isn't your fault, it's that crowd they hung out with. So we're let off the hook on one level, but does that mean we can shrug off responsibility?

The other side of the coin has to be that if they turn out to be little saints (like you!) we can't take the credit either. What was it all for: that careful parenting, the long talks about life, love and morality? The forgiveness when you behaved so badly (like when you were drunk at 2:30 A.M. and got me out of bed to collect you)? Did I give you all that, so a group of kids can make you in their images? No way.

Love,
Mum

Dear Mum,

Although I understand your views, I feel that you fail to see the importance of friends in a teenager's life. You always tease me about the close relationship I have with my girlfriends, saying it's more like a love affair. Yet we go through everything together—my friends know more about my life than you do and have more influence over me.

They see me outside the home, in nightclubs, in lessons, when drunk . . . I talk to them when I've had a fight with my boyfriend or you. Peer pressure is always seen as a bad thing but this is wrong. When friends criticise or offer advice, it is far easier to listen and take on board than when parents do so.

Many of my friends don't have a stable parental structure and so it's friends they turn to. If I give advice on drugs or sex (areas parents find difficult to face with their own children) my friend will know that what I say is from an equal's view, someone who knows and understands the situation, which a parent can never fully do.

So Mum, although it's you who I call for when I'm ill, my friends are very important to me and have helped shape me into the person I am. I think we both know that you are just the tiniest bit jealous.

Love,
Kitty

Listen Missy,

I admit I am jealous sometimes, because I value our closeness so much. I want you to be *my* friend! I boast that you tell me everything, and then I'm

✒ Who Influences Children More, Their Parents or Their Peers? *continued*

put out when it's proved untrue. Last weekend, Dad and I were walking along Princes Street in Edinburgh and bumped into some girls you were at school with, one of whom had a pierced nose. I said, "Kit would never do that because she knows I hate it." The next night we took your cousins to hear some jazz, and they informed me you'd just had your nose pierced—and were really worried what I would say about it! So, was I wrong about my influence on you? Yes, otherwise you wouldn't have had it done. But you did care what I thought; which is something to celebrate.

The thing is, this nose-piercing (like the panther recently tattooed on your tummy) happened when we were away on holiday and you were with your friends. I'm not saying you bent to peer pressure to decorate your body thus—but sometimes I get fed up with all of you and the "culture" you inhabit. Too much talk about sex and clubbing, too much loafing about watching TV, too little direction, not enough interest in great issues. Sometimes I feel that all of you—lovely, bright girls—drag each other to the lowest common denominator. Or is this unfair?

Love,
Your confused mother

Dear Mum,
That is not only unfair but *wrong.* Far from dragging each other down, we encourage each other. Part of the reason I love and respect my friends is that they are all intelligent, sensitive girls. You say we talk too much about sex. Come on! For the amount of time I spend on the phone I couldn't just be talking about sex—there's not that much to talk about, is there? In fact we discuss everything from the trivial to the bombing in Omagh, when we were all moved to tears. About my tattoo and nose: I am my own person—moulded partly by you but still me, an individual, Kitty. You know I hate it when people think I have only achieved things because of you and Dad—well, I hate it just as much when you attribute what I do to my friends.

I respect you and what you think but I also know (and hope) that you respect and trust me to make wise decisions. You *have* to let me make my own mistakes. I could have been friends with girls who think drugs are cool; instead we all feel they are sad. You've done a good job but I owe the person I am to three "people"; my family, my friends and *me.* There are some parts of my life where you can't be there to guide me, and others where it's only you.

Love as ever,
Kitty

Darling Kit,
So much of what you say is right—and we're both too intelligent not to see there has to be a compromise. Anyway, who always welcomes your lovely friends? But I remember when you were little—bullied at school or miserable because some horrible little cow wouldn't play with you—and I realised there was nothing I could do to protect you from the hurt your peers

Who Influences Children More, Their Parents or Their Peers? *continued*

might do you. Dad and I gave you our genes, and a stable family life, but after that . . .

Yes, you will go on being formed by people you love (both genders), things you experience, books you read, pain you feel. I hope I don't cling to the bright balloon that's tugging in the wind already. But I don't think you should bear children unless you take responsibility and go on mothering forever. Glad I put you first in the past. Is it wrong to feel that in the future, when you've lost contact with friends who are so important now, your old Ma will still be at the centre of your life, and that you will still be influenced by me?

All my love,
Mum

Dear Mum,
Of course it's true and always will be. I hope you'll mother me all your life just as I'll go on loving and respecting you all mine. Yes, I had a hard time when I was younger and just as my grandmother couldn't stop you being called names, you were powerless to help. At my age you realise that far from being the gods of your childhood, parents are flawed. You've made mistakes, and (at times) I've taken care of you. Remember when I forfeited a friend's birthday because you had food poisoning? The mother–daughter role reversed.

You have given me so many of the things I love: literature, theatre, poetry, ideas—sometimes I hear myself speak, and think I am my mother. That doesn't stop me resenting it when you tell me to go and do some work—I'm old enough not to be told. I look up to you so much, and am proud of you as I hope you are of me, not as your child but as another person. Think of me as a jigsaw puzzle—if any part of me were missing (you, Dad, my friends, my boyfriend . . .) I would not be whole.

Your ever loving daughter,
Kitty

Activity Two: The Loop Writing Process

Loop writing consists of a series of short pieces of writing that help you think more productively and write more interestingly. It is called a "loop" process because as you do many of these short pieces, you allow your mind to slide away or digress from full concentration on the exact question or topic, but afterward you loop back to focus on your topic as you revise. While doing these loops, trust that the pieces will actually yield good insight in the end. By turning slightly away from the topic and writing little stories, portraits, and even lies, your mind will find insights that it can't find otherwise. (In the dark we can sometimes see a faint star or the hands of a clock from the corner of our eye that we cannot see when we look directly.) But these insights are often implied, not directly expressed. So you often have to reflect on the loops you wrote in order to see what they are telling you about your topic.

Your teacher may invite you or your group to choose your own topic, or she may set a topic. Here are a couple of topics we consider useful and appropriate to explore using the loop process:

- Explore the relationship between speaking and writing. What's useful and problematic about each of them? Are there differences between how your mind works when you speak and when you write? Is your language different? Is the "talking on paper" that you did when you wrote a dialogue more like writing or talking? In what ways is e-mail "talking" and in what ways is it "writing"? What roles do speaking and writing play in your life?

- Consider your gender, race, religion, socioeconomic class, or cultural background (or perhaps more than one) to explore three things:
  - The strengths and virtues they have given you (i.e., what are you proud of in your inheritance?).
  - The ways they have tempted people to stereotype you or even be prejudiced against you.

Exploring the Writing Process
On Riding Digressions

I just figured out what it is I'm trying to say—found my point or assertion. I've been wrestling for three days and unable to figure it out—knowing that I've been saying good stuff—knowing that long passages I've been writing are good (some as long as 3–4 pages)—but unable to *say* exactly what it is I'm really trying to say.

I found it when I started to write out a slightly tangential thought. I realized this was a side thought and started a new sentence in parentheses. In midsentence I recognized it was even more tangential than I had realized and almost just stopped and crossed the whole thing out as an unhelpful side road. And then I just said what the heck and kept going, and all of a sudden it led to a sentence that zeroed in on the precise issue that was at the heart of the 15–20 pages I'd so far written but been unable to sum up.

It's simple and clear once it's said. But *I* couldn't see it. Or I couldn't see it till late in the game—and not till I let myself ride on this digression.

Peter Elbow

- The ways they might have led you to stereotype or even be prejudiced against other people.

These are not easy topics. They might seem too large or too personal or too academic. We think they are important in themselves, but we also chose them because we want to show you how the techniques of this workshop—dialogue, loop writing, and collaboration—are all helpful when you are faced with a complex topic *you* didn't choose.

We suggest that you write a collaborative collage for this workshop, but you can use the loop writing whether you are writing collaboratively or alone, and whether you want to produce an essay or a collage. The loop writing process will be the same in any case.

We'll show you five general kinds of loop writing:

1. First thoughts, prejudices, preconceptions.

2. Moments, stories, portraits.

3. Dialogue.

4. Change of audience, writer, and time.

5. Lies, errors, sayings.

You can't normally use all of the loop processes on one writing task, but it's worth trying them all and becoming comfortable with them. That's why we're asking you to try them out quickly for this workshop. If you are writing collaboratively, make sure that you and your partner use all the varieties (even the variations or subvarieties). See if you can write for at least 10 minutes on each of the subvarieties. (When writing your loops, it's best to write on only one side of the paper, so you can later cut out and save the best passages for rearranging and pasting.)

1. First Thoughts, Prejudices, Preconceptions

You have already sampled this kind of writing if you did focused freewriting in Workshop 1. It is a matter of putting down whatever first comes to mind about your topic. Focused freewriting might have felt like a mere exercise, but writing first thoughts is a good way to start out writing a serious essay: You always know more about a topic than you realize. The important thing is to jump in and keep on writing and let yourself get past what you already have in mind.

A helpful way to write first thoughts is to use what might be called narrative thinking. Simply write your thoughts in the form of a story about what's happening in your head from moment to moment as you explore the topic: "When I think of this topic, what first comes into my mind is a feeling that _____. Then I think of _____. Then it occurs to me that _____. And then I wonder about _____," and so on. This procedure takes the emphasis away from the question of whether your thinking is true or right or sensible. It puts the emphasis instead on a different kind of truth and validity: that these thoughts, feelings, images, hunches, and wishes are going on in your mind, that these are snapshots of what you bring to the topic. This approach adds to the sense of adventure in the process and often encourages more exploration.

You might worry that an acceptance of prejudices will lead you to wrong ideas or bad thinking. Remember that you're treating this early writing not as "the answer" but as exploration. If you want to do good thinking on a topic, you need to understand your own prejudices and preconceptions. The best way to understand them—and to prevent them from infecting your careful writing—is to get these candid snapshots of your initial feeling and thinking out on the table.

For example, let's say you've decided to focus on the relationship between speaking and writing. Let's say further that you're sick of writing and tired of people (like us) glorifying it. You could call this a first thought or preconception. Take it seriously. Explore it: It may lead you somewhere useful. Why are you sick of writing? What about it has been glorified too much? What happens to you when you write? Why do teachers, textbook writers, and journalists glorify writing so much? We think you're more likely to understand writing this way— by acknowledging and exploring your first thoughts—than by pushing those thoughts aside or defending them as gospel.

Give yourself permission to go along with your preconceptions— even to exaggerate your prejudices. You might want to start off by saying something as extreme as "There is no longer any need to learn how to write now that we have telephones." Once you've written this, you may react so strongly against its absoluteness that you'll want to cross it out. But we suggest that you follow through, push it, nurture it a bit, and protect it from your own criticism for a while. As you allow yourself to get carried away by your extreme idea, you may discover some unexpected problems with writing—or why writing has been so important to humankind. You'll begin to understand some of the significant differences between talking on the telephone and writing things down. Almost invariably there are interesting insights tangled up with early careless thinking. People seldom come up with good new thinking except through some obsession or exaggeration.

If you are doing a research project and have to do a lot of reading or research before you write, use first thoughts and prejudices *before* you do that reading and research. By putting on paper all the ideas you already have—even writing out a quick 20-minute fantasy of what you hope your research will show—you'll find that your reading and research become far more interesting and productive. You'll already have ideas of your own to compare with what "authorities" say; you won't be reading with a blank mind. You're more likely to remember what you read and have more reactions to it.

2. Moments, Stories, Portraits

- *Moments:* Quickly list the moments or situations you can think of that somehow seem connected to your topic.
- *Stories:* Quickly list the stories or sequences of events that come to mind in connection with your topic.
- *Portraits:* Quickly list any people who somehow seem central to your topic.

Look over your list, choose at least one from each category, and write for 5 or 10 minutes about it. But you may discover that one or two of these are so important that you need to write at great length. You can do that now or wait till later. At this point don't spend any time trying to connect separate pieces to one another or to elaborate on the significance of them unless that just comes to you while you're writing. (We didn't use the term "loop writing" in Workshop 1, but that's what you were doing there when you wrote moments, stories, and portraits to create a collage about you as a writer.)

The cognitive power here comes from using *experiential* writing (description and storytelling) for the sake of *cognitive* or *expository* writing or thinking. We are often smarter when we tell stories and think about actual people than when we give ideas and reasons. Try testing this idea sometime by asking someone his ideas about the relationship between speaking and writing. After he has said a few things, ask him to tell you some moments, incidents, and people that come to mind when he thinks about speaking and writing. After he's talked some more, ask him to reflect on these moments, stories, and portraits to find insights or implications about speaking and writing in each of them. It's very likely that he'll come up with more and better thinking by means of this roundabout loop path than by starting off directly with "trying to think." He's very likely to surprise himself and discover that what he said about speaking and writing when you first questioned him is different and not as valid as the reflections he comes up with after telling stories and reflecting on people. Loop thinking is concrete and specific thinking that cuts a path around generalities, pieties, and prejudices. Thus writing up remembered moments sometimes works against first thoughts in a productive way.

3. Dialogue

It seems as though describing and storytelling are easier and more natural than abstract kinds of discourse like explaining, giving reasons, and making inferences. Describing lets us close our eyes and see what to say; storytelling carries us along on a stream of "and then, and then, and then." We've been describing and telling stories from infancy. Giving reasons sounds more like "school discourse."

But there's an important exception here. Ever since we could talk,

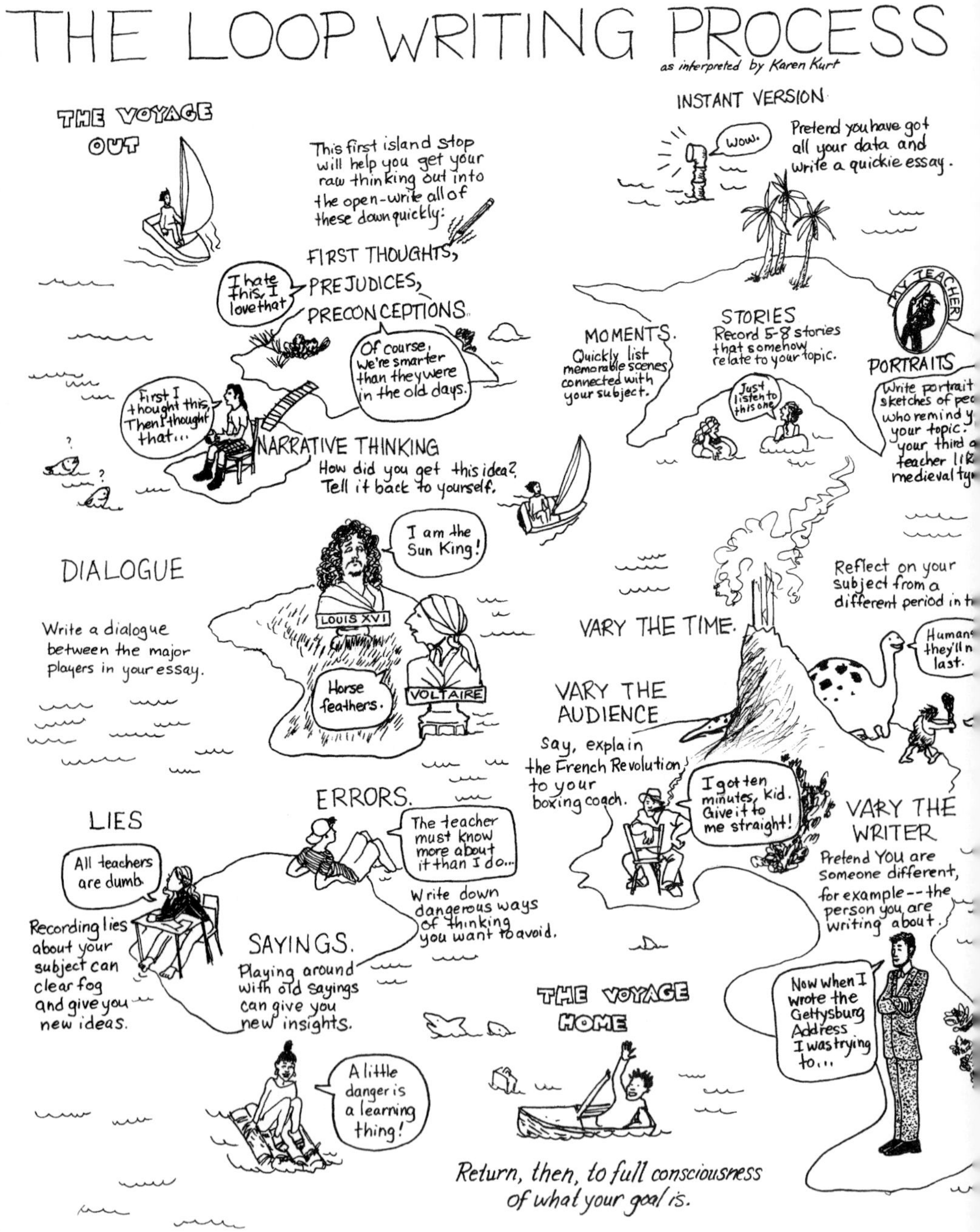

Figure 1 The Loop Writing Process

we've engaged in dialogue too, and dialogue tends to consist of explaining, giving reasons, and making inferences. When someone told us that we couldn't have ice cream before lunch or that we had to go to sleep after our snack or asked us why we thought the flower was "sad," we fell naturally into giving reasons, explaining, and making inferences. We've been doing it ever since. That is, dialogue pops us right into the kind of conceptual and reason-giving uses of language we need for writing essays. (Of course, it doesn't organize that conceptual language and thinking into an essaylike form, but we can do that later.)

There are other powerful advantages to dialogue. A dialogue injects unusually strong energy into language and thinking. A dialogue makes you speak and think from your own point of view and yet forces you to imagine someone else's point of view while you are doing so. A dialogue leads you to the very stuff of essays: assertions, summings-up, reasons, arguments, examples, counterexamples—and probably all in down-to-earth, clear language.

Thus one of the most powerful ways to do exploratory writing for essays is simply to write a dialogue. Probably the easiest way to do this is to find a friend or classmate and write a collaborative dialogue between yourselves. But it works fine to write a dialogue all by yourself. In writing this dialogue yourself, you must first choose someone to have your dialogue with. Choose someone who seems important to the topic you want to explore. The person can be real or fictitious, living or dead, someone you know well or someone you've never met. And, as we mentioned earlier, you can have a productive dialogue with objects or concepts (e.g., a dialogue between speech and writing).

4. Changes of Audience, Writer, and Time

It is classic advice to write to someone who doesn't understand your topic, even if you are really writing something for experts. Writers have traditionally benefited from writing their technical material as though to children. Dr. Samuel Johnson, one of the most prolific and popular writers of the eighteenth century, used to read his writing to his unschooled servant and not stop revising till it was clear to her. It's not simply that this process forces you to be clear. The most important effect is that you see your topic differently when you direct your thinking to a different audience—and this process gives you new perspectives and new ideas. So, for this topic choose one or two people you would enjoy sharing thoughts with.

You can achieve comparable benefits by varying the time. Try writing about speech and writing as though you were living in the future or during some period in the past. You will notice many things about the topic that you wouldn't otherwise notice.

Varying the writer—that is, your own identity—will change your perspective even more directly and give you new insights. You might pretend that you've never learned to write, or that you could only write and not speak, or that you are a professional writer. You could imagine you were a court stenographer or a caption writer for TV and spent your workday doing nothing but turning speech into writing.

If you want to end up with something fair and judiciously detached, spend some time writing from the point of view of someone who is extremely biased and involved in the subject. Then write as someone with the opposite bias. Obviously this category can merge into a dialogue.

This mode is good for experimenting: Start out writing to various audiences and at various times and as various people. Ask yourself, Which are most fruitful to continue with?

Writing as Play — Lies, Errors, Sayings

For some reason, most people find a kind of pleasure in writing down what they know is false. It seems to go against the grain of how writing is supposed to work (careful and true). And yet deliberately writing down what you know to be false can also help thinking. It opens a back door into creativity.

We're not asking you to write extended pieces of writing (unless you want to)—just single sentences.

By *lies* we mean statements that are obviously and flatly wrong. (Examples: "When I manage to write the right words on paper, the paper itself magically speaks out loud what I have written." "I will never again in my life write another word." "Writing is always false.")

By *errors* we mean something slightly and interestingly different: statements that are *almost* right—tempting, but wrong. For errors, write down things that many or most people believe, or things you're not sure of, or things you wish were true but probably are not. (Examples: "To get a good grade, you have to give a teacher exactly what she asked for." "Speaking is always more informal than writing." "I can always speak my thoughts better than I can write them.")

Sayings tend to carry useful "folk wisdom," and they also teach you to squeeze a lot of meaning into a pithy and memorable chunk of language. You can use sayings that already exist: "The pen is mightier than the sword" or "Those are words writ in water." But we encourage you to make up your own sayings and phrases: "Speaking is forever but writing disappears before you know it." You don't always have to know exactly what you mean by sayings you make up. Playing with "proverb phrasing" will lead you to formulations that are interesting to explore: "Speak softly but carry a big pen."

Lies, Errors, Sayings *continued*

Writing as Play

If it sounds merely foolish to write lies, errors, and sayings, try answering these questions and you'll find some good insights:
- In what respect is this lie true?
- Why do some people think this idea is true?
- Are there times when this is true and times when it's not?
- What would follow if this were true?
- What is it that makes this untrue?

Discussing lies, errors, and sayings with your partner or group is particularly fruitful. You can also make up good ones collaboratively with them.

MAIN ASSIGNMENT
Using Loop Writing to Create a Collage or Essay

Our suggestion for this workshop is to produce a collaborative collage. But it's easier for us to explain how to do it if we start with directions for a solo collage (and we also want to emphasize the usefulness of loop writing for solo writing).

Read through all the pieces you've written. As you read, decide which passages are the most interesting and successful. Which ones throw the most light on the topic? These passages might be anywhere from a few sentences to a couple of pages. Keep the good ones and arrange them in whatever order seems most interesting and effective. (If you remembered to write on only one side, you can simply cut out the good ones with scissors, spread them on the floor, and play with various arrangements.)

You can set your sights on any of three outcomes: an open collage, a focused collage, or an essay.

Open Collage. If you want to produce an *open collage,* you can move at this point toward a final version. Just edit your pieces by making minor revisions: cuts, tightenings, changes. Arrange them in the best order—the order that feels most interesting or enlightening or dramatic—not necessarily in the most logical order. Of course, this process may spark other bits you can write and use in your collage. Now proofread. Your collage will be a lively piece of writing that will throw good light on the topic. In short, an open collage doesn't have to be completely unified with a clear conclusion. It doesn't have to state explicitly what it is "saying." It can simply plant seeds in the reader's mind. When such seeds bear fruit, the effect on readers is usually more powerful than if you had told them exactly what you want them to think.

Focused Collage.   You can produce a *focused collage* by working more with your material. A focused collage is also made up of interesting short pieces—diverse "blips"—but it is more clearly unified and has a conclusion: It says what it is saying. For this you need to carry your thinking further and force yourself to figure out what all these pieces of loop writing mean. Thus you would have to write one or more additional passages that tell what all the others add up to. These pieces would answer the question "So what?" and would probably come near the beginning or the end. A focused collage is more carefully framed than the open collage: It doesn't leave so much up to the reader.

As an example, we provide here a focused collage on child abuse done by Darci Jungwirth, a student:

> Sara was afraid to come home at night. When she got there she would always find the same thing: her father with a beer in his hand and his breath smelling of alcohol. His hair was all messed up and he was sitting in the brown recliner with the ripped seat that he never bothered to get patched after an incident with a cigarette left burning. He always greeted her the same way. "Hi, darling, how was your day?" He would try to be nice first but always ended up getting out of control or going off the handle over nothing. She would end up huddled on her bed, both her body and soul wincing in pain from this man, her father. She lay on her soft old bed with the dusty pink comforter for hours. When she could finally get her strength up she did her homework that had to be completed adequately to avoid another beating.

> *Child:*   Dad, why do you hit me?
>
> *Dad:*   Son, I don't know why. I had a bad day at work and bills are due tomorrow. I had so much tension and anger built up inside me that I was just mad at the world and you happened to be there.
>
> *Child:*   But Dad, you do it all the time; don't you realize that you make me scared to be around you at all. I'm always worried that you are going to haul off and hit me at any moment. You say things that make me feel bad too. I don't think that you love me. I feel like everything that goes wrong in your life is my fault and that I am worth nothing.

Dad: I don't mean to be mad at you son; it is just that I feel so bad myself and then I see you and it makes me feel even worse that you are not happy either. I don't want the responsibility to feed you all the time and to keep you entertained—it all adds pressure to the stress I have already.

Child: What would you do if you didn't have me, Dad? Who would you take your anger out on then? You already went through Mom; that was why she left. You make me feel like the lowest piece of garbage on the whole earth and you made her feel that way too. You need to realize that it is you who needs to deal with your problem first. I am only a child and I should not have to deal with your frustration—it is not my fault. The bruises I get from your beatings will go away on the outside but inside they just keep getting bigger and bigger. They will never heal. The panic and fear I feel when you go off on me cannot be erased from my memory—how can you forget that kind of terror? It is like watching a horror movie. I am watching but there is nothing I can do to help.

The abuser who comes to mind is about 35 to 40 years of age; he has painful eyes and dark hair. He stands nearly six feet tall, average build. He is your average guy; he does not look like he could ever hurt anyone but after you've seen his anger you can. He is not really a bad person but he has had a hard life. When he was a child the same kind of father did the same kinds of things to him. He always vowed never to turn out like him but for some ironic reason he is the mirror image of that man he hated, the same looks, the same eyes.

He walks a tad bowlegged and seems to have self-confidence. He wears nice business clothes to work and casual clothes at home. On the weekends he takes care of the house and mows the yard. He lives alone with his daughter now. She does all the household chores while he does all the "men's work." He does not lay a hand on the dishes or a pan.

Your Daddy does not hurt you because he hates you. He loves you very much. He does not want to hit you and say mean things but he is very sad. Since your Mommy left he has been very unhappy and he wishes she would come back. Do you know how you feel when you go to school and the teacher tells you that you have to come inside because recess is over; sometimes you get mad at her because you are having such a good time playing on the playground. You get mad at your teacher but it is not her fault that recess is over. You are not really mad at the teacher but you act like you are mad at her. Well, when your Daddy hurts you, it is the same thing. Your Daddy is not really mad at you; he is just angry about other things that are happening in his life.

You are not being a bad girl or doing anything wrong when your Daddy hits you. When your Daddy does this to you, you need to go tell someone so that your Daddy can get help from the doctor. The doctor will help your Daddy get all better and then he will not hit you anymore. He will be the Daddy you remember who used to take you to the playground and play catch with you in the front yard. You are a very good girl and I am very proud of you.

The children are victims; they are the ones who have to live with the torture for the rest of their lives and try to deal with an abusive parent along with all the other growing up they are doing that is tough enough already.

The line between spankings as punishment and when they turn into beatings is a very fine line that is difficult to draw. Many people receive spankings in childhood for getting out of line or doing something that is not acceptable to their parents.

LIES—OPPOSITE VIEWPOINT: The parents are right; there is no such thing as child abuse. It is all a misconception and the people who try so hard to put child abusers behind bars are all people who should mind their own business. They should worry about their own families. The kids were being brats so they deserved to get a good whipping. They are at fault and they can be blamed for everything. Kids are worth nothing and they should be treated like they are nothing. Parents are always right and never do anything wrong. The parents who abuse their children should not be punished; they should be rewarded for doing justice to the whole society. It was the kids' fault that the dog came and wet on the rug and that they did not get A's in every subject at school. It was the kids' fault that their mother ran out and is never coming back; they made her cry and leave. I never hurt her; it was just the damn kids, always screaming and yelling. I was right to hit them. Parents are too lenient on their kids these days. There is nothing like a good whipping to leave purple marks all over their puny little bodies to teach them a good lesson. They will thank me for it when they are older. I hope that they can beat their kids too, or else they will never learn discipline. All the anger I feel right now is because of them. If I did not have the kids in my life everything would be perfect. Kids cause all the problems. Nothing is my fault; it is all theirs. I know I am right.

They are not just beating their children for the fun of it. The children are scapegoats for their parents' frustration. They need to get help for the sources of the anger that cause abuse in the first place.

They are still to be held responsible for their acts and it is never acceptable to beat a child.

Almost more important than counseling for the parents is counseling for the children who actually have to go through this hell. They feel trapped, unable to get out, and helpless. They need a hand to grasp, a person to talk to.

A successful collage gives its pieces to the reader in intuitive order and lets the reader enter into a kind of interaction or collaboration with the pieces to make sense of them. That is one of the advantages and pleasures of the collage for readers: It's a more participatory form. Actually, all language has gaps and ambiguity and requires the participation of the reader, but the collage highlights this interactive dimension in all language.

Exploring the Writing Process
On Improvisation

What you finally read in the published text is what's been collaged and montaged (can one use these words like this?) from all my various improvisations. In other words, writing for me is also a way of splicing stuff together. That's real writing for me, and not that initial spontaneous flow of words. That's in the final text too, but buried inside the other levels of improvisation. It's in the various *re*-workings and *re*-writing sessions that the real elements of improvisation (and not inspiration) come, because improvisation is always something that builds on something else.

Raymond Federman

Essay.   You can also use loop writing to produce an *essay*. Indeed, one of the best ways to understand the nature of the essay as a form is to explore how it differs from a collage. The essay asks for two things that are not necessary in a collage: full explicit unity and full coherence.

- *Unity*. A collage can be perfectly successful if it is only "sort of unified"—that is, if all the parts are related, yet don't all connect perfectly to a precise center. But an essay insists that you work out what the center is and keep everything related to it.
- *Coherence*. A collage invites you to jump from point to point with no connective passages, and sometimes to jump quite a distance. But an essay insists that you work out your train of thought so that each part follows with a smooth, coherent connection.

To produce an essay, then, you have to push your thinking harder: Work out exactly what you want to say and make sure all the parts really fit it; work out your train of thought and make sure all the parts follow. The crucial process will probably be to look back over all the pieces of loop writing you did and figure out more clearly in your mind what each of them is telling you. Then arrange your points in a coherent sequence. This is where an outline is very helpful. An essay requires more work, of course, but the benefit is that your thinking is more developed and careful. In other words, the collage is best for throwing light on an issue and making people think; the essay is best for working out your thinking fully and reaching a conclusion with maximum validity.

Suggestions for Collaboration

It will probably be obvious by now how to make a collaborative collage from your loop writing, and why a collage is such a helpful way to get used to collaborative writing. First, get together and listen to each other's pieces of loop writing or share them on paper. Then decide together which pieces seem most interesting and successful, and which ones you want to choose for your collaborative collage. The pieces don't need to agree with each other or have the same voice or tone. In a collage, contrasts are a benefit: a source of energy that stimulates thinking in readers. In effect, you are putting together a collection of pieces, each written from an "I" point of view, for the sake of a "we" enterprise: a gathering of individuals toward a collaborative purpose. Whether or not you actually use the first person singular in these pieces doesn't matter. If you make it clear to readers on the title page that this work was written by multiple authors and that it is a collage consisting of individual and distinct passages separated by asterisks rather than smoothly connected, readers will get the picture.

They will understand what's going on when different "I's" say conflicting things or tell conflicting stories in different voices.

If you want an *open collage,* you can now move to completion: Agree on an order for your pieces; work collaboratively to edit, tighten, and proofread. If you want a *focused collage,* you'll have to collaborate a bit further in your thinking. That is, after listening to everyone's loop writing, you need to decide more explicitly on your focus, and decide more clearly how your pieces hang together or relate to each other. You *don't* have to agree with each other on a single point of view or conclusion; it's fine to disagree completely. But you do need to agree on your disagreement; that is, you'll have to agree on how to describe the relationship between your conflicting opinions, and on that basis write a few collaborative passages that represent your *larger collaborative joint view* of your disagreements. These collaborative passages would probably occur near the opening and/or the closing. In effect, the focused collage might be a collection of "I" pieces, but they would be framed by some crucial "we" pieces that express joint or collaborative thinking to focus the whole thing.

Take a look at the collaborative collage produced by students Laura Corry, Elija Goodwin, Matt Ludvino, Denise Morey, and Tassie Walsh:

Collaborative Collage about Writing a Collage

Laura Corry, Elija Goodwin, Matt Ludvino, Denise Morey, Tassie Walsh

We sat around the table hearing the audible roar of gun blasts and explosions from the video games over at one end of the cafeteria. Several conversations went on at once. We spoke about anything. The work was the last thing on our mind. We were just getting to know each other.

❧

The first day that we met together as a group alone, I felt kind of awkward. I didn't really know these people. Would I want to spend the semester working with them or would things be strained? I worried that perhaps there might be some kind of "impenetrable barrier" between us. However, as we sat down and began the process of getting to know each other, I began to feel more at ease and comfortable. We talked for quite a while and there was really no awkwardness, no strained moments, no long periods of quiet. As a group we seemed to hit it off. I did not feel shy about saying what I really felt.

❧

When five people, different in every way, share experiences with each other, there is going to be something there. Different ideas and opinions, mannerisms, and mind-sets, sharing different pieces of themselves with

Collaborative Collage about Writing a Collage   *continued*

each other. There is something to be learned there. Something intangible will be received whether anyone wants to or not. The ideas were already out there for everyone to see. Something will be absorbed. I have a yearning for knowledge and I have a problem with understanding people: Any insight gained is definitely appreciated.

I think working as a group was hard because no one wanted to. No one wanted to meet for a long time and try to figure out something to write and then sit and write it. We seemed to want to find something we could do on our own and yet put it together as a group. I think part of why this happened is because we did not fully trust each other. Time is very hard for all of us, and it always seems that one person does not show up or cannot stay. How can we put our grade in the hands of a group of peers yet strangers?

The situation was strange. We all had ideals with no way to express them. Well, maybe it's just me. This group project really brought me down in the beginning. I've never written with anyone else before. I tried to be reasonable but no ideas would come.

As I sat down at the computer my mind froze up. I had had all these ideas running around in my head and now nothing. I stared at a blank screen. The hum of the computer lulling me asleep at this late hour. I started to write just to get anything down. What came out wasn't what I wanted, but it was a start. I think just the thought of writing with a theme, a topic, for the group was stifling my thoughts and creativity. Suddenly, an inspiration hit me. Yes, that was more like it. But it still needed work and more added. So I saved and shut the computer off to let the ideas ferment a little bit.

It was a couple of Thursdays ago; we were all determined to figure out what our group project was going to be. We thought about reviewing a book or movie. This was not a unique enough idea. We then as a group talked about writing a play. "Yeah, that's it; write a play." "How will we approach it?" Yes, this would be very creative, but as a group we felt that there was a lack of time to challenge ourselves and make this work. After just telling the group that my brain was dead (mental block), I had an idea.

I remember when we decided on our collaborative project. Suddenly the mood changed. We all had smiles on our faces and our body movements became more relaxed. It's amazing how decision making can cause such stress and how the larger the group the harder it is to make a decision.

It is harder to write in a group. I feel like these writing exercises are helpful, but each time that we are asked to do them I wonder about the

Collaborative Collage about Writing a Collage *continued*

content of my writing compared to the others'. I feel like I have a responsibility to the group to write well and please them.

We shared the writing we did by reading it out loud. This was almost ritualistic when the group met.

Even in a small group, it is hard to get together at a set time. Everyone is so busy. It got easier when the group got comfortable with each other because we realized that we would do fine even with the absence of one person.

Everyone must be there and contributing. When one person doesn't show or can't make it, like when I had exams, it really seems to disrupt the group. It is hard to make decisions, and you miss that person's input to bounce off of. Once a group is formed, each piece is sort of essential for it to work. When someone has another obligation, things really seem to fall apart.

When I work in a group I get very nervous. There have been too many times when I have had to do more work than others and yet we got the same grade. Or, because of something someone else did, I did not get as good a grade as I should have. Because of this, I don't like working in groups. If I have to, I am always the one asking if people have finished their part and making sure that they know exactly what they should do.

Here I am again, back at the Newman Center, staring mindlessly at the grain of the table top. I can barely hear the others' discussion over the bang of my thoughts. It's not that I don't care; it's just that after a while you get burnt out and need to drain the cluttered pool in your head. I sometimes feel a little suffocated this semester. Not because of this class alone, but because of the combined workload of all my classes. It seems like I'm being held underwater for two minutes at a time. I thrash at the invisible hands until they let me go, but only long enough to catch a gasping breath. Then I'm submerged again in a block of water looking up as the sun's rays hit the surface, distorting the skyline.

Whenever the group found itself confused about something, I always tried to give my best input and knowledge. In the group, I always made sure that I knew what the assignment was, when it was due, and so on. Knowing myself, I am aware that when I am involved in any group I like to participate in this way. Yet I am shy and I feel timid when I have to speak aloud. This weakness became less noticeable as I became more comfortable with the group.

Collaborative Collage about Writing a Collage   *continued*

When I work in a group I am sort of on the outskirts. I stay fairly quiet, occasionally voice ideas when I feel they are important, support others' ideas when I feel they are good. But when it comes down to making decisions, I usually can be happy and work with any decision that is made, so I let others battle it out while I watch.

When I work in a group I am sort of on the outskirts.

The best part of working in a group is being able to bounce off each other's ideas. When we start talking, even about seemingly unrelated topics, we start identifying with each other or disagreeing, and that makes us think about things in ways we hadn't before. Soon we are coming up with a pretty good description of school and how we have reacted to it. Problems we've had in the past and why. It starts off pretty informally and soon we have a wealth of learning and potential papers.

As another example of a collaborative collage, we present the following—an interesting hybrid form published in *The New Yorker* as an obituary for Robert Bingham, a longtime contributor to that magazine:

Robert Bingham (1925–1982)

He was a tall man of swift humor whose generally instant responses reached far into memory and wide for analogy. Not much missed the attention of his remarkably luminous and steady eyes. He carried with him an education from the Boston Latin School, Phillips Exeter Academy, Harvard College—and a full year under the sky with no shelter as an infantryman in France in the Second World War. Arriving there, he left his rifle on the boat.

One of his lifelong friends, a popular novelist, once asked him why he had given up work as a reporter in order to become an editor.

"I decided that I would rather be a first-rate editor than a second-rate writer," he answered.

The novelist, drawing himself up indignantly, said, "And what is the matter with being a second-rate writer?"

Nothing, of course. But it is given to few people to be a Robert Bingham.

To our considerable good fortune, for nearly twenty years he was a part of *The New Yorker*, primarily as an editor of factual writing. In that time, he addressed millions of words with individual attention, giving each a whisk on the shoulders before sending it into print. He worked closely with many writers and, by their testimony, he may have been the most resonant sounding board any sounder ever had. Adroit as he was in reacting to sentences before him, most of his practice was a subtle form of catalysis done before he saw a manuscript.

Robert Bingham (1925–1982) *continued*

Talking on the telephone with a writer in the slough of despond, he would say, "Come, now, it can't be that bad. Nothing could be that bad. Why don't you try it on me?"

"But you don't have time to listen to it."

"We'll make time. I'll call you back after I finish this proof."

"Will you?"

"Certainly."

❦

"In the winter and spring of 1970, I read sixty thousand words to him over the telephone."

❦

"If you were in his presence, he could edit with the corners of his mouth. Just by angling them down a bit, he could erase something upon which you might otherwise try to insist. If you saw that look, you would be in a hurry to delete the cause of his disdain. In some years, he had a mustache. When he had a mustache, he was a little less effective with that method of editing, but effective nonetheless."

❦

"I turned in a story that contained a fetid pun. He said we should take that out. He said it was a terrible line. I said, 'A person has a right to make a pun once in a while, and even to be a little coarse.' He said, 'The line is not on the level of the rest of the piece and therefore seems out of place.' I said, 'That may be, but I want it in there.' He said, 'Very well. It's your piece.' Next day, he said, 'I think I ought to tell you I haven't changed my mind about that. It's an unfortunate line.' I said, 'Listen, Bobby. We discussed that. It's funny. I want to use it. If I'm embarrassing anybody, I'm embarrassing myself.' He said, 'O.K. I just work here.' The day after that, I came in and said to him, 'That joke. Let's take that out. I think that ought to come out.' 'Very well,' he said, with no hint of triumph in his eye."

❦

"As an editor, he wanted to keep his tabula rasa. He was mindful of his presence between writer and reader, and he wished to remain invisible while representing each. He deliberately made no move to join the journeys of research. His writers travelled to interesting places. He might have gone, too. But he never did, because he would not have been able to see the written story from a reader's point of view."

❦

"Frequently, he wrote me the same note. The note said, 'Mr. _____, my patience is not inexhaustible.' But his patience *was* inexhaustible. When a piece was going to press, he stayed long into the evening while I fumbled with prose under correction. He had pointed out some unarguable flaw. The fabric of the writing needed invisible mending, and I was trying to do it with him in a way satisfactory to him and to the overall story. He waited because he respected the fact that the writing had taken as much as five months, or

Robert Bingham (1925–1982) *continued*

even five years, and now he was giving this or that part of it just another five minutes."

"Edmund Wilson once said that a writer can sometimes be made effective 'only by the intervention of one who is guileless enough and human enough to treat him, not as a monster, nor yet as a mere magical property which is wanted for accomplishing some end, but simply as another man, whose sufferings elicit his sympathy and whose courage and pride he admires.' When writers are said to be gifted, possibly such intervention has been the foremost of the gifts."

If you want to increase the need for cooperation, you can write a *collaborative essay.* It would consist not of separate blips in separate voices, but an extended piece of writing that readers would feel as connected and single. That is, it needs to consist mostly of "we" thinking and writing, not "I" thinking and writing. Thus when you are writing a collaborative essay, you have to keep discussing your individual loop writing and what it all points to until you can pretty much come to some agreement.

But even in this connected essay, you can use quite a few of the "I" passages from your loop writing if you transform them into examples or points for your essay. That is, you might frame some of these passages with wording like this: "One of us had the following experience that illustrates what we are saying here: . . ." Or "One of the authors, however, points out a difficulty with the idea we have just explained: . . ." In short, it can be an essay from the "we" point of view representing corporate agreement, yet it can have some genuine diversity of thinking and perhaps even plurality of voice. You can even have an essay that clearly explains and explores a disagreement: This would be a case of agreement about the terms of disagreement.

Harness the Power of Disagreement for Collaborative Writing—and Also for Solo Writing

Notice how we are introducing you to collaboration by suggesting a progression from less agreement to more agreement. The dialogue and the open collage provide good starting places because, on the one hand, they require some agreement—but not very much. You have to agree only on which pieces to choose and how to arrange and edit them. The dialogue and open collage spare you the two hardest forms of collaboration: reaching full agreement in your thinking and finding a common voice. The focused collage pushes you a bit further into collaboration by asking you to agree in your thinking and find a common voice, but only for a few short passages. Finally comes the essay, which asks for full agreement.

Or does it? Even for the essay, please don't struggle for more agreement than you really need. What we consider the most important point in this workshop lies here. When you are trying to write a coherent essay—a seamless piece—you don't have to make it *too* seamless. You can *keep* some of those conflicting ideas and voices. It's fine in an essay to break out at various points with passages that might start like this: "But wait a minute. Let's look at this issue from a contrasting point of view." Or, "Notice what follows, however, when we consider what an opposing voice might say." Or, "There are some serious objections, however, to what we have just been saying." In each case, you can go on for a paragraph or even for a long section stating this contrasting idea or arguing this conflicting point of view.

Exploring the Writing Process
On Collaboration

About collaborating [on an essay with Andrea]. Lots of talk. LOTS of talk. Out loud brainstorming, a woman's conversation, many wandering diversions to create the wide beautiful track, lots of explaining our ideas and that touching off new ideas and coming around in a circle and laughing about not knowing what we were getting to or exactly where we had been. A long time— the clock surprised us by saying it had been over three hours! The logical part of my brain saying at the end of that session: But have we gotten any farther than agreeing mostly on the ideas I came to her with three hours ago? Yes, we had, I believe: We had begun some new entity called Our Project. We had sparked ideas and validated thoughts and begun to shape something—even though it still looked shapeless. Couldn't quantify it, but it was a learning *process* even if it didn't result in a paper right then to judge, or even a definite direction. . . . During the second meeting, in the middle of us blabbing on about the paper, I heard myself stop and say, "Do you feel comfortable enough to tell me if you don't like an idea I come up with?" Andrea said yes, which I figured she would say, and I felt that way too. So then we plunged right in again to full speed brainstorming and thinking and discussing.

Jana Zvibelman

And the conflicting point of view can even be in a contrasting voice—with or without quotation marks. Most readers experience these breaks or this internally "dialogic" quality as a strength rather than a weakness in an essay.

Thus we are not introducing the easy forms of collaboration (the dialogue and the collage) simply because they are easy—though that's a big benefit too. These easy forms bring into your writing and thinking a dimension that is often missing in much collaborative writing. A good deal of collaborative writing is weak in its thinking because the writers settle for the few things they could agree on. And much collaborative writing has a weak or fake voice because the writers hid their individual voices. The collage may be easy, but it shows you a way to bring to essay writing what is rare and precious and often lacking: some internal drama of thinking and voice.

Indeed, the collage will have the same benefit on your *solo* writing if you let it. Too much solo writing—especially by inexperienced writers—suffers in the same way we just described. The thinking is dull and obvious because the writer latched too soon onto one idea or thesis and timidly backed away whenever he felt perplexed or came across a conflicting view; he nervously swept the complication under the rug and hoped no one would notice. And the writer tried to use a "proper" or "impressive" voice and came out with something fake or stilted. Most good solo writing represents a single writer having some internal dialogue with himself—having more than one point of view and using more than one voice. Critics often praise this dialogic quality in good writing.

So, if you need to turn your collage into a single and coherent piece of writing, don't make things too "single" or one-dimensional. Look for ways to save as much of the dialogical drama of thinking as you can—even the drama of voices—while still getting it all to hang together. Try for rich thinking and complex voices harnessed to a single and coherent task. Any good passage from your loop writing that fits your topic probably *belongs* in your essay. It might have to be moved, reshaped, or reframed, but good thinking and lively voices are what most people are looking for in essays.

Some colleagues tell us that this is dangerous advice, so perhaps you should take it with a grain of salt. They would argue that one of the main problems with inexperienced writers is their tendency to save too much—to be too scared to throw things away. But we'd reply that the other main problem with inexperienced writers is their tendency to throw away the lively, perky passages in their rough writing and replace it with "proper writing"—smooth writing from which all the mistakes have been removed, but writing that is so dull and timid that no one would ever read it by choice.

Down-to-Earth Suggestions for Working with Others

Students have sometimes reacted to what we are saying with frustration: *"But you two keep putting off the question of how to actually reach agreement and find a common voice! You keep giving us ways to avoid it and telling us it's no problem. But we've suffered in collaborative groups that break down because people couldn't agree. We've been forced to work with people we don't want to work with. We've been taken advantage of by loafers. We've had our time wasted when we could have done a better job alone—and quicker too."*

This is a valid objection. There's no getting away from the real difficulties of working together, whether or not people need to agree. And sometimes your task requires you to agree and to find a common voice. For this nitty-gritty difficulty, we offer some nitty-gritty rules of thumb:

- Never try to generate actual prose together. It will drive you crazy: One person suggests a sentence; the person with the pencil writes it down; someone else objects; the writer erases and writes something different; someone else tries. And so on until everyone is crabby. Don't argue about or even discuss actual wording until you have some rough drafts to work from. There are various ways to avoid this killing situation:
  - Use something like the loop process so that everyone produces prose (everyone takes the risk). Then people can proceed positively rather than negatively: Choose the bits they mostly like rather than criticize what they don't like.
  - Brainstorm. Encourage and accept all ideas and have someone take them down. No criticism. Then hear them and discuss and pick the ones that appeal. Have one person take notes on the agreements and then write up a very rough draft. Share it; hear some general kibitzing as to strengths and weaknesses about the thinking. No arguments about wording yet! Have another person take notes on that discussion and write up a slightly better draft. Now that you have this draft, you can start to discuss wording. And so on.
  - Meet and discuss the topic and reach general agreement on certain points. But then each person writes up one section. Come together to hear the sections; discuss the strengths and weaknesses of the thinking and voice. Then one person does a quick rewrite of the whole thing. Hear it and get feedback. Someone else does the final write-up.
  - Here's a risky, difficult method, but it can work well if you have the right mix of people. After only a bit of discussion,

one person writes a very rough discussion draft. This must be a brave and nondefensive person who can write quickly with very little effort, for much of what she writes will be rejected and virtually all of it changed. After discussion, someone else writes the next draft. A bit more discussion and copyediting, and someone else does the final copy.

- When hard choices have to be made, of course you will sometimes have to argue against each other's thinking. What helps most is a spirit of supportive cooperation. And one concrete technique is helpful: Avoid "God statements" and stress "I statements." That is, avoid saying, "This is wrong for the following reasons," and instead say, "This doesn't seem right to me because I had the following reactions." In short, remember that you are seeing things from only one point of view and you may be wrong. Be prepared to change your mind. Someone has to change his or her mind or you won't get the job done. But if you are supportive of each other and creative, it won't be fighting where one person "wins" and the other "loses." It will be a process of collaboratively figuring out new ideas that are better than those held by any of you individually.

- When you get close to a final draft and are trying to think about a voice, make sure to read things out loud. Get different members to read. Try to hear the different voices in the pieced-together writing. Try reading with exaggeration to bring out different possibilities of voice. Then you can decide which voice (more or less) is the one you want to try for. The person who can "do" that voice is probably the one who should do the final polished version.

- Be concrete and assertive about spelling out everyone's task. Write it down. Collaboration almost never works without an explicit schedule. Be tough-minded about insisting that people fulfill their responsibilities, and on schedule. If you are doing more than your fair share, maybe it's because you haven't insisted that others do their fair share. Be tough and expect others to be tough about this.

Take heart. Despite the real difficulties, we still think you will do best if you realize that collaboration is mostly a matter of getting the right attitude, or spirit, or feeling among you. That's exactly what our introductory dialogue and collage activity—the "easy collaboration"—will do for you: give you practice and experience working together and reaching agreements.

Attitudes or feelings make the biggest difference. If collaborative writing feels weird, stop a moment and reflect on the fact that it is probably the most common kind of writing in the world. In business, industry, and government, most writing is collaborative. Most research in the hard sciences and social sciences is written collaboratively. And it helps to notice the collaborative dimension even in most "regular" solo writing. Whenever you write something yourself, you tend to use the ideas and voices that you have absorbed from those around you. Collaboration is a common thing that humans naturally do. It's only in school that people tend to say, "Make sure you don't get any help from others."

It's helpful to realize, by the way, that we all learned collaboration before we learned to do things by ourselves. The collaborative use of language precedes the solo use of language. Babies learn to speak by first having dialogues with parents. Only through these dialogues do they gradually learn to "internalize" language enough to speak or think extended strings of language on their own.

Realize too that moving from difference to agreement is not just a difficulty; it is also an opportunity. If you have to struggle to work out some agreements, that very process will carry your thinking and analysis further. It will help you find weaknesses in your present views and lead you to new ideas that none of you could find alone. Collaboration is the most powerful way to expand your thinking about something because it brings multiple minds to bear on it.

Sharing and Responding

If you are writing collaboratively, you will probably do most of your sharing among yourselves in the process. In particular, as you read over your dialogue in order to edit it, and as you share your loop pieces in the first steps toward the collage, remember this: Mostly listen—listen for what is good. Put your effort into picking out the good bits and see if that process will show you what to use so you don't have to spend much time criticizing the ones you don't like. The spirit of collaboration is best served if you can make your choices by means of positive enthusiasm rather than by means of negative criticism.

If you want to get responses from others on your dialogue or collage, some of the main questions would be these:
- Which words or sections or pieces are strongest?
- What do you hear the best sections saying—and almost saying?
- What do you hear the whole piece saying?
- What happens as you listen? What are the steps or stages in your response? That is, tell us how the sequencing of pieces in our collage works for you.

For other response options, see "Sharing and Responding" at the end of this book.

Process Journal and Cover Letter

You may be trying more new processes here than in most work-shops—and some of the most unusual and perhaps difficult processes too: dialogue, loop writing, collage, collaboration. You will have your hands full simply talking about the ones that were most important to you: What was helpful and not helpful? difficult and easy? surprising or interesting?

But for future writing decisions it will be helpful to answer these questions:

- Which loop processes did you find the most helpful for getting involved in the topic and expanding your thinking? Do you think the other loop processes will be helpful for you if you get more familiar with them?
- Describe the collaboration you engaged in. What were the sticky points, and how could you deal with them better next time?
- How can you get more of the drama of contrasting thoughts and voices into your future solo writing?

For your cover letter, it's good to include some or all of your process writing. But don't forget to answer some cover letter questions. Here are the main ones: What is your main point and what effect are you trying to have on readers? What do you feel works best in your paper and where are you unsatisfied? What changes did you make on the basis of any feedback? And most important: What feedback do you want now from a reader? But your teacher may ask you particular cover letter questions that pertain to this assignment.

RUMINATIONS AND THEORY
Loop Writing versus the "Dangerous Method"

The Dangerous Method

Many teachers and textbooks say that to produce a "good" piece of writing, you must figure out what you want to say before you start writing: "Think before you write," they say. Toward this goal, they often suggest that you make an outline of your whole paper. Only then are you to start actually writing.

This advice sounds sensible. But this process of holding off writing till you get your meaning clear in your mind—so that you can write something right the first time—is what we call "the dangerous method." It's dangerous because it leads to various writing difficulties that most of us are familiar with.

- You find yourself procrastinating: "I can't start writing yet. I haven't thought this through well enough. My outline isn't right. I've got to do more reading and studying and thinking."
- You spend hours trying to figure out what you want to say—perhaps even making a very careful outline—but you don't really come up with much that's interesting.
- Even when you *do* figure out lots to say beforehand and get it neatly outlined, it's hard to write from your outline. You start to wander away from the outline, which makes you feel guilty. You think of a new idea you love, but it doesn't fit. Or worse yet, your outline starts to unravel as you write: You think of new problems or objections to something in your outline, or you can't quite explain the idea or the transition that seemed so right when it was in outline form.
- You agonize over every sentence in an effort to get it right. You constantly cross out, change, revise, start over.
- Finally, when you get a draft written, you can't bring yourself to make major revisions—or throw even a sentence away—because you've poured so much sweat and blood into writing every word.

Perhaps you don't have these difficulties. Perhaps you are actually good at the dangerous method of getting everything clear before you start writing. If so, by all means write that way. And of course there are a few writing tasks where you must get your meaning clear before writing, such as for exams that allow no revising time.

But usually when we write, we need to do more thinking about our topic. Even if we believe we understand quite well what we want to say, our thinking can benefit if we do our early writing in an exploratory mode. It helps us find new thoughts and new ways of talking about our old thoughts.

Of course writing does require getting your meaning clear in your mind, often even making an outline. And writing certainly means communicating to others what you've already figured out. But these processes usually work *best* after you've already done enough exploratory writing to produce good raw material—and if possible after you've felt the mental click that tells you, "Ah! That's it! Now I see exactly what I want to say." This insight is often accompanied by some clues about organization.

"It's Impossible Not to Think of Something"

So wrote the poet William Stafford. Whenever we pay attention to our mind, we find words and thoughts there; we may not always be satisfied with them, but they're there nevertheless. If we put these words on paper, other words take their place inside our heads. This process is infinite. But we're quite likely not to believe in it until we feel it proved: We need to put down the words we find in our head and then find others taking their place. The only limit to what we can write comes from our muscles: how long we can sit up, hold a pen, type.

When we write something down and don't stop to look back inside our heads, more words come anyway, and these words begin to appear on the page. If we continue to write, we become conscious of new sets of words only as they appear on paper. This can give us the intriguing sense that the words are writing themselves. In truth, much writing happens this way, whether it's exploratory or not. We rarely plan any written sentence out entirely in our heads. We start off a sentence with an intention to go somewhere with it and with the faith that we can do that. And we continue the same way when we've finished that sentence.

This is not to say that we don't get stuck. We do. Think of yourself as being in a maze. You come to a junction and are baffled. You could just sit and try to reason through the alternatives, but if you've never been in this maze before, that's hopeless. Your best chance of getting to the end is to try possibilities. Since every piece of writing is unique, you can think of each one as a maze you've never been in—even though you may know something about mazes in general. When you're stuck, it isn't because you don't have words; it's because you're trying to figure out in advance whether they're the right words. But the only way to know that is to write them out.

At first it may seem as though they're "wrong" words, but if you keep writing, you may arrive at some good ideas that you would never have gotten to otherwise. Even if you come to a dead end or feel irreversibly discouraged, you can always return to the point in the maze where you were stuck in the first place and take a different path. And remember: If your aim is to learn more about mazes themselves, you should deliberately take as many routes as possible.

This, of course, is analogous to loop writing. You start off a certain way that seems to be heading where you want to go, and travel wherever that takes you. If you are blocked in some way or don't like what you're doing, you can return to your original subject and start from it again in another way. You may well discover that there are quite a few effective approaches to your topic. Once you know that, you have choices. So if your aim is also to learn more about writing, it pays to explore as many paths as possible.

Revising

PART II

Drafting and Revising

Essential Premises

While all your writing is a product of your own thinking plus what you've taken in over the years through observing, listening, and reading, drafting asks you to pull your thoughts out of what's already in your mind, and revising asks you to focus far more pointedly on what others can help you see and add.

Writing is not just a recording of what you've already thought, but a way of building or creating new ideas on the basis of old ideas; that is, often you cannot start with the ideas you end up with because these ideas come to you only as a result of your writing or revising.

It isn't always easy (and certainly not always necessary) to separate drafting and revising. Sometimes we draft new ideas in the middle of revising. That's good.

Most of what we see in print has been revised.

Revising is hard work.

Main Assignment Preview

If you did the preceding workshops, you've already done some drafting and revising. Any writer's first writing on a subject is a draft. Sometimes the final versions are very close to the first drafts; sometimes they're so different as to seem totally unconnected. Most of the time, they're both connected and different. You've probably discovered that for yourself already.

In Workshop 1 you did quick revising (but nevertheless major revising) by simply cutting heavily to make a collage. In Workshop 4 (loop writing), you were faced with a mass of disorganized, rough, exploratory material from which to produce a coherent draft: You had to go through and choose, discard, shape, and rewrite.

Thus, we've already asked for lots of drafting and revising—just treating both activities for what they are: namely, inherent parts of the whole writing process. We don't want to give you the idea that composing is a linear process, proceeding lockstep from early drafts to first revisions to proofreading and final revisions. Sometimes you don't revise at all, sometimes you mostly revise, and sometimes you're doing new thinking and revising all mixed together. But because of their significance, it's worth making drafting and revising the main focus of a workshop.

This workshop's *main assignment* will be to choose a piece of writing you've generated previously, and revise it at three different levels of intensity. Our goal in this workshop is to help you better understand the ways in which a draft, through revision, becomes a final piece. We also want to help you understand, as a result of actual practice, how important revision is to good writing. Most of all, we want to show you strategies to help you get better at it.

Many people believe that good writers write something and send it off to a publisher, who prints it exactly as it's written. That's not how it works. When we read something published, we have no way of knowing what it first looked like and what changes the author made—first on his own and then on the advice of editors. But many writers testify to how much they revise and what a struggle revision can be. Here are two writers talking about revision:

> I am a witness to the lateness of my own vocation, the hesitations and terrors that still haunt all my beginnings, the painful slowness with which I proceed through a minimum of four drafts in both fiction and nonfiction.
>
> **Francine du Plessix Gray**

> I had a difficult time revising this piece. I was never sure if my ideas made sense. I wasn't sure of what I really wanted to say. My feedback groups helped a lot by offering opinions on different directions my original paper seemed to be taking. They helped me to see where my thoughts got hidden somewhere in the words I used. After a lot of rethinking and reorganizing (and also with the help of a classmate's "literary analysis" of my paper), I found my way through my thoughts and realized where my paper should go. The revision process was long and difficult, but I feel it did a lot of good.
>
> **Stephanie Curcio (student, process writing)**

You will have sensed the note of pain and struggle in the preceding quotations, and you may have painful revising memories yourself. Most of the time, there's no way to make revising easy or fun. Inherently it involves going over work again and again, evaluating, criticizing, and throwing away what sometimes seems like part of yourself. Nevertheless, we hope to counteract the tendency to be too grim or tense about revising and show that, like generating, it benefits from a spirit of playfulness. And, when finished, revision can generate immense satisfaction.

Writing Centers

All colleges and universities that we know of, plus many high schools, have writing centers or writing labs staffed by trained tutors. We urge you to make use of these tutors. Too often such centers or labs are thought of as grammar fix-it shops, but that is not an accurate assessment. Tutors can help you with all stages of the writing process, from coming up with topics to drafting, revision, proofreading, and reflection. Once students have discovered for themselves what valuable resources writing centers can be, they usually continue to use them for all their writing assignments—not just those for writing classes. We urge you to seek out your center and discover for yourself how useful it can be.

Drafting

Drafting is essentially whatever you do first when you begin work on a piece of writing. Some writers make lists; others do some form of clustering; still others (like us) do lots of freewriting. (In other texts, you'll often see these techniques labeled "prewriting." Though these texts describe the same process we're describing here, we prefer "generation," or simply "drafting," since they, too, produce writing—they don't precede it.)

In this workshop we are going to use, as an extended example, the entire revision process as worked through by one student, Beth Spencer. But we want you to see how she started this piece of writing also. So on the following pages we have reproduced her beginning notes and first rough drafts, which she wrote while responding to the Perl Guidelines laid out in Workshop 3.

What's important when drafting is to concentrate almost solely on what you want to say. Sometimes an early draft is getting ideas clear for yourself even though you may already have an audience in mind. While drafting, you don't need to worry about paragraphing and transitions or spellings. Some writers end up with a plethora of crossings out in a first draft; that's fine. What this should mean is that you're struggling to get at what you want to say. The two of us often hear a little voice in our heads during this early stage that says, "No, that's not quite it; try again." So we'll cross out what we've written (or delete it from the screen) and rewrite. This isn't truly revision at this point, but a search for matching works to intended meaning.

It's important to stay at this stage and not get bogged down in spelling or punctuation or even with writing grammatically complete sentences. Too many beginning writers don't struggle enough at this stage but move toward conclusions far too quickly. Try holding yourself back by setting your alarm clock for 30 minutes and not allowing

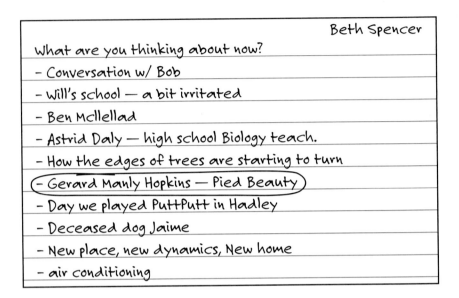

Beth Spencer

What are you thinking about now?

- Conversation w/ Bob
- Will's school — a bit irritated
- Ben Mcllellad
- Astrid Daly — high school Biology teach.
- How the edges of trees are starting to turn
- (Gerard Manly Hopkins — Pied Beauty)
- Day we played PuttPutt in Hadley
- Deceased dog Jaime
- New place, new dynamics, New home
- air conditioning

- Rick Bragg's book: <u>All Over but the Shoutin'</u>
- Next two books ① Dorothy Allison <u>Cavelands</u>
  ② Kaye Gibbons <u>On the Occasion of my Last Afternoon</u>
- Warm coffee w/ cream
- brown recluse
- minutes, minutes, minutes
- Bob as Will's stepfather — a good match
- ceiling lights here — just like the ones in first grade
- chocolate pudding — lunch

Figure 1   Figure 1 shows the front and back sides of a card Spencer filled in response to the question "What are you thinking about now?"

yourself to go back to revise until the alarm sounds. And don't forget that at first revision may well make your writing more chaotic rather than less chaotic. Think about what happens when you add eggs to cake batter; at first they make it less uniform and more messy, but if you keep beating, the batter becomes better and better. It's almost as though the eggs disrupt the batter—and revision often does that, too.

It's particularly important to keep yourself from spending hours on

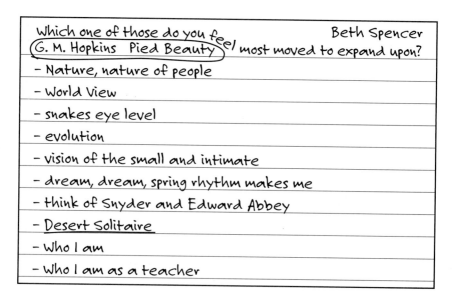

Which one of those do you feel most moved to expand upon? Beth Spencer
(G. M. Hopkins   Pied Beauty)
- Nature, nature of people
- World view
- snakes eye level
- evolution
- vision of the small and intimate
- dream, dream, spring rhythm makes me
- think of Snyder and Edward Abbey
- Desert Solitaire
- Who I am
- Who I am as a teacher

- Spiritual life — expressed as psalm, poem, prayer
- Act of writing as prayer — nontraditional mode
- Bittersweet "and so I did sit and eat"/-(Love III)
- Being in love colors everything around you.
- Becoming lost in the words and in between the words

        william Morris ⟶ PreRap

Figure 2   Figure 2 shows cards with Spencer's response to a follow-up question, "Which of those do you feel most moved to expand upon?"

an introductory paragraph, which can be the hardest part of a piece to write. You can always come back to it, and that's often preferable because you may discover, while drafting, that you really want to say something other (and better) than the idea you started with. It's pointless to waste time on introductions you will have to discard.

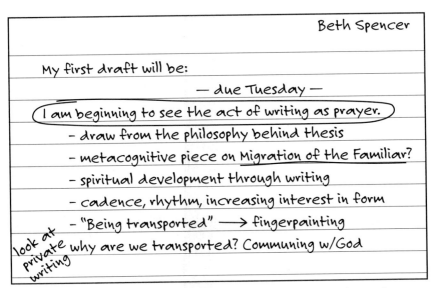

Beth Spencer

My first draft will be:

— due Tuesday —

I am beginning to see the act of writing as prayer.

- draw from the philosophy behind thesis
- metacognitive piece on Migration of the Familiar?
- spiritual development through writing
- cadence, rhythm, increasing interest in form
- "Being transported" ⟶ fingerpainting

look at private writing why are we transported? Communing w/God

Figure 3 This card shows Spencer beginning to focus on her topic.

Having said that, we recognize that some writers may have trouble getting started if they don't have a fairly solid point from which to start. If you're one of these writers and struggle with opening paragraphs, we suggest that you limit yourself to writing only a short statement of your main purpose or idea (which you may or may not use later), and go on from there.

Quick and Dirty Writing. Before we go into greater detail on revision strategies, we want to make you aware that there is something we call quick and dirty writing. This is writing that merely records something fairly routine whose content you're absolutely sure of. If you want to leave a note for your roommate explaining why you won't meet him as planned, you probably don't need to make a draft and revise it several times. If you want to explain to your parents where you are, you can simply write something like this: "I took the dog for a walk—be back soon."

The message here is that revising is important, but you don't have to revise everything, and revising doesn't have to be a quest for perfection. And sometimes revising may even squeeze the life out of language: "When I arrived home, Fido appeared restless and kept barking at the door, so I took him out for a walk; I didn't want you to worry about where the two of us might be. We certainly will not be gone for long. I'll see you soon."

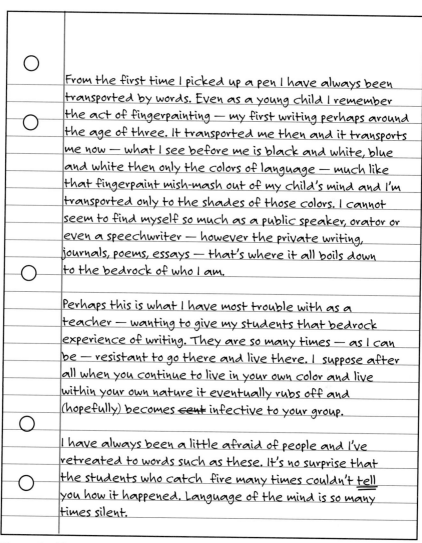

From the first time I picked up a pen I have always been transported by words. Even as a young child I remember the act of fingerpainting — my first writing perhaps around the age of three. It transported me then and it transports me now — what I see before me is black and white, blue and white then only the colors of language — much like that fingerpaint mish-mash out of my child's mind and I'm transported only to the shades of those colors. I cannot seem to find myself so much as a public speaker, orator or even a speechwriter — however the private writing, journals, poems, essays — that's where it all boils down to the bedrock of who I am.

Perhaps this is what I have most trouble with as a teacher — wanting to give my students that bedrock experience of writing. They are so many times — as I can be — resistant to go there and live there. I suppose after all when you continue to live in your own color and live within your own nature it eventually rubs off and (hopefully) becomes ~~cent~~ infective to your group.

I have always been a little afraid of people and I've retreated to words such as these. It's no surprise that the students who catch fire many times couldn't tell you how it happened. Language of the mind is so many times silent.

Figure 4   This is Spencer's first rough draft.

Quite a bit of the writing that occurs on e-mail networks is quick and dirty. Those doing the writing sometimes send a correction notice almost immediately if they see they've given the wrong information. In an e-mail message, you may even see a kind of discursive revision: "When I said 19, I really meant 29 in the first sentence" or "but that's not really what I mean—what I really mean is . . ." Some writers apparently prefer not to go back and revise errors; and some systems make such a move a bit complicated. When ideas become complex, what often happens is that the writer is forced to revise what she first wrote because someone will call into question what she has said or may seek clarification. However, such idea revision does not result in revising the original text, which in any case is already out in cyberspace somewhere. In truth, most writing appearing on discussion lists is quick and dirty and stays that way. But we also know of instances where what someone has written in an e-mail message, probably modified and clarified in response to questions, has become a conference paper or a chapter in a book. In other words, the original e-mail serves as an early draft.

Additional Drafts

When you move beyond quick and dirty writing, drafting begins. We advise, once you have a complete first draft, that you seek feedback. If you're really struggling, it's often helpful to share incomplete drafts, too. Your teacher may provide time for giving feedback in the class, or she may not. But you can always find readers and ask for feedback. At this early stage, you should ask for feedback directed at the content rather than the form. Sharing strategies 1 through 9 in "Sharing and Responding" (at the end of this book) will be most helpful.

When moving through subsequent drafts or moving toward your final draft, you may well find strategies 10 and 11 most helpful. Or you may want to borrow strategies we cover next as part of our discussion of reworking or reshaping.

For an example of this stage of the writing process, see Beth Spencer's draft of "The Act of Writing as Prayer" below.

First Word Processed Draft

I am beginning to see the act of writing as prayer. Just a few months ago I sat before three professors, each of whom held a copy of my collected poems in their laps, asking me to explain both the genesis and evolution of my poetry to date. I will never forget the way they looked over their respective bifocals at me: one with a half-grin; one with a mock-scowl and the other with the unabashed delight beaming on his face. There, in that 15 × 25 foot cinderblock office, I recounted how writing had taken hold of me at a young age, the sins of omission and commission admitted through poetic language, and always, always how the act of writing *transported* me beyond my physical body. I tried to explain that it was not so much the words, but the space between the words that compelled me beyond the hard swivel chair and bad lighting to a place which both exhilarated and humbled my spirit. The act of writing for me, then becomes that silent space of fear and perfect clarity.

Writing demands that I abandon the notion that I am the source of all creation. I dab words onto the page in fear that I really don't understand what will overtake the process. Journals, lists, couplets, and clusters of words are my markings against a white surface that are like little fists clasped together and pressed to my forehead. They plead with the universe to show me, show me the way. Not knowing where I'm going makes the shock of clarity that much more exhilarating. When I am writing, I am pushing against the notion of what I think I know. In the stillness of the morning, I may be moved to describe the beauty of migratory birds: *I have one rose-breasted grosbeak and eight indigo buntings at the feeder. Where will they light next? Will they make the journey back to Central and South America?* At night I fall into sleep scrawling: *a china moon a straw hat and deacons and jackals everywhere. Oh set the coffeemaker in the morning. I wish that . . . [sleep].* My language always knows where it's going; my hand does not.

It is the physical act of going into the unknown that, for me, is getting down on my knees and humbling myself at the foot of the bed first thing in the morning. It is sitting in a half-lotus trying to follow my breath. It is letting the trains of thought barrel past me until I am receptive to my breath alone. I am transported away from the clamor of my daily life and into the presence of what churns the universe around. And it seems, without fail, that once I reach that place where the pen takes on a life of its own I cannot imagine wanting to be anywhere else again. I come away from each session thinking *why did I resist?* I am intrigued by what is before me. Tomorrow I will unravel it some more.

Peer Responses to Spencer's Draft

First Response

1. Where does the writing really become interesting? Why?

I am captured by your idea!

To me the writing is interesting from the title forward. Comparing writing to prayer is a very interesting idea because, as you state, "Writing demands that I abandon the notion that I am the source of all creation." I don't think a lot of writers would be comfortable looking for practical advice for their writing by beginning with the acknowledgment of their powerlessness. And yet, there it is: We don't control the muse.

Somehow, after reading this piece, I feel that sharing useful or utilitarian insights on how the writing process works for you must "transcend" the idea that all creativity is an impenetrable black box. An interviewer who would ask Miles Davis or any other artist the standard question, "Where does your creativity come from?" is very likely to receive a response that is useless information for the audience in a pragmatic sense, something that will only harden the separation between the viewing and creating art. Prayer, however, is like writing in the sense that we all can and must do it for ourselves first: We can be the ultimate judge of its value. Your comparison of writing to prayer reinforces the private, vital and independent nature of the act of writing.

2. Where does it go flat? Why?

In general, the piece ends too soon for me. I enjoy your creative metaphors, especially the description of "clusters of words" as "little fists clasped together against my forehead."

While one of your strengths lies in your convincing voice speaking through your personal experiences, I keep waiting for you to close the circuit: Can (should) you define prayer more clearly? Could you then compare writing to prayer more directly? Although the creative process is something that traditionally resists interpretation, it seems that you've isolated that act with the act of writing together for the reader to see, but then stop before you really start to draw more specific comparisons of prayer to writing and vice versa. I think that there is room here to be more specific, more literal, about what prayer and writing each involve without becoming pedantic or reductive. It seems like a real wealth of fruit has yet to be harvested . . . what comes next?

3. Do you as a reader make a real connection with the idea of writing as "prayerlike"? Why or why not? What can the author do to illustrate this idea more?

Without turning this into a religious tract, I think that God must be found within this idea. Quite simply, there can be no prayer without a "higher power." I think you hint at this when you remark that "[w]riting demands that I abandon the notion that I am the source of all creation."

That said, how do you talk about that spiritual connection in a way that is honest, and yet doesn't exclude readers who either don't share your religious convictions or, perhaps most importantly, come to your piece seeking a fresh and useful perspective to apply to their writing and not a religious experience? Connecting prayer to writing is an exhilarating and powerful idea that can also misfire if not handled carefully.

What about some good, old-fashioned audience analysis here—whom are you writing to? If it's other writers, my feeling is that they will be captured by the honesty of your experiences—your journals, your morning habits, your feelings of regret for not having written sooner—and yet also demand that you "push" this idea further toward some conclusions. I think I see the evidence of some of the conclusions already: Why do you "fall asleep scrawling" at night? Why do you think the writing habits that you do have tend to work for you?

4. Which areas of this essay need more discussion?

Again, I think that I'd find it helpful to couple more pragmatic suggestions and conclusions with your experiences. Bluntly put: What about writing is like prayer? I think you can return to this conceit time and time again with numerous new avenues each time you compare a specific aspect of prayer to a specific aspect of writing.

This is a powerful idea: You have found an analogy that is revealing some profound truths for you and your readers. Good luck!

Another Response

Dear Beth,

I like your essay a lot; I'm very intrigued—pulled in. Here are some responses you can think about as you revise. Thanks for the questions. I won't really answer them so directly, but will use them to guide me.

Here is some *pointing*: places that come out strongest for me, hit me, stick in mind.

—The opening image of being with the professors; cinder blocks; glasses. I've been there. Here it's called an "exam" and, though people usually pass, still a little tense.
—"fear"—big word here. And "perfect clarity."
—fists clasped to forehead.
—stillness of the morning.
—those lines about birds.
—my language always knows where it's going.
—churns the universe around.
—why did I resist?

Here are some *movies of my mind* as I'm reading—but also paying attention to your questions:

I get involved in that opening image, having been there. I have feelings about those sessions where I've been a participant. I hate those meetings and discussions about someone's work being framed as an "exam." But perhaps it was dandy and nice for you.

But then somehow I'm moved to a different universe in the second and third paragraphs—not noticing that it's happening—

when you start talking about writing as prayer. In your question you asked if I connect to it. Yes, I do, though I wouldn't say that writing is prayer for me. But somehow it feels a *right* and *important* thought. Perhaps I wish it were true for me. And certainly I sometimes feel that writing surprises me and gives me thoughts and even feelings I didn't expect; takes me to the unknown. That's what's most exciting to me about writing; this mystery. So I get excited that you have a different lens for getting at that mystery and excitement.

A simple question flits across my mind. Do you actually get down on your knees to pray? I love the childish simplicity of being on knees with hands to forehead—though I also know that plenty of sophisticated nonchildren do that. I like the combination of frank religious exploration here and the lack of dogmatic language.

Here are some movies after I've read again—a day or so later—and more than once—thinking back over it and reflecting.

I'm perplexed by what I experience as a gap between that first paragraph and the rest. I'm in one world and then another. Somehow I can't bridge the gap. Wanting help. Maybe there's something wonderful about that first world being so completely different—so worldly compared to the rest of the paper. Writing as satisfying a university requirement vs. writing as prayer! Amazing. But I can't hold them both in mind at the same time.

But I love where the main part of the essay is going. You are giving me language for a vague religious position I feel: that there's something there if we listen and don't resist. And I love the link between that and writing.

And yet at the end I'm not satisfied. I feel there's something missing; I want more or want some change. I feel it could be a lot stronger. But I feel kind of helpless in not having anything concrete or useful to say. But maybe that's a point too: It's not a matter of being clever and figuring something out—it's about being quiet and *waiting* more for what's missing—or at least for what could carry us further.

Maybe I want a bit more concreteness about you and your writing life. It's quite general. What you have is somewhat general. I find the specifics precious: the opening image in that room with those particular people; those particular words or lines that you actually wrote (or said). Maybe I want to see more of your actual writing life. It's "spiritual" but there's not much "incarnation"— embodied particularity. Not sure.

Thanks for writing it and opening a door.

Best,
Peter

Process Writing on "The Act of Writing as Prayer"

Dear Peter:

I think I'm moving into an area with this essay that definitely makes me uneasy—which is always a good indication that the mind is reaching another stage of metamorphosis. As I look over the essay, the thing that strikes me is my capacity to be really honest and not skirt the main issue at hand: spirituality. This is no pat on the back, mind you—it's actually a little unsettling. However, I'd like to be more honest and *more* to the point of what I'm trying to say. I am very aware that the subject can go awry quite easily and fall off into "dogmatic" language (as you mentioned) if I'm not careful. But I really believe what's driving me in this essay is *attempting to explain* the force of The Spirit and how it guides my life and my writing. Prayer is such an intense and private and potentially volatile subject—I'm sort of wondering how I got here in the first place. But then, if I've really submitted myself to the process then it's not really up to me to worry about the outcome and just remain receptive. Another little shock of clarity, eh? The parallels between the two subjects seem to keep exposing themselves even more as I write. I realize that for the first time in my life I could really write a book on this whole idea.

But then there is fear. It can be such a stranglehold, can't it? But I've discovered if you can really find out what you're afraid of and "get its number" then you are free to write, unfettered and unafraid. That whole section on fear really hit a nerve with me and it felt good to get that down on paper. It was good to enumerate all of the factors that keep me from simply coming forth with my stranger ideas and emotions. I believe that looking at this self-centered fear in my personal life and getting honest with it is the best method to getting honest in writing. It's also definitely something that spills over into the classroom: I can convey a certain confidence to my students when they seem most frustrated and confused with an assignment. I can assure them that they are just where they need to be: in process. I sort of secretly know they are pushing into that mystery I mentioned (I want to say so much more about that!).

I would have to say that if I can narrow down the "subthemes" of this essay they would be: "fear," "mystery," "the ultimate audience" (thesis committees and the like), "waiting," "The Spirit," and something like "liminality and composition." Writing really does put us between two different worlds if taken seriously and I guess I can only speak to my own experience of negotiating these two worlds. I'm not sure that I've accomplished this exactly in this draft but it is something to bear in mind.

As a parting thought, some feedback that would be helpful from other readers would be the issue of clarity and style. I feel as though my initial draft had more "prose poetry" in it and this subsequent draft is more "essay-ish." Does it water down my first thoughts or help to clarify them? What areas seem to give an "ah-ha" response (felt sense, right?) and what areas make you sort of wince? Any areas where you doze off? Does the spiritual tone become a religious tone at any point? Your ideas are most welcome.

Sincerely,

Beth

Three Levels of Revising

For purposes of the main assignment in this workshop, we are going to think of revision as any stage that occurs after you have a complete piece, though—as we've already said—revision usually occurs at all stages of the writing process.

Many students equate revision with correcting mechanics or copyediting. Experienced writers never confuse the two. For them, revision means entering into a conversation with their previous thoughts. They match what they have already written against what they now wish to say and create out of the two a new piece that suits their present purpose. For example, now that we're revising this textbook for a second time, we are aware of the need to include instructions for using electronic media. That awareness has generated the need to revise, not just add. What our premises imply is that revision never stops. But of course writers need to finish things for particular deadlines, and so they revise what they have and submit it—usually with the recognition that if they submitted it later, they'd make additional changes.

Since this is how revision actually works, no one can say exactly what revising is. Probably the best definition is that revising is whatever you do to improve a piece of writing in terms of getting closer to what you want to say to a particular reader or readers—whoever they may be (e.g., friends, colleagues, an editor at a publishing house, the general reading public of a particular publication, a teacher, or even oneself). But to help us talk about revision, we're going to distinguish three levels:

1. Reseeing or rethinking: changing what a piece says, or its "bones."

2. Reworking or reshaping: changing how a piece says it, or changing its "muscles."

3. Copyediting or proofreading for mechanics and usage: checking for deviations from standard conventions, or changing the writing's "skin."

1. *Reseeing or rethinking: changing the bones.* When you read over something you've written, you often realize that it doesn't say what you now want it to say. You now see you were wrong, or you've changed your mind, or you need more, or you left something out, or you didn't understand the full implications of what you were saying. The process of writing and rereading changes you. At its most extreme, this level of revising may mean that you crumple up what you've written and aim it toward the trash basket: The cartoon image of a writer surrounded by wads of discarded paper is not far from the truth. Most writers feel they have to discard lots before they come up with something they can use. When *A Community of Writers* first came out, Workshop 5, which is now all about collaboration—using the loop process and the collage as methods—had no mention of collaboration. It was only about the loop process. As we were revising, we mentioned collaboration only briefly. In the intervening years we got more and more interested in collaboration. Consequently, we added a whole new Workshop, Workshop 4, on collaborative writing.

2. *Reworking or reshaping: changing the muscles.* This second level of revising means that you're satisfied with what you are saying (or trying to say) but not with how you've said it. Working on "how" tends to mean thinking about readers: thinking about how your thoughts will be read or understood by people other than yourself. Thus feedback from readers is particularly useful for this level of revising. One of the most common kinds of reworking is to improve clarity. Sometimes this may mean adding clarifying sentences or transitions—or even whole paragraphs. Perhaps you realize you need to change the order you present things in; or you need an introduction, conclusion, and some transitions; or you've implied ideas or suggested attitudes that you now consider unnecessary.* Most common of all,

---

* In the reworking level of revising this book, we found ourselves giving a good deal of attention to the subtitles scattered throughout the workshops: adding some and clarifying many. Having finally figured out what we were trying to say—where we were going—we were now trying to improve the road signs others would try to follow.

Exploring the Writing Process
On Changing Your Mind

I just figured out that all this stuff about revising is simply "man-talk" for changing your mind—which I have done and been made fun of for my whole life.

Andrea Warren

you simply need to leave out parts that may be OK in themselves (or even precious to you) but that don't quite belong now that you've finally figured out what the piece of writing is really saying. These passages clog your piece and will distract or tire readers. (You may not believe we left out a lot of the first draft of this book, but we did.)

3. *Copyediting or proofreading: changing the skin.* This third level of revising is usually what you do right before you hand something in or send it to its most important readers. At its simplest, it means finding typographical errors. At a level slightly above that, it means fixing sentence structure and checking spelling, punctuation, subject–verb agreement, and other features of usage. The spellchecker on your computer can help, but be careful about pairs such as *their/there* and noun and verb endings such as *s/ed*. Your spellchecker won't pinpoint these for you.

A writer needs to do all three kinds of revising and ideally in the order we've described them. After all, there's no point in fixing the spelling of a word or the style of a sentence if you're going to cut it, and no point struggling to reword the presentation of an idea until you know you're going to keep it. But of course writing activities don't always stay in a neat order. Sometimes it's not until you rework the presentation of an idea that you realize that it needs to be cut.

Beth Spencer continued revising and editing "The Act of Writing as Prayer," which you've already seen in several stages. The *latest* draft of her essay appears here:

The Act of Writing as Prayer   *Beth Spencer*

I am beginning to see the act of writing as prayer. Just a few months ago I sat before three professors, each of whom held a copy of my collected poems in their laps, asking me to explain both the genesis and evolution of my poetry to date. I will never forget the way they looked over their respective bifocals at me: one with a half-grin, one with a mock-scowl, and the other with the unabashed delight beaming on his face. There, in that 15 × 25 foot cinderblock office, I recounted how writing had taken hold of me at a young age, the sins of omission and commission admitted through poetic language, and always, always how the act of writing *transported* me beyond my physical body. I tried to explain that it was not so much the words, but the space between the words that compelled me beyond the hard swivel chair and bad lighting to a place which both exhilarated and humbled my spirit. The act of writing, for me, then becomes that silent space of fear and perfect clarity.

I once remember battling a deep resentment towards a person who

The Act of Writing as Prayer   *continued*

had probably brought the most pain to my life. I was caught in a thicket of brambles, playing this resentment over and over in my mind. I wanted a way out, wanted to free myself of the barbs that clung to me. The more I resisted, though, the more desperately entangled I became. I forced myself to pray for the person every day for two weeks. I submitted myself to the process, against my better judgment. At first, I remember praying: *please, God, give that sonofabitch what he deserves.* Each day, I prayed a similar sentiment. And each day the words became less and less powerful—revealing that, to my surprise, they were not the truth of my spirit or of my Creator's spirit. By the last few days the prayer changed to *God, bless this person with peace and abundance. I now see, too, that they are as trapped and fearful as I have been.* Again, thinking I knew the truth about a person was changed through prayer. Writing, for me, has the same effect.

Every time I hover above my journal, scrawl a thought on a restaurant napkin or tap out clumps of phrases onto my keyboard, I am submitting myself to an uncomfortable process. Writing demands that I abandon the notion that I am the source of all creation. I dab words onto the page in fear that I really don't understand what will overtake the process. Journals, lists, couplets, and clusters of words are my markings against a white surface that are like little fists clasped together and pressed to my forehead. They plead with the universe to *show me, show me the way.* Not knowing where I'm going makes the shock of clarity that much more exhilarating. When I am writing, I am pushing against the notion of what I think I know. In the stillness of the morning, I may be moved to reach for my pen and describe the beauty of migratory birds: *I have one rose-breasted grosbeak and eight indigo buntings at the feeder. Where will they light next? Will they make the journey back to Central and South America?* At night I fall into sleep scrawling: *a china moon a straw hat and deacons and jackals everywhere. Oh set the coffee maker in the morning. I wish that . . . [sleep].* My language always knows where it's going; my hand does not.

Prayer, too, requires that I simply submit myself to a process and trust that it will guide me into a deeper sense of understanding. It insists that I pay attention to that stillness of the morning and wait for a nudge. A nudge of clarity at first, and nothing more. *God,* I think. *I do not do not understand your will for me right now. You know me, God, you know me. You know that I need big arrows. Wide maps. Bright colors. I am here. Show me.* Then, when I least expect it, a nudge—no, a push—that moves me from one place to another in my mind; a feeling of powerlessness until I engage in prayer and feel how it transforms me in ways I could never imagine.

Above all, prayer is humble. Prayer keeps me striving for humility just as writing does. Both prayer and writing are a negotiation between humility and ego. I'm not the best at that—I have a tendency to think I have all the answers. And then there are times when I think I know nothing. And,

The Act of Writing as Prayer *continued*

ultimately all I really do know is *nothing* and that is what writing, like prayer, reveals as we go along. It reveals nothing new under the sun and, at the same time, it reveals everything. Revelations about human nature, ourselves, the way our minds work, our prejudices—yes, our prejudices—those wonderful stopgaps that really get us to the door of mystery. I recently found myself thinking a first line of poetry such as "The houses coil together in my mind / the framed yards, bald patches, places marked / with a single acorn" was the most perfect opening to a poem. In fact, I thought, *this is really pretty outstanding. Brilliant, perhaps. How I love it when it comes this easy.* And then I let it sit for a few days—*perhaps* let another pair of eyes take a look at it. And, thank goodness, my focus begins to sharpen. Umm . . . maybe that first line is a bit overstated. No, I was wrong. It's *quite* overstated, although I do genuinely feel that the second and third lines give some nice, clean visual images. I'll let them stay for now. Writing through my prejudices, if done long enough, will ultimately paint me into a corner, pull the rug out from under me and *force me to see things differently.* If I can remember that my writing is fed by a dialogue with the God of my understanding, The Spirit, The Muse—whatever you want to call it—I will be able to smile and laugh a little at myself when I move into that shock of clarity: mystery.

Writing and prayer, for me, are connected through mystery. Mystery is what churns the universe around. What's tricky about this connective tissue between writing and prayer is that it is the incentive that gets me *to the keyboard, on my knees, drawing the breath and saying o.k. I really want to enter into this. I'm going to "strap in and close my eyes."* Mystery is the one thing that drives me beyond the fear. Writing, like prayer, only reveals a truth to the writer who is ready, who is putting herself out there with a conviction of faith that constantly pushes through the formidable fear. Fear of being misunderstood. Fear of inarticulateness. Fear of looking and sounding stupid. Trusting and not trusting the muse—moments of weakness where the voice of the potential reader is louder than the voice of The Creator. Fear that someone will take your thoughts and words and twist them into something they were never meant to be, taking the beauty of being vulnerable to the creative process and destroying it with an unmovable, arrogant heart.

It is the physical act of going into the unknown that, for me, is getting down on my knees and humbling myself at the foot of the bed first thing in the morning. It is sitting in a half-lotus trying to follow my breath. It is letting the trains of thought barrel past me until I am receptive to my breath alone. I am transported away from the clamor of my daily life and into the presence of what churns the universe around. And it seems, without fail, that once I reach that place where the pen takes on a life of its own I cannot imagine wanting to be anywhere else again. I come away from each session thinking *why did I resist? I am intrigued by what is before me. Tomorrow I will unravel it some more.*

MAIN ASSIGNMENT
Revising on All Three Levels

Choose a piece of writing that you want to revise at all three levels. It probably makes the most sense to pick something that you feel dissatisfied with so that you know you won't mind doing extensive work on it.

There are two principal resources for good revision: time and new eyes. The best source of new eyes is other people; but if you let time go by, you've changed since you did your last draft, so in a sense your eyes are different. You don't see things the same way any longer. This is why it's so important to try to put something aside for a while and do your serious reviewing after a week or more has passed. This is why we've arranged this text so that you revise something a week or more after you first explored and wrote it.

Step One: First-Level Revising—Reseeing, Rethinking, or Changing the Bones

Share your piece with your group and use them to help you discover aspects of your subject that you have neglected, or explore possible major revisions: ways in which you might change your mind or disagree with your earlier draft or reach different conclusions. Or perhaps it's a descriptive piece or story, and you want to change the whole approach. Here are two suggestions to guide your group work:

1. When you've finished reading your piece (before oral discussion), allow a few minutes for freewriting. You can write down any additional thoughts you have on your topic or story, any doubts you now have about what you've written—anything at all about what the piece says. Those who have been listening to you should simply pretend that they've been assigned your subject and write their thoughts about it. At the end of this freewriting period, each group member can read what he's written. All this can serve as starters for discussion, but since this is your paper, you should guide the discussion and follow up on what is particularly interesting to you. (The others will have this same chance to be in charge when they read their papers.) You may want to ask your group members to give you copies of what they've written so that you can reread them at your leisure.

2. Another way to approach this level of revision is to ask each group member (including yourself) to pick out the most interesting sentences and freewrite about why they are interesting, what they

mean, and so forth. For this exercise you'll have to read your paper twice to your group, but reading twice is always a good idea. (It's best not to provide copies for your group since you want them to focus on your ideas, not on specific wording.) While doing this, it isn't necessary or even advisable for any of you to try to stick to your main idea. Remember, you're trying to explore all aspects of a topic no matter how unrelated they might seem at first.

Revision for the sake of revision can be a deadening chore. That's why we ask you to practice first-level revision as a pretending game. Joining the game with your classmates may lead you to new insights about your subject that you'll want to incorporate into your writing. (Of course, you don't need the game if you discover you actually do see your subject differently.)

On the basis of your group's discussion, decide what you now want to say and then rewrite your paper. Don't be surprised if you find yourself doing more revising than you expected. You may even discard the ideas you started to revise with. That's part of what should happen.

If you find this difficult—for example, if you find you don't want to change what you've said or what the story deals with—do some experimenting anyway. Play with your ideas or story. Revision is usually done in the spirit of clenched teeth and duty, but it can be done better in a spirit of play or even fooling around. The most reliable (and enjoyable) technique for changing the bones of your writing is to role-play. Pretend to be someone else who has a different outlook on your topic or issue: one of your group members, perhaps, who disagrees with you, someone else you know, or even an imagined person.

Another technique is to pick a paragraph (or even a sentence or image) and build a whole new essay or story around it. In other words, deliberately try to write something different even if you're satisfied with what your original piece says. It helps to start with a fresh sheet of paper or a new computer file to free you from the original way you developed your ideas.

If you give yourself half a chance, you can get caught up in this kind of play. The words you produce will create their own complex of ideas, which in turn will lead to other words, sentences, and paragraphs.

Let the process change your mind-set so that you are no longer striving to write something different from the original version; you're working toward fulfilling some new goal or purpose, one that has grown out of the writing itself.

We know that much revision in the working world is probably reworking, not reseeing. If your boss tells you to write a report about a meeting of a special planning group, you can hardly revise it into suggestions for improving company management (even if that's what you'd rather write). Still, if you learn that you don't have to stick slavishly to what you've already written, you can free yourself to use the first drafts as seeds rather than constraints. There are always deadlines, of course, so at some point we have to stop new thinking about our subject and focus instead on refining what we've already said. We think that most students, however, get to this second step too soon; they don't recognize the power and pleasure of the prior step. That

Exploring the Writing Process
On Discovering Ideas

I've just written and revised a paper about freewriting I was writing for a conference.

I procrastinated, as I always do, waiting for special inspiration—it didn't come (usually it doesn't). So I forced it, felt like I was stammering on paper. After 10 minutes, though, I was rolling.

After about 30 minutes of this nonstop writing, I had a good amount of stuff on paper, although I still wasn't particularly pleased with what I had come up with. Still, I had to get it done, so I started working with it. As I did that, more and more came out. Soon I had a rough draft of my paper. But I didn't particularly like it, so I fiddled with it some more. Since I had agreed to read it at a get-together of a group of us who meet about once a month to work on our writing, I had to get it in some sort of presentable form.

I told everyone before I started reading it that it sort of did what I wanted it to do; I just didn't think it did it very well. After I finished reading, the members of the group started talking about the ideas in it—not criticizing anything and not giving me many suggestions, just talking about it.

As I drove home that night, it came to me—I knew what I had to do. I had to reorganize, present what I wanted to say as a story of an intellectual quest, what started me on the quest, what I found along the way, and what I concluded when I finished the quest. I don't know why I hadn't seen this before, but I hadn't. Something about sitting in the group and reading it, hearing it discussed a bit, made it (my text) into an object I could look at from a greater distance and shape in a more logical way. The next day I made these revisions with very little effort.

Pat Belanoff

is why, in this workshop, we require you to do first-level revision even if you are satisfied with what you've already written.

Once you've made your revision, you can decide whether you want to use it or your original for the remainder of the work in this workshop. Remember: Revisions aren't necessarily better—they're different. Once you understand this, you'll be willing to take risks as you revise: changing everything almost totally, exploring something which seems at first odd or silly to you, trying new approaches, developing some ideas that you don't even agree with. You can throw it all away if you want to. Almost invariably, though, you discover something substantial that you like—something that you'll want to incorporate into your original. Whatever happens, there's no reason to use a revision simply because it's a revision. And you may now decide you've got two pieces you want to finish up.

Step Two: Second-Level Revising—Reworking, Reshaping, or Changing the Muscles

When you've decided which version of your essay to use, you're ready to practice the second level of revision—reworking. For this, prepare a good legible copy of the version you've selected and use very wide left- or right-hand margins—say, about three inches. Make copies for your group. Before going to class, write a brief paragraph just for yourself that states briefly your purpose for writing the paper and the reasons why you chose to accomplish your overall purpose in the way you did. (Workshop 6 focuses more on purpose as the guiding principle of revision.) Then, on your copy of the essay, write in the margin some notes about each paragraph. These notes should include a *summary* of what the paragraph says and does (its purpose) and how it fits in where it is. These subsidiary purposes can include introducing, restating, giving examples, setting a scene, building suspense, giving your opinion(s), describing, moving to another aspect of your paper, concluding, and so forth. (See "Skeleton Feedback and Descriptive Outline" in "Sharing and Responding" for more about this powerful activity.)

Here's how one student writer summarized the purpose of a paper she planned to revise at the second level:

> I wanted to make readers see the disco scene, so I described it. But I also wanted to show how silly it is—poke fun at the people in it.

And here are the marginal summaries she wrote about the first few paragraphs of her essay. Notice that she had already begun to think of possible changes:

Outside the crowd waits. Guys clad in their outermost layer of skins, their pants, are nervously looking for their ID's within their wallets. Of course they make sure every girl sees the big wad of bills. What they don't know is that there is always a girl in the crowd who decides to light a cigarette and upon doing this sees that the big wad of bills is in fact one dollar bills. News travels fast and soon everyone is laughing at the guys. Then there are the young enticing girls. They look about 20 with their makeup caked upon their faces (you'd need a Brillo pad to scrub it all off), skin-tight Spandex and heels. These "women" are in actuality 14 or 15 years old; what gives them away is the way they smoke. They simply don't inhale. The drag of smoke enters and exits in the same dense cloud; they need to fan the air with their hands so as not to die of suffocation.

Introducing, setting the scene, describing people.

Also trying to set the tone—being sarcastic. I'd like readers to wonder what's going to happen.

The tension is building, and it seems to hang in the air like a low-lying cloud. The people are moving closer and closer to the entrance as if stalking prey. The doors open and everyone pushes in. Suddenly a pink Cadillac screeches to a halt and the driver gets out. The multitude of people stop! It's as if a spell were cast upon them. "It's him!" a young girl cries.

Showing what happens right before the doors open, trying to get suspense going. Paragraph introduces Mr. Big—sarcastic about him too.

He is tall, dark, and rich! He is wearing a white suit (polyester of course) with a black silk shirt. His shirt was, of course, opened to his navel in order to display his jewelry. The jewelry consisted of three rope chains, each varying in length and width, and the fourth was an inch-thick rope chain bearing the Italian phallic symbol, the horn. The crowd, still mystified, parted like the Red Sea, allowing Mr. Big to enter the disco. The two-ton bouncers who were once mountains of malice became little pups when greeting him. "Can I help you,

Describes and makes fun of Mr. Big. Moves the story ahead a bit. Shows how people react to him and how phony everything is.

Mr. Big?" "Your table is waiting for you, Mr. Big." "You look very nice today, Mr. Big," and so on.

Once that awesome happening settled and passed, the crowd went back to pushing and shoving through the doors. It's really ridiculous to see people who are supposed to be grown-ups react like little children when they see a circus for the first time. If they only realized that the circus they're watching (Mr. Big) gets his ears boxed by his mother if he comes home too late.

Gives my opinion about all this, although I'm not sure why I put it here—maybe because I'm now going to move the scene inside.

Once inside, the eardrums shatter like a drinking glass does when it encounters a high-pitched voice. This calamity happens because of the booming music that seems to vibrate the entire building. Ah, there's Mr. Big and his harem. All the women flock around him as if he were a mirror. He'll make his grand entrance on the dance floor later on.

Describing the scene inside, including Mr. Big. I'm making fun of the women who hang around him. I want to describe everything step by step as people would see it when they went in.

Upon entering, the bar is to the left, and a few steps below is the dance floor. By the way, the steps are notorious killers since many, under the influence of alcohol, forget they exist. On the other side there is the seating area consisting of dozens of tables and black velvet, cushiony, recliner-type chairs. They are the type of chairs you lose yourself in.

This is more description of the inside. The thing about the steps is something I always think about when I look down at the dance floor because I fell on them once. Maybe this should all be added to the paragraph before since it's all description.

Ask your group members to write the same kind of marginal notes on their copies of your essay. Also ask them to jot down a few words specifying any emotional reaction they may have to each paragraph: Are they curious, bored, annoyed, offended, excited, informed, hostile, or something else, and can they pinpoint the words or phrases that cause their reactions? They can do all this at home or in class. If this work is done at home, your teacher will probably give you some time in class to share and get clarification.

Using the feedback you've gotten, decide what changes, if any, you want to make. Most of your changes will probably be aimed at making your meaning clearer. This can include *restructuring* (reordering paragraphs, adding transitions, providing or reworking introductions and conclusions), rewriting (reworking sentences or phrases to alter their emotional impact or clarify their meaning), and *adding* (everything from background information to new points, to examples, to clarifying phrases). If, while doing this, you find yourself moving back to the first level of revision (altering what you say), don't be surprised. We told you that the three levels of revision cannot be fully compartmentalized. You need to keep in mind, too, that form and content are inextricably linked: Changing *how* something is said almost always affects *what* is said.

One final note about this level of revising. Your paper is yours, and you need to trust your own instincts about how you say something. We think that before ideas get into words, there is always an impulse toward meaning, a felt sense. Once we put an idea into

Exploring the Writing Process
On Revising With Scissors and Tape

Exploring the Writing Process Thank you for reading my "rough" (sure took a lot of work to produce something so unfinished—on the computer I lose track of how many drafts I've gone through). When I tried breaking up the exposition, as you suggested, I discovered the need to equally break up the narrative. Then I became more aware of the importance of linking particular episodes with specific discussions (and also discovered a lot of redundancy). I ended up doing a lot of literal cutting and pasting: printed up the whole article, cut it up almost by paragraphs, and then rearranged and taped things together. So I ended up moving from computer back to a physical scroll. (I know the writing process is supposed to be recursive, but doesn't this sound positively retrogressive?) I've never produced anything quite this way before, and I honestly hope that future articles won't be so emotionally demanding. I think I'd now like to tackle some "safe," comparatively dull piece of literary analysis.

**Deborah Klein,
University of Jos, Nigeria**

Note: This is the writer's observation after completing a revision of an article that appears in the November 1999 issue of *College English.*

Figure 5   Revision: Start to Finish

words, we test it against that original impulse; and when the words and the impulse match, we know we've got the idea right for ourselves. Sometimes this felt sense of rightness comes immediately;

sometimes we have to rewrite several times before we feel it; and sometimes we just give up and recognize that, for the moment, we can't achieve it. Our point is that only you know exactly when you've said what you want to say. Someone else may suggest a very nice sentence, but it's no good if it's not what you are trying to say.

Step Three: Third-Level Revising—Copyediting and Proofreading

When you've finished this second level of revision, type up a final, clean copy of your paper—double- or even triple-spaced. This can be the copy you hand in to your teacher. Make at least two copies of this almost-final version. You will use the extra copies for copyediting and proofreading, the final level of revision.

Your teacher might not be able to provide time in class for you to proofread and copyedit every paper you hand in. But you should find the time for it. Typographical and usage errors can destroy the best piece of writing; once you've spent a lot of time getting your thoughts straight and in good order, it's foolish not to take a little extra time to make them readable. Surface flubs can make readers decide not to read your piece at all or to read it in a hostile mood.

You will benefit tremendously from the comments of your fellow students here. If your teacher sets aside class time for this activity, proceed as below:

1. Make two copies of the almost-final version of your paper. Give one copy to another student, asking her to copyedit and proofread your paper, and doing the same for her.

2. Read your classmate's paper very carefully, and pencil in any corrections you think appropriate. You are looking for errors in mechanics or typing (capitalization, underlining, abbreviations, and so forth) and all violations of the rules of Standard English. You'll particularly want to check spelling, punctuation, sentence structure, subject–verb agreement, and pronoun reference. If you aren't sure about a change you've made, put a question mark by it. If a sentence doesn't sound right to you—and you can't pinpoint exactly what's bothering you—draw wiggly lines under it. Be sure to sign your name to the paper as editor. Your teacher may want to collect all edited copies of each paper in order to pinpoint particular students' problems.

3. Once you get the copies of your paper back, you'll need to make a decision about each correction or comment made by your editor(s). If you're sure they're right (perhaps your mistake was

carelessness or poor typing), make the correction neatly in ink on your good copy. If you're sure they're wrong, don't erase the change; leave it, so that your teacher will know what you've made a decision about. If you're not sure one way or the other, you'll have to check with some third-party authority: a handbook, your teacher, a tutor in the writing center, or a proficient classmate, roommate, or family member.

4. If your teacher gives you additional class time, you can share your findings and problems with others in the class. All of us store rules about language in our heads, even though we may not be consciously aware of them. If we didn't have such rules, we couldn't talk or write at all. If you can become consciously aware of the rules you use, you can discard or alter those that are unacceptable (as defined by your teacher or the grammar book you are using) and sharpen those that are valid. Class discussion will make you aware of which you should keep and which you should discard.

If you do not have time for this activity in class, you may be able to make arrangements with classmates to do it outside of class. Otherwise, ask your roommate, a friend, or a family member. You can even hire a tutor to help.

You can also copyedit and proofread productively on your own, of course. Sometimes the best strategy for dealing with problems you can't clearly define is to rewrite the problem sentence in a different way. Try to think yourself back into the idea you had when you wrote the sentence, and see if you can write it in a way that matches your idea more clearly. Say what you mean aloud to yourself, talk it through, and then try writing it again. You may want to rewrite the sentence several ways. You'll probably recognize which one is the best. If you do rewrite an entire sentence, you should reread the paragraph it's in to make sure you haven't disrupted the flow of the ideas and language. If, when you've made decisions about all suggested changes, you discover you've made so many that it's hard to read your paper, ask your teacher if she'd like you to retype it or make the changes on your computer and reprint the paper. If you have to retype it, remember it needs proofreading again. (This is one of the many advantages of writing on a computer.)

If you make a relatively high number of usage errors, you'll need to do some extra work. Set aside several pages in your journal or notebook to list the errors you make. In this way, you can discover which errors recur and concentrate on avoiding them. What you'll probably discover is that you're not making many different errors, but the same errors over and over. Your teacher may expect you to do some extra work to begin clearing up your particular set of errors.

Suggestions for Collaboration

You might want to switch papers with a classmate at each level of revision, then switch back, and compare notes on what recommendations you've both made. The final—or latest—draft should be produced *collaboratively,* incorporating the revisions you've decided jointly to implement.

Sharing and Responding

A major portion of the activity in this workshop already involves sharing your writing with your peers and receiving and making responses. Your classmates have already undertaken a version of "Believing and Doubting" during the first level of revision. They pretended your topic was theirs. In the second level of revision, you and your classmates have provided a kind of "Descriptive Outline" in the margins of papers. The other sharing-and-responding activity that we recommend for this workshop is "What Is Almost Said?" You will find it useful to ask your classmates this question as you're working through the first and second levels of revising.

Process Journal and Cover Letter

You've probably done some process writing in previous workshops about the revising you did there. But since we haven't until now made revising the focus of a workshop, it's important to try to learn as much as you can about what happens for you in this slippery process. Try to re-create and describe as much as you can of what you did in all the revising activities of this workshop: feelings, thoughts, reactions, things you can learn. If you need help, these prompts may be of use:

- Simply gather as many memories and reactions as you can under the three stages:
  - First-level revising of bones, or what you said.
  - Second-level revising of muscles, or how you said it.
  - Third-level, skin-deep copyediting or proofreading.
- Freewrite about your own revision processes in the past and about how you feel about revision. Do you revise a great deal? If so, why? What writings of your own are you the most reluctant to revise? Why? When you revise, at which level do you tend to work at most?
- At what points in your writing do you tend to stop and fix things? Are they frequent? What triggers you to stop the flow of words and go back to change something?
- Read "Ruminations and Theory: Revising and Grammar" and write in your journal about some of your experiences with grammar.

Writing as Play   Mechanical Revision

1. After you've finished the sequence we set forth in this workshop and have a paper ready for final submission, select one of its paragraphs that seems particularly leaden or energyless to you. Replace every form of to be in that paragraph with a verb that captures some of the action of the sentence itself.

   Example: Look back at the paragraph in our sample essay (page 134) beginning "Upon entering, the bar is to the left [. . .]." Here's how that might look according to this exercise:

   Upon entering, you immediately see the bar to the left, and a few steps below, the dance floor. By the way, the steps have a reputation as notorious killers since many, under the influence of alcohol, forget that they exist. A seating area consisting of dozens of tables and black velvet, cushiony, recliner-type chairs lines the other side of the dance floor. In this type of chair, you can lose yourself.

   OR

2. Examine your almost completed paper, and take one of the middle paragraphs or the end paragraph and put it first. Notice what changes you have to make.

   Example: Here's what might happen when the paragraph beginning "Once inside, the eardrums [. . .]" is placed first:

   The eardrums shatter as a drinking glass does when it encounters a high-pitched voice. This calamity happens because of the booming that seems to vibrate the entire building. Ah, there's Mr. Big and his harem. All the women flock around him as if he were a mirror. He'll make his grand entrance on the dance floor later on.

   Now that we've gotten in, the noise of the waiting crowd outside fades away, but we know the rest of them will be there most of the night. The scene out there was something else [. . .].

   (Look to see what other changes you might need to make in this paragraph as well as throughout the piece.)

   Since this is just a for-fun exercise, you do not actually have to rewrite your entire paper—unless of course your teacher asks you to, or, just perhaps, you might like it better this new way. Fun can be productive!

For your cover letter, it's good to include some or all of your process writing. But don't forget to answer some cover letter questions. Here are the main ones: What is your main point and what effect are you trying to have on readers? What do you feel works best in your paper and where are you unsatisfied? What changes did you make on the basis of any feedback? And most important: What feedback do you want now from a reader? But your teacher may ask you particular cover letter questions that pertain to this assignment.

RUMINATIONS AND THEORY
Revising and Grammar

Many people think that learning to write means learning grammar. When we ask students at the beginning of a semester what they expect from our course, many say they expect to be taught grammar. They rarely understand that grammar mistakes (subject–verb agreement, tense forms, sentence completeness) and deviations from standard usage (spelling, inappropriate word choices, and word forms) do not usually lead to a distortion of meaning, though, of course, they can. But deviations from standard usage can be quite distracting for many readers. Each of us can probably tolerate a different level of deviation. Some people can read a whole paper in which the final "s" is missing from present-tense verbs and not react. Others will react to even one missing "s."

Errors in usage often force readers into giving attention to the words instead of to the meaning. Continually distracted in this way, readers begin to believe that the author's meaning is unclear, the organization poor, or the quality of thinking mediocre. Or they'll judge the writer as not very committed to the ideas she's presenting; and if that decision reinforces itself through ongoing usage and grammar errors, readers may conclude that the writing does not merit their continued attention either.*

---

*One of the reviewers of this textbook commented (in reference to the Writing-as-Play box of this workshop) that we had overused forms of "to be" in our "Ruminations and Theory" section. As a result, we revised this paragraph. Following is the original paragraph:

   The real problem with errors in usage is that they force readers into giving attention to the words instead of the meaning. If readers are continually distracted in this way, they begin to believe that the author's meaning is unclear, the organization is poor, or the quality of thinking is mediocre. Or they'll think that the writer is not very committed to the ideas she's presenting, and if that's the case, why should the reader give them much attention?

There is a continuing debate in scholarly and pedagogical journals about whether to teach grammar and usage in writing courses. Here is our position:

- Instruction in grammar cannot serve as a substitute for instruction in writing.
- What students learn from doing grammar exercises rarely transfers to their writing.
- There is a need for discussion about what people mean by "standard usage"—along with its function in society and its relation to nonstandard dialects.
- Elimination of certain usage errors (particularly the dropping of an "s"—as in "she see"—and the use of phonetically induced forms—"she could of done it") is a slow process. We cannot expect students to alter something so basic to their natural language very quickly.
- Instruction in standard usage should focus on the errors students actually make and the contexts in which they make them.
- Students should be forced to articulate for themselves the reasons why they use nonstandard forms. Only in this way can they begin to build different rules into their personal language.
- Students should be required to submit final copies of their revised pieces that are free from errors in typing, usage, and grammar. We believe in giving students some help in achieving this, but what's most important is making them realize that they have to find whatever help they need. Students who are poor spellers, for instance, may always have to find someone who is willing to check their papers for all misspelled words. Spellcheckers on computers are a godsend for such students. Remember, however, that a spellchecker cannot tell you that "there" should be "their," and it won't tell you that "form" is incorrect when you meant "from." It may well be that computers will soon be supplied with easy programs for checking some other aspects of usage. In any event, we believe students must find ways to write Standard English whenever they want or need to—for example, on job application letters and forms. This does not mean we consider Standard English superior to other varieties; in fact, we encourage students to hold on to their native dialects, whatever they may be. Such dialects give language life and often gradually serve to renew Standard English.

Revising through Purpose and Audience

Writing as Doing Things to People

Essential Premises

Experienced writers know when to think about their audience and when to forget about them. When revising, you need to do both—though not at the same time.

All language—spoken or written—has a purpose and all language does something, though it may not always be what a writer intended.

Revision requires becoming consciously aware of your own purposes, but also aware of the effects your language is having on others.

Main Assignment Preview

The goal of this workshop is to help you learn to shape your writing better by thinking more pointedly about what you want your words to do, and to whom—that is, about purpose and audience. The *main assignment* is to revise a paper you wrote for some other workshop in this textbook. In Workshop 5, we laid out one way to go about revision. In this workshop, we're going to suggest other ways to work on revision.

We almost always have a *purpose* in mind when we speak. We may be just expressing ourselves ("Ouch!"), making contact ("Hello, how are you?"), conveying information ("It's 10 o'clock"), or persuading ("It's much too hot to work—come to the beach with us"). Even when we talk to ourselves, we probably have some purpose: to buoy our spirits ("C'mon, you can do it"), to keep from being frightened ("It's only the cat"), or to get something off our chest ("I hate him, hate him, hate him!").

In addition, we almost always have an *audience* in mind when we speak: maybe just anyone ("Help! I'm drowning!"), a good friend ("I've missed you"), a parent ("I've studied all week; can I use the car?"), a teacher ("Do you take off for misspelling?"), peers ("Let's do something different this weekend"). And we sometimes just speak to ourselves. Since writing usually takes more time and effort than speaking, we're even more likely to have a purpose in mind when we write compared to when we speak, even if the purpose is mostly to fulfill an assignment for a teacher.

Purpose and audience interact to influence what you say. In all likelihood, if you want to borrow a friend's car, you wouldn't persuade him to let you have the car by saying you had studied all week. You'd be more likely to say, "Are you really my friend?" If you're writing to convey information about the popular music scene to your teacher, you'd probably include more background information than if you were writing an article for your campus newspaper. When we write only for ourselves, though, we can use whatever language and approach we please—and say whatever we want—since there's no fear of hurting or annoying someone or getting a baffled look.

Audience in Writing

Let's work up to purpose by way of audience. Sometimes you know who your audience is—for example, your parents or a particular committee or group of friends. Perhaps your audience is your classroom partner or group.

Exploring the Writing Process
On Writing Letters (and Not Sending Them)

To write letters to friends & *not to send them.* . . . When you are on fire with theology, you'll not write it to Rogers, who wouldn't be an inspiration, you'll write it to Twitchell, because it would make him writhe and squirm & break the furniture. When you are on fire with a good thing that's indecent, you won't waste it on Twitchell, you'll save it for Howells, who will love it. As he will never see it, you can make it really indecenter than

he could stand; & so no harm is done, yet a vast advantage is gained. . . . Often you are burning to pour out a sluice of intimately personal, & particularly private things—& there you are again! You can't make your mouth say them. It won't say them to any but a very close personal friend, like Howells, or Twitchell, or Henry Rogers.

Mark Twain

But sometimes you don't know your readers. You may have to write a letter explaining why you're returning some faulty merchandise or a letter requesting information from a government agency. You may be writing an essay of application to law school and have little sense of who the admissions people are and what they are impressed by. Sometimes you know *who* your readers are but not what they're *like*. That is, you may write something for a particular newspaper or magazine that gets all sorts of readers with all sorts of views and feelings. Or perhaps you have nobody and everybody in mind as your audience: You're writing about an issue for people in general or just for yourself.

There's nothing wrong with writing when you are unclear about your audience. Very good writing can be produced in that frame of mind. Besides, you often have no choice: You must write and you don't know the audience. But even when you are very clear about your audience, you may get confused when you think about them; in that case, it pays to forget about them and write your first draft to no one in particular or to a friendly audience. If your audience is not a problem, however, you can usually focus your thoughts and language better if you keep them in mind.

Two Kinds of Audience Analysis

The obvious kind of audience analysis is to think about who your readers are and where they stand on the topic you are writing about. If you are writing something persuasive or argumentative, you will probably think most about where they *disagree* with you; after all, that's why you're writing—to change their minds.

But watch out. Yes, you need to understand the points of disagreement, but your best hope of persuasion is usually to build from a platform of agreement or shared assumptions. Your audience analysis needs to focus on figuring out some of those points of agreement. Even if your disagreement is very large and even if you feel you are trying to persuade people who are deeply different from yourself, there are probably crucial *assumptions* that you share. (For example, die-hard pacifists and hawks in this country often agree about the desirability of democracy and individual freedom.) To put it another way, if you cannot find any shared agreement or feel some kinship with the "enemy," it's probably a waste of time writing to persuade them.

Whether you know your real audience or not, you can analyze the audience that your writing implies. For if you look closely at any piece of your writing, you can find clues about whom you were unconsciously assuming as the reader. For example, does your piece have little touches that imply your readers are smart or dumb? informed or uninformed about the topic? likely to agree or likely to fight you? frivolous or serious?

Following are two different versions of an editorial that have much the same purpose:

1. It is time now for this country to cease its bombing of Afghanistan; the price in innocent lives has become far too high. We cannot applaud a victory that comes from shedding the lives of children, old people, and women who have known little in their lives but poverty.

2. Rebuilding the lives and environment of the Afghani peoples must now become our first order of business. For too long these suppressed groups have been subjected to lives of poverty and overly strict cultural codes. We can best begin this rebuilding by ceasing our bombing of the country.

The first of these two versions assumes an audience that views cessation of bombing as crucial; the second of these two assumes an audience that may not be favorable to such a course of action. Thus, the first version assumes that cessation is a good in itself, whereas the second provides other reasons for ceasing the bombing. Chances are those who approve of continued bombing would not even read the remainder of the piece introduced by the first version. They might, perhaps, continue to read the second version.

The "implied reader" is a subtle dimension of a text (and an im-

Exploring the Writing Process
Staying Engaged

Though my writing process has certainly changed due to this class, I think that my process of writing is still suffering. My major question: how can we become re-excited by our writing and ideas after the first draft is said and done? I spoke to several classmates during the semester who were having similar trouble reentering and reengaging with their work after setting it aside for a week or two. It seems that a lot of us have gotten used to losing interest in our work, or even deploring it, after it has left us for a bit. And that doesn't seem right.

Leslie Edwards

portant, critical concept in literary criticism as well as composition). Most of us need the help of responders to discover the implied reader in what we write. For example, sometimes a responder will show you that your text gives off contradictory audience cues. Perhaps at one point your writing implies that the readers are already interested in your topic, and at another point that they are uninvolved. The contradiction may undermine your writing by alienating *all* readers: Everyone feels, "He's not talking to me."

One of the most common kinds of implied reader is a "reader in the head"—that is, some past reader who continues to be a powerful influence on you. For example, responders may show you that your letter to a newspaper is full of confusing qualifications because you are still unconsciously writing for a teacher who told you never to make a broad generalization when writing about a controversial subject. It may not be suitable advice for this audience. Or your essay for an economics teacher is full of impressive verbal fanciness that had always won praise from English teachers, but it's inappropriate for this audience.

The differences we touch on here are ones that you will face (or are already facing) during your college years as you write for different teachers in different disciplines. You will also encounter such differences in audience in your personal life both now and after you leave school. But right now we're going to concentrate on the writing you do for school.

We have provided next an example of an essay written by Gary Kolnicki, a former student, that was explicitly revised to suit two different audiences. Read the two versions, and consider these questions:

- What specific changes did Kolnicki make to the essay for general readers to make it better suited to teachers or those knowledgeable in physics?
- Does the shift in audience imply a shift in purpose as well? Why might general readers want to read the essay? Why would a teacher read it?
- Is Kolnicki successful in tailoring his information for the two different audiences?

What Keeps an Airplane Up?   *Gary Kolnicki*

VERSION FOR GENERAL READERS OR STUDENTS IN THE WRITING CLASS

At least once in the course of your life while sitting in an airplane, you must have asked yourself, "What keeps this thing from falling out of the sky?" You may think you understand. You've probably studied it or had it

What Keeps an Airplane Up? *continued*

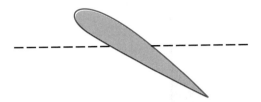

Figure 1 Cross Section of a Wing

explained to you. But ask yourself, as you sit there looking out at nothing but clouds, if you can explain it to yourself and the answer will probably be No.

Two dynamic effects supply the lift for an airplane in flight. The simplest and most obvious source is what is called "the kite effect." Because the wing of the plane is slightly tipped upwards like a kite (see Figure 1), and because the plane is moving forward through the air, molecules slam with high speed into the *bottom* surface of the wing, pushing it upwards. Clearly there would be no kite effect if the plane were not moving forward. (It's true that the kite may not seem to be moving forward, but in fact it is moving forward with respect to the air around it—for the kite only flies if there is a good breeze.)

But the kite effect supplies only about one-third of the lift in an airplane. Two-thirds of the lift comes from what is called the "dynamic lift effect." This effect also depends upon the plane moving forward very fast. (Thus planes don't try to take off till they have a good velocity.) But to understand the dynamic lift effect, the major source of support for an airplane, you need to understand how gas particles exert pressure at a microscopic level.

Air is a gas that consists of a very large number of particles or molecules in high-speed motion. These molecules travel in straight lines in all directions. Because air is so dense, these molecules continuously collide with one another, bouncing off in all directions in zigzag paths. But because there are so *many* molecules moving randomly in this way, it turns out that at any given moment about the same number of particles are moving in all directions—with a result that there is no net movement of air. There's lots of motion, but as a whole it's getting nowhere.

But these molecules do exert pressure on any surface that they run into (and the more molecules, the more pressure). For when the randomly moving molecules hit the wall, they transfer their momentum to the wall—causing pressure. In an air-filled box, for example, an empty cigarette box on the table, the air exerts an *equal* pressure on all the walls since there are an equal number of particles bouncing off each wall. Thus the box stays where it is on the table: all those molecules are hitting on all walls equally.

An airplane wing is shaped in such a way as to make an "airfoil." It is

What Keeps an Airplane Up?   *continued*

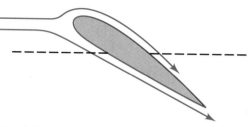

Figure 2   Path Difference

rounded in the front, and arches to a point in the back. Because of this air-foil shape (and because it is somewhat tipped upward) there is an *imbalance* of pressure as the wing passes through the air.

As the wing passes through the air, the air takes two distinct paths across the wing: above and below (see Figure 2). Since the upper stream travels a longer path than the lower stream, the lower stream reaches the back of the wing first.

Because the upper stream hasn't yet reached the back, the air above the rear of the wing has lower pressure, causing the lower stream to curl up and back rather than to continue in the same direction. The upper stream meets this curling stream and forces it in a circular flow, called a vortex (see Figure 3). The upper stream is accelerated due to the lower pressure under the vortex.

The Bernoulli principle predicts dynamic lift under these conditions. According to this principle, a higher speed results in lower pressure. The stream above the wing has a higher velocity and produces a lower pressure—thus a net upward force or lift. Remember that this effect is all being produced by molecular collisions at the microscopic level.

To illustrate this principle more schematically, consider a piece of paper in horizontal position with three volumes of air: one below, one above, and one in front, as shown in Figure 4.

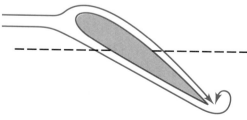

Figure 3   Vortex

What Keeps an Airplane Up?   *continued*

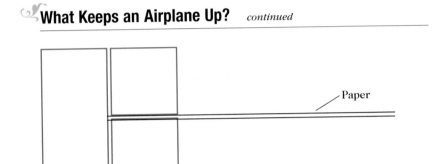

Figure 4   Small Volumes of Air

This picture describes a case in which no motion results. Look now at Figure 5 with the top box moving to the right. The force which moves the upper box must result from an imbalance in pressure between it and the larger box in front. Since the large box's pressure hasn't changed, the upper box must have a lower pressure in order to be moved to the right. It follows that the faster the motion, the lower the pressure. The lower pressure above results in a net force upwards, or lift.

Flaps, movable deflectors at the trailing edge of the wing, control the amount of lift. If a flap is in a downward position, it increases the curvature of the wing and thus makes the path difference between upper and lower flows even greater. This results in a process similar to the one just described and lift increases. The opposite occurs if the flap is in an upward position.

Of course, more can be explained about the complicated subject of flight. Basically, however, the physical processes described above prevent an airplane's falling out of the sky. Though not magical, the effects which describe the way air alone can hold up a jumbo jet are quite fascinating, complicated, and unexpected. Even a person with basic physics knowledge may not be aware of the sources of an airplane's lift on a fundamental level.

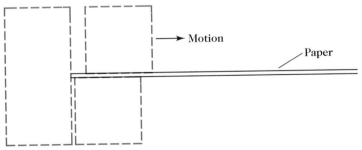

Figure 5   Motion from Pressure Imbalance

What Keeps an Airplane Up? *Gary Kolnicki*

VERSION FOR TEACHERS OR FOR PEOPLE WHO KNOW A BIT ABOUT PHYSICS

Even though many people believe they understand the way an airplane flies, very few truly know the physical processes which occur.

Two dynamic effects join to supply nearly all the support, or lift, for an airplane in flight. For an airfoil or wing, dynamic lift and the kite effect provide nearly all the lift.

Instrumental in understanding dynamic lift and the kite effect is a fundamental understanding of the gas particle theory along with a concept of pressure at a microscopic level. The Bernoulli equation predicts that these two effects will bring lift but does not aid in explaining them.

Air, a gas, consists of a very large number of particles in high-speed motion which travel in straight lines in all directions. Because air is so dense, particles continually collide with one another, bouncing off into other directions, in zig-zag paths. Since there are a large number of particles in this random motion at any one time, about the same number of particles move in all directions causing no net movement of air.

Pressure of a gas on a surface is a force due to collisions of molecules of the gas with that surface. As the molecules in random motion move in a way so that they hit the wall and transfer their momentum, pressure results. Therefore, the more particles in the gas, the more particles that will be moving in that certain direction, colliding with the wall, and putting more pressure on it. In an air-filled box, the air exerts an equal pressure on each wall, since there are an equal number of particles bouncing off each wall.

An airfoil is shaped and oriented so that an imbalance in pressure results as the wing passes through the air. The following effect accounts for the majority of this pressure imbalance. It is called dynamic lift.

A wing's cross section appears in Figure 1. It is rounded in the front and arches to a point in the back. Figure 1 also illustrates the upward direction in which the wing points.

As the wing passes through the air, air takes two distinct paths across the wing: above and below. Since the upper stream travels a longer path than the lower stream, the lower stream reaches the back of the wing first. This is illustrated in Figure 2. Because the upper stream hasn't yet reached the back, the air above the rear of the wing has lower pressure, causing the

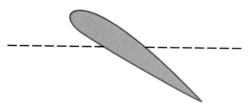

Figure 1 Cross Section of a Wing

What Keeps an Airplane Up?   *continued*

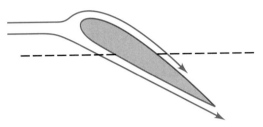

Figure 2   Path Difference

lower stream to curl up and back rather than to continue in the same direction. The upper stream meets this curling stream and forces it into a circular flow, called a vortex. Figure 3 shows this flow. The upper stream is accelerated due to the lower pressure under the vortex. Once the upper stream has reached a velocity so that the upper and lower streams simultaneously reach the trail end of the wing, a pressure difference will no longer exist to curl up and back the lower stream. The vortex then moves away and dissipates, leaving this continuous flow of air above the wing.

The Bernoulli principle predicts dynamic lift under these conditions. A higher velocity results in lower pressure, according to this principle. Above, a stream with higher velocity than the lower produces lower pressure. Therefore, a net upward force, lift, results.

Microscopically, this effect is caused by molecular collisions.

Consider a piece of paper in a horizontal position with three volumes of air: one below, one above, and one in front (see Figure 4). This picture describes a case in which no motion results. Focus now on Figure 5 with the top box now moving to the right. The force which moves the upper box must result from an imbalance in pressure between it and the larger box in front. Since the large box's pressure hasn't changed, the upper box must have a lower pressure in order to be moved to the right. It follows that the faster the motion, the lower the pressure.

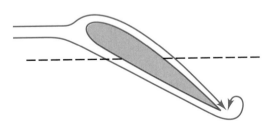

Figure 3   Vortex before Constant Flow

🌀 What Keeps an Airplane Up?   *continued*

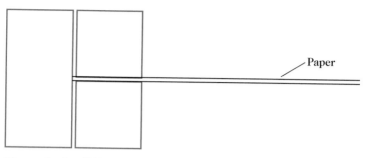

Figure 4   Small Volumes of Air

Now, think of air passing across a wing in steady flight. As shown earlier, the upper stream has a higher velocity than the lower stream. Since the air in front of the wing exerts the same pressure on both these streams, similar to Figure 5, the upper stream must have a lower pressure than the lower stream. The greater velocity is the result of a larger force, or greater pressure imbalance. The lower pressure above results in a net force upward, or lift.

The kite effect is also described in a microscopic way. This effect occurs due to the upward orientation of the aircraft's wing. As the wing proceeds through the air, molecules slam with high speed into the slightly upturned bottom giving more lift to the plane.

The kite effect accounts for about one-third of total lift. Dynamic lift claims the majority of lift—almost two-thirds. Aircraft velocity is necessary for both these effects, and, therefore, thrust must be supplied. For this reason, aircrafts are designed to minimize friction. In some ways, an airplane is designed to slip through the air like a paper airplane.

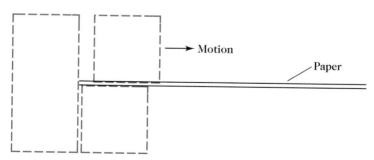

Figure 5   Motion from Pressure Imbalance

What Keeps an Airplane Up? *continued*

Flaps, moveable deflectors at the trailing edge of the wing, control the amount of lift. If a flap is in a downward position, it increases the curvature of the wing and thus makes the path difference between upper and lower flows even greater. This results in a process similar to the one just described and lift increases. The opposite occurs if the flap is in an upward position.

Of course, more can be explained about the complicated subject of flight. Basically, however, the physical processes described above prevent an airplane's falling out of the sky. Though not magical, the effects which describe the way air alone can hold up a jumbo jet are quite fascinating, complicated, and unexpected. Even a person with basic physics knowledge may not be aware of the sources of an airplane's lift on a fundamental level.

Bibliography

"Aerodynamics." *Britannica Online.* Vers. 99.2. April 1999. Encyclopedia Britannica. 25 May 1999 <http://search.eb.com/bol/topic?eu=3920&sctn=1>.

"Airplane." *McGraw-Hill Encyclopedia of Science and Technology.* 8th ed. 1997.

Halliday, David, Robert Resnick, and Jearl Walker. *Fundamentals of Physics.* 5th ed. New York: Wiley, 1996.

Digression on Teachers as Audience

Teachers read differently from most readers. They read not for pleasure or information, but because it's their job. They read as coach or director. Think about how a director watches a play she's directing— as opposed to how the audience watches it. The director is certainly a *real* audience; she is "really" watching the play, probably more carefully than the "real" audience. Yet, of course, the performance is not for her but for those who buy the tickets. They pay to see the play; she's being paid to watch and kibitz. She's not so much trying to tell the actors how she reacts to the play (she may be tired of it by now), but rather how *she* imagines the audience will react.

School writing situations are often comparable. For example, your writing teacher may specify an audience other than herself for a writing assignment (for example, the readers of the editorial page of the local newspaper). Or she may simply assume that the writing is not only for her but also for general readers or other students in the class. In either case you have some kind of *double-audience* situation, especially if you are graded on the piece.

It is rare that we write something only for the teacher. Notice the difference if you write a letter to her arguing for a change in your grade. Usually you write for *the* teacher who is a stand-in for other readers. Teachers occupy a tricky role as readers. On the one hand, they try to read as coach or editor, telling you not so much how they react but how they think your real audience will react. On the other hand, of course, their own reactions will color their understanding of the reactions of others.

A "coach" or "editor" is a nice image for the writing teacher. For a coach or editor is an ally rather than an adversary. A coach may be tough on you, but she is not trying to be the enemy; she's trying to help you beat the real enemy (the other team). There's no point in fighting the coach or being mad at her, or for the coach to fight you. The better you and the coach work together, the better chance you both have of achieving your common goal of winning against a common adversary.

But you may have noticed that teachers can easily fall into being *grumpy* coaches. Sometimes it seems as though the only thing we teachers do is criticize your writing. One reason for our attitudes arises from the conditions under which we have to read student papers. As writing teachers we almost always read student writing in stacks of 25, 50, or 75 papers at a time. Consequently, we tend to fall into what you might call schematic reading. After the 10th or 15th paper (especially if all the papers are on the same topic or in the same genre), we often develop a kind of ideal paper in our heads. Instead of reading a paper just to see what is there, we check it against that model—looking for certain points that need to be made or certain features that this assignment calls for. We fall into looking at each paper in terms of how well it fits or doesn't fit what we are looking for. (Notice how we teachers often talk in terms of what we are "looking for," and how you students ask us, "What do you want us to do in this paper?") In normal reading conditions, the reader isn't checking what he reads for the presence of something he *already knows;* he's looking to find things he doesn't know.

We're not trying to blame teachers. This kind of reading is an inevitable consequence of the *role* of teacher and the conditions in which we read. A director can't enjoy a play in the way a paying audience can. Frankly, we think most writing teachers are overworked and underpaid. But the role and these reading conditions can lead teachers to be grumpy or to emphasize mistakes. That's why we urge you so much in this book to use your fellow students (in pairs or small groups) as another audience for your writing. Fellow students may not be as skilled in reading as your teacher, but they can read your writing as real readers—take it on its own terms and simply look for pleasure or usefulness—and not feel they are reading as a job or duty or to teach you.

In short, we want you to get the best of both audiences: Use your teacher for her professional expertise in diagnosis and advice; use your fellow students for their ability to tell you what actually happens when real readers read your words. You get the *worst* of both worlds if you try to get your fellow students to give you professional diagnosis and advice and ask your teachers not to be critical. It is worth having some frank discussions about this tricky double-audience situation in school writing: for students to tell honestly how they experience the teacher as audience, and for teachers to talk honestly about how they experience their situation as readers. It is a painful area, but not one for blaming: There are no right answers here. It's a question of gradually seeing clearly something that, as far as we know, no one yet understands well.

A Brief Exercise

Look closely at the remarks your teacher made on an essay you are planning to revise. Copy each of her comments into your notebook and write a response to each one. One good format for this is called a double-entry notebook.* Here's how it works: Divide a notebook page into two columns (or use facing pages). On the left-hand side, copy your teacher's comments; on the right-hand side, state in your own words what you think your teacher said and add your reaction to this paraphrase. Once you have worked your way through all your teacher's comments, write a brief paragraph describing your teacher as an audience. What is it he focuses on? What does he particularly like? Dislike? What does he most urge you to do: rethink? rewrite? correct? What this paragraph ends up being is a description of your teacher as an audience for your papers. In truth, you might find this a useful exercise to do for all your teachers. Whether to share the end result will be your decision.

Purpose in Writing

It's hard to imagine a situation in which someone could write and have no purpose at all. Perhaps it's to dump emotion or to get yourself to see some dilemma more clearly: That is, your audience is re-

---

*This strategy is developed and explained by Ann Berthoff's "A Curious Triangle and the Double-Entry Notebook; or How Theory Can Help Us Teach Reading and Writing."

ally yourself. For this workshop, though, we want you to focus on purpose in the sense of what you want your writing to do in relation to some audience other than yourself.

We can highlight *purpose* in writing if we consider the interesting situations where writing itself undermines its very purpose. For example, sometimes you can persuade better by *not* writing, by sitting down with your reader and *talking*. If you write to him, that written document may put him off with its formality and distance. Indeed, sometimes the most persuasive thing you can do is not even to talk but to *listen*. Often your only hope of persuading someone is to show him that you respect his thinking and are willing to adjust yours on the basis of what he's saying.

But sometimes writing is a better mode of persuasion than speaking because, in some situations and with some people, speaking just leads to fruitless arguments. A piece of writing can be less disputatious, less intrusive, calmer. Writing can give you a chance to express something quietly to the person without the need for him to answer back to you: a chance to plant a seed and avoid all arguing.

This digression—questioning whether to write at all—highlights the practical and, as it were, nitty-gritty approach you need to take concerning purpose if you want to make an actual difference through your writing. If you really think about who your audience is and what you want to do to them, you may have to rethink a lot of things you took for granted. Most of us tend to stress what words mean, not what they do. Of course, some of the best and most highly paid writers in our society—writers of advertisements—think very much in terms of what words do. There are a number of things that will help you to articulate your purposes more clearly in this concrete and specific way:

1. Practice *responding* to writing by telling what the words actually *do* to you—that is, by giving movies of your mind as a reader. (See Section 7 of the "Sharing and Responding" part of this textbook.)

2. Hear movies of the minds of readers as they read what you've written. (You'll get more chance for this later in the workshop.)

3. Look at advertisements in print and on radio and TV, and analyze them for their purpose: What was the writer trying to make *happen* in us?

4. Force yourself to come up with specific statements of purpose for your own writing. Consider the following examples:

   • To make readers *act* in a certain way (buy something, vote for someone, give a contribution, write a letter to their representative, and so forth).

- To make them *feel* a certain way (for instance, to feel sympathy for a particular person), or to give them a vicarious experience—that is, to make them feel as though they've actually been there (to show them, not just tell them).
- To make them trust you, or make them laugh.
- To impress readers (teachers?) that you've really learned a lot of material and thought things through.
- To convince readers that you are right.
- To make readers feel you understand how they see or feel things.
- To bowl readers over.
- Instead of wanting to bowl readers over (with the danger of making them feel threatened or making them want to fight against you), just to plant the seed of a difficult or alien view.
- To give readers information. (But notice that this is falling short of the task. No advertising writer would let herself stop there. Why are you giving readers information? What do you want the information to make them feel or do?)

Exploring the Writing Process
On the Question of Audience

I have a really hard time with writing a diary or journal because I can never figure out who the audience is supposed to be. Is it me? Is it the teacher? I can't write just for myself when I know someone else is going to read it.

Student

Writing as Play | Writing for an Inappropriate (possibly) Audience

Think of some audience that is somewhat irrational: a five-year-old child, your dog or cat, an alien from another planet, someone who lived 500 years ago, and so forth. (Samuel Johnson, the eighteenth-century essayist, once said that he insisted upon revising everything he wrote until his house-cleaning help could understand it.) Alternatively, think of the audience as someone whom you want to alienate or someone from whom you want a very important favor. Then begin revising the piece you are working on with this new audience in mind. It will probably help if you write out for yourself first exactly what your purpose now is.

MAIN ASSIGNMENT
Analyzing Purpose and Audience in a Piece of Writing

The assignment for this workshop is to analyze audience and purpose in a piece of writing you have already written, and then to revise that piece on the basis of your analysis. With your teacher's permission, you may even use a paper from another class. You can choose any piece of writing to work on—from a collage to a descriptive piece to an argument (though your teacher may ask you to work on one particular kind of writing). Here are the main questions you need to address in your analysis:

1. *Audience.* Whom did you see then as your audience and whom do you see now? If your group members are the wrong audience for this piece, what differences do you think there would be between their reactions and those of the right audience?

2. *Purpose.* Were you consciously trying to do something to readers when you were writing your piece? Can you now see any unconscious purpose you had? Would you specify a different purpose now?

3. *Actual effects.* What actual effects does your writing seem to have on the readers in your group? What specific words or features seem to cause their reactions?

4. *Advice for revising.* Finally, make sure your analysis includes some advice to yourself for revising.

The goal of this analysis is not to *judge* but to *describe.* That is, we're not trying to get you to congratulate or criticize yourself ("I tried to make them laugh but they sat there stone-faced!") but rather to write a paper that describes *purposes* in writers and *effects* on readers—relating those purposes and effects to specific words and features on the page. In performing this analysis, you might find it helpful to make references and comparisons to other pieces you've heard and discussed in your group.

Ways to Proceed

There are many ways to complete the assignment for this workshop, but here is a sequence of steps you will probably find helpful:

1. Pick out the piece of your writing that you want to analyze. Perhaps it interests you because you are pleased with it and want

to look more closely at something that worked for you. More likely, it's a piece that still troubles you and needs revision, in your opinion.

2. Do some fast exploratory writing about the audience and purpose you had in mind in your original writing. Do you have any different feelings now about audience and purpose for this piece? Can you now see any unconscious purpose you had?

3. Look at any response you got from your teacher on this paper and see what you can learn about the effects your words had on her.

4. Share your piece with your partner or group and ask them to tell you in detail about the effects the writing has on them. Ask them to give you careful movies of their minds. It will help a lot if you make them stop periodically and report specifically what is happening to them as readers. Then, changing to a more analytic mode, ask them to relate these effects to specific features of the text. If a reader got bored or hostile, can she figure out what words or tone or structural feature in the writing caused it? You can join in on this analysis.

5. Then ask your partner or group to talk about whom they see as the audience and what your text implies about audience. Does the text imply that readers are professional or amateur? emotional or cool? Can they see any old audiences in your head that led you to shape your writing inappropriately? Again, you can join in.

6. If your group is the wrong audience for your piece, ask them to speculate on any differences between their reactions and those of your intended audience. In this discussion, don't overestimate *differences* between readers. You can learn a great deal from seeing what your words did to the wrong readers. For example, your group might say they felt intimidated by your tone. Probably your teacher would not feel exactly intimidated, but there may well be something problematic about your tone.

7. To complete your analysis, ask your classmates for advice about revising. Give yourself advice too: On the basis of what you have learned about audience, purpose, and effects, what changes do you plan for your revision?

8. Revise your piece on the basis of your analysis. Show your revision to your partner or group and tell them what you have done and why. Ask them for any further suggestions.

You do not need to go through all these steps to revise something you write and make its purposes clearer to your intended audience.

But we believe that good writers have an intuitive sense or feel of audience and purpose that guides them as they revise. Our hope is that if you consciously go through the steps we've suggested, you'll discover how attentive you need to be to all of this when you revise. As you develop into a more experienced writer, this sense of audience and purpose may go underground, but it will still be a source of intuition or feel for whether your words are matching your intentions. So whenever you're struggling as you revise, look back at the steps we recommend here, and this may get you going again. Take from our suggestions whatever helps you in a specific instance of revision.

Variations on the Assignment

1. Instead of actually revising an earlier paper, make your final piece for this workshop a written *analysis* of that earlier paper. Be sure to include an extended proposal for revision.

2. Revise an earlier paper *and* produce a written analysis of it. Your discussion of specific revisions in the analysis essay need not be as extensive as for variation 1.

3. Instead of concentrating only on analyzing your essay, make your final piece a comparison of your writing with the writing of someone else in your group: the audience, purposes, and effects of two pieces of writing.

4. Make your final piece an essay about purposes and audience in *three or four* papers in the group. Your analysis would have to center on one or two key issues of audience and purpose (for example, trying to get hostile readers on your side or trying to make readers experience a certain emotion) and explore those issues in examples and illustrations from all the papers.

Suggestion for Collaboration

Write a collaborative essay with two or three people in your group whose writing is also being analyzed. This essay can take the approach of either variation 3 or 4 described previously.

Sharing and Responding

To get material for your analysis and revision, you'll need to get feedback from classmates. If you're analyzing a paper you wrote for an earlier workshop, locate that feedback, but now make sure you get readers to give you emotional as well as logical reactions to the paper you plan to revise. "Movies of the Reader's Mind" (Section 7 of the "Sharing and Responding" part of this text) is probably the best technique for this.

If you are doing this workshop's assignment collaboratively, enlist others outside your group to give you feedback both on the paper(s) you're analyzing and on the essay you produce as a result of the analysis.

For feedback on your analysis, you'll find the following sections of "Sharing and Responding" particularly useful: (3) "Summary and Sayback"; (10) "Skeleton Feedback and Descriptive Outline"; and (11) "Criterion-Based Feedback," especially the criteria traditionally applied to expository writing.

In addition, you might ask your readers and listeners the following questions:

- Do you agree with me about whom I have identified as the audience of the paper(s)? about what I have identified as purpose(s)?
- Do you understand what I would do if I did revise? What other suggestions would you make for revision?

When sharing your revised paper, ask readers and listeners the following questions:

- Have I taken my own advice from my analysis of this paper?
- Whom do you now see as the audience for my paper, and what do you see as its purpose?

Process Journal and Cover Letter

- Do you usually have a definite audience in mind when you start to write? How do various audiences affect your writing? teachers? your writing group? Which audiences do you find most helpful and most problematic? Do you find it difficult to ignore audience?
- How do you see and experience the teacher as audience?
- Do you usually have some definite purpose in mind when you start to write? Or do you discover purposes after starting? How does purpose function for you as you write?

For your cover letter, it's good to include some or all of your process writing. But don't forget to answer some cover letter questions. Here are the main ones: What is your main point and what effect are you trying to have on readers? What do you feel works best in your paper and where are you unsatisfied? What changes did you make on the basis of any feedback? And most important: What feedback do you want now from a reader? But your teacher may ask you particular cover letter questions that pertain to this assignment.

RUMINATIONS AND THEORY
More on Purpose and Audience

Purpose, Genre, and an Overview of Rhetorical Terrain

In Workshop 3 we emphasized genre; in this workshop we empha-size purpose. It's worth exploring how genre and purpose are similar and how they differ.

It seems as though certain genres are designed to accomplish certain purposes. If you want to persuade someone, you're likely to assume you should write a persuasive essay, not a poem or a story. (In this case the genre's name even carries the name of the purpose—to persuade.) And yet if you take it for granted that you shouldn't write a poem or story, you should think again. You would be putting too much stock in genre and not thinking concretely enough about purpose.

For really there is no necessary connection between genres and purposes. Poetry, for example, may seem to express personal emo-tion more often than informational essays do, but that's just a matter of how poetry has tended to develop since the romantic period in the nineteenth century. Essays can express personal emotion, and poems can convey information. (Until the romantic period, poetry was treated as an appropriate genre for conveying information, even sci-entific information. The first version of atomic theory came in a long Greek poem, "On the Nature of Things," by Lucretius. Alexander Pope wrote an important poem called "An Essay on Man"—which is, indeed, an essay.) The important practical point here is that the per-suasive essay is not the only way to persuade. Stories, novels, poems, and letters can sometimes persuade better than essays. And the essay can be a form of lyric or autobiography.

It turns out that the grading of writing is often linked to assump-tions about genre. If someone says, "This is a poor persuasive essay," he may well mean that the piece violates what he expects of the per-suasive essay genre; yet it may in fact persuade many readers. Or a teacher may say, "This is an excellent persuasive essay" (and even give it an A)—and yet not actually be persuaded by it.

Some writers don't care whether their pieces fit the traditional forms and conventions. That is, some story writers don't care if some readers say, "This is a very peculiar story—there's no real ending" or "I can't figure out whether this is a story or an essay." Some business writers don't care if readers say, "This writer doesn't seem to know the rules for proper memos." Those writers simply want to have a certain effect on readers, and they have decided they can do it better by breaking certain rules or conventions about genres. Of course, they must recognize the risk in this approach: They will annoy those readers who don't like departures from genre, but it is through this process that genres change. For example, it's no longer clear that the story genre demands a climax or an ending that resolves all the loose ends.

Another way to say this is that there isn't a perfect genre for each purpose. You can do many things with any one genre; for example, you can use a story to amuse, to persuade, or even to convey information. (Think about the purely informational qualities of novels like Arthur Hailey's *Airport* and James Michener's *Hawaii.*) The point is that you need to think concretely and realistically about purpose— and not take things for granted.

In Workshop 3, we focused on how topic and audience interact with genre. In this workshop, we also focused on audience—in this case, how audience interacts with purpose. Thus, it is a good time now to stand back and see how all these facets of writing—purpose, genre, audience, and topic—are distinct, yet intertwined.

- To focus on purpose is to focus on people—what the *writer* intended and what happens to *readers*—the audience—as they read.
- To focus on the *topic* is to focus on the world or the message.
- To focus on genre is to focus on the *text*—the form and the conventions used.

And, of course, you always have to keep in mind the context in which purpose, topic, and genre function: in a classroom, among friends, among enemies, in an office, and so forth. When you focus on one dimension, you may leave other dimensions vague or ambiguous for a while. There's nothing wrong with that. For example:

- We may get quite far in writing a poem about something (thus knowing genre and topic) but not be sure of audience or purpose.
- We may be engaged in writing a letter to someone (knowing genre and audience) but not be sure of the topic or purpose.
- We may start to write something entertaining about a subject (purpose and topic) but not be sure of the audience or genre.
- Indeed, we may know only that we want to write about a particular topic and remain vague about all three other dimensions: audience, genre, and purpose. We simply need to write in an exploratory way and see where it takes us.
- And, of course, context matters much: We may be writing in school, out of school, or on the job; we may be writing in a situation that feels threatening, or in one that feels friendly and accepting of us and of our ideas.

Each rhetorical dimension is related to the other. Any change in one is likely to cause a change in the other. But as we have seen, the lines of connection are a bit rubbery. Thus, before you are finished with any piece of writing, you should be sure of all four dimensions. Indeed, one way to check over a piece of writing and move toward revision is to make sure you are clear and consistent about audience, purpose, genre, and topic (or message).

About Audience

Most teachers and theorists of rhetoric say that you should think about your audience before you write and keep audience in mind while you are writing. Yet we find that it often helps our writing to forget about audience as we write, and then revise later to fit the readers.

Your preference may well depend on your temperament. Or it may be that keeping readers in mind is better for certain writing tasks (or for certain readers) than for other tasks or readers. The issue of audience is a complex tangle, but an important one. We are going to work toward untangling it here and end up with some practical advice on how to make audience work for you and prevent it from working against you.

A Balance among the Four Possible Relations to an Audience

Many students have never written except in school: all their writing has been assigned, read, and evaluated or graded by a teacher. If you never write except for evaluation by teachers, you can drift into unconsciously feeling as though that's what writing is: performing for someone in authority in order to be judged. Many students have no sense of writing as a way to communicate with real readers. And they may lack any sense of writing as a way to communicate privately with themselves, to explore thoughts and feelings on paper just for the sake of exploring. It is useful to become more conscious of the four main ways of relating to or using an audience in writing:

1. *Keeping your writing to yourself.* This is a case of not using an audience—keeping readers out of your way, out of your hair. Many people who were blocked in their writing and then learn the knack of private writing say, "I discovered that the problem wasn't *writing*: it was writing for an *audience.*" If you have kept a diary that you don't intend to share, you have participated in a venerable and traditional form of writing for no audience other than oneself. But of course you can also use private writing to help you produce material that is eventually intended for an audience.

2. *Giving your writing to an audience but getting no feedback or response from them: sharing.* When you share but don't get feedback,

it emphasizes writing to communicate rather than writing to perform or be judged. Obviously communication is the most common and natural way to use words—the way we are most skilled at.

3. *Giving your writing to an audience for nonevaluative feedback or response.* Sometimes in school we fall into assuming that the only thing to do with a piece of writing is to try to talk about how good or bad it is or diagnose its strengths and weaknesses or give suggestions for improvement. It is crucial to realize that we can get helpful responses to our writing without any of that. And we can get it from readers other than a teacher: from peers, friends, parents, and any others who might be interested in us or what we write. Really, one of the least interesting things we can ask about any piece of writing is how good or bad it is. It's usually much more fruitful to ask questions like these: "What does it seem to be saying? Does it say different things to different readers? Why did the writer write it? Why should we read it, or what can we get out of it or apply to our experience? How is it put together, and how does it function?" We have plenty of suggestions for useful nonevaluative response in the "Sharing and Responding" section of each workshop and in "Sharing and Responding" at the end of the book.

4. *Giving your writing to an audience for evaluative response.* When we use readers in the other three ways just described, then it makes good sense sometimes to get evaluative response from them. Evaluative response is only a problem if that's all you ever get, or if you trust it too much—forgetting that even the best professional critics cannot agree in their evaluations.

Audience as a Focusing Force on Our Minds

Think of audience as exerting a kind of magnetism or focusing force on our minds. The closer we are to our listeners or readers and the more we think about them, the more influence they have on our thoughts and feelings. That is, when we are with people or very aware of them in minds, we are more likely to feel their concerns or see their point of view. When we go off by ourselves or forget them, we ignore their point of view. Both these situations have harmful and helpful outcomes.

Some audiences are helpful because they make it easier to write. Such an audience usually consists of a person or a group who likes us and respects us and is interested in what we are interested in. People who want to hear what we have to say tend to make us think of more things to say and to write more fluently. Their receptivity opens our minds. And the act of writing to such readers tends to shape and focus what we are thinking about—even if we had been confused before sitting down to write.

But other audiences are unhelpful or problematic because they intimidate us or make us nervous. Most of us have had the experience of finding it harder and harder to write for a teacher because the teacher did nothing but criticize what we wrote. There are other kinds of problem audiences too. If an audience is completely unknown (for example, an admissions committee or a prospective employer you've never met or someone from another culture) or vague (the general public), you may find it hard to write for them.

The trick then is to notice when an audience is being helpful or not helpful so you can decide whether to think about them or forget about them as you write.

Even though audience is a tricky theoretical issue, the practical answer is simple if you think in terms of a little three-step dance with readers: first a step *toward* readers, then *away* from them, and finally back *toward* them.

- *Toward your audience.* Start by bringing your readers to mind. Imagine them; see them. Doing so may help you focus your

Exploring the Writing Process
On Ways of "Imaging" Audience

I don't consciously think of audience when I write. In writing for this course, I knew I was going to share my writing with the class but I didn't think of this or imagine them in some way. Right now, I guess I'm directing this writing to you but I'm not really thinking of that. Does this make any sense? I'm not sure where I go in my mind when I write. The feeling I have is of moving upward and to the sky, kind of out of body: a suspended state once I get moving and forgetting time. This is why I tend to write late at night. There are fewer interruptions and the time is more open-ended. I do this weird consciousness thing even when I write letters. Then I have a person in mind but I direct the writing to their gut or heart and occasionally their mind. When I first fell in love with my old boyfriend, he was living far away. I wrote to him often and I remember imaging a kind of moving cloud or smoky essence that I directed my writing toward: the part of him I loved and wanted to connect with.

Nancy Blasi

thinking and your approach to your topic. You may well find more to say, just as you would naturally find things to say if you were standing there in front of them and they asked you what was on your mind. If things go well, you simply keep this first relationship to the audience for the whole writing process.

- *Away from your audience.* If you have any difficulty with your writing, it may be because your audience is getting in your way: because they are unknown or intimidating or because thinking about them makes you worry too much about trying to get your writing right. Try putting them out of mind and writing for yourself: Get your thoughts straight in your own mind—even if you know that this process is leading you to write things that are not right for your intended audience. If you can once put clearly on paper what you think, then it's not so hard afterward to make changes or adjustments to suit your words to the audience.
- *Finally, back again toward readers.* No matter how clearly you see things for yourself, you must consciously bring your audience to mind again—as a central part of your revising process. In doing so you may realize that what is clear for you is not clear for them; or you may realize that for them you need a change in approach.

Can We Forget about Purpose and Audience?

We have spoken of the value of thinking about audience and purpose; then we turn around and say it is sometimes useful to forget about audience and purpose if your hands are full just trying to figure out what you think (rather than worrying about how to convey what you think to others). However, it's important to acknowledge that in a sense one can never avoid orientation toward audience and purpose in any use of language: To open our mouths is to have the impulse to say something to someone for some reason. Our language is often shaped quite well by audience and purpose without our having any conscious awareness of who the audience is and what our purposes are.

But even if we can't get away from audience and purpose (or, putting this in its most general form, even if human intelligence is deeply social and human behavior is deeply purposive), there's still a big difference between *being* conscious of audience and purpose and *not* being conscious of them. There's also a big difference between trying to make your writing *fit* audience and consciously allowing your writing *not* to fit audience and purpose (for example, in exploring a topic). In short, there are advantages in trying to plan and know and control what we are doing, but also advantages in leaving quite a lot to intuition or the tacit dimension.

We recognized this same issue when we spoke of organization versus messiness in freewriting. Does doing fast and furious freewriting and not worrying at all about the organization mean you are getting away from organization? No, for it's impossible to get away from organization; everything has organization. But it does mean three important things:

- You are getting away from *thinking* about organization.
- You are inviting messy organization.
- You are inviting your *intuitive* or *tacit* power of organizing—your imagination. For we can often make a more interesting organization by intuition than by careful planning.

What it all boils down to is trying to learn to take the best advantages of both dimensions of the mind: careful conscious planning and intuition. For even though we are often more intelligent in our unconscious intentions than in our conscious ones, intuition can also lead us down the garden path. Therefore, before we are finished with a piece of writing, we do well to try to invoke the careful and conscious side of our minds: to become clear about audience and purpose and organization.

Exploring Voice

Main Assignment Preview

There are three possibilities. Your teacher may decide on one (or more than one).

1. Write an essay that explores the various voices you find in your writing and in your speaking. Explore how they relate to each other—and perhaps how they relate to your sense of who you really are. Or you could focus your analysis on the speech and writing of a friend or classmate—or the voice of a published author.

2. Choose a paper you have already written, and revise it with special attention to voice. Revising in terms of voice—perhaps even trying to change the voice—can be an ideal way to improve a paper that doesn't satisfy you.

3. Gather passages from your writing that illustrate different voices you use in writing. Then create a collage of your written voices.

Ⅼanguage as Ⅼlay   Saying "Hello"

Try out different performances of the single word "Hello." You can do this yourself, but it's more fun with a pair or small group or even in the whole class. The goal is to see how many different messages you can send by just pronouncing the single word. You may be surprised at how many there are. (Think about the different ways people of different ages and genders use the single word to flirt—and the subtly different flirting messages we can send. Think about how people say "Hello" when they want to make fun of someone else's dimwittedness.) As each person says "Hello," listeners discuss the messages they hear in it. Other words you could try: "OK," "Yes," "Now."

About the Nature of Speaking and Writing

In contrast to the huge variety of ways of saying "Hello," there's only one way to write it. Yes, you can underline it or print it in color or write it in italics or use different typefaces. You can try different spellings—"Helloooo." But the possibilities in writing are miniscule compared to the infinite resources of the human voice. Let's think about these resources for a moment. With our voices we have loud and soft, fast and slow, high and low, stress and no stress, and all the variations in between. Or we could use none of them and talk in monotone, but that would carry a message too. We have pauses and rhythms and timbres (breathy, gravelly, whiney) and so forth. Written words just sit there silently, mutely.

Spoken words have other advantages over writing too. When we hear someone speaking, it usually seems as though that speaker has done the work of getting the meanings into our heads. But when we read someone's writing, it usually seems as though *we* have to do the work of getting the meaning into our heads.

In truth, things are not so simple. Writing is not really so impoverished. The point we want to get across in this workshop is that writing *can* have a voice. It is possible to get all those interesting rhythms and melodies of the spoken voice into writing and thereby make it do all the things that speech can do. That is, some written words have a live voice: When we read them, we hear the sound of a person in there and it seems as though the writer is doing the work of getting the meanings up off the page into our heads. If you get voice into your writing, readers will pay better attention and your meaning will come through stronger. One of the goals of this workshop is to help you breathe a voice into your writing.

There's a sense, however, in which *all* writing has a voice of some sort. That is, there's a potential voice in all writing if we listen hard enough. And it turns out that one of the most useful ways to talk about the differences between pieces of writing is to talk about the voices in them.

Certain kinds of voice are frowned on in certain kinds of writing. In highly formal kinds of writing such as we find in business reports and scholarly journals, readers and writers seem to want formal voices: quiet, dressed-up, well-behaved, and impersonal voices. "Keep it dignified; keep it decorous; don't raise your voice." With more informal kinds of writing, such as we find in newspaper feature stories and many magazine articles and literary essays, readers and writers invite casually dressed, informal voices: personal, lively, idiosyncratic voices.

And how about writing in school and college? Should it be formal or informal? Can it have a personal, lively, casual voice, or must it be dignified and restrained? As all students know, teachers don't agree. Some teachers are happy to get an informal voice while others want a dignified, impersonal voice. And some teachers who are open to both nevertheless don't like a mixing of voices: They don't like to hear a casual spoken voice bumping into a formal academic one. Yet some teachers don't mind a mixing of voices if it's done well—as with a well-placed piece of slang or colloquial rephrasing to give emphasis in an otherwise formal paper.

Because of this variation among teachers and other readers too, we have a second goal for this workshop: not just to learn how to breathe voice into your writing, but also how to vary or adjust your voice according to the situation or your reader's needs. To do this, you'll also have to learn to listen well to differences in written voice.

And there's a third goal we have—one that might have occurred to you already: "I don't want just any voice in my writing. And I don't want just the voice my reader wants to hear. I want *my* voice in there. I want the voice in my writing to fit *me!* Even if I adjust my voice to fit different audiences, I don't want to sound artificial or fake. I still want to sound like me." This is a feasible goal. That is, even though people's voices usually change in different situations when they talk to different people (we can sometimes tell who someone is talking to on the phone just by the tone of voice he or she is using), some people nevertheless manage to sound "like themselves" even when they use different voices. They always sound genuine, not like they are uncomfortable or pretending. Other people can only sound like themselves when they talk to some people. Most of us don't quite sound like ourselves when we are nervous or afraid. Often we develop certain slightly artificial voices to deal with certain audience situations. For example, certain teachers use a "folksy" or "stern" or even "friendly" voice, and we can feel that this voice is not really "them." Other teachers can shift toward a folksy or stern or friendly tone of voice, and yet we still feel that they are being themselves. Voice is a mysterious matter.

We have designed the exercises in this workshop to help you learn not only to vary your written voice as needed but also, if possible, to still sound like yourself.

Exploring Voices in Writing

We spend a good part of our lives noticing how people talk. From the earliest age we can "hear" people's moods just from listening to their voices. For example, we can often tell if someone is mad at us even when they say, "Oh no, I'm not mad at you." We can do this even if we are listening to them on the phone and voice is the only cue we have. There are a multitude of expressive words that describe how people talk—words for tone of voice: cheerful, chirpy, sarcastic, breathy, haughty, scared, timid, flat.

Written words just sit silently on the page. But writing will speak to us if we "listen" to it well enough—with our ears and our mouths. In order to help you learn to apply your sophisticated voice-listening skills to writing, we are providing you with three short activities. Each one will help you learn to hear, understand, and describe the voice in a piece of writing. These activities are done best in pairs or small groups.

Activity One: Try Voices Out Loud

What does the voice in the writing actually sound like? The best way to find out is to speak the words out loud in order to "enact" or "inhabit" or "render" the voice. That is, don't just say the words, but give them a reading that brings out the voice—the tone, mood, feeling, or character.

Try to get two or three readings of the same passage. You can do this yourself, but it's better to get help. Others can often hear a voice you didn't hear. Of course, you may well disagree about whether a voice is "there" or fits the text. This is appropriate. Different voicings can be equally in the text—but it's always a matter of interpretation. For example, the same passage could be read as sarcastic or straight.

In addition, a single passage can change voices or tones as it goes along. For example, it might gradually build up to more excitement; or it might suddenly slow down and become quietly meditative. It might even change to angry. Since the goal is to hear voices on the page—that is, to explore voice in written language—it's fine to play around, stretch, or even exaggerate a bit. Then you can discuss your reactions to these readings and try to decide when a reading fits the written words well and when it isn't right for the words.

You can apply these activities to pieces of your own writing or pieces that your teacher suggests. (You could also use passages of our writing. We wonder whether you have sensed some passages in this book as more in Pat Belanoff's voice and others in Peter Elbow's voice.) But here are four passages you could also use if you prefer.

a. INTELLECTUAL WOMAN SEEKS REAL GUY. I'm a 50-year-old babe, slender, divorced, mother of one. You're a smart Mr. Fix-it with muscles. You hate classical music, love Motown, never set foot in a museum, read only when forced to. You like hanging out, eating pizza, and drinking beer. Financially secure. Send note and photo (of you and/or your truck).

Personal advertisement, *New York Review of Books,* **February 18, 1999**

b. You see, there's a simple reason our elected officials consistently fail to function. They are stupid. (Not all. There are 17 who actually know what they are doing.) Please don't look for anything more complex. They are dumb, that's all. End of story.

As a matter of fact, if you take a close peek at them you will see a herd of peabrains who are today—this very moment—holding the best job they will ever have. And they're lucky to be employed, because who would hire them?

Exploring the Writing Process
On Using Voice to Revise

I reread the experimental changes (I keep saving each draft under a new file name so if I don't like the changes I've made I can go back to one of the previous drafts) and got disgusted because I was hit over the head with a major issue I hadn't attempted to deal with at all in the previous night's work—the two different voices I was using in the piece. At that point I asked Deb to read it (unfortunately for her, she wandered into the computer lab at just the *wrong* moment . . .). I asked her for just a quick, initial reaction to the tone. She reaffirmed my feeling that it was a schizo piece—a different person took over at the bottom of page two. Then she made a practical suggestion that really helped get me on a steadier track—"Why don't you just delete the first page and three quarters and begin the paper with Voice #2?"

Kathy Reckendorf

You wouldn't put them behind the counter at the J&J Variety in Waltham because they steal. You couldn't have them wait tables at the Stockyard because they are so slow they could not remember a food order.

Pick up trash? Why, they take 12 months to do eight hours of work as it is now; your Christmas tree would still be at the curb on Decoration Day.

Mike Barnicle, *The Boston Globe,* **January 5, 1993**

c. *Simplified Method.* The following discussion outlines the rules that apply for using the Simplified Method. *What Is the Simplified Method?* The Simplified Method is one of the two methods used to figure the tax-free part of each annuity payment using the annuitant's age (or combined ages if more than one annuitant) at his or her (or their) annuity starting date. The other method is the General Rule (discussed later).

From the Internal Revenue Service's *Tax Guide for 1998: Individuals*

d. What's in a name? A reader noticed something funny about Dassant's *New England Pumpkin Spice Bread & Muffin Mix:* It has no pumpkin. Dassant's *Hood River Apple Spice Cake & Muffin Mix*? Yup. No apple. You add those yourself. Moreover, the two mixes list the same ingredients, in the same order. A customer service representative confirmed that the mixes are "basically the same," and gave us permission to put pumpkin in the apple mix, as long as we followed directions on the pumpkin box. "Gosh," notes our reader, "Maybe they should call it New England Pumpkin, Cranberry & Walnut Spice Bread & Muffin Mix. Then they'd suck in the cranberry and walnut lovers . . . without adding a thing to the mix inside!" We didn't have the heart to ask the company what New England and Hood River had to do with anything.

Consumer Reports, **Feb. 1999**

We'll try to illustrate what we are asking for with this sample passage from a student, Deb DuBock:

Fun. Fun. Did I say this was fun? A curse, that's what the computer is. In process. Nothing's ever done. You can always find a new way to rework things. Example: the ending. That came to me while I was working on another paper. It probably doesn't work, but hell, enough is enough. I've got shopping to do, cards to send, laundry, you name it. I'm calling it quits. OK, so I'll give it one more read tomorrow in school.

Since we didn't include a tape recording with this book, we can't give you out-loud renderings of this passage, but we can talk about the renderings we've heard from students working on this passage. Some students read it with a voice of cheerful, amused exasperation;

others heard a voice of serious, hair-tearing frustration; one reader even gave a kind of frenzied Dr. Strangelove voice to the passage—spitting out those first two words through tightly clenched teeth like a mad scientist going crazy ("Fun. Fun.").

Notice the rich possibilities in just those first two words: Some people gave the second "fun" a very different mood or tone from the first one—more angry and sarcastic; others gave the second "fun" a tone of questioning as though the writer had suddenly noticed what she had just said and now is questioning it. ("Fun. *Fun?*"—the second one saying, in effect, "Are you kidding?")

Quite a few students changed voices in midpassage. A number of students put in a big pause before that last "OK, so I'll give it one more read tomorrow in school." Some of the pausers made that last sentence sound discouraged and dejected, while others gave it a voice of amused self-mocking—the voice of someone who knows that she always gives in to the need for more work and has come to accept that fact about herself. What we see here is what all actors know: that the same words have a number of potential voices in them.

Activity Two: Inhabit the Voice and Play the Role

What kind of person talks this way, and how does she see the world and talk about all kinds of things? To answer this question, try to *get inside* the voice in the passage—try to pretend to *be* that person or play the role of the speaker in the passage. Now that you have a new voice and are a new person, just talk (or write) in your new voice. Here's what we wrote when we did the exercise and tried taking on the voice and identity of that same passage by Deb DuBock:

> My mom called me last night. Saturday night! What made her think I'd be here. The nerve! But there I was. I thought it was going to be someone else and I answered all happy. I know she could hear my voice fall when I heard it was her. But what did she expect? She wants me to come visit next weekend. Next weekend! Give me a break, I'm not going. I'm just not going. I'm an adult, OK? I'm earning money. I'm taking care of myself. N. O. No. OK . . . so what are you making for dinner?

Activity Three: Describe the Voice

How would you describe the voice? After you have tried inhabiting or enacting the voices in a piece of writing in these exercises, you will find it much easier to find *analytic* language to describe the voices you hear in it. What are the tone, character, and mood of this voice? Here is one possible description of the voice Deb DuBock used:

It's a voice of exasperation and frustration. But there's also a note in the voice of self-awareness—that this frustration is not the end of the world—a faint note even of amusement or enjoyment. And that last sentence has a smile of amused self-mocking underneath the discouraged giving in.

It can also be useful to describe voices in metaphors of clothing (baggy sweater?), weather (stormy?), or color (gray?).

With these activities, we are trying to illustrate a large principle of both learning and teaching. You don't actually need to be able to describe voices to be able to hear them, understand them, and use them. Thus, people can usually describe and analyze almost anything better *after* they have entered into it or enacted it or "tried it on." Describing the voice requires a somewhat detached and analytic ability. Of course, this analytic ability is useful and interesting not only for

Exploring the Writing Process

On "Speaking" Writing

Toward the end of his life, Mark Twain started dictating his autobiography to a secretary—lying in bed each morning smoking cigars. He wrote about this method to William Dean Howells.

You will never know how much enjoyment you have lost until you get to dictating your autobiography; then you will realize, with a pang, that you might have been doing it all your life if you had only had the luck to think of it. And you will be astonished (& charmed) to see how like *talk* it is, & how real it sounds, & how well & compactly & sequentially it constructs itself, & what a dewy & breezy & woodsy freshness it has, & what a darling & worshipful absence of the signs of starch, and flatiron, and labor &

fuss & the other artificialities! Mrs. Clemens is an exacting critic, but I have not talked a sentence yet that she has wanted altered. There are little slips here & there, little inexactnesses, & many desertions of a thought before the end of it has been reached, but these are not blemishes, they are merits, and their removal would take away the naturalness of the flow & banish the very thing—the nameless something—which differentiates real narrative from artificial narrative & makes the one so vastly better than the other— the subtle something which makes good talk so much better than the best imitation of it that can be done with a pen.

Mark Twain

analytic school assignments, but also for handling countless situations that come up in life. We've all been in situations where the tone of voice matters a lot—and where people argue about it. ("I apologize. I'm sorry I hurt you." "I don't believe you are really sorry." Or, "Stop being sarcastic with me!" "Oh, come on. Here we go again. I wasn't being sarcastic; I was just making a friendly joke.")

Exploring Your Own Voices

Our goal now is to give you a better sense of the different voices that already exist in your writing. On the basis of what you learn, you will be able to take more control of the voices you use in order to fit them better to different readers—and to fit them better to yourself. Use the following activities to get started.

Activity Four: Harvesting Your Own Voices

Start by gathering passages from your own writing. Look among all the pieces and kinds of writing that you can find—writing you've done in this course and writing you've done for other reasons—and find as many passages as you can with *different* voices or tones or moods. Short passages of just a paragraph or two will do just fine. If you think that you always write in the same voice, look carefully—listen carefully—and you'll find much more variety than you expected.

You'll probably find different voices in the different papers you've written for this course. But if you have old papers around, they may show changes in your written voice over time. And don't just look at papers. You've done much more writing. Look at stories, poems, freewriting, early drafts, journal writing, personal notebooks, notebooks you keep for other classes (where you sometimes write notes to yourself or friends), notes to roommates, letters to friends or family, or more formal letters you've had to write such as job applications. If you use e-mail and can find copies of things you've written, you'll probably find passages with notable voices. (E-mail is particularly interesting because it is *writing,* but people use it more as though they were speaking. Notice the little smiley faces and "emoticons" people use to signal tone of voice.)

But don't forget—and this is one of the most important things to investigate—you can often find different voices in just one paper or letter. Papers often start off in one voice, sometimes a somewhat stiff or neutral or careful voice. Then they may change voice as the writer gets warmed up. Sometimes writers slide into yet other voices when they provide examples, relate anecdotes, and make asides or digressions. (And how about those parentheses? You never know what you're going to sound like once you step inside a parenthesis.)

Try to find one or two passages that you feel comfortable with that somehow feel "like you"—sound the way you want to sound. You can probably find *different* voices that still feel comfortably like you. But try also to get passages that feel *uncomfortable*—to illustrate what happens to your voice when you somehow sound "off" or "wrong." How about a voice you almost never let yourself use, but that feels like you? It can be productive to get a friend to help you look for passages with different voices. Sometimes other people have an easier time noticing differences in voice.

We hope that you'll gather enough passages—at least 10 or more—to make a rich, full collage of your writing voices.

Activity Five: Bringing Your Own Voices to Life

The goal now is to work on hearing and understanding your different writing voices better and figuring out how they work. Get into pairs or small groups and try out the three activities you did earlier in this workshop (pages 174–179)—but this time apply them to some of the voice passages in your *own* writing.

1.   Try the voices out loud to see what they sound like.

2.   Inhabit some of the voices and write in them about something completely different.

3.   Describe the voices.

The first two activities will probably benefit you most, because the main way that you learn about voice and develop your voice is not by analyzing but by getting voices into your ear and mouth and body—so that the voices just *come out of you.*

It might feel a little uncomfortable or unsafe to let other people do these role-playing activities on your writing. Other people are likely to exaggerate or even slip into a bit of parody. So it's fine to do the first two activities yourself and let others describe the voices they hear in your passages. But if you feel brave and don't mind a little play or stretching of your voices, you will learn a lot from letting others do the first two exercises on your passages.

In any event, the goal is to find the voices in your writing and bring them to life. It helps to experiment. Remember that your ultimate goal is to get more awareness and control over voice in your writing, to use different voices depending on the situation, and to develop and use a flexible or versatile voice that feels right for you— probably one that you feel comes from a deeper part of you. When you get such voices, you and your listeners will often know it right away. They'll feel a resonance or solidity or trustworthiness.

Sometimes a problem crops up. A reader says to you, "Yes, that's it; that's strong; that's you," but you feel, "No, that's not me." This is an interesting dilemma. There are no easy answers here. In our experience, voices that are stronger and more resonant with you are not necessarily voices you like. Certainly our strongest voices may not be "nice." In his *Writing with Power,* Peter Elbow observed that sometimes you have to choose between a voice you *like* and a voice that is *strong*—strong enough so that others will actually sit up and listen to you. Some people have been taught to like a voice that doesn't cause any trouble. But the more you use your strong voice, the more

Exploring the Writing Process
On Writing Across Cultures

I feel caught between two cultures. When I have to write a letter to my family and friends back in Korea, I realize that I have lost the eloquence of my native language. In particular, I have forgotten lots of Chinese characters that are used frequently in written Korean. I hardly read or speak Korean these days since I have to write, read, and speak English every day. While I feel sad about losing touch with my native tongue, I also strongly feel that as a foreigner living in this country I must master English in order to survive. Instead of feeling as though I am lost and split between these two cultures, I should feel enriched since I am bilingual and can enjoy both cultures.

I used to write poems when I was in college back in Korea. The colors that emerged from my poems were frequently black and white as I would write about darkness, human suffering, snow, and so on. I remember that I used to be afraid of darkness when I was little, but as I grew up, I became fascinated by the secrecy that darkness implied. While I, as a college student, searched for some meaning in life, black became my favorite color. I thought that black meant negation and nothingness, but it also could be thought of as a point of beginning from which all things can happen. Since I came to America, I have hardly written any poems. I used to feel inspired to write when I was younger. I wonder whether the reason that I stopped doing creative writing is because English is not my native language, or because I am getting older and don't feel inspiration anymore, or because I have to do academic writing all of the time.

I still dream in Korean even though I dream in English most of the time now. Sometimes, I speak in English to my family in my dreams but I don't remember whether they understand me or not.

Eunsook Koo

versatile and flexible it will become; you will develop more voices that are resonant.

Of course, you are not necessarily trying to decide on *one right voice* for you. There probably is no such thing. You need different voices for different situations. Nevertheless, try to get a feel for when a voice feels right for you and when it doesn't. You may begin to get a sense of a kind of voice or range of voices that you recognize as yours, and other voices that seem definitely wrong or unfitting for you.

All these activities are about *listening* for voice in writing. What about the other goal of *getting* more voice into writing? You'll find that all the trying out, rendering, and inhabiting different voices—*out loud*—will help you *breathe* more voice into your writing. The crucial thing is to hear more as you write, to get comfortable with your speaking voice, and to be brave about making a noise. If you do these things, your writing will gradually come more alive.

Correct and Clear Writing—But Still in Your Voice

When you try to write something with no mistakes at all, do you end up making your writing stiff, awkward, and impersonal? The problem comes from assuming that because a piece of writing has to end up completely correct and without errors, you need to *start off* trying to avoid all errors. The cure is quite simple: Don't worry about correctness at all as you get your early drafts written; just think about your topic and use your comfortable voice (or whatever voice you want). Correct mistakes later.

Try out the following quick activity. It will illustrate an important principle: Writing can be completely, perfectly, 100 percent correct without having to be formal, stiff, or impersonal.

Activity Six: Minimal Revising

Find a short passage of your freewriting—or a piece of your writing (an e-mail, perhaps?) that is completely casual, informal, and comfortable, but that has plenty of mistakes. (Of course, some passages of fast freewriting do not have a comfortable voice; some passages get tangled and garbled. Don't use a passage like that for this activity.)

Go through your passage and make whatever changes are necessary to get it clear—not formal, dignified, or elegant, just clear. Also, correct all the mistakes in grammar and usage. (You might get a fellow student to look for mistakes you've missed.) *But make as few changes as you can!* Therefore, when you find a mistake or a place that doesn't make sense, don't rewrite the whole passage. Simply make the smallest change you can and use as much of the original, comfortable language and voice as possible. What you should end up with is a passage that is not only *absolutely correct* but completely *informal, casual, personal,* and *comfortable* in voice. It will have no mistakes in what we call Standard Written English.

Peter Elbow did this activity with a piece of his informal, private freewriting. Here is a passage from his original, fast, casual writing:

> Screen is something halfway between mind and paper.
>
> Mind is a mess: paper supposed to be neat. When I'm writing on screen, it feels like it's sort of—half—still in my mind. It's a second mind—It's not still partly in me. Like my mind I can't look at all of it at once, I can only put my attention on one bit at a time. I don't yet have complete detachment from it til I print it out. It gives me a second mind.
>
> Another mind. Sometimes I make such a mess that I feel in a swamp—too many options—once I remember feeling Oh I wish I were writing in ink on expensive velum so I would just choose a word and be done. Not feel like I have to keep revising and changng. I want something final (must find that process piece I wrote when I was in that situation.
>
> Sometimes I try to revise too much on screen. Too much chaos in the mind.

When he did minimal revising to get rid of mistakes and get the passage clear—but to make as few changes as possible—he came up with this:

> What I find on the screen is halfway between the thoughts and feelings in my mind and writing on paper. Mind is a mess; writing is supposed to be neat. But when I'm writing on screen, the words seem half in my mind. So the computer is a kind of second mind. The words are still partly in me. The computer text is also like my mind because I can't look at it all at once. I can only put my attention on one screen at a time. I don't have complete detachment from it until I print it out.
>
> Another mind. Who says two minds are better than one? Sometimes I make such a mess with my two minds that I feel in a swamp—too many options. Once when this happened I remember feeling, "Oh, I wish I were writing in ink on expensive vellum so I would just have to choose each word and be done, and not feel as though I have to keep revising and changing. I want something final." I still have some process writing I did when I was in that situation.
>
> Sometimes I try to revise too much on screen. This makes for too much chaos in the mind.

Our point here is that correct writing doesn't have to be formal or impersonal or stiff in any way. When a teacher says, "I want your paper to be absolutely correct," you may think that she hates an informal, personal voice, whereas she *may* hate only mistakes and unclear sentences. In such a situation (and this is also the situation for most magazine and newspaper writing and many committee reports), your best route is the one in this exercise: Write in your most comfortable voice and then correct and clarify it afterward. Of course, you can't use slang or ungrammatical constructions if the audience wants correctness, but you can keep an informal personal style: There is no conflict between writing in an informal voice and writing correctly.

Impersonal Formal Writing—But Still in Your Voice

Sometimes teachers or other readers ask not only for correctness but for writing that is *impersonal* and *formal.* Many teachers of science say that scientific writing should be impersonal. When you *set out* to produce formal or impersonal writing, you often produce language that feels stiff, awkward, or artificial. This is not necessary. You can produce impersonal or formal writing that still seems comfortable and natural—if you go about producing it in the right way.

Activity Seven: More Minimal Revising

The crucial process here is to start out informally in a voice that feels comfortable for you. Don't worry about correctness or the need for formality. After you've written it, go through and remove *only* the personal and informal features (just as you removed only the mistakes in the previous exercise). You will end up with something impersonal and formal, but it will not be stiff or dead; it will still have your voice in it. But if you start off trying to *write* it in a formal voice, your language will often feel very stiff and uncomfortable.

Here is what Peter Elbow came up with when he removed the personal, informal elements.

> What we find on the screen is halfway between the thoughts and feelings in our minds and writing on paper. Mind seems like a mess; writing is supposed to be neat. But when we write on screen, the words still seem half in mind. So the computer seems like a kind of second mind.
>
> The computer text is also like the mind because we cannot look at it all at once. We can put our attention on only one screenful at a time. We don't have complete detachment from what we've written until we print it out. Are two minds really better than one? Some people, when their writing creates a mess, feel as though they have too many options. They wish they were writing in ink on

expensive vellum so they had to choose each word and be done with it. When we feel we have to keep revising and changing, we often wish for something final.

Revising too much on screen can make for too much chaos in the mind.

Here is Peter's process writing, reflecting on the choices he made:

When I looked for informal or personal elements to remove I came up with these: contractions; dashes as punctuation; sentences without a verb; conversational words like "till" and "bit"; conversational expressions like "just have to choose" (changed to "simply have to choose").

It was also informal to write in the first person ("I") and refer to my own individual experience. I decided I could make it fairly formal and impersonal by changing to first-person plural ("we"). I suppose a few teachers might even call "we" informal. I could have made my language more definitely formal and impersonal by talking about "people" instead of "we," but that seemed needlessly stiff. But I did use "some people" toward the end for experiences that felt more personal.

It was interesting to deal with my question, "Who says two minds are better than one?" It gives a personal flavor because it is addressed directly to the reader. First I changed it from a question to a statement ("Conventional wisdom tells us that two minds are better than one"), but that also felt needlessly stuffy. I decided I could keep it as a question if the question isn't pointed so directly at the reader ("Are two minds really better than one?"). I could use a kind of formality and impersonality while still keeping things livelier and closer to my voice.

Our point here is that your writing (and your sanity) will benefit enormously if you remember these distinctions. You can have writing that is perfectly *correct*—but is still personal and informal. And you can have writing that is *impersonal* and formal—but is still lively and sounds more or less like you, not stiff, awkward, and dead.

Let us conclude by summarizing our advice: Start off writing in a way that feels comfortable for you—in a voice that feels like the right voice for you (unless you are actually trying to mimic someone else's voice). Don't worry about correctness or level of formality. Afterward you can do the minimal revising needed for correctness—or even for formality. If you try to start off writing in a formal voice, you will often get tangled into artificial language.

Nevertheless, if you really want to sound like someone different from yourself, someone with a completely different character (perhaps someone older or more formal or more authoritative), *then* it may pay to start out trying to *use* that voice from the beginning. Try to imagine and see that person in your mind's eye and hear him or her talk in your mind's ear. Try a bit of speaking as that person would speak. Role-play that character a bit: How would the person sit or stand or walk or hold his or her head? Try to enter the role and *be* the person. *Then* write from within that role. But you don't need to pretend to be someone else just to write something correct or formal.

One additional piece of advice: When it comes to correctness, formality, and voice, a great deal depends on the first few paragraphs or the opening page of a piece of writing. If you can start by establishing the voice and the level of formality that is called for, many readers will not notice differences in the rest of the piece. And readers are a bit more forgiving about mistakes if the first page or two are totally error free. In short, if you get the beginning right, you have more leeway in what follows. Look around, for example, at formal pieces of writing (perhaps scholarly essays or business memos), and you'll see that they often establish their formality in the first page or so and then actually lapse gradually into much more informality. When the informality is in the beginning, readers say, "This writer can't write formal prose." When the informality comes later on, many readers say, "This writer has a real facility with formal writing."

MAIN ASSIGNMENT
Exploring Voice in Your Writing

There are three possibilities here:

Option 1: Write an essay that explores your voices—the various voices you find in your speaking and your writing—and the question of whether you sense a single voice—"your" voice—in or underneath or behind them all.

Option 2: Choose one of your papers that you would like to revise by changing the voice. It could be a finished paper, it could be a draft, or it could be a long fragment from your private writing or freewriting.

Option 3: Create a collage of your written voices. (See Workshop 4 for guidance in building a collage.)

If you choose **Option 1,** the following questions might help you:
- What are your important voices? Think back to times when your speaking or writing voice was notable or important. Examples:
  a. Think of a person you feel comfortable and easy talking to. What is your voice with this person? What does it tell about you? What side of you does it bring out?

b. Think of a time when you felt particularly awkward in talk-ing—tongue-tied or artificial or "not you." What was your voice like then? Where did that "not you" voice come from?

c. Think of a time when you spoke with particular intensity and conviction. Perhaps you were mad or sad or excited. As you spoke, you could feel, "Yes. This is right. I'm saying what I re-ally need to say and damn it, I'm saying it so my listener *has* to hear it." What was your voice like? What part of you was it bringing out? In short, think about how certain people or oc-casions bring out different voices in you. Try freewriting or role-playing in those various voices. See what those voices want to say.

- What are some of the voices of others that have been important in your life: family, friends, teachers, coaches? Have you ever heard echoes of a parent's voice coming out of your mouth? A bunch of friends who hang around together often start sounding alike. Most of our voices have even been influenced by voices of characters in public life, on TV or radio, in books, in church, and in school—voices we hear often that carry weight or authority. Think of phrases that reverberate in your ear or your memory from some of these people. ("I have a dream." "Winning isn't the main thing, it's the only thing." "Just do it.") Listen to the impor-tant phrases in your mind's ear—listen to *how* the person says it—and write about that voice and its meaning for you.

- What voices and parts of yourself do you show in your speaking but have a hard time using in your writing? What parts of your-self come out in your writing but don't show in your speech?

- Where would you put yourself on this continuum? At one end are people who feel they have a single, "real" voice that represents a single "real" self (despite variations in tone for different situa-tions); at the other end are people who feel that they have vari-ous voices and various selves, and that there's no such thing as a "real" voice or "real" self. In short, what do you see as the rela-tionship between your self/selves and your voice/voices?

One of our former students, Bryant Shea, wrote the following essay on finding his voice(s) in response to Option 1 of this workshop's main assignment:

Voices I Hear   *Bryant Shea*

Two years ago I read a Charlie Brown comic strip and the last frame read "The worst thing to have is a great potential." Boy, can I relate to that. In four years of high school sports I never lived up to what anyone thought I could do, including myself. Freshman year it was great: "You have great po-tential," I would hear, and even if I screwed up they would let me try again.

Voices I Hear   *continued*

By senior year, though, it was "He had so much potential." It was ridiculous; I was a two-sport All-Star and had gone to the state finals or semifinal in three different sports. I started for all the teams I played on, but still I did not live up to my "potential." Every time I do poorly at something I hear that voice in my head: "You had so much potential—if only you had worked harder." It rings in my head constantly, "you had so much potential . . . you had so much potential." I really wish I could walk into something and have everyone think I sucked. At least this way it would be a surprise that I was good. Instead good is the expected: great is my "potential." Charlie Brown was right: the worst thing to have *is* a great potential.

That is probably the most memorable voice that rings in my head, but there are others as well. Whenever I do anything stupid I hear my mom's voice saying "Oh, Bryant, why?" No matter how old I get, I still remember her saying that all the time when I made a stupid mistake. She did not get upset; she got disappointed, which I think was probably worse. The first time I can remember her saying that, I was about five. I had gone outside and played in the mud wearing my school clothes. When I came in I knew that I had done something stupid and I was getting ready to get yelled at, but my mom just came in the room and said "Oh, Bryant, why? You know better than that." It was worse than getting yelled at; I felt like I had really disappointed her. Now when I hear that voice I do not worry so much that my mom will be disappointed but rather that I have disappointed myself. Another voice that I constantly hear is that of my basketball coach. Whenever I am doing anything physically demanding and I want to quit, I hear his voice in my head saying, "Come on, Bryant, you know you can do this, work it, work it." I think in the six years I knew my coach, he said "work it" about a million times. When I first met my coach he was a basketball instructor at my camp. He used to push everyone to the limit and if you gave less than one hundred percent he got mad. By the end of the week we called him the "Work It" man, because he used the phrase so much. Little did I know that I would have to hear it for four more years in high school. I will admit this, though; his voice ringing in my head has pushed me along many times when I thought I was going to give up.

It is funny how you can translate people's voices into your own. The three voices that I talked about above were all from people I know, but when I hear them, it is me talking. I get upset when I do not live up to my potential, I am the one disappointed when I do something stupid, and I am the one pushing myself to do better when I hear "work it." I guess that everyone has the same thing happen to them; it is part of growing up, I would assume.

Along with these voices that I have of other people, my mind has its own voice. It is the voice that I talk to when I have to figure something out; it's the voice that right now is saying, "Okay, think: what else do I have to write about?" This voice is my conscience and it is what I hear when I do something wrong. It says, "Should I really be doing this?" or "Wow I didn't think you could be so mean." Everyone has a voice like this and without it we would probably be in a lot of trouble. This voice is what interprets the

Voices I Hear   *continued*

other voices that I hear and then says, "Listen to what they have to say." I think it would be great sometimes to hear what other people are saying to themselves when they're talking to you. The voice inside your head tends to be much more honest than the one that comes out of your mouth, and most of the time we would be better off listening to our inner voice.

If you choose **Option 2,** try to find a piece where the voice feels bothersome to you or "off." Perhaps it is wooden and stiff—timid writing. Or perhaps it is a piece where you got carried away with a voice you now don't want to use in a final draft—for example, one very hostile to the reader. Or perhaps the paper seems to be dominated by a strong voice that now feels corny or fake or overdone to you—for example, too jolly or pretending to be 60 years old and wiser than the rest of the world.

The activities you have done for this workshop will put you in a good position to do this assignment, but there is no right sequence of steps to follow. Perhaps you will start work on this paper with nothing but a sound in your ear and a feel in your mouth for the voice(s) you are trying to create or with some awareness of the voice(s) you don't like. Or perhaps you can start by describing or explaining to yourself analytically what those voices are. Our only advice is to use *both* kinds of understanding: first, the understanding that comes from inhabiting the voices by speaking them out loud and getting the feel of the words in your mouth and the sound of them in your ear; second, the understanding that comes from analysis and explanation. Use each kind of understanding as a check against the other.

As you do this assignment in revising voice, you might have the impulse to change the *ideas* or *content* of the paper. Even if this is a faint impulse, listen to it. When you use a different voice, you are being a different person, or at least are taking a different point of view or speaking from a different part of yourself. It's not surprising if this process leads you to think different thoughts. Thus, you might think you are doing only what we call second-level revising or changing the muscles, but you will probably find yourself drifting into first-level revising or changing the bones. (More on this in Workshop 5.) When this happens, it's a good sign.

Suggestions for Collaboration

Write a collaborative essay comparing the voices of two or three of you. Each of you should start by making a collage of passages of your own writing—passages that illustrate your different voices. This first step can be done individually, but it's helpful to enlist the aid of your partner(s) in choosing among possible passages and deciding what order to put them in. Then write your collaborative essay comparing the constellation of voices each of you has. Possible questions: Does one of you have a wider or narrower range of voices? What are the feelings that each of you has about various voices and their range? How do the voices seem to relate to the person's identity as seen by herself and seen by others? Do certain voices seem less legitimate? Do certain voices have a particular history?

Sharing and Responding

For the essay about my voice:
* What can you learn from my essay that you can apply to your own writing?
* Summarize what you hear me saying or implying about voice and self—and tell me your views on the issue.

For the revision assignment:
* Describe the main voice or voices you hear in my revised version. How is it (are they) different from the voice(s) of my piece be-fore it was revised? Try describing the voices in terms of cloth-ing—jeans? baggy sweater? jacket and tie?
* Describe any changes or variations of voice you can hear within the single piece of writing (for example, from confident to timid or serious to humorous). Do these changes or variations work, or are they a problem for you?
* Do you hear any echoes of outside voices—voices that are not mine? Have I made them part of my voice, or do they seem undi-gested or unassimilated?

For the collage assignment:
* Among the various voices in my collage, tell me which are most striking and interesting to you. Describe those voices and tell me why they interest you.

For other response possibilities, see "Sharing and Responding" at the end of the book.

Process Journal and Cover Letter

* Talk about how you experienced the three exercises for explor-ing voices in writing: performing a voice, role-playing the person in the voice, and describing the voice.

- Did this workshop make you notice voices of yours that you hadn't noticed before? Or change your feelings about some of your voices?
- When you were revising your paper for voice, what changes in content or point of view did you notice?
- Which parts of you were brought out by the voice you used in your revision?

For your cover letter, it's good to include some or all of your process writing. But don't forget to answer some cover letter questions. Here are the main ones: What is your main point and what effect are you trying to have on readers? What do you feel works best in your paper and where are you unsatisfied? What changes did you make on the basis of any feedback? And most important: What feedback do you want now from a reader? But your teacher may ask you particular cover letter questions that pertain to this assignment.

RUMINATIONS AND THEORY
About the Human Voice

Here are some facts about the human voice. These are not quite innocent facts since we intend them to show why voice is such a suggestive and resonant term for the understanding of writing. But we think you will agree that they are nevertheless true facts.

- People almost always learn to speak before they learn to write. Normally we learn speech at such an early age that we are not aware of the learning process. Speech habits are laid down at a deep level. Also, in the development of cultures, speaking comes before writing.
- Voice is produced by the body. To talk about voice in writing is to import connotations of the body into the discussion and, by implication, to be interested in the role of the body in writing.
- We can distinguish two dimensions to someone's voice: the raw *sound* of their voice and the *manner* or style in which they use that sound. The first is the quality of noise they make based as it were on the physical instrument they are playing. The second is the kind of tunes, rhythms, and styles they play on their instrument.
- We identify and recognize people by their voices—even when they have a cold or over a bad phone connection. We often recognize them by their voices even after a number of years. Something constant persists despite the change.
- People have demonstrably unique voices: Voice prints are as certain as fingerprints for identification. This might suggest the

analogy of our bodies being genetically unique, but our voice prints are less dependent upon genes than our bodies are.

- Despite the unique and recognizable quality of an individual's voice, we all display enormous variation in how we speak from occasion to occasion. Sometimes we speak in monotone, sometimes with lots of intonation. And we use different tones of voice at different times—for example, excited, scared, angry, sad. Furthermore, we sometimes speak self-consciously or artificially, but more often we speak with no attention or even awareness of how we are speaking. The distinction between a natural and an artificial way of talking is theoretically vexed, but listeners and speakers often agree in their judgments of whether someone is speaking naturally or artificially on any given occasion.

- Our speech often gives a naked or candid picture of how we're feeling: Our voice quavers with fear or unhappiness, or lilts with elation, or goes flat with depression. People sometimes detect our mood after hearing nothing but our "hello" on the phone. Our moods often show through in our writing too—at least to very sensitive readers—but it's easier to hide how we're feeling in our writing. We can ponder and revise the words we put on paper. Speaking is harder to control, usually less self-conscious, closer to autonomic behavior. Cicero says the voice is a picture of the mind. People commonly identify someone's voice with *who* he or she is—with his or her character—just as it is common to identify one's self with one's body. (The word *person* means both body and self, and thus it suggests a link between the person and the sound of the voice as produced by the body. *Persona* comes from a Greek word for the mask used in dramatic performances, a mask that amplified an actor's voice.)

- Audience has a big effect on voice. Partly it's a matter of *imitating* those around us; just as we pick up words and phrases from those we spend time with, or pick up a regional accent, so we often unconsciously imitate the ways of talking that we constantly hear. Partly it's a matter of *responding* to those around us; that is, our voice tends to change as we speak to different people, often without awareness. We tend to speak differently to a child, to a buddy, to someone we are afraid of. Peter Elbow's wife says she can hear when he's speaking to a woman on the phone. Some listeners seem to bring out more intonation in our speech.

- There are good actors, on and off the stage, who can convincingly make their voices (and faces) seem to show whatever feeling or character they want—irrespective of how they actually feel.

- People can become just as comfortable in writing as in speaking. Indeed, we are sometimes deeply awkward, tangled, and even blocked in our speaking.

- Though voice is produced by the body, it is produced out of *breath:* something that is not the body and that is shared or common to us all, but always issues from inside us. Also, breath is a prime sign of life. This may partly explain why so many people have been so tempted to invest voice with "deep" or even "spiritual" connotations.
- Voice involves sound, hearing, and time; writing or text involves sight and space. The differences between these modalities are profound and interesting. Sight seems to tell us more about the outsides of things, sound more about the insides of things. In evolution, sight is the most recent sense modality to become dominant in humans—and is dealt with in the largest and most recent parts of the human brain. Sight seems to be most linked to rationality—in our brain and our metaphors—for example, "Do you see?"
- Spoken language has more communicative channels than writing. That is, speech contains more channels for carrying meaning. For example, there is volume (loud and soft), pitch (high and low), speed (fast and slow), accent (yes or no), and intensity (relaxed and tense). Note that these are not just binary items, for in each case there is a huge range of subtle degrees between extremes. In addition, each case has patterned sequences; for example, tune is a pattern of pitches; rhythm is a pattern of slow and fast and accent. Furthermore, there is a wide spectrum of timbres (breathy, shrill, nasal); there are glides and jumps; there are pauses of varying lengths. Combinations of *all* of these factors make the possibilities dizzying. And all these factors carry meaning. Consider the example of the subtle or not so subtle pause as we are speaking, the little intensity or lengthening of a syllable—and all the other ways we complicate the messages we speak. We can't do those things in writing.

  It's not that writing is poverty-stricken as a communicative system. But writing has to achieve its subtleties with fewer resources. A harpsichord cannot make gradations of volume the way a piano can, but harpsichordists use subtle cues of timing, such as slight hesitations, in order to communicate the *kind* of thing that pianos communicate with volume. Mozart had fewer harmonic resources to play with than Brahms. He did a lot, but with less. To write well is also to do a lot with less. If we are angry, we sometimes press harder with the pen, break the pencil lead, hit the keys harder, or write the words all in a rush. In such a mood our speech would probably sound very angry, but none of these physical behaviors shows in our writing. Nevertheless, it is *possible* to get our tone of voice down on the page so that readers hear it.

  To conclude this chapter, we'd like to offer another essay on voice, this one by a student, Minh-Ha Pham:

How Can I, a Vietnamese Girl . . .   *Minh-Ha Pham*

How can I, a Vietnamese girl brought up on food stamps and green stamps, living in a one-bedroom house with an extended family of eleven on El Paseo Street, have a voice?

My mom warned me never to marry a writer. She said that writers are too sensitive and would never make good breadwinners. She said he'd see a wilting flower and be too depressed to go to work—if he had a job. But probably, he'd just sit at home all day and get in my way.

When I decided to be an English major, she was hurt. *"Con hu qua,"* she would say. She would do anything for me, why couldn't I do this for her? Why waste her money reading books and studying writing? Why couldn't I do that on the side, for fun? In the meantime, law school was where I needed to put my mind. This argument continued through my bachelor's degree, through my master's degree, and through the day I moved to Amherst to begin work towards my doctoral degree in English. In some Sunday morning phone calls, law school is still hinted at.

My parents were more invested in our education than any other parents I knew. I would listen to my friends talk to their parents. Their conversations *sounded* like conversations. They would talk about the weather, new boyfriends or girlfriends, new movies, new books, upcoming parties or events. The conversations I had with my parents sounded more like this:

What are you doing right now?

Nothing. I just got up.

Are you eating well?

Yes.

Are you saving money?

Yes.

Have you had any tests lately?/How did you do on the test?

Yes, I did OK.

Just OK?

In these conversations, I never told my parents which books I was reading or what my essays were about. I never told them the discussions that went on in my classes or my thoughts about the canon, literary tradition, or literature. While I reported back grades and results, I never told them what these grades meant. And they never asked.

I was completely alone in my decision to be a student of literature. I don't say this with any bitterness or sadness. It was just a matter of fact. I knew, as I was making this decision sophomore year in college, that my parents could not support this decision in the same way that they supported my sister's decision to be pre-med or my brother's decision to study chemistry. While I wasn't sad about this, I found that my writing environment wasn't conducive to the liberal and romanticized notion of "the writer" that I was learning at school.

How Can I, a Vietnamese Girl . . . *continued*

First and foremost, being a writer meant being an author, having an authorial or authoritative voice. This was very nearly an impossible expectation for me. How can I, a Vietnamese girl brought up on food stamps and green stamps, living in a one-bedroom house with an extended family of eleven on El Paseo Street, have a voice, much less an authoritative voice? I think of Gloria Anzaldúa's quandary, "Who am I, a poor Chicanita from the sticks, to think I could write?"* If I were ever to presume the authority to voice my opinion, I would quickly be reminded of the position of my voice by any one of my family members. Clearly, the question of voice would have to be reworked if it was going to work at all.

The second requirement that I learned writers needed was an audience. You're not a writer until you have an audience. Further, your writerliness is measured by your publications—more publications means more audience which means better writer. But what happens when you don't have an audience? Because all of my writing is personally and politically motivated, my main audience is my family and my Vietnamese community. So to rephrase my question more accurately, what happens when your audience believes that writing is a bad use of your time and their time? Who has time to sit around the house and write? And if they had any extra time to listen to me read my writing, don't I think they'd be working overtime like they do every weekend so that they could make ends meet this month? Clearly, the audience question was going to have to be renegotiated as well.

I lay out the terrain from which my writing had to grow in order to map out the conventions of writerliness that I had to displace in order to make writing feasible. The map of writing as it was laid out to me didn't include all the sidestreets and alleys in which my writing had to maneuver. So, what makes me a writer? Why do I write? Probably the best way to answer these questions is to examine the ways in which I'm *not* a writer, to look at the conventions of writerliness and show the ways that my experience breaks with these conventions.

First of all, I don't write because I love it. Writing has caused a lot of pain for me within my family and within my community. Family secrets or abuses are not meant for the public to know. Talking badly about one's family in public is an unforgivable crime. The subjects that I would consider taboo are topics that many of my peers write about. This is not self-imposed censorship, though, because I don't write to share my experiences or to heal myself either. That has never been a motivation for me. I never wanted to tell anyone about my family's suspicions of writers because it would be misunderstood as a lack of familial support, a suggestion of a domineering family, another nod reaffirming the tired Asian stereotype of a cold, strict family.

*Gloria Anzaldúa and Cherrie Moraga, *This Bridge Called My Back* (New York: Kitchen Table Women of Color Press, 1984), p. 163.

How Can I, a Vietnamese Girl . . .   *continued*

I don't write because it is the only thing I know how to do or the only way I know how to express myself. Writing *is* a luxury. It is a devotion of time to selfish reflections, hubris, and fantastical imaginings in a language that is not nearly as rich as my own. I am not too naive to believe that I deserve to write because this would also mean that I deserve to sit and read and think while many of my family members work 14-hour days in factories and assembly lines to barely make ends meet.

Finally, I don't write because I want to be a writer. That term is as suspicious to me as it is to my mother. The delineation of writing as a profession is a difficult category for me to buy into. My mother would never be considered a writer by the conventions I've laid out because she's never been published, her audience is often a private one, and her writing isn't an expression of voice so much as it is a method of communication. Yet, she is a writer. She writes more bill payments every month than she would care to, she writes family members in Viet Nam often to tell them how we're doing, she writes notes to herself to remember to pick up this or that for my dad or one of us. She's constantly writing. In fact, it would be impossible for her not to be a writer because we live in a writing society. We are all writers.

Of course these explanations only cryptically locate my position as a "writer." The problems with voice and audience still need attention because my voice is not my own and because audience is not an essential correlative to my writing.

My voice is meaningless if you don't understand where it comes from. It's a traditional Vietnamese voice, it's an immigrant voice, it's a once-middle-class-Vietnamese-turned-lower-class-American-made-back-into-middle-class-now-hyphenated-American politicized voice. It's a female voice. It's the daughter of a first son and second daughter voice. It's an older sister voice and a younger sister voice. My voice never exists on its own. It only exists in relation to the past and my family. I do not own my voice because ownership makes no sense in my family. My voice belongs to my parents who would say that it really belongs to my grandparents who would say it really belongs to my great-grandparents, etc. My voice is a tool, an heirloom, perhaps, that was handed down way before time began. It was important for me to understand this so that I could know how to use this tool, how to cherish this heirloom.

Needing an audience means that the reason I write isn't genuine. I don't write because I want someone to hear me. I write because I have something to say, something to get off my chest. Once it's written, the point of writing has been achieved. The cause of my writing is synonymous with the effects of my writing. There is no need to wait for a response because there's no time for that. And, as I'm reminded, if my intended audience had any extra time to listen to me read my writing, *don't I think they'd be working overtime like they do every weekend so that they could make ends meet this month?*

PART III

Important Intellectual and Academic Tasks

Reading as the Creation of Meaning

Interpretation as Response

Essential Premises

The process of reading is a process of *constructing* or *creating* meanings that are only potentially there.

It's helpful to capture our reading process in more detail by observing it closely, which we can easily do by stopping periodically in midprocess and writing what we find in our heads.

Whenever we read a text out loud with full meaning or expression, we automatically create an interpretation of that text. The interpretation we create by entering into a text through speaking is often more interesting than the one we come up with if someone asks us directly for our interpretation.

Main Assignment Preview

Your main assignment will be to write an essay about a text. We will lead you through a series of activities to help you read and think specifically about "Song," a poem by W. H. Auden. Bear in mind, however, that these techniques are useful with *any* text—prose as well as poetry.

On Reading

Reading may look passive: We sit quietly and let the images of the words come into our retina and then pass inward to our brain. But reading—indeed all meaning making—is a deeply active process of creation. In fact, when we have trouble reading it's often because we've been mistakenly trying to be passive—trying to make ourselves into good cameras. We've been trying to become perfect little photographic plates on which the meanings on the page print themselves with photographic accuracy. But since reading doesn't work that way, we have trouble understanding the words. Even the simple act of seeing is exploratory and active. The eye may be like a camera, but the brain is not. It cannot take in retinal images, only electric impulses.

The important thing to realize is that not only reading but even seeing or making sense of what is around us is always a process that occurs in stages. It takes place gradually through the passage of time, not instantaneously like an image passing through a lens. In the first stage, our mind takes in the first pieces of information—the first trickles of electrical impulses—and quickly makes a guess or a hypothesis about what we might be looking at. Then the mind repeatedly checks this guess against further information that comes in. Often we have to change our guess or hypothesis as new information comes in—before we see what's really there.

Because normal perception occurs so quickly, we seldom realize that this process of guessing-checking-maybe-revising is going on, especially since we don't think of vision in these terms. But if you will keep this explanation in mind in the days and weeks ahead and watch yourself in the act of seeing—particularly when you are trying to see something obscure or something you've never seen before—you'll catch yourself in the act of making these visual guesses or hypotheses: "I'm pretty sure that's a white car going down the highway," but then in a second, "Oh no, wait. Why is a white boat coming up the highway?" In short, we tend to see what we expect to see until evidence forces us to revise our expectation.

If seeing and hearing are such active creative processes, so must reading be: In fact, it's exactly the same process. When we read words or hear them, we understand what we expect to understand till evidence forces us to revise our expectation. Even in the process of reading individual words, research shows that as soon as we see a few letters or the shape of the whole word or the phrase that it's part of, we guess what it is and then, as we get more data—or as our guess doesn't seem to fit—we revise our guess. And so the same constructive process goes on in all reading, whether for words, phrases, sentences, paragraphs, chapters, or whole books.

Consider the opening sentence of Hemingway's story, "A Clean Well-Lighted Place":

> It was late and every one had left the cafe except an old man who sat in the shadow the leaves of the tree made against the electric light.

It's not a hard sentence; we know all the words. "It was late" looks clear enough, but is it? Actually we know very little about what it means here. Is it late afternoon or late night? By the end of the sentence, we probably guess it's nighttime—because "the electric light" is mentioned—but we can't be sure. Similarly, "old man" seems clear, yet the only meaning we can get from it is the picture *we create* from our experience of old men. Each reader's creation or picture will be different, and each picture will be that reader's "hypothesis" about the meaning of the word. But each picture will get modified when succeeding sentences come along and provide a fuller picture. Most readers will probably have to change the picture or meaning they have unconsciously formed as a hypothesis. This is the process of reading. Over and over a word or phrase gives us a *bit* of meaning, but it doesn't make sense till we flesh it out a bit—create a meaning—but we continually have to change our creation as succeeding words come along. We are always having to hold something in mind uncompleted while we wait for a fuller meaning gradually to unfold—in time.

We see here why some people have a hard time reading. They think they are supposed to be clear about the meaning of one word (or phrase or sentence or paragraph) before going on to the next word (or phrase, sentence, paragraph). But that's impossible. The meaning of X is seldom clear till we get Y and Z and much more. So they feel bad: "I guess I'm just a bad reader." Or they hate the insecurity of having to create guesses and move on before learning which guesses are right. To read well, one has to learn to be comfortable continually taking in little bits of partial meaning and creating hypotheses or hunches (*interpretations*) about what the words really mean—and being ready to change those interpretations with new information. And while they're getting later information about that first sentence, they are in the midst of the creative uncertainty about the second sentence. When the previous paragraph or page gets clearer, the present one is probably still dicey.

In this workshop, we will highlight this creative, interpretive process of reading so you can see it more clearly and learn to be better and more comfortable with it. We will show you three activities or exercises for interpreting a text—in this case a poem—by means of responding and actively creating meaning. There's quite a lot to do here; if your teacher has to skip an activity, we hope you'll experiment with it anyway on your own.

We have two other goals in exploring the reading or interpreting process: helping you do better with hard texts, and helping you use the collaborative dimension of reading. The activities here will get you started.

Activity One: Looking Closely at the Reading Process by Giving Movies of Your Mind as You Read

This activity is a kind of mini-laboratory in the reading process: a three-step procedure designed to help you monitor your conscious and unconscious reactions as you read. In this activity we interrupt you as you read a poem—we stop you twice midpoem and ask you what's going on in your mind—so that you can take note of your responses and reactions and interpretations as they happen. The poem we're using has 15 short stanzas. We have printed five stanzas on this page, five more on page 204, and the last five on page 206. We've done this so that you can record your reactions to each section before you see the rest of the poem. If this strikes you as highly artificial, you are right. But this artificial process will help you capture some of the mental events in your reading and interpretation that you don't usually get a chance to see.

Step One: Capturing Reactions on the Fly

Start, then, and read the first five stanzas of the poem in the box on this page.

Read them however you would normally read. But when you finish, freewrite for at least five minutes to get down on paper what was happening in your mind *as* you were reading the stanzas—and also what's happening in your mind now as you are reflecting and mak-

"Song"   *by W. H. Auden*   *(first section)*

As I walked out one evening,
    Walking down Bristol Street,
The crowds upon the pavement
    Were fields of harvest wheat.

And down by the brimming river
    I heard a lover sing
Under an arch of the railway:
    "Love has no ending.

I'll love you, dear, I'll love you
    Till China and Africa meet,
And the river jumps over the mountain
    And the salmon sing in the street.

I'll love you till the ocean
    Is folded and hung up to dry,
And the seven stars go squawking
    Like geese about the sky.

The years shall run like rabbits,
    For in my arms I hold
The Flower of the Ages,
    And the first love of the world."

ing sense of the words. If you wish, go back and read the words again. What meanings or partial meanings come to mind? What thoughts, feelings, or memories are you having? Which words linger? Try to get your mental events on paper. (You could do this whole exercise with a tape recorder, speaking your reactions as you go rather than writing. You might capture more that way.)

Of course sometimes we read something and our only reaction is, "I'm confused." That's fine. Write it down. But try to write a few more words about what kind of confusion this was: frustrated? bored? angry? In this situation, read the passage again and see what sense you can make this time and what goes on in your mind and feelings. Jot down some notes on this too.

When you finish, go on and go through the same process with the next five stanzas on page 204. Read them and freewrite and record whatever happens in your mind as you are reading, thinking, and trying to make sense—and enjoying the poem, too. You are giving yourself movies of your mind as you read. Then repeat this process for the last five stanzas on page 206. Finally, read through the *whole* poem again and write about what goes on in your mind then.

There's an interesting question about the reading process that is highlighted by this exercise: When we read, should we try to "finish" or "master" or "settle" one section of a poem (or any text) before going on to read the next one? There's no right answer. We all read in different ways—and differently for different pieces of writing. Do what you normally do. However, it's worth pointing out that one of the biggest problems some people have in reading is a tendency to spend too long trying to *nail down* one part before moving on. This usually gives you needless frustration since there's often no way to really find out what an early part means until you see a later part. That's how language works.

Notice that there's an interesting correlation here between the processes of reading and writing: In both cases, we tend to get in trouble from trying to do it right the first time. It's an impossible goal. Most people read better and write better when they let go a bit and learn not to work so hard to get it right before moving on, but come back again and again. This is really an issue of revising: Revising is involved in good *reading* as well as good writing.

Before you have finished, make sure you have read the whole poem at least twice from start to finish rather than in bits. When you read it straight through, you may well have new responses and thoughts and interpretations—new feelings, memories, frustrations, associations. Or you may simply become more convinced of how you saw it before. (But even "becoming more convinced" is something going on in your mind.) So make sure you stop after these read-throughs and freewrite for a few minutes to record what is then going on in your thoughts and feelings.

What we are asking for is really process writing—but it's about your reading process. This writing will help you understand better how your mind works when you read: your habits, your preoccupations, your blind spots, your strengths, and the things you'd like to do better. Breaking the poem into parts is like putting the camera on slow motion so you can see more clearly the details of how your mind gradually makes meaning out of words. Athletes often watch slow-motion pictures of how they function in order to learn to function better. (By the way, it's interesting to notice similarities and differences between how your mind works as you write and as you read.)

You can look at examples of this kind of process writing on pages 221–224 of the Readings section at the end of this workshop: reactions by students while reading Richard Wilbur's "The Writer" (printed on page 220). What we are asking for is the same as "movies of the reader's mind"—a method of giving feedback to fellow writers, which

ℒ **"Song"**   *by W. H. Auden*   *(continued)*

> But all the clocks in the city
>   Began to whirr and chime:
> "O let not Time deceive you,
>   You cannot conquer Time.
>
> In the burrows of the Nightmare
>   Where Justice naked is,
> Time watches from the shadow
>   And coughs when you would kiss.
>
> In headaches and in worry
>   Vaguely life leaks away,
> And Time will have his fancy
>   Tomorrow or today.
>
> Into many a green valley
>   Drifts the appalling snow;
> Time breaks the threaded dances
>   And the diver's brilliant bow.
>
> O plunge your hands in water,
>   Plunge them in up to the wrist;
> Stare, stare in the basin
>   And wonder what you've missed.

we explain and illustrate in a separate section of "Sharing and Responding" at the end of this book.

Step Two: Share, Compare Notes, Create Meaning with Others

At this point it is useful and interesting to share the movies of your mind with one or two of your classmates. Indeed, it makes sense to do this earlier in the reading process; for example, even after you have read only the first section.

Most people find it interesting just to see how other people's minds react to the same words. It's often a relief to see other people's "really rough drafts of reading." When we are reading, sometimes we feel, "Oh dear, everyone else but me understands it perfectly," and it's fun to see that it's a messy, imprecise process for everyone. Students often think, "Teachers and critics have a magical ability to see the hidden meaning in poems—whole and complete—but I don't have that ability." As with writing, it's a relief to discover that everyone's mind tends to be a mess at the early stages, no matter how skilled they are. Some people hide the mess more (sometimes even from themselves), but the mess is there. And it helps to see that everyone has different reactions and feelings, even when they happen to agree on the main outlines.

In addition, we want to emphasize the collaborative dimension that is inherent in reading and making meaning. It's not that we usually read in groups—we usually read alone—but we usually discuss what we read with others if we have the chance. Lawyers, scientists, and businesspeople as well as literary critics usually reach conclusions about what something means and implies on the basis of discussion with colleagues. Even when we can't actually discuss our reading with others, we often hold bits of mental discussion with them in our heads anyway.

So find an occasion at some point to share your written reactions with others (though don't feel pressured to share things that are too private). The goal is to see the poem through their eyes. Then do a few more minutes of writing to record how their reactions and interpretations did or didn't affect how you see the poem. What new meanings, reactions, feelings, or thoughts come to you on the basis of hearing what others wrote? You may experience large changes or only tiny readjustments. Sometimes someone else's reaction or memory or association becomes prominent in your mind.

We're not saying you should try to agree with other readers. Just *use* other readers; try out their readings to help you find a meaning or interpretation of the poem that satisfies you. The goal is simply to see and understand the poem better.

Reading "Right" and "Wrong"—Reading With the Grain and Against the Grain.   Every piece of writing implicitly asks us to become the right kind of reader for it, the reader who will take the viewpoint and feel the feelings and get the meanings that the writing asks for. When we have difficulty reading something, it's usually a case of "I can't—or I *won't*—become the kind of reader that this piece asks me to be." Some women, for example, have called attention to how often pieces of writing (or art) ask the reader to take on a male point of view, sometimes even asking readers to take pleasure in the criticism or exploitation of women.

We're not asking you necessarily to become the kind of reader you feel this poem is asking you to become. It's fine to be a *resisting* reader, to read "wrong," or to read "against the grain." Notice in the Readings section how Barbara Hales and Julie Nelson are resistant readers of Richard Wilbur's "The Writer." In their dialogue, one of

---

"Song"   *by W. H. Auden*   (*concluded*)

[Note to readers: In the first four stanzas that follow, we are still hearing words spoken by "all the clocks in the city."]

The glacier knocks in the cupboard,
    The desert sighs in the bed,
And the crack in the tea-cup opens
    A lane to the land of the dead.

Where the beggars raffle the banknotes
    And the Giant is enchanting to Jack,
And the Lily-white Boy is a Roarer,
    And Jill goes down on her back.

O look, look in the mirror;
    O look in your distress;
Life remains a blessing
    Although you cannot bless.

O stand, stand at the window
    As the tears scald and start;
You shall love your crooked neighbor
    With your crooked heart."

It was late, late in the evening,
    The lovers they were gone;
The clocks had ceased their chiming,
    And the deep river ran on.

them vehemently refuses to read the poem the way the poem seems to ask to be read. The only thing we ask is that you not stop reading: not stop with "Huh?" or "I hate this piece" or "I hate being the kind of person this poem asks me to be—or having the kinds of feelings it's asking me to have." Please stick with the poem and work out a reading even if it is only a description of what you sense the poem is trying to do to you and why you refuse and insist on having a completely different set of thoughts and feelings. In short, the goal is not to read "right" but to read attentively and capture a record of how your mind makes meaning out of words.

Many people who care about good reading feel that students must choose between a "careful process of objective reading that looks for what's really there" and (what they think of as) "a careless process of giving movies of the mind that is nothing but 'reading in' personal subjective ideas." We insist that this is a false choice. Paying close attention to events in your mind does not mean ignoring what's on the page. Giving movies of your mind, as we describe it, means paying close attention to your reactions *while you are paying close attention to the words on the page.* So this process doesn't mean accepting any old meaning as correct or valid: of course, some readings or interpretations fit a text well and others don't. But since no words *actually contain* meanings till readers put them there, we think it's more valid—and much more interesting—to pay close attention to what actually happens in our minds as we try to read well.

Yes, this process *can* lead you to subjective readings—some of which in the end can fairly be called "wrong"—unsupportable by the text. But even a "wrong" reading can help us notice a faint tinge of a meaning that is actually there but just hovering around the edge of the text. For example, an essentially serious or mournful text might have a wisp of humor or satire that's hard to notice unless someone goes a little overboard with that reading. If we add the *social dimension* of reading—the process of comparing and discussing our individual readings with others—we usually get better and more valid readings than if we start out "trying to be right" and "scared of being wrong."

Step Three: Learning about Yourself as a Reader

Read back over everything you have written so far and try to see what you can notice about your habits as a reader. Notice which parts of the poem struck you most and which parts left you unaffected. Try to notice which parts of the poem you did not comment on. How did your reactions differ from those of others? Think about which dimensions of your self or character played a role in your reacting and interpreting. Look in particular for life positions and life themes:

- *Life positions.* How is your reading affected by your age? your gender? the region where you live? your race? your nationality? your class? your sexual orientation? your occupation? We cannot actually step outside of our positions, but reading can be one way to imagine ourselves differently or to enter vicariously into other positions. Nevertheless, our own life positions exert a strong force on how we read.

- *Life themes.* Can you see any powerful experiences or interests or preoccupations that shaped your reactions? Here are some examples of life themes that affect many people's reading: relations between parents and children, divorce, love, sex, eating, the outdoors, fighting, loneliness, adventure, breaking free of obligations.

It's interesting to get a better picture of *who we are as readers*—what lenses we read through. There is no such thing as perfectly neutral reading. But insofar as we can get a sense of what lenses we read through, we can get a better sense of what kinds of things we might miss. Do you think, for example, that women read and notice and react differently from how men do? It can be interesting to share this last writing, too—about yourself as a reader—but we think it's more important to write these things for yourself. Share only what you want to share.

Alternative to Activity One: Double-Entry or Dialectical Notebook*

Here's another way of paying attention to how you read and thereby improving your reading. This activity is particularly useful if you are reading difficult material that you need to study or master for an exam—but as you'll see it's good for very different kinds of reading,

---

* This section draws heavily on Ann Berthoff's "A Curious Triangle and the Double-Entry Notebook; or How Theory Can Help Us Teach Reading and Writing." The notebook is her idea. But see also Peter Elbow's "Methodological Doubting and Believing" in *Embracing Contraries.* Full listings for both works can be found in the Works Cited section of this book.

Exploring the Writing Process
On the Process of Composition

In the actual process of composition or in preliminary thinking, I try to immerse myself in the motive and *feel* toward meanings, rather than plan a structure or plan effects.

Robert Penn Warren

too. Let us quote Ann Berthoff (who devised this activity) as she describes it:

> I ask my students (all of them: freshmen, upperclassmen, teachers in graduate seminars) to furnish themselves with a notebook, spiral bound at the side, small enough to be easily carried around but not so small that writing is cramped . . . What makes this notebook different from most, perhaps, is the notion of the double-entry: on the right side reading notes, direct quotations, observational notes, fragments, lists, images—verbal and visual—are recorded; on the other (facing) side, notes about those notes, summaries, formulations, aphorisms, editorial suggestions, revisions, comments on comments are written. The reason for the double-entry format is that it provides a way for the student to conduct that "continuing audit of meaning" that is at the heart of learning to read and write critically. The facing pages are in dialogue with each other.

That's all there is to it. But if you do this regularly, you will notice how that dialogue—that continuing audit of meaning—gradually helps you read both more accurately and more creatively and thus helps you get more out of your reading.

Try it. Choose a piece of reading that you can learn from and reflect on—not just something you read to pass the time. Start reading it and, as you do, pause to write down (on the right-hand side of your notebook) words, details, images, or thoughts that strike you. You're not taking notes. Don't try to capture or summarize everything; just encourage yourself to write about what you *notice* in the reading and in your own reactions to the reading. If you find yourself reading more than a few pages without any writing, stop and ask yourself what you noticed in those pages you just read, or how you were reacting. At the end make a few more notations to capture quickly what's in your head as you finish reading.

If possible, let an hour or a day go by and then read over these entries slowly. As you do, jot down on the left-hand side of your notebook whatever comes into your mind as you read the right-hand side. There is no right way to do this, but here are some suggestions of entries you could make:

- *Second thoughts.* What further ideas do your recorded notes suggest?
- *Connections.* How do your notes relate to other parts of your life—to your deepest concerns or interests?
- *Reactions to your reactions.* What do your notes tell you about how your mind works or what you are interested in?
- *Dialogue with the author.* What do you have to say? How would he or she reply?

- *Dialogue with others.* Whom do you want to talk to about these things? What would you tell or ask them?
- *Summary.* What's the most important thing you notice about your notes as you read them over? What kinds of connections can you find in your notes? What conclusions about your reading do your notes make possible? What parts now seem particularly important or unimportant?

Don't worry about the exact difference between what to write on the right and on the left. There's no rigid distinction. Mainly it's a difference in time: As you are reading something for the first time, whatever you write goes on the right-hand side. As you read this over later, whatever thoughts you have go on the left. Thus the important thing about this process is to get your thoughts to be in dialogue with each other. The dialectical notebook makes it possible for you to exploit the advantages of being two people—having two different viewpoints or having discussions with yourself.

Try the same thing with a recent experience: an important conversation, argument, or interchange with someone; a walk that was important to you (perhaps in a beautiful place or at a time when you needed to think something over); an activity that was important to you (such as participation in a deciding game, taking a crucial exam, surviving a harrowing ordeal, or being invited to a party with new friends). On the right-hand side, put down first-stage notes: what you can remember, what you notice. Then, after a day or more, go on to write second-stage reflective notes on those notes on the left-hand side of your notebook.

If possible, share both sides of your notebook with others and listen as they read theirs. This will give you some hints about the ways others read, ways you may want to try out. Others will learn from you in the same way.

Activity Two: Interpretation as Rendering or Animation or Performance

Whenever you read something out loud, you interpret it. That is, you can't read something out loud without automatically deciding what the words mean, and that meaning can be *heard* in your reading. (Of course you can settle for pronouncing words disconnectedly without any sense of meaning—but that's not what we usually mean by "reading out loud.") Often we don't have to figure out the meaning before reading out loud because the act of reading out loud in itself leads us to figure out the meaning of words that we had been stuck on—it puts the meaning there on our tongues. The mouth can be smarter about language than the eyes. Thus, the minimal task we have in mind here is simply to read the poem out loud in such a way as to make the meaning as clear as possible to listeners.

But please don't settle for the minimal task. Critics have often noted that the best interpretation of a text may be a rendition or performance of that text. To figure out how to render a text out loud is usually the quickest and most insightful way to figure out an interpretation. If you read the words with any spirit or animation—if you don't cop out and use a timid monotone—you will convey much more than the meaning of the words. You will convey the spirit or tone of the words—the implications.

Just by trial and error, using your mouth and your ear, you can decide how a sentence or paragraph or stanza should sound (or a whole essay, poem, or short story). Once you figure out your reading, you *have* interpreted it. Then you can *work out* the interpretation that you have already enacted in sound. Most important, this interpretation, based on voice and sound, is usually more insightful and sophisticated than the interpretation you come up with if you go straight to analytical "interpretation talk."

We suggest using groups to put on a rendering or animation or performance of the Auden poem you've worked on in this workshop, or a couple of the most central pages of an essay (or the poem by Richard Wilbur printed in the Readings at the end of this workshop). It is fine for performances to be playful and even take some liberties with the poem. Here are some techniques that student groups have used for renderings of Richard Wilbur's "The Writer" (printed on page 220).

- *Using more than one reader and varying readers.* For example, one group used all their voices for stanzas one, four, five, and eleven (the stanzas that seem the most "choral"). They used only one reader for the first line of the second stanza and the first two lines of the sixth (where there is an "I" speaking). And they used a pair of readers for most of the second and third stanzas (the extended image of the typewriter and the boat) and for the extended story of the trapped bird.

- *Echoing or repeating lines.* One group had one person repeat certain lines after they were said the first time—quietly and intermittently in the background. This reader repeated "My daughter is writing a story" until the group got to "I wish her a lucky passage"; then he repeated that phrase intermittently until the group got to "I remember" and he kept on with that phrase until he stopped for the last stanza. Another group treated the poem like a round: Reader two didn't start until reader one had finished the first stanza. They had only three readers and the effect was interesting. It was like having waves wash over you. Yet as listeners, we understood more than we expected we would. Still, the goal wasn't to put across a clear understanding: it was to give a "musical" or "sound" rendition.

- *Putting parts in different orders.* Some groups experimented by starting with the story of the bird, or the extended image of hearing the typewriter and the boat. When we hear things in a different order, we notice new relationships; we learn more about the text.

- *Staging and interpretive movements.* One group had someone playing the father—walking meditatively around; another person playing the daughter holed up in a room—struggling with writing; another person acted out the trapped bird in a kind of dance. All this while a couple of others read the poem. A few adventuresome groups always try rendering pieces entirely with movement and sound—no words at all. This is interesting and fun. Remember, these performances are for people who already know the poem. For one enactment, a person who knew American Sign Language did a signed version while another person read the words; that was extraordinarily beautiful and moving.

- *Adding words—creating a dialogue with the poem.* One group added words for the daughter to speak. Some groups interjected some of their own interpretive responses, adding thoughts or memories or reactions of their own. In one performance, one person kept interjecting the phrase "Get a life, Dad!" (See Hales and Nelson in the Readings section.) There are limitless possibilities. Any strong reactions or even background material can be added to a performance to make it a *dialogue* between your voice and the voice of the poet.

After the renderings, do some freewriting about what you learned from working out your own rendering and seeing those of others.

This performative approach is helpful in thinking about the question of whether there is such a thing as a correct interpretation. As you'll see from the performances of your classmates, most sets of

---

Language as Play   Sound Effects

Create a kind of rendering or accompaniment to the poem consisting wholly of *sounds*. When students did this for the Richard Wilbur poem, some groups used the sound of a typewriter either intermittently or throughout the poem. Another got the sound of a bird banging against the window. One group made some abstract or nonrepresentational sound effects to go with the rendering.

words can be performed in more than one plausible way. Some texts lend themselves to a multiplicity of readings or interpretations (these are more "open" sets of words), while other texts seem more "closed" or determined and seem to ask for only a few or possibly only one interpretation. We can usually notice when a reading is implausible and notice the various degrees of pressure when a reading is pulling the text where it doesn't seem to want to go. But sometimes a very talented reader or actor can show us a new reading we never would have dreamed of and might even have called absurd, and succeed in making it seem absolutely plausible. For the purposes of this exercise, however, the goal is not right readings but variations in reading. It can be helpful to push and pull and even distort the text. Sometimes even a very "wrong" reading—satiric or parodic—can show us something in the words that we hadn't noticed.

Activity Three: Interpretation as the Creation of New Meaning

In schools and colleges people usually assume that writing about literature means writing some kind of essay of analysis or interpretation. But it doesn't have to work that way. When *poets* respond and write about a poem, their response often takes the form of another poem: some kind of answering poem that in some way relates to or bounces off the poem they read. The way they appreciate a poem is to do a piece of work that somehow shares the same thematic or formal space as the poem. They create a companion poem. Many of the famous poems we read and appreciate (and write essays about) are, directly or indirectly, companion pieces or response poems to previous poems. In effect, the poet is saying, "I found this poem powerful and enabling, and I will write this new poem somewhat in its shadow." Virginia Woolf wrote that the best way to understand a book is "not to read, but to write; to make your own experiment with the dangers and difficulties of words."

Perhaps you don't normally write poems and even find it a bit scary to think about doing so. This is true for both of us too; we are in no way poets. What helps us most if we want to write a poem is to find a poem that we like and connect with, and then use it or borrow from it: to use its theme or some of its words; to borrow some of its form or some of its spirit and energy; to ride on its coattails and make a poem of our own. What we find most useful is not deciding what the poem will be about beforehand, but letting the borrowed elements somehow lead us to start writing some lines and writing some more lines and seeing what this *new* poem wants to be about and where it wants to go. It's an exercise in letting the words or the structure lead us.*

Here are some suggestions for writing a poem in response to the Auden poem:

- *Borrow some of the texture* of Auden's poem to make your own. Try writing a poem that uses the rhythms of popular songs and poems. Auden seems to mix echoes of ballads and folk songs ("As I walked out one evening"), children's songs and nursery rhymes (Jack and Jill and the Giant—"And the river jumps over the mountain/ And the salmon sing in the street"), and popular songs in general. He also uses the rhymes and the sing-song three-beat line that go with those kinds of songs. You could draw on the same sources. But it would be just as good, if not better,

---

* We've learned about these techniques from Kenneth Koch, Theodore Roethke, and Charles Moran.

Exploring the Writing Process
Two Theories of Inspiration

There are two theories of inspiration. One idea is that poetry can actually be dictated to you, as it was to William Blake. You are in a hallucinated state, and you hear a voice or you are in communication with something outside—like James Merrill's new poem, which he says is dictated through the Ouija board by Auden and other people.

The other idea is Paul Valéry's, what he calls *une ligne donnée,* that you are given one line and you try to follow up this clue, pulling the whole poem out of it. My own experience is that a rhythm or something comes into my head which I feel I must do, I must write it, create it.

For example, I recall looking out of a railway window and seeing an industrial landscape, factories, slag heaps, and the line coming into my head: "A language of flesh and roses." The thought at the back of this was that the industrial landscape was a language, what people have made out of nature, the contrast of nature and the industrial, "A language of flesh and roses." The problem of the poem was to work this connection out, trying to go back to remember what you really thought at that instant, and trying to recreate it. If I think of a poem, I may spend six months writing, but what I am really trying to do is remember what I thought of at that instant.

Stephen Spender

to try for echoes, words, and rhythms from more recent popular songs that are loud in your head or that you think might be in the heads of people you would like to write for—even popular love songs or rock songs or rap. We strongly suggest that you not try for rhyme unless you enjoy it and are pretty good at it. Poems are often pulled down when rhymes don't come easily. Poems can be terrific without rhyme; plenty of songs don't rhyme.

- *Borrow some structural features* to lead you to a poem of your own. It needn't be about love. Here's one way to use Auden's structure: First, write a short section where you speak in the first person and name a time and a place—and overhear someone else saying or singing something. Second, write a section in the voice of that someone. Third, write a section that starts with "But" where an object or many objects ("all the clocks") reply or contradict the first speech. These words seem to be addressed directly to us ("O let not Time deceive you" "O stare, stare in the mirror"). Finally, make the last section an impersonal statement rather than spoken words addressed to someone. But it should use a number of words from preceding sections (Auden uses "lovers, clocks, river")—and one prominent word from the first stanza ("evening").

- *Simply make use of a grab bag of prominent elements.* Here are some elements you could use to spark your mind: Use the name of a street; name two places (continents?) in one sentence; use at least one surprising metaphor where something is something unexpected ("the crowds were fields of wheat"); use elements from one or two nursery rhymes; mention a road or path to somewhere and then describe that place ("a lane to the land of the dead. Where . . ."); somehow manage not too obtrusively to repeat words more often than usual (plunge, plunge; stare, stare; look, look, look; blessing, bless; stand, stand; crooked, crooked; late, late).

- *Use some actual words.* There are so many striking words here that if you use too many, you'll probably echo Auden too closely. But if you choose a set of six or eight, these could spark you into your own poem. The trick is to pick ones that are interesting but, in a way, random. Here is a possible set that could be generative: pavement, brimming, arch, China, conquer, shadow, coughs, basin, wrist, distress, scald. Or use your intuition to pick another set. However, try to pick ones that simply catch your eye before having any sense of what your poem will be about. Let the words lead you to your poem.

- *Use the theme.* Try writing a poem (it could be a prose poem) where there is some kind of meeting between a belief in love and a doubt that love is real or possible.

- *Reply*. Try writing a poem of reply. What does this poem lead you to want to say? Perhaps something about how this poem makes you feel? Something about your experience with love? A story of a very different dialogue about love?

What's crucial for this process of writing a poem is to give yourself permission to do something just for the heck of it—to see where the process leads you. Allow yourself to be dissatisfied—even embarrassed. When *we* do this, we have to force ourselves to keep writing, almost like freewriting, so that much of what we put down is simply junk or filler. We end up throwing away more than half of what we've written, but we didn't suffer to write it so it doesn't hurt. You have to be playful and not too reverent about the process of writing a poem.

After you have a draft, you can make big changes so that no one would ever see any relation to the Auden poem. But there's nothing wrong with leaving very direct links to his poem. It's an act of respect to write a poem that has echoes of someone else's poem. (If you have a hard time connecting to this poem, perhaps your teacher will let you write in response to a different one.)

MAIN ASSIGNMENT
An Exercise in Interpretation

Write an essay about the Auden poem. In your essay, see if you can somehow speak to the following three questions: What do you think the poem means or conveys? How does the poem function or mean or convey what it does? How did the activities of this workshop help

Exploring the Writing Process
Poem

How Poetry Comes to Me*

It comes blundering over the
Boulders at night, it stays
Frightened outside the

Range of my campfire
I go to meet it at the
Edge of the light.

Gary Snyder

*Try writing a poem with the same title—or perhaps change the second word of the title.

you (or not help you) come to your understanding of the poem? (Don't forget about the role of other people.)

Before we leave this workshop we want to reassure you that we're not trying to persuade you to go through these extensive processes every time you read something. We all often want to read quickly for pleasure. But these processes we are demonstrating here, once learned, will enrich your fast, casual reading. And if you have an assignment to interpret a piece of literature for a class, you might indeed find it helpful to go through all the response steps we've set up. Poetry might even be defined as language that's rich and well built enough that it invites the kind of reading and reflecting on your reading that we suggest here. The pleasures and the meanings in poems don't get "used up" in one reading.

Suggestions for Collaboration

Work with one to three others sharing all the writing you did in Activity One (movies of the mind while reading). Write a collaborative essay that compares and contrasts your reading processes. See if you can figure out any of the influences on the ways in which your minds worked similarly and ways in which they worked differently: for example, school experience, personality or character, family, gender, class, race, sexual orientation.

Sharing and Responding

For responses to your poem:
- Which of my words and images somehow linger, work, or have an impact on you?
- What meanings, feelings, and associations do those words produce?
- What new views, ideas, or insights does my poem give you about the Auden poem?

For responses to your essay:
- How do your reactions and understandings of the poem differ from mine?
- What new views, ideas, or insights does my essay give you about the Auden poem?
- What are some things that are "almost said" or implied in my essay?

For other techniques, see "Sharing and Responding" at the end of the book.

Process Journal and Cover Letter

- What did you learn about yourself as a reader? About the effect of life positions and life themes on how you read?
- What did you learn about yourself from the process of rendering or performing the poem? How did this change your reading?
- Reflect on your process of trying to produce a poem. What would it take to get you to do this more often?
- Reflect on the similarities and differences between your writing process and your reading process.
- How did you respond to the readings and interpretations of others? And they to yours? Do you tend to be a believer or a doubter of what other people say?
- How have your prior school experiences with literature influenced how you read and respond to literature?

For your cover letter, it's good to include some or all of your process writing. But don't forget to answer some cover letter questions. Here are the main ones: What is your main point and what effect are you trying to have on readers? What do you feel works best in your paper and where are you unsatisfied? What changes did you make on the basis of any feedback? And most important: What feedback do you want now from a reader? But your teacher may ask you particular cover letter questions that pertain to this assignment.

RUMINATIONS AND THEORY
About the Artificiality of Giving Movies of Your Mind While Reading

These exercises in the reading process might seem odd and artificial to you, so we want to spell out now why we are asking you to use them. Our goal is to *both* illustrate what you already do when you read—*and* help you read better in the future.

What You Already Do.   Yes, we keep interrupting you in the middle of your reading and asking you questions to write about, and so we are clearly producing an artificial reading process. We may cause you to think of things that you never would have thought of if you were just reading quietly on your own. But reflect for a moment about these things "we made you think of." We didn't give you anything but the poem; we didn't put anything in your mind that wasn't there already. Any "new" thoughts or memories must have been already in your mind. We merely interrupted your reading and made you pause so that more of what was in your mind came to conscious awareness.

Our point is that these unconscious reactions would *still* have influenced your reading subliminally—even if you read quickly without any interruptions. What's new in our exercise are not the thoughts and memories, but your *conscious awareness* of them.

For example, our artificial exercise may have triggered a memory about rabbits or about a time when someone read you the nursery rhyme about Jack and Jill. Those memories might not have come to mind during a fast reading, but they probably influenced that fast reading without your noticing it. Research on reading gives more and more evidence of how quick and active our thinking and remembering are when we read—how much goes on below the level of awareness. Since words never *contain* any meanings except for the ones we *put* there, what we put there must be based on all the thoughts, feelings, and experiences already inside us.

Think about where meaning comes from. There are no meanings in words; only in people. Meaning is what people bring to words; and the meanings people bring are their own meanings—amalgams of their own individual experiences. When readers see the word *chat,* for example, they will bring different memories and associations—all having to do with informal conversation. Some people may have a very warm, cozy feeling about chat. Others, however, might find the word irrevocably colored by an experience when a powerful person said, "I think we'd better go to my office and have a little chat." And yet a French reader will bring to those same four letters, c-h-a-t, meanings having to do with cats.

We might assume that the reading of straightforward prose is "regular reading," while the reading of difficult stories and poems is "irregular" or "exceptional." With difficult literature we have to stop and puzzle things out; we get one idea and then we have to change it when we get to something that contradicts it. But the process of reading difficult pieces simply shows us more nakedly the very same process that goes on quickly and subliminally in all reading.

What You Will Do in the Future: If you engage now and then in this artificial exercise—going slowly, pausing, looking inside at memories and associations, making hypotheses—you will learn to be more active and imaginative in your fast reading. You will learn to pay more attention to the words on the page and their relationships with each other; and you will pay more attention to the richness—the meanings, reactions, and associations—that you already bring to words. By being more skilled at the active and exploratory process of making meaning, you will simply understand more. You will be better at seeing the meaning even in very difficult pieces of writing.

Readings

The Writer   *Richard Wilbur*

*Richard Wilbur (b. 1921), a Pulitzer Prize–winning poet and former
Poet Laureate of the United States, is also a translator, a teacher, a
Broadway lyricist, a critic, an editor, and an author of children's books.*

In her room at the prow of the house
Where light breaks, and the windows are tossed with linden,
My daughter is writing a story.

I pause in the stairwell, hearing
From her shut door a commotion of typewriter-keys
Like a chain hauled over a gunwale.

Young as she is, the stuff
Of her life is a great cargo, and some of it heavy:
I wish her a lucky passage.

But now it is she who pauses,
As if to reject my thought and its easy figure.
A stillness greatens, in which

The whole house seems to be thinking,
And then she is at it again with a bunched clamor
Of strokes, and again is silent.

I remember the dazed starling
Which was trapped in that very room, two years ago;
How we stole in, lifted a sash

And retreated, not to affright it;
And how for a helpless hour, through the crack of the door,
We watched the sleek, wild, dark

And iridescent creature
Batter against the brilliance, drop like a glove
To the hard floor, or the desk-top,

And wait then, humped and bloody,
For the wits to try it again; and how our spirits
Rose when, suddenly sure,

It lifted off from a chair-back,
Beating a smooth course for the right window
And clearing the sill of the world.

It is always a matter, my darling,
Of life or death, as I had forgotten. I wish
What I wished you before, but harder.

Response to "The Writer": Movies of the Mind While Reading   *Elijah Goodwin*

[Written after reading only the first quarter of the poem]

The sea imagery gives the act of writing power. I feel as though his daughter is writing something passionate. I almost picture a ship in a storm or a ship crashing through large waves. She is adventuring and exploring through her writing. What she is writing is something that she believes in, is excited about, rather than an assignment or the like. The chain hauled over the gunwale represents the lifting of her mental anchor as she is free to write. It represents freedom of ideas and creativity. She has let go of the anchor that holds back the creativity.

[Written after reading only the second quarter of the poem]

Each moment in life is important and can be very incredible. Even though she is young, she has had a lot of experiences, good and bad, and she carries them with her. It is possible for a young person to have a more incredible meaningful life than an old person. Sometimes I feel that way myself. That if I died tomorrow, I would die contented, knowing I have lived a full life.

[After reading almost to the end of the poem]

It keeps reminding me of the subject that I have been thinking of, the struggle to live freely. We will continue to batter ourselves against the walls as the bird continues to struggle to make the wrong choices and to recover and try again. And perhaps we may make it to the freedom of flight before we hit that wall or window one too many times. To find that entry into the wide open.

[After finishing the poem]

The romance of the ocean has always held a place in my heart. When I was young and even now, I travel to the ocean often, so I reacted right away because of the powerful effect the ocean imagery had on me. Lately I have been almost obsessed with the idea of being free and exploring. Being open to experiences, opening my mind, taking my body to its physical limits. I have been looking for the ultimate sensory and mental overload. To experience things so purely that you threaten to just burn out. And this is the angle I approached this poem with. I pictured the girl freeing her mind from preconceived ideas and pressures and the blocks of society. It was easier for me to react to the poem in pieces than as a whole. It is because of the way I think. Quick, fleeting, powerful images, glimpses through a window at high speed. It is not a matter of attention span; it's just that simple is more powerful.

Response to "The Writer": Movies of the Mind While Reading   *Tassie Walsh*

The first thing I do is picture the scene. At first I imagine a young girl, but as I am told she types, I picture her to be a teenager in high school. She has a sunny room with her window open and the lace curtains blowing. It is late afternoon in the late spring or early summer. Her room has old teddy bears, mirrors, and pictures.

Her father is middle aged. He wears slacks and a shirt and a sweater without sleeves. The stairwell goes up then turns left. The stairs are carpeted beige and there are old family pictures on the wall going up.

I don't want to be here [at school]. I want to be in my sunny room. I want my home. I want warmth. I want my room. I want my bears and my mirrors and pictures. I want my dad to be interested in what I am doing.

It is about a wish for life. He wants his daughter to fly. He wants her to keep trying. It will be hard, she will fall, but he wishes her a lucky passage.

Collage Dialogue on "The Writer"   *Barbara Hales and Julie Nelson*

The father is proud of his daughter who has chosen the solitude of her room to write a story. He's curious and thinks she's too young to be interested in writing. She's excited, can't sleep and started writing even before the dawn arrived. She doesn't want to be disturbed and has sent the message out to her world by shutting the door. The keys continue at a steady pace. She's driven to get her thoughts and feelings onto the paper. The father stops by her door to listen. He continues to wonder what could possibly entice her from sleep at that early hour.

ALL THIS NOISE OF CHAINS!

WHY CAN'T HE GET ON WITH HIS OWN THING AND STOP FUSSING ABOUT HIS DAUGHTER?

I SENSE HIM THERE—OUTSIDE THE DOOR—

I WANT TO BASH HIS FACE IN.

Her struggle for freedom reminds him of the day they together witnessed the hurt and fear of a starling caught in that very room. They assisted only by raising the sash and staying present to send their healing energy to the bloody bird. They were delighted to watch it regain its strength and fly to freedom.

YUCK

"HUMPED AND BLOODY"—COME ON, IT WOULD DIE OF SHOCK IF IT WAS THAT BADLY OFF.

Collage Dialogue on "The Writer"   *continued*

HOW ABOUT FATHER OWNING HIS OWN FEELINGS. HE IS ASSUMING THE STRUGGLE IN HIS DAUGHTER—IT MAY OR MAY NOT BE TRUE.

THIS ASSUMPTION ANNOYS ME.

I IDENTIFY WITH THE DAUGHTER WHO WOULD BE FURIOUS IF SHE SENSED HER FATHER HOVERING OUTSIDE THE DOOR AND WOULDN'T BE ABLE TO WRITE.

Life will present traumas—even small things will sometimes feel like a matter of life or death. The father would like to protect her from the harshness and pain of life's experiences. But from the wisdom of his years, he knows wishing her a lucky passage is all we can ever do for another person.

. . . the concerned, supportive parent . . .

. . . the child fighting, albeit prematurely, for her independence . . .

. . . the eternal "generation gap". . .

. . . the eternal parent/child dynamic . . .

Some Thoughts about "The Writer" on the Occasion of the Death of Isaac Bashevis Singer   *Laura Wenk*

I read the poem "The Writer" by Richard Wilbur just after hearing of the death of the great Yiddish writer, Isaac Bashevis Singer. My interpretation of the poem is wound around the feelings I had at that moment.

For me the poem is about the ways that, while the young and old cannot always truly communicate—cannot be fully in each other's worlds—there can be a knowing. There can be a true, felt sense about each other's lives that can be gratifying, that can fill our hearts and give us hope. So, it is a poem about connections, although imperfect ones. As such, it is also a poem about being able to let go and feel oneself as separate.

The father in the poem had given as much as he could to his daughter. He had helped her build a solid sense of self and let her follow her own heart. To my mind this means that, among other things, he must have given her a sense of the past—of who she is as understood by what has happened to those who came before her. For growth and understanding of self is connected to understanding one's parents, and them their own parents—so a chain is built.

In reading this poem, I became the daughter. Isaac Bashevis Singer became the father. He stood watching through the door along with other people who have been important in creating an atmosphere in which I could grow to be a strong, independent person. I sat inside typing, secure enough in my past to feel the turbulence of the present and dream of the future.

Some Thoughts about "The Writer" on the Occasion of the Death of Isaac Bashevis Singer   *continued*

Even though I must do my own writing, I want to know that I am not entirely alone. I want to know that there are people near me—people who have come before and will come after—who are thinking clearly and acting out of a place of conscience.

I want to feel a thread running from the past to the knot where I hold it and onward into the future. I want this thread to sometimes become a live wire. There have been people who can turn on the current for me. They tell me that, while I, like the starling in Wilbur's poem, must find my way through that window alone, they have opened the window wider for me and will watch my flight through it.

There have been writers, like I. B. Singer, who have helped make the world of my grandmothers real to me—that have let me look back through that window to understand just how I got into this room to begin with. There have also been family members, friends, and political activists whose presence, stories, and work have strengthened my understandings, and made solid the ground on which I walk. I mourn the death of each living link to this rich past, and worry that in their absence the looking back will become impossible—the thread will be severed.

My grandmothers formed another link to a much more personal history—a family history. Each in her own way helped me to see patterns woven by the threads of their sisters and brothers, parents and grandparents. They wove a nest from which it was safe for me to venture outward—no matter how tentative my starts.

I don't think I will ever understand how my grandmothers found the strength to test their own wings in an air so filled with blood—so many losses. What lampposts lit their way through pogroms and gas chambers? How did they manage to trust that I could have a "lucky passage"?

Elsie, you were brave to open a window for me that you were too frightened to look out yourself.

Gerti, I still plant columbine and violets for you, and the smell of linden brings me to your side.

Persuading and Arguing

Essential Premises

Persuasion and argument share certain traits, but they also differ in important ways.

The first step in persuasion is getting someone to listen. Persuasion relies less on formal rational argument and more on reaching out to an audience, particularly through appeals to experience and emotion.

An effective argument presents a point of view through careful reasoning, but there is no single *right* way to argue. In fact, the nature of argument differs from field to field.

There are powerful procedures for working on argument that don't depend on the formal study of logic.

Good arguments don't have to be aggressive or confrontational.

Main Assignment Preview

The emphasis in this workshop is first on writing persuasively and then on translating your persuasive piece into argument, so the *main assignment* is in two parts. Your persuasive piece will take the form of a letter to the editor of your school or local newspaper. Using the same subject, but perhaps selecting a different audience, you will then write an argument that lays out carefully your reasons for your point of view on this subject. As an alternative, you may wish instead to analyze someone else's already written argument on this subject.

We'd like your thinking on persuasion to be grounded in your own experience, not just in theories. Therefore, please stop now and freewrite (this will remain private writing) about an occasion in your own life when someone's words played a big role in affecting how you felt or thought about something—or even changed your action. Anyone who has done this has persuaded you. Or write about an occasion when *your* words affected someone else's thinking, feeling, or behavior. Tell the story of this event in some detail. What really happened? And then speculate about how or why these words managed to be persuasive. If something else besides logic and hard evidence was important, what was this something else?

Evaluating Letters to the Editor

Consider the fact that more people read letters to the editor in the newspaper than read the news or editorials or even sports. What distinguishes these published letters is that they are short, and they consist of people speaking out to others. If you want the quickest and best way to affect the thinking of the community you are part of, get a good letter published in your student or city newspaper or in a magazine that publishes letters. Here are some examples:

To the Editor:

The women's magazine editors whose Sept. 25 letters criticize Elizabeth Whelan's Sept. 8 Op-Ed article on their health reporting ignore the main point: it is contradictory for magazines presumably concerned about women's health to carry advertising for a product, namely, cigarettes, that brings disease, miscarriages, premature widowhood or death to women.

They declare "we have cautioned women repeatedly about the hazards of smoking," but how can anyone take them seriously when their advertising promotes smoking? If these magazines have women's best interests at heart, they will drop their cigarette ads.

Louise P. Dudley, *New York Times,* October 12, 1992

To the Editor:

(A previous letter writer) feels women with children should be prohibited from going on spaceflights. If there is to be such a rule, it should also prohibit men with children from going on spaceflights. The loss of a father is just as bad as the loss of a mother.

Daily News, March 20, 1986

To the Editor:

The Oct. 17 killing of a Japanese exchange student in Baton Rouge, La., described in "Another Magnum, Another Victim" (Op-Ed, Oct. 31) could not have been prevented by restricting the Second Amendment rights of Americans to ownership of hunting weapons alone, as the authors recommend. Hunting arms are intended to kill with a single shot, and the .44 Magnum round used in this killing is widely used in low-power hunting rifles. It is unproductive to blame American attitudes about guns for a problem that is rooted in white American attitudes toward members of other races.

I have little doubt that the young victim, Yoshihiro Hattori, would still be alive today had he been as white as his companion the evening of his murder. The white friend of the victim was alongside Mr. Hattori the instant the victim was gunned down, and so gives witness to the murder.

Deterring bias crime by vigorously prosecuting gross incidents such as this one will save more lives than retricting a homeowner's right of self-defense.

Ludwig R. Vogel, *New York Times,* November 1, 1992
Note: *The writer was, at the time of writing, chairman of the New York State Libertarian Party.*

To the Editor:

Mothers Against Drunk Driving Long Island supports New York City's initiative in seizing the cars of drivers arrested on drunk driving charges. There's no question that these offenders are using their vehicles as lethal weapons.

The more than 16,000 deaths every year in the United States from drunk driving accidents attest to the horrific toll of this violent crime. We hope this initiative will lead to more rigorous enforcement of current state law that already allows forfeiture of vehicles owned by repeat offenders.

New York City's initiative will empower the police to seize vehicles from drunk drivers on the first offense. A "first offense" does not necessarily mean the first time an offender is driving drunk. It means that it is the first time that he or she has been caught. The typical offender drives drunk between 200 and 2,000 times before he or she is arrested. Too often the first time they are caught is when someone has been injured or killed. It is better for the offender to lose a car than for an innocent victim to lose a life.

The initiative does involve some legal complications, and even logistic concerns—where do you keep all the impounded cars? But complications or inconvenience should not deter justice; and certainly should not deter any reasonable and positive action that can save lives.

In 1998, law enforcement agencies on Long Island made an estimated 13,000 Driving-While-Intoxicated arrests. MADD Long Island will monitor the progress of this, creative, life-saving initiative by New York City as a possible way to strengthen the dedicated work of law enforcement on Long Island.

Peter Jones, *Huntington Station Newsday,* February 1, 1999
The writer is president of MADD Long Island.

Questions for Evaluating Letters to the Editor

By yourself—or better yet with your group—answer as many of the following questions as possible. (Your teacher may specify how many of the letters you should read for this part of the workshop.)

1. *Most persuasive.* Which letter persuaded you the most? the least? Answer the question using quick intuitive judgment. After answering the following questions, come back to this one. You may discover you've changed your mind.

2. *Claim.* For each letter, state the claim (the point the writer wishes to make) in as short a sentence as possible.

3. *Support.* What is the support for the claim of each letter? Try to summarize it in a sentence. What do you think the writer was relying on: logic, information, example, emotion, language, or something else?

4. *Language.* In each case, did the language add to or detract from the writer's presentation? Try to be specific about exactly which language had what kind of effect on you.

5. *Your position.* What was your position on the topic of the letter before reading it? Did the letter change your position? What influence did it have on your thinking and feeling even if you didn't change your mind?

6. *Listening and trust.* Which one made you listen most, even if it didn't change your thoughts or feelings? Why? Was it because you trusted the writer?

7. *Assumptions.* What did each letter writer seem to be assuming as true? Do you agree with these assumptions? What does that have to do with your reactions?

8. *Audience.* For each letter, do you think you're the audience the writer had in mind? How does that affect whether or not you're persuaded? If you're the wrong audience, what sort of audience do you think the writers had in mind?

9. *Voice.* Go around your group and read each of the letters aloud at least twice. Does hearing the words change your reactions? "Put on" or "enter into" the voice you hear, and write as though you were that person.

Here is what one of our students, Janine Ramaz, wrote as an evaluation of the first three of the letters above:

> People who write short letters to the editors of their local newspapers know that they have to make their points briefly and clearly. Readers of newspaper Letters to the Editor sections are mainly interested in knowing what their fellow citizens think on issues the newspaper has printed articles on. If they want to read long, detailed arguments, they will look for them elsewhere in the paper. So letter writers must use few words to get across their opinions. In this paper, I'm going to look at how three short letters do this.
>
> All the letter writers know that they have to say right away what letter or article they're writing about. So they identify that in the very first sentence. This is good because then people who aren't interested in these particular subjects will probably go on

and read something else. But then when the letter writer says also briefly what the content is, readers who missed the other letter or the article but are interested will go ahead and read the letter. So every one of the writers of the letters I'm looking at says quickly what the issue is.

This issue is the subject of the letter. The issues of my three letters are advertising cigarettes in a woman's magazine, parents on spaceflights, and owning guns. I believe that the most effective of these three letters is the one about spaceflight.

The first of the letters I read, the one about women's smoking, was really too long. The writer of this letter made the same point twice. Furthermore, the second time she says it she uses the words "but how can anyone take them seriously." I hear a whiny voice here which makes the whole letter less strong.

The third of these three letters is criticizing those who are using a particular unfortunate incident to argue against gun ownership. To me, the argument is weak because the writer avoids the whole issue of banning all kinds of guns which might have saved the young man's life. Since I was sure the writer would not approve of banning all guns, his point got weaker for me. And, too, not all accidental gun shootings involve people of different races.

The letter I thought most effective was also the shortest. The writer made his point (I'm not really sure if the writer was male or female because there was no name) in plain simple language: "The loss of a father is just as bad as the loss of a mother." Furthermore I think this letter will have a broader appeal than the other two because the first one would appeal mostly to women and perhaps turn men and nonfeminist women off. The third letter appeals mainly to gun lovers, though it would also have some appeal to those with strong beliefs in good racial relations.

The letter about spaceflights really made me think about something I hadn't thought of before and even to come to a new conclusion that parents shouldn't go on spaceflights. It should just be single people or married people with no children. That's the main reason I consider this letter the best: it made me do some thinking after I read it and didn't burden me with unnecessary words.

Conclusion about Informal Persuasion

On the basis of these examples and the answers you came up with to all the questions, can you reach some tentative conclusions about what is most helpful and least helpful in short informal persuasion—

in trying to get readers who disagree with you to listen to you? In trying to get an audience to look and perhaps act in a particular way? What do you see as the chief difference between how these letters persuade? Keep in mind that complete arguments that "prove" that *our side* is right and *their side* is wrong are usually effective only for our side: for gatherings of our team to help us clarify our thinking, to help us remember why we believe what we believe, and to make us feel better about our position. They are seldom read by the other team (except when they are doing research about why we are wrong).

But this view is not so discouraging if you look closely at how words affect people. After all, it would be odd if people changed their minds all at once. And we see that though progress in persuasion is always slow—and we may not be good at creating airtight arguments—the main act in persuasion is something we *are* all good at: sensing the other person and somehow reaching out and getting the other person to *listen*. Best of all, persuasion doesn't require length. The main task is to get readers to open the door; too many words only make resistant readers close the door tighter.

MAIN ASSIGNMENT I
Writing a Letter to the Editor

Step One: Writing the Letter

Spend some time reading and scanning newspapers: neighborhood papers, local papers, school newspapers. Pick several issues out of these newspapers that you feel strongly about and begin freewriting, telling why you feel strongly about them and why you think others ought to as well. In your freewriting, concentrate on *your* reasons for your strong feelings on your topic. Don't think yet about persuading others. It's your own emotional and intellectual commitment that you need to tap now.

One approach is to think back to the time you first became aware of your feelings about the issues you want to write on. Describe the experience that led to your stance. Writing out this experience will help you get a firm grip on why you believe as you do.

Push yourself to write at least 10 or 15 minutes on each topic you select. You might even want to rant and rave about your topics a bit—no harm done; this is not what you're actually going to send off, and the ranting will help you get at the core of your feelings and thoughts. After you've done this exploratory private writing, set it aside for a bit—even an hour helps. Read it over when you come back and decide which issue now appeals to you the most, the one you want to use for your final letter. Isolate the point you want to make about this issue, and state it as directly and concisely as possible so that you can incorporate it into a letter.

Now you're ready to write a first draft for sharing with your classmates. And you must begin to think about your audience. Chances are you may want to address the same audience as the one addressed by the article you're reacting to. Other students in the class can help you characterize this audience on the basis of the original article.

Another good way to approach this first draft is to come up with some possible objections to your views. You may or may not have done this as you were freewriting. But now you can make a list of all the reasons that might keep people from accepting your assertions. To make these clear, try writing a dialogue with yourself where you speak on both sides of your issue. You can, of course, enlist a classmate to write out the opposing side. (For more on the specifics of writing collaborative dialogue, see Workshop 4.)

Exploring the Writing Process
On the Persuasive Power of Grades

Professors' grades even had the power to change my own opinion about what I'd written. For example, last semester I wrote a nice paper on *The Faerie Queene.* I put a lot of effort into it and really cared about the subject matter. . . . However, I received a fairly mediocre grade, the same grade I received on a previous paper that I had spent much less time on. I thought to myself, "Well, all that work went for nothin'." Immediately, I negated the paper just because of the grade I received on it. I started to believe that my paper was worthless.

However, looking back on it, I now realize that the paper helped me appreciate *The Faerie Queene.* I don't believe that I would have read it as closely, cared about what the story was telling me, if I hadn't been writing a paper on the poem. In short, I took ownership of the work and I made sure that the paper remained mine as well. I did not let my professor kidnap my paper by putting a grade on it. The paper was important to me, the writer, and that's what matters.

Jerry Boyd

After you've done your freewriting or dialogue, decide on your focus and whether you want to take objections into consideration. It's not *necessarily* a good idea to answer opposing opinions; sometimes too much responding to objections can make your piece sound defensive, and you are better off with a shorter and more direct piece.

Step Two: Writing Your Explanation

After reading your letter to your group and perhaps discussing it with them, try freewriting answers to the following questions:

- What is my purpose in writing this piece?
- Who is my audience? How do I expect them to react? Why would they react this way?
- What am I assuming to be true? How does that work for my piece?
- What sort of voice have I embedded in my letter? Why did I choose this voice? (We suggest you read your piece aloud and exaggerate the voice you think is there.)
- What claim am I making? How am I supporting it?
- What decisions did I make about the language of my letter? What was the basis for these decisions?

Through your reflections on all these questions, you should be able to produce a solid first draft to share with your classmates.

Step Three: Publication

Your teacher may ask you to revise your letter and send it out for publication. If that is the assignment, your class may want to keep a folder or notebook with copies of all the letters after they've been mailed to the chosen publications. To this folder, everyone can add copies of letters that do get published in addition to any responses to them.

Moving to Argument

As we talked to you about persuasion, we emphasized the central skill in persuasion as getting someone to *listen*—to open the door of his mind; we downplayed longer, more formal, carefully reasoned arguments. But obviously there are certain situations where it is valuable to use a long, careful argument. We turn now to a consideration of such arguments. Our first goal is to help you see through any essay to the skeleton of reasoning at its heart in order to better evaluate the arguments of others and to construct better arguments of your own.

We have another goal here too; namely, for you to become more sophisticated about the *nature* of arguments, to become more critical as you read and listen to arguments. That is, even though argument is a subject complex enough for a whole book—indeed for a whole discipline (called logic or rhetoric)—we can give you substantial help with it in this workshop.

Analyzing an Argument

Summaries of the rules of reasoning tend to be wrong unless they are long and complex enough to describe many, many exceptions. Reasoning is too complicated; the effectiveness of reasons in *particular* arguments depends on too many variables. For this workshop, then, instead of trying to give you brief rules, we'll help you harness and extend your *tacit knowledge* (which is enormous and complex): that shrewd common sense you have built up over years of practical reasoning.

We present here a simple but powerful method for working on reasoning or arguments. You can learn to use it best if you practice it first on someone else's writing. After learning to use this method with the writing of others, you'll be able to apply it to your own writing. For practice, you'll find several examples at the end of this workshop.

To begin work on your own project, you will first need to locate an argument on the subject you focused on for your persuasive letter. Thus, you may need to do a bit of research. We speak at much greater length about research in Workshop 11, but for now, do not hesitate to enlist the support of the reference librarians at your college or local library. And, certainly, if you are working collaboratively with one or more others in your writing class, you can share the task of tracking down an appropriate piece of argument for analysis.

The word "analysis" implies two different tasks:
* *Breaking down* an argument into its parts. This is a *descriptive* task of learning how to isolate, identify, and understand the main elements of an argument.
* *Assessing* the effectiveness of an argument. This is an *evaluative* task.

It helps to realize that the first task—seeing what the elements of an argument are—is actually more important and more feasible than the second task of trying to evaluate the effectiveness of those elements. Evaluating an argument is usually a matter of unending dispute, whereas seeing it clearly is something you can manage. You can often get agreement among readers about what a reason is and what supports that reason, even though they can't agree on how persuasive the reason is.

Breaking Down an Argument into Its Parts

1. Look at the Main Claim, Reasons, and Support

Main Claim.   Decide what the main claim, the point the writer is most strongly arguing for, is and summarize it in one sentence. Perhaps the main claim is obvious right from the start ("I wish to argue in favor of the value of sports for education") and remains clear throughout. But sometimes the claim is not so clear; there may be slippage between an earlier statement of the claim or thesis and the final summary statement.

Take care to summarize the main claim in the simplest language you can manage; wording counts a lot. There's a crucial difference between saying "Terrorism can be countered without violence" and "Terrorism can be reduced if the democratic nations of the world take certain firm actions." Make a note if you find a problem determining the main claim: if, for example, the writer changes claims or if you think the real claim is different from what the writer says it is. You might decide there are actually two slightly different arguments in the piece you're analyzing.

If it's hard to decide on the main claim, go on to the next step and come back later.

Reasons.   Read through the piece again and decide what you think are the principal reasons that argue for the main claim you have identified—or tentatively identified. It's possible to pick out reasons even when you're unsure of the main claim. Summarize each reason in a *simple short sentence.*

For a three-page essay, you could choose three main reasons— or ten. It's a question of how closely you want to examine the thinking. Use your judgment. Try it out different ways.

List these reasons in the order you find them. If you are aiming to revise a piece of your own, you can reorder them later if you wish.

Support.   For each reason, what support is given? Support might take the form of evidence, illustrative examples, anecdotes, even other smaller subreasons that you didn't list as major reasons.

2. Look at Assumptions

What assumptions or unstated reasons does the argument seem to make? Read through the argument once more with only this subtle question in mind: What did the writer seem to take for granted? Assumptions are slippery and often insidious because the writer gets them into the reader's head without saying them. And if you share the writer's assumptions, you'll have an even harder time uncovering them. For example, the following assumptions might function as un-stated reasons in an argument: "What is modern is better than what is old-fashioned"; "Saving time is always a good thing."

To find assumptions it helps to imagine what kind of person is making the argument—perhaps even make an exaggerated picture of him in your mind—and try to think of what that kind of person takes for granted. Finding assumptions in a piece of our own writing is par-ticularly difficult because we usually don't realize we have them. They're just there. It's best to seek help from other readers as you search for assumptions in your own writing.

3. Think about Readers or Audience

What is the implied audience? Does the writer seem to be talking to people who already agree or to people who don't agree? to peers? professionals? teachers? to a large or a small audience?

How adversarial is the writer? Does he take an either/or stand, in-sisting that others have to be wrong if he's right? Does he use a lot of energy in showing that others are wrong?

How does the writer *treat* the audience? What's his voice or stance? Is he respectful? talking down? distant? hesitant? To get at this, two or more of you can read the argument aloud. Think about your own reactions. Did the piece annoy you, make you angry, defensive?

Assessing the Effectiveness of an Argument

Look back at what you have figured out so far: the reasons, the sup-ports, the assumptions, and the audience implications. Try to decide on the effectiveness of each one. This is the messy and arguable part; there are no rules for what works and what doesn't. Different arguments and

Exploring the Writing Process
On Trusting the Act of Writing

Anybody who finds himself in this situation of writing to a prescribed notion or to illustrate or to fill in what he already knows should stop writing. A writer has got to trust the act of writing to scan all his ideas, passions, and convictions; but these must emerge from the work, be *of* it.

E. L. Doctorow

supports work for different readers. Some people are impressed by tight logic; others are made suspicious by it. But at least you are looking at smaller elements, and so judgments are a bit more manageable. A few techniques might help:

- Look for counterarguments, counterevidence, or attacks that could be made against each reason, support, or assumption. That is, play the doubting game with each element.
- Ask what kind of person would agree and what kind of person would disagree with each reason, support, or assumption. What kind of person would do or think what the writing seems to be urging? This humanizing approach sometimes opens doors.
- See Section 10 in "Sharing and Responding," "Skeleton Feedback and Descriptive Outline," for an example of this procedure used on a sample essay.

If you have done a careful job with the main task of summarizing, then the task of evaluating becomes more manageable.

MAIN ASSIGNMENT II
Writing, Revising, and Analyzing Your Own Argument

Step One: Building an Argument

Since you've already done a fair amount of thinking about your subject as you wrote and discussed your letter to the editor, you probably feel quite satisfied with your point of view on it. You're convinced you know what is right and you want to convince others. But to create a reasonable argument, you need to see the point of view of others. *Imagine* someone who disagrees with you. Perhaps you can think about what kind of life experience would lead someone to feel differently than you do. Be careful not to characterize that person as stupid; you need someone intelligent and fair-minded if you're going to get a useful dialogue in which you move back and forth between your ideas and the ideas of that imagined other person. Of course, if you can find someone in your class who disagrees with you, you can write a collaborative dialogue. Make it a dialogue in which you listen to each other, not one in which you try to shoot each other down.

Your dialogue should help you come to a clear position on your issue. But it may also lead you to modify your stance somewhat. Just keep in mind that a clear position doesn't necessarily have to be a definite pro or con position. You can write a good argument for a position something like this: "We need to understand better the place of competitive sports in education," as well as for the position either that competitive sports are good for education or that they are bad for education.

Once you have your position, you can complete your draft. It's sometimes possible to produce an effective argument by smoothing your dialogue, removing digressions, elaborating on significant points, and providing transitions, an introduction, and a conclusion. In effect, you will be presenting a narrative of the development of your thinking.

If you're aiming for a more traditional essay, you can isolate significant points in your dialogue and build an informal outline before completing your draft. Notice how Kimberly Graham builds her argument at the end of this workshop.

Step Two: Revising Your Own Argument

Use the analytic procedure we set forth earlier to revise your argument. Since you are working on your own piece, however, you can't just stop with deciding what's strong and weak in your piece; you need to figure out how to improve it.

Here are a few suggestions:

- When you list main reasons, write each one on a 3 × 5 card or on a half-sheet of paper. This way you will find it easier to play with a different order of points or to restructure the whole piece.
- Define your main claim. If you are not sure, try a bit more exploratory writing.
- Finally, figure out the best order for your argument. Even though an argument operates in the realm of reasoning, this doesn't mean that there's some perfect order you have to find. There are always a host of possible organizations or sequences that could be effective.

Arguments are not necessarily more effective if they present reasons step by step in the most logical sequence, as in a geometry textbook. Obviously it pays to hide the logic in a poor argument, but even a strong argument is sometimes clearer and more persuasive if presented differently from the way a logic or geometry text would present it. So try different orders; you can start with the most powerful reason, or end with it, or give reasons in the order you thought of them (with a kind of narrative thread), or arrange them by resemblance.

In short, don't feel you have to have mastered logic to be good at this process. Use your intuition; follow hunches. Of course intuition alone can be wrong. That's why you need the two powerful tools we've suggested here: an X-ray of the skeleton of reasons in the argument and an assessment of the effectiveness of these reasons. And don't forget the value of collaboration in doing all of this.

Writing as Play   Writing Extreme Arguments

Instead of writing a serious letter to the editor or a serious argument, try extremes. Example: "Athletics and competitive sports are so important to education that we should make them the focus of college. Let's eliminate English and math classes; who uses that stuff, anyway?—but almost all of us are going to be involved in sports in some way all our lives—as participants or observers." And so forth. Another example, perhaps as main support to your argument: "A recent survey of college undergraduates uncovers an important truth: Watching team sports is the most popular college activity. We know that everyone is more likely to hang in there when doing something they really enjoy. If watching team sports became the central activity on a college campus, the president and other administrators would no longer have to worry about attrition; alumni financial contributions would undoubtedly also increase dramatically."

Suggestions for Collaboration

Any one of the possible assignments listed in this workshop can be begun and completed collaboratively, discussing each step as you go. Such a process gives you the opportunity to experience directly how productive it is to do joint thinking. But you can also work separately at the beginning (each write a letter and explanation or each take one aspect of the analysis or construction of your argument) and then compare notes and decide whether to go your own ways or actually produce something jointly written.

Sharing and Responding

With persuasive texts in particular, we need to know what readers' reactions are. Thus, the main feedback technique might be "Movies of the Reader's Mind" (Section 7 of "Sharing and Responding"). This sort of feedback encourages readers to start by telling you their original opinion on your topic. The early forms of feedback (Sections 1 through 5) are useful for early drafts—helping you develop your own thinking. Getting people to describe your voice tells you how trustworthy you sound (Section 6). "Believing" feedback can help you develop your argument further, while "doubting" can help you see what objections readers could raise (Section 9). Certainly you can ask for feedback on your letter by suggesting that readers use the letter analysis we include in the workshop, and on your argument by suggesting that they use our analysis procedure.

When doing sharing and responding on the assignments in this workshop, you should try to give readers written texts, particularly for later drafts, because it's difficult as a reader to follow prose closely unless it can be read. It probably makes sense for readers to give you feedback in written form too—keeping the tape recorder as an option.

Process Journal and Cover Letter

- How did you choose your topic for the letter assignment? Did you find yourself believing your assertions more and more as you wrote—or less and less? What's the significance of this change?
- When persuading or arguing (either orally or in writing), did you find yourself putting more emphasis on why your own view was better or on why the other views were wrong? How did this affect your writing for this workshop?
- Do you find yourself more comfortable working with short, informal persuasive pieces or longer, more careful arguments? What was different for you about doing these two pieces?

For your cover letter, it's good to include some or all of your process writing. But don't forget to answer some cover letter questions. Here are the main ones: What is your main point and what effect are you trying to have on readers? What do you feel works best in your paper and where are you unsatisfied? What changes did you make on the basis of any feedback? And most important: What feedback do you want now from a reader? But your teacher may ask you particular cover letter questions that pertain to this assignment.

RUMINATIONS AND THEORY

Informal Persuasion and Formal Argument

We find it useful to lay out two opposite answers to the question of how words can persuade. At one extreme is the _extended, formal argument_—the careful, elaborated "proof"—in which you are as logical as possible and you don't resort at all to feelings or emotional, persuasive language. At the other extreme is _informal persuasion_—more intuitive and experiential. This kind of persuasion doesn't try to mount a full argument; in fact it may not use an argument at all, but simply convey an important piece of information or tell a story.

Extended formal argument requires readers to read carefully and at length. They've got to be interested enough in you or in what you are saying to give you lots of time and attention. Extended, careful argument is what you might be expected to write for an audience that is *expert* or *professional*—for example, if you were writing a report for a college task force about the location of a new building or about a particular health care plan. Such an audience isn't interested in emotional arguments or in being persuaded. You don't have to coax them to read and to think carefully about the matter; they're already interested in figuring out what's the best view. It's their job to read with care. They want good analysis and good reasons. If they find you trying to persuade them with an emotional appeal instead of reasons and evidence, they'll likely start to distrust you and say, "What is this pesky writer trying to hide? What are the 'real' reasons he's covering up?" Clever persuasion gets in their way.

Informal persuasion, at the other extreme, is the kind of thing you find in editorials, leaflets, advertisements, short spoken interchanges, and of course letters to the editor in newspapers. It's usually shorter than formal argument, settling for making a couple of the best points, and perhaps giving a reason, some information, and some personal experience all wrapped up together. Often this kind of argument doesn't try to *change* someone's thinking but just to plant a seed. This is the kind of piece you need to write if you are trying to reach readers who have no special reason or commitment to read what you've written.

Brevity is the most common solution to the problem of readers who are liable to wander away at any moment. Whatever you want to say to such an audience, you have to say it fast. You can't take it as your goal to completely change their thinking. Planting a seed or opening a door is probably the best you can hope for.

But informal arguments aren't always short. The crucial thing that marks informal argument is a decision to forgo full argument and instead to *reach* or *interest* readers, perhaps by getting them to experience something or by telling a story. Again, for example, *Uncle Tom's Cabin* is a story that functions as a piece of persuasion, and it had a powerful effect on national sentiment about slavery before the Civil War. Informal persuasion may make points, but more often it succeeds by conveying *experience* or appealing fairly strongly to readers' emotions.

Nonadversarial Argument, Reasoning, and Grammar

Nonadversarial Argument

"Construct a thesis; state it forcefully; line up evidence to prove that your thesis is correct; prove that contrary opinions are wrong; conclude by restating your thesis." Are these the kinds of directions you've received for writing an argument? Writing that is structured this way is often seen as the only valid kind of argument—at times, as the only valid kind of writing.

We are not going to question the validity of adversarial arguments absolutely, for we recognize that there are contexts in which such a form is the most effective one. But we do question its universality as the best (sometimes the only) form taught in schools.

This model of persuasion and argument seems to be grounded in either/or, right/wrong, good/evil stances: "If I am right, you have to be wrong." Consider the result of these approaches: The reader who thinks differently has to define herself as wrong or stupid or bad before she can take your position seriously. This explains why most persuasive pieces and arguments are exercises in wasted energy and tend to become mere displays of the ability to follow prescribed form. We'd like to push for a different conception of argument, a less aggressive, less adversarial conception.

In truth, there may be a way in which writing by definition is monologic and authoritarian—after all, there's one voice speaking. And while you're reading what someone else has written, it has more power than you do because you can't answer it and argue with it and make it change its mind. This power can have two opposing results: Either we can succumb and be submissive to what we're reading, not question it at all, or we can resist it—perhaps even overdo our resistance—because we resent our inability to express our opinion to the author. We can even have both of these reactions to the same piece. The more strongly the author presents opinions, the more likely we are to have these reactions. The question is, "What effect does the author's opinion have on us?" We would answer our own question by saying "Very little." If that's the case, the writer has not accomplished much.

One way to encourage dialogue is to contextualize what you're arguing for. Arguments that are absolute—"My point is true for all people in all situations at all times!"—probably provoke the most resistance from readers. If you can set what you're arguing for in a context and acknowledge that what you believe is conditioned by certain circumstances and experiences and present those, you may provoke less resistance from a reader.* A reader can enter into the dialogue by bringing up other circumstances and experiences. (In Workshop 11 we stress the importance of contextualizing all research,

---

*We have (we hope) provided contextuality for the arguments we're constructing here. See the second paragraph of this section. Do you think that's a useful strategy here? What was your reaction to that paragraph?

of recognizing the limits within which all research functions and thus the limits to what one can conclude. This same strategy is important in argument, too.)

Does this mean that you can't argue for something if you believe it's absolutely true: the existence of a supreme being, the necessity for preserving the natural environment, the value of loving others, and so forth? No, of course not. What it does mean is that you're more likely to be genuinely listened to if you say something like, "This is what I believe and this is why I believe it" rather than "I'm right, you're wrong, and this is why." Again, argument doesn't always have to be the aggressive sort that hits readers forcefully over the head. An argument for your point of view can be just as effective, perhaps even more effective, if you think of your reader as a partner in discussion and your aim as a desire for conversation that will result in your both being better informed about the issue.

All of us have a much better chance of being persuasive if we can present a train of thought that says, in effect, "I'm not asking you to give up your beliefs; you can think whatever you like." We might even go so far as to say, "I'll bet your beliefs or opinions make a lot of sense. Continue to think whatever you want. But let me show you some of my thinking that I'll bet you'll find useful and interesting. Don't worry if what I say seems to contradict what you think. We might both be right in some way that we can't yet understand." This approach invites dialogue.

If it's true that you want your opponent to listen to you, then you have to listen to him. While you're drafting an argument, you can create an opponent as we suggested in this workshop. Writing out his side of the issue will make you a better proponent of your position.* Paradoxically, you have a greater chance of arguing successfully with others the more you can enter into *their* position. What you are trying to produce in readers is a glimmer of feeling that says, "Hey, this writer isn't crazy. I can really see why he feels that way." It can be scary for readers to enter into the skin of "the enemy," especially if they think that position is immoral, uninformed, or stupid. The scariness comes from the fear: "Well, if they are right, even a little bit right, then I must be wrong." But this isn't true. It often happens that two opinions or positions that appear to be opposite—and that make people fight tooth and nail—can *both* be right in certain senses. In

---

*Notice the paragraph following this one in which we briefly present arguments in opposition to our own. Does this make you feel more or less favorable to our point of view.

short, you can argue your position without having to argue that the other position is wrong.

We've heard the claim that in beginning writing courses, a teacher's chief goal must be to prepare students for the writing they will do in other courses as they move through their college years. Those who make this claim then claim additionally that these other courses usually will ask for a strong statement of a main point backed up by a logical ordering of reasons and a final forceful conclusion. We're not in a position to deny this claim; that's why we can't and won't make a universal argument against the need to teach such a form. But we do question whether the form is as uniform as some textbooks and teachers say it is. Our experience with writing-across-the-discipline programs and writing-in-the-discipline programs doesn't always support this claim. And, furthermore, we believe that writing courses should prepare students to do the kind of writing one may be asked to do on a job once school is finished—and also to do the kind of writing one may do freely because she or he wants to.

We know there will always be situations where a person has to argue for an absolute acceptance of her point of view and a complete refutation of every opposing opinion—for example, when a lawyer argues against a death sentence for her client. But even here we believe that the principles of nonadversarial argument are worth considering.

Reasoning and Grammar

To figure out what makes good argument is like figuring out what makes good grammar. Indeed, reasoning and grammar are deeply similar: Grammar is a picture of the regularities in the way people use *language;* reasoning is a picture of the regularities in the way people use *thought.*

Take grammar. Though there are certain universals—certain regularities in how people use language whether they speak English or Chinese—for the most part grammar is a story of local peculiarities: Different languages and different dialects are composed of different regularities. Grammar is largely an empirical business; there is nothing but "what native speakers do." That is because at its most basic level, grammar is what makes language possible. Mistakes are either momentary lapses or, more likely, not mistakes in grammar but mistakes in *usage.*

If we let grammar include matters of usage (such as whether you may split infinitives or begin sentences with "And" or "Hopefully"), grammar then becomes defined more narrowly: what *prestige* native speakers *approve of* or call *appropriate for writing*. At the level of usage, dictionaries may tempt you to think there are right answers, but dictionaries do nothing but record what natives (or prestige natives) do or approve of. Thus dictionaries continually change their minds as the years go by and as people change their habits. At any given moment, dictionaries disagree about the usage and even spelling of certain words.

Although there is no such thing as "correct grammar" built into the universe (or at least very little of it, and it won't help you choose between "who" or "whom"), if you want to get a good grade in most classes, get certain kinds of jobs, or persuade your readers, you have to get rid of what your audience will call "mistakes."

The same situation holds for logic or reasoning. Here too there seem to be few universals. In *The Meno,* Plato stresses the universals, concluding that all humans seem to agree about the rules of geometry or mathematics. But most of our reasoning is not about geometry and mathematics, and it turns out that good reasoning in most realms (like good grammar at the level of usage) depends on what different groups of people call good reasoning—that is, upon conventions that are different in different cultures or disciplines. Recently a number of critics have posited differences between feminine and masculine ways of presenting points of view. To reason well is to learn the conventions of a particular community of writers within a particular area of knowledge or practical functioning. And, increasingly, we are becoming aware of the different conventions for successful argument in cultures other than our own.

Are we saying that grammar and reasoning are nothing but a set of random rules to memorize—like batting averages or capitals of the states? No. There is a rational and orderly science of grammar that you can study and master. It's a lovely science—in a sense the science of the human mind. The same goes for reasoning. But fortunately we don't have to study and master the science of grammar to make our language strong (or to get rid of most of what others call mistakes). So, our point in this workshop is that we don't need to study the science of logic to get our reasoning strong (and get rid of our worst mistakes in thinking).

The reason we can do well without studying and memorizing rules is that we've done so much talking, listening, discussing, and writing that we already have an enormous amount of tacit or unconscious knowledge of grammar and reasoning. Can we get good grammar and good reasoning just by putting pen to paper and writing? Don't we all wish! No, we can only benefit from all our tacit knowledge if we go about using it in the right way. In this workshop we suggest tools to harness our tacit knowledge of reasoning effectively and, in doing so, gain more control and conscious awareness of that tacit knowledge.

Steps to Help You Make the Best Use of Your Tacit Knowledge of *Grammar*

1. Start off writing as naturally and comfortably as possible. *Don't* think about grammar or about any minor matters of phrasing or spelling; think only about what you want to say. *Talk* onto the paper. In this way you are making the most use of your intuitive knowledge of grammar. The most tangled writing almost always results from slow and careful writing: You stop after every three or four words and worry about whether something's wrong—and then think about how to finish the sentence. Or you search a thesaurus for a different word or search the dictionary for a spelling. You lose track of the natural syntax in your head. If instead you can get yourself to talk on paper naturally and comfortably, you will produce mostly clear and correct syntax to start with.

2. Next, using whatever revising process you find best, get your text to say *exactly* what you want it to say—but still without worrying about minor matters of phrasing, grammar, and spelling. Thinking about these things will only distract you from paying attention to what you are trying to say. Why fix up the grammar and spelling in a sentence you may well throw away or rewrite anyway?

3. Now turn your attention to phrasing, spelling, and grammar. Read your draft aloud slowly and carefully to yourself and see what improvements you can make and what mistakes you can eliminate. If you read it *aloud* to yourself—slowly and with expression—you will find even more ways to improve it.

4. Read your piece aloud to one or two listeners: for their help, yes, but also because their presence as audience will help you recognize more problems and think of more improvements.

5. Give your final, typed version to another person to copy-edit. As part of third-level revision in Workshop 5, we included a structured method for getting proofreading and copyediting help from others.

Thus, in this book we do not summarize the rules of language or grammar or usage for you. You can easily find other books—handbooks—that do so. (Unfortunately, however, such handbooks tend to be wrong unless they are enormously long and complex. Any simple rule will have too many exceptions that depend on the context.) However, you will do a better job of strengthening your language and fixing your writing if you work in the more empirical—and more enjoyable—fashion we've just described. The strength of our approach comes from (1) using language unself-consciously to tap your tacit knowledge; (2) examining and revising what you've produced in a self-conscious, systematic, and controlled frame of mind; and (3) collaborating with others.*

These same three steps can make your *reasoning* effective too: (1) write out your argument and its support by talking naturally and unself-consciously on paper; (2) examine and revise what you've written, in the self-conscious, systematic way we've outlined in this workshop; (3) get help from others. By going about writing an argument this way, you use both intuitive and systematic modes of thinking; exploiting them together leads to powerful argumentative writing.

Some Sample Arguments

The Great Campus Goof-Off Machine   *Nate Stulman*

Op-Ed from The New York Times

Conventional wisdom says that computers are a necessary tool for higher education. Many colleges and universities these days require students to have personal computers, and some factor the cost of one into tuition. A number of colleges have put high-speed Internet connections in every dorm room. But there are good reasons to question the wisdom of this preoccupation with computers and the Internet.

Take a walk throught the residence halls of any college in the country and you'll find students seated at their desks, eyes transfixed on their computer monitors. What are they doing with their top-of-the-line PC's and high-speed T-1 Internet connections?

They are playing computer games instead of going to chemistry class, tweaking the configurations of their machines instead of writing the paper due tomorrow, collecting mostly useless information from the World Wide Web instead of doing a math problem set—a host of activity that has little or nothing to do with traditional academic work.

I have friends who have spent whole weekends doing nothing but playing interactive computer games. One friend sometimes spends entire evenings—six to eight hours—scouring the Web for images and modifying them just to have a new background on his computer desktop.

And many others I know have amassed overwhelming collections of music on their computers. It's the searching and finding that they seem to enjoy: some of them have more music files on their computers than they could play in months.

---

* You will have a harder time at this task if you are not a native speaker or if you don't read a fair amount. But don't underestimate your ear: If you've heard a lot of radio and television, you've heard plenty of Standard English and developed a keen sense of the differences between levels of formality.

The Great Campus Goof-Off Machine   *continued*

Several people who live in my hall routinely stay awake all night chatting with dormmates on line. Why walk 10 feet down the hall to have a conversation when you can chat on the computer—even if it takes three times as long?

You might expect that personal computers in dorm rooms would be used for nonacademic purposes, but the problem is not confined to residence halls. The other day I walked into the library's reference department, and five or six students were grouped around a computer—not conducting research, but playing Tetris. Every time I walk past the library's so-called research computers, it seems that at least half are being used to play games, chat or surf the Internet aimlessly.

Colleges and universities should be wary of placing such an emphasis on the use of computers and the Internet. The Web may be useful for finding simple facts, but serious research still means a trip to the library.

For most students, having a computer in the dorm is more of a distraction than a learning tool. Other than computer science or mathematics majors, few students need more than a word processing program and access to e-mail in their rooms.

It is true, of course, that students have always procrastinated and wasted time. But when students spend four, five, even ten hours a day on computers and the Internet, a more troubling picture emerges—a picture all the more disturbing because colleges themselves have helped create the problem.

Nate Stulman is a student at Swarthmore College.

**RESPONSES TO THE "GREAT CAMPUS GOOF-OFF MACHINE":
LETTERS TO THE EDITOR OF *THE NEW YORK TIMES***

To the Editor:

Nate Stulman (Op-Ed, March 15) inserts a healthy "byte" of caution into the discussion of classroom technology. New technologies clearly offer great opportunities for learning and research. In my introductory courses, for example, I suggest Web-based resources to help with researching and writing papers.

The problem is that while offering a great time-saving resource for collecting information, the new technologies do not easily teach students how to search in a discriminating manner or how to think critically about the information they download.

Our enthusiasm for cyber-pedagogy should not prevent us from at least recognizing its potential negative impact on students who are far more likely to have surfed the Web than to have visited a library before they enter college.

Mark Cassell Kent, OH, March 15, 1999.
The writer is an assistant professor of political science at Kent State University.

The Great Campus Goof-Off Machine   *continued*

To the Editor:

As an undergraduate, I understand Nate Stulman's point that our fellow students spend way too much time on the computer ("The Great Campus Goof-Off Machine," Op-Ed, March 15). But Mr. Stulman's notion that universities are doing a disservice by providing Internet access—which will revolutionize the way we live—is downright foolish. High school and college students get in car accidents all the time; does that mean they shouldn't drive?

The bottom line is that college life is a learning experience, a time in which students learn to live independently and to acquire self-discipline. I spend a lot of time on the Internet, and maybe I should be doing my schoolwork instead. But I have also learned to limit my surfing time, spend hours studying, and learn to enjoy life.

Paul Hogarth, Berkeley, CA, March 15, 1999

Too Much for Too Little   *A Student*

Opinion piece written for campus newspaper

When was the last time you sat down and really enjoyed dinner, let alone any other meal in the cafeteria? Can't remember, can you? Neither can I. Don't you think you deserve better service and a higher grade of food? Most students believe they deserve better treatment, so why isn't anything being done? Most students on campus are paying large amounts of money for room and board and also tuition. And a large amount of this money goes towards each student's meal plan during each semester. If you are a commuter student, you suffer too when you have to eat in school cafeterias. There's an old saying, "You get what you pay for," but unfortunately we are not.

Did you ever realize how a good meal and quality service affect your attitude and motivation for the day? Sometimes it's the only thing people look forward to. But of late, most people are left aggravated and hungry after making a trip to the cafeteria. The management on campus is in disarray at the moment. Their poor decision-making and actions cause a great number of hold-ups and mass confusion. If waiting in a long line that moves once every ten minutes isn't bad enough, try finding a seat.

Let's get to the heart of the matter: the food. Lately the quality of the food has gone from mediocre to downright pathetic. Management should put a little variety in their choice of food. They should give students a few alternate choices. Part of the time dinner is cold and sometimes unidentifiable. To cover up they say it's Chinese food. But once you taste it you realize you are eating last week's leftovers. So you say to yourself, "Maybe I'll have a hamburger, they can't mess that up." Wrong again. The burgers are pretty close to hockey pucks, and there are no french fries. The two usually

🖋 Too Much for Too Little   *continued*

go together hand in hand. And to finish off dinner maybe one would like some dessert—a piece of cake, for example. Well, let's just say when the fork started to bend I kind of figured the cake was not for me.

So when is it all going to change? The school says they improved their food program from the previous year. Well, I guess I should consider myself lucky. If I take into consideration how the food is now, I can merely assume either that last year the food was really terrible or that they just have not made much progress at all. Changes won't come over night, and they may not come at all. It's up to the students to make the choice and to decide what's right. If you like the way the food is now, then by all means enjoy yourself. But I would prefer some better quality food. I'm not asking for shrimp and lobster (though I wouldn't mind). But a little more efficiency in the kitchen may save a lot of aggravation.

🖋 The Male Bashing Stereotype   *Kimberly Graham*

Academic paper in 3 drafts

[Early Draft]
Why did we, as a society, need to create a term such as "male bashing"? What is it? Who is guilty of it?

Many women are now feeling dissatisfied with aspects of their lives that they once accepted. They want to be more than housewives. Some want to go back to school in the pursuit of an education and a better job. Many who are in the work force want more power and prestige. Some of these women believe that men are to blame for their dissatisfaction; it was men, after all, who controlled most parts of their lives. They married men and became housewives. Most of their bosses are men. Are women needing a scapegoat? Women are very demanding; they like to intimidate men, and if they do not get what they want, they do not see a future in their relationship with them. To vent their frustrations they resort to male bashing. They blame men for everything. If their car wasn't fixed right, it was because the mechanic was a man. When a crime is committed against a woman, they blame all men. If a female co-worker was sexually harassed by her boss, they assume all male bosses would do the same thing. Male bashing is an overgrown tendency to blame men for every dissatisfaction and to assume all men are alike. It's too bad that we had to come up with this term because it is dangerous and self-destructive.

The media and certain medical circles played a big part in the creation of the term "male bashing." Almost every week on either The Oprah Winfrey Show or Jerry Springer there is one segment on the state of male-female relationships. Most of the segments include panelists who have just written a "revolutionary" new book, or a group of women (or men) talking

The Male Bashing Stereotype   *continued*

about their problems. Inevitably one show turns into a male bashing event because of either a panelist's views or the comments from a participant in the studio audience. One *O.W.S.* was originally about why women marry men who are less financially successful or intelligent than they are. The view at the end of the show turned out to be that women were sick of the games men usually play and they wanted someone they had control over. Men they were used to going out with were egotistical, selfish, cruel, stupid, immature, afraid of commitment, and the list continued. Phil Donahue presented one panel of all men that had formed a "men's club," and the women in the audience felt that they were weak and immature for wanting to be with each other instead of women. There has also been a rapid flow of books written by psychologists and therapists on the state of the sexes. *Men Who Hate Women and the Women Who Love Them* was a bestseller in hardcover and paperback. *Women Men Love, Women Men Leave* is a fairly recent one describing types of women and why men leave them. Books like these give male bashers fuel for their arguments because, as the titles suggest, they put men in a bad light.

One of the most controversial books of late is Shere Hite's new one entitled: *Women and Love: A Cultural Revolution in Progress.* It presents the views of 4,500 women and Hite's conclusions from those views. Critics of the book called it inaccurate and false and also think Hite is guilty of male bashing. She based her report on findings from only 4,500 women when the number should have been much larger. She assumed that the views of the participating women were also those of the rest of the female population. For instance, she has concluded that about ninety-three percent of all women are unhappy with their current relationships and about seventy percent are unfaithful but believe in monogamy. It's inaccurate to judge for the many with data from only the few. The book is presented as a testament to the unhappiness of women because of men, and it should be presented more objectively.

The first draft ended here. Following, in boldface type, are questions and comments from the writer's group members and, in regular type, the writer's responses to them.

Do women have a reason to bash and holler? I have to admit—I have met some stupid, immature, egotistical men. But I don't think that all men are alike and I haven't blamed all my frustrations on them.

Why do some women resort to mental violence? The media has provided many groupings for men and women. There are the "men afraid of commitment," "the older men only interested in younger women," "the men obsessed with getting ahead in their careers," and "all men in their twenties."

Many women tend to find one fault in a man and turn it into a basis for criticism of all men who have the same fault. Then they find

The Male Bashing Stereotype   *continued*

a media grouping and conclude that all men are alike. There are also slots for women: "tired housewives and mothers not wanting sex," "women only interested in having a career," "women living off the men who marry them," and "all women in their forties." If we stopped creating these groupings maybe there would not be bashing against anybody because people would be judged as individuals.

Male bashing is dangerous because it gives men the idea that all women are out to get them. That's not true. Yes, some are, but not all of us are violent militant feminists. It gives society the impression that feminism is to blame and that things were fine before it started. Women guilty of male bashing also put down the concept of feminism. They are fighting for equality, yet they are discriminating against all men for the actions of a few of them. We seem to be going backward in our struggle.

[Second Draft]

What women want—recently there has been a lot of publicity on what women were not getting. And who do we point our lotioned, perfumed hands at? MEN—who else? If we are unhappy, then men, as a race in themselves, are to blame, right? We don't have anyone else to blame. The whole female population is unmistakably guiltless. Why the propensity to turn men into scapegoats?

Him: (While watching the Minnesota Twins win the World Series): Yeah!!! GO, GO, GO!!!

Her: Let's go to a movie or something. Do you want to talk?

Him: Umm.

Her: Was that a yes or a no?

Him: Umm.

Her: Why don't you ever want to talk?

Now, there is a definite problem going on there. The woman (we'll call her June) obviously wanted to talk about something, and she tried to communicate her desire to the man (he's Ward). But her timing was off. Asking her husband, or boyfriend, if he wanted to talk while the World Series was on is like his asking her to meet his mother-in-law while she is applying a deep-cleaning, pore-rejuvenating, look-twenty-years-younger facial mask. Neither the game nor the mask are necessarily important things, but to the person involved, they constitute a sort of livelihood. June could have waited until Ward was done watching the game to ask him to go out. It's common courtesy. Just because it was a man (inarticulately) refusing to talk does not mean that all men would do the same thing. If June had realized how she would feel if Ward did the same to her, then she might have understood his grumbling disinterest. Many frustrated women today are trying to pin the source of their dissatisfaction onto men only, when a more

The Male Bashing Stereotype   *continued*

constructive activity would be to look inside themselves and find the core of their pain. It is a difficult thing to do when the easy way out is to blame, accuse, and complain.

A spotlight has been lit on one woman of the last few turbulent decades who has analyzed the state of relationships in the horrendous romantic environment of the eighties: Shere Hite. Her new book, entitled *Women and Love: A Cultural Revolution in Progress*, is fast on its way to becoming a very controversial bestseller. In it she explores the mentality of dissatisfied women and concludes that men play a large, if not total, role in the creation of female frustration.

I say: poop on her. Yes, there are some disgusting examples of the male species—men who proudly and continuously examine just how many decibels their next belch can create (and whether it will crack the tempered glass of their bathroom windows); blind dates who show up displaying their impressionist renditions of nine tattoos scattered extremely artistically upon their mud-splattered arms; college letches who, when confronted with a group of two women and seventeen inebriated fraternity brothers, suggest consuming and emptying all the bottles of Rolling Rock Beer to start a game of strip spin-the-bottle; polyester-clad barflies ambling up to a woman and, in less than two steps, managing to regurgitate the evening's content of alcohol consumed into her lap . . . Need I go on? But it is very important to remember (I know . . . even I am having a hard time after the last sentences) that not all men are responsible for women's anguish. Many people search for scapegoats because they are afraid to admit that they might have made a mistake. A lot of women find it easy to blame men because they know they will receive sympathy from many other women. Ms. Hite has perpetuated the myth of male-created frustration by presenting the views of 4,500 women and applying them to the national population. She has not stated what women want—she has stated what unhappy women want.

Why are we bringing up the question of what women want, anyway? Why now? Don't get me wrong; it's not that I think the question is not an important one. On the contrary; I consider it crucial. But why all the clamor now?

I think I have an answer. Now that women have gone out and "done it all"—worked, had babies, entered politics, entered space, developed an argument supporting the metaphysical qualities and the transcendental properties of the color black, drunk a six-pack of Jolt—they are beginning to realize that maybe they overdid it. Stress and burnout are beginning to catch up. In their struggle to prove themselves to society, some women went too far and are now afraid to say, "Hey, I made a mistake. This isn't what I wanted." I can understand why they would be afraid to admit it. Some men would turn around and reply, "You should have stayed in the kitchen where the little woman belongs!!" They have also seen many stressed-out men continue with their struggles, and the women do not

The Male Bashing Stereotype   *continued*

want to be the ones to quit. Women have had to prove themselves to society by going beyond what men have done, and for that reason they voice their unhappiness to their boyfriends, husbands, lovers, and so on.

This society would not have to wonder what women (or men) wanted if there were no sexual barriers. Just suppose that there were no physical differences between male and female bodies. Yes, folks, it would be mighty boring, but for the sake of argument, imagine. (Here comes another scenario.)

> *Ward:*   Hello Ms. Flintstone. How did the reports on juvenile penguins in the South Antarctic come out on the IBM/PC with color graphics?
>
> *Wilma:*   Just fine, Mr. Cleaver, but I had problems in the area of young penguin street gangs terrorizing the arctic corners.
>
> *Ward:*   Well, why don't you work on it some more and I will get back to you.

Neither Ward nor Wilma has any distinguishing sexual characteristics, so Ward is not wondering what color Wilma's lingerie is while he curses her feminine lack of computer literacy, and Wilma is not wondering if Ward wears boxers or jockeys as she tears apart his masculine egocentricity. Without sexual characteristics people would not be considered men and women separately, but people . . . just people. Then our society would wonder about the wants of everybody as a whole. Definition of this fantasy land: UTOPIA.

[Final Draft]

What do women want? Recently there has been a lot of publicity on what women were not getting. What Do We WANT?? Who has the answers?? Shere Hite? Oprah Winfrey? Ronald Reagan? My plumber? I don't know if I even understand the question.

The original question—what do women want—has turned into the question: What kind of men do women want? I cannot speak for the whole female population, but I know what I want in a man—or rather, what I don't want.

I do not desire any man who proudly and continuously examines just how many decibels his next belch can create (and whether it will crack the tempered glass of his bathroom windows). So he drank sixteen cases of Ballantine Ale—big deal! He must be able to control his bodily functions in mixed company. Besides, I do not appreciate his friends' attempting to grade the intensity of the belch by holding up their callused fingers.

Nor do I remain at my door, awaiting blind dates who show up displaying their impressionist renditions of nine tattoos scattered extremely artistically upon their mud-splattered arms. A date is an occasion for which one showers, washes, scrubs, DISINFECTS, FUMIGATES!! And I am not the least bit interested in hearing that the tattoo "artist's" name was Anthony "Michelangelo" Giancanna.

Since I am a female University of Massachusetts student, this next

The Male Bashing Stereotype   *continued*

type of man particularly makes me ill. College letches who, when confronted with a group of two women and seventeen inebriated fraternity brothers, suggest consuming and emptying all the bottles of Rolling Rock Beer to start a game of strip spin-the-bottle. What's even more terrifying is when one of them shows up with a Twister mat and a bottle of Mazola. I'm just as fun and exciting as the next person, but, hey, public displays of sweltering lust just aren't my style.

The least desirable of this lengthening list of odd personas is the pseudo-feminist pig who claims to respect Gloria Steinem's every word, while secretly wondering if there exists a small, white, cotton flower embroidered in the center of her brassiere. It is this same sad excuse for a man who, after suggesting an evening at the Four Seasons, thinks convincing a date to pay for a thirteen-course dinner with raspberry crepes and two orders of baked Alaska constitutes a feminist attitude. After all, if she wants to be equal then she should pay for his dinner, theater tickets, Brooks Brothers' suits, an IBM/PC with full-color graphics, a diamond-blue metallic Porsche, a fifty-three-room chateau in the Swiss Alps, etc. The pseudo-feminist pig is also very articulate concerning women's issues and proves it with a phone bill of $3,975.87 to Dial-a-Porn. He is the most dangerous of the undesirables since he has the ability to con unknowing women into thinking that he is compassionate and charming, while secretly wanting to cover them with instant banana Jell-O pudding while handcuffed in the back seat of a mint-green 1974 Chevy Impala.

I do not want to dwell on the above descriptions because, as a feminist, my imagination concerning the various mutant abnormalities of the male species may . . . how can I say it subtly . . . run rampant through the hellish field of sarcastic literary discourse. I have determined what kind of men I don't want. Hopefully these caustic exaggerations will not offend any male egos. As unbelievable as it may seem, I do have a glimmer of hope in the existence of desirable men. But where are they? Do I have to travel to southwest Kansas to find an underpaid tractor salesman who loves to wear the color pink? I suppose there is an Antarctican ice fisherman who is more than willing to relax and enjoy the benefits of my making fifty times more income than he would ever make. Maybe there is a Holiday Inn pool maintenance staff person living in Acapulco, Mexico who knows how to cook homemade turkey soup and double German chocolate cake while diapering an infant. WHERE ARE THEY?

So what does this paper prove? I have come up with an answer to the question of what women want. Or have I? No, the statement is too vague. Society should not generalize—it's an emotional question. I do know what qualities I like in a man: compassion, sense of humor, intelligence, sense of equality toward women, respect for the human race, the ability to read aloud the works of D. H. Lawrence while stirring instant banana Jell-O pudding . . .

Interviewing as Research
How Do Writers Write?

Essential Premises

We can understand writing better by investigating the *kinds* of writing in the world—writing that people do for school, for work, and on their own.

It's also helpful to investigate the many *ways* people go about writing. It is usually reassuring, whether we discover similarities ("Wow—she has the same experience I do") or differences ("Isn't it amazing that he can get things written using that odd method").

Interview essays liven up our style by getting us to incorporate speech into our writing.

MAIN ASSIGNMENT
Conducting an Interview and Writing an Interview Essay

For this workshop we ask you to conduct an interview and find out as much as you can about what and how someone else writes. Our main goal is for you to learn about the great diversity of kinds of writing and ways of writing in the world so that you'll see more options when you approach a writing task. As you hear the interviews written by your classmates, you will gain much more perspective on all the things writing can do.

But we also have other goals for this workshop:

- You'll learn to conduct interviews: to ask questions and to listen to what another person is saying, but also to hear what's behind what she is saying.
- School writing and academic essay writing are always in danger of going dead. The interview is good for helping you get lively speech qualities and voice into your writing because you will use lots of quoted speech.
- As you work through this assignment, you'll get practice in how to find or carve out a theme or develop a conclusion from a mass of diverse material.

- We invite you to think about how writing is often the blending together of your own ideas and the ideas of others into a text you can call your own.

Your main assignment is to conduct an interview and write an interview essay. Here are the three things that most readers will be looking for in an interview essay:

1. Rich information about what and how your interviewee writes and how she thinks and feels about writing.

2. A feeling for what the person is like.

3. Your own thinking as you make sense of all your data: a conclusion of your own.

Six Steps to the Main Assignment

Step One: Choosing Someone to Interview

Pick someone who writes a significant amount and cares about writing. Four possibilities suggest themselves:

- An adult who writes as part of her job—perhaps someone in a field you are considering for yourself. (You may be surprised how much people have to write in fields that seem distant from writing. Recent research shows that engineers, for example, spend an average of 25 percent of their week writing.)
- An adult who is devoted to writing, though it is not part of her job. (Ask around. You may find relatives or family friends who write magazine articles or fiction or poetry or who do research—all in their free time.)
- A junior, senior, or graduate student who is majoring in a subject you would like to explore.
- A member of your writing class. (Probably you'll think of someone who particularly likes writing, but it can be very useful to interview someone who particularly hates writing in order to learn how that can happen to people and what the effects are.)

If you are working in groups, you'll all learn the most if you each choose a different kind of person to interview. Adult subjects make the most sense for students who live at home or off campus, since they can easily work with an adult from their home environment. But of course there are adults on any campus—and not just faculty—who write seriously, whether or not it is part of their job.

You'll need *two* interviews with your subject (at least two hours in all). Set up these interviews early and follow through to make them happen. Busy people sometimes have to change appointments, so you may need to push to get your interviews. The important thing is to make sure the person has enough interest in writing to give you the time you need.

Step Two: A Practice Interview with a Classmate

Some of you may have done some interviewing in the past, perhaps as a reporter for a school newspaper, perhaps as part of an assignment for a particular class. If so, you can help others in the class who haven't had this experience. Interviews can be fun, but they do take some practice and skill, especially if the process makes you nervous. We suggest a short practice interview with a classmate.

This practice session can be as little as 15 or 20 minutes, but it will help you with the essential process in interviewing: asking only a few key questions, getting your subject to talk, holding back and being quiet, listening hard, and taking notes.

The two main questions or requests are utterly simple:

- Please tell me about as many important writing occasions or incidents from your life as you can think of right now.
- Tell me as much as you can about the most interesting or important one.

Your classmate may not be able to think of many occasions in response to the first question, but that's all right. Just get her to pick *one* occasion and tell you as much as possible about it. Telling the story of one writing occasion usually makes people think of more. Get the person to choose different kinds of writing.

Your main job is to get your subject talking—and to listen. Your best tool is to be genuinely curious and to listen attentively with involvement. You can show your interest by asking follow-up questions. ("How did

Exploring the Writing Process
On Revising for Spontaneity

Galbraith writes longhand—"That is the speed at which my mind works"—and revises a great deal. It is usually at about the fifth draft, he says, that his trademark note of casual spontaneity enters the prose.

John Cassidy, The New Yorker, November 30, 1998 [from a profile of John Kenneth Galbraith (b. 1908), one of the most influential twentieth-century writers about economy and culture]

you feel when that happened?" "Was it noisy or quiet?") But don't try to steer too much. Let your interviewee determine the direction and the main topics. Your job is to find out how this person understands and feels about the world of her writing.

As you listen, take some notes. Don't be shy about it; do it proudly. Most people are flattered that you care enough about what they are saying to take notes. But you don't need to try for full, extensive notes. Simply jot down phrases and single words as each topic or point goes by—words and phrases that are somehow important or striking and that are connected to all the main points. That's enough —as long as you go back over these abbreviated notes very soon after the interview so you can flesh them out with fuller notes of what your subject actually said.

If this were a longer interview, you would be going over your notes alone. But for this exercise, do the reconstructing aloud in front of the classmate you interviewed. As you go through your notes repeating and reconstructing what she said, she can help you by making corrections. And after you finish, she can mention things from the interview that *she* thought important or interesting that you didn't mention—just to give you another perspective on what you recorded.

If this were a longer interview, you would also be jotting down some of *your* reactions, observations, and trains of thought as you reconstruct the interview. But for this quick in-class exercise, simply *tell* some of these observations after you have reconstructed your subject's words. After going through this exercise in interviewing-and-

Exploring the Writing Process
On Interviewing

Interviewing made me sort of nervous because I just didn't know whether she wanted to talk to me about this or was just being nice or polite. I took some notes at the beginning but they didn't mean much; when I tried to figure them out I couldn't even remember talking about those things. I was just too nervous. When she started talking about trying to write a novel and how her daughter knocked milk on the pages and then the dog sat on them I just laughed. I remember that and I didn't even take notes. I remember so clearly that she said "My dog's an author!" Then I wasn't so nervous anymore.

Marsha Koons

reporting-back, switch places and give your classmate a chance to interview you and report back.

It's important at the end for you and your partner to spend a few minutes talking about what it was like being interviewed. What approaches made you feel most comfortable? Which questions were most effective for stimulating memory and thoughts? What got in the way?

Option in Threes.   This same interviewing exercise can be rich and interesting in groups of three. One person interviews another, as before, but the third person functions as onlooker—either listening or also taking notes. Then when the interviewer reconstructs his notes, the onlooker can chime in to help capture the words actually spoken and comment on things he would have tried to record that the interviewer omitted. Or they can both reconstruct notes, compare them, and learn from each other—with, of course, the help of the interviewee.

Step Three: Your Real Interview—First Session

You may be nervous as you start, but once you get going you'll probably enjoy the session. This interview will be as simple a process as your practice interview, for the same two questions or requests are virtually all you'll need. Just go back and forth between getting your subject to remember various writing occasions and getting her to talk about certain ones in more detail.

Again, try to ask broad, open-ended questions and be a listener. Because this is a longer interview and you are trying to find out more, we suggest three other kinds of questions you can use during the interview.

1. *Supplemental questions* you can toss in as your subject is talking about various writing occasions, especially if he or she seems to run out:
    *   Tell about the process of getting this written.
    *   Did it go through stages or drafts or changes?
    *   What was satisfying or pleasing?
    *   What was hard?
    *   What was perplexing?
    *   What was the occasion (assignment, need, situation)?
    *   Who was the writing for?
    *   Was the writing required or voluntary?
    *   How high were the stakes for this writing—how much did it matter to you?
    *   What surprised you?

- How did you feel about the process of writing it?
- How did you feel about what you had produced?
- What were you trying to achieve with this writing—what effect were you trying to have on your readers (for example to inform them, persuade them, entertain them, impress them, make them realize how you feel, get something off your chest)?
- Were there other possible readers or past readers in your mind as you were writing?
- How did readers react?
- Where did you do this writing and what were the conditions like in that setting?

2. *Conclusions or reflections* from the writer herself: "Do you have any thoughts about all this? What strikes you as interesting about all that you have been telling me?"

3. *A fuller picture of the range of writing* that this person has done. After she has told you about several writing occasions, she'll be in a better position to give an overview of the kinds of writing she does most and the kinds she does least. If you ask for this overview at the beginning, she is more liable to forget about certain kinds of writing that might be interesting and important. For example, she might forget that she is a big list maker or a writer of tiny notes to family or friends.

Exploring the Writing Process
On Writing to Understand

This year I had a fight with my best friend, so I'm much more into my studies. For the first half of the summer we had a job, but when we came back to school we weren't talking or anything. I would talk to my mother about what was happening. I guess for the first week she listened, but then she said, "Why are you letting this affect you?" I didn't know what I was upset about, so I went upstairs and I just started writing why that had happened. I felt better about it. I reread it and I saw that it was probably partly my fault. I guess that was a good idea to write it down. I never got a chance to tell her because she was always with her [new] best friend.

From an interview with "Lisa," in Linda Miller Cleary's *From the Other Side of the Desk: Students Speak Out about Writing*

If you feel your interview falling into a lifeless question-and-answer pattern, try to use more open-ended questions, such as "Tell me a story about a time when you were really pleased or disappointed" or "Tell me more about that" or "How did you feel about that?" and so forth. And don't be afraid to wait for a while after you ask a question and again at the end of an answer. Be willing to leave long silences hanging in the air. People often give their best answers after a long pause for reflection. Remember that one of the best things you can say is simply, "That sounds interesting; talk some more about that."

Tape Recorder.   You might use a tape recorder for your interview if you prefer, and if you have one available and your subject doesn't object. It will let you quote your subject's words exactly. Most people don't mind being recorded and soon get over being self-conscious. You won't have to take notes during the interview (except to jot down some of your own thoughts and reactions). But a tape recorder doesn't solve your recording problems. You'll still have to take notes as you listen to the tape. And taping can deceive you into becoming a lazy listener during the interview. You can capture much more in notes than you might expect, and note taking is an important skill to develop.

Step Four: Reconstructing Your Notes after Your First Interview

Don't forget: It's crucial to make time right after the interview to go over your sketchy notes.
- Write out explicit notes for the main points.
- Try to quote some of your subject's most interesting or striking words.
- Don't forget to include a few *physical* details such as the setting (the room and the atmosphere) and the person's appearance (how she was dressed, how she spoke and moved).
- Write out some of your *own* observations, reactions, questions, and trains of thought about what the person has said.
- If you had to decide now on a "moral of the story," what would it be? You don't have to settle it yet, but what's the most interesting conclusion you could draw at this point?
- Work out some new questions for a second interview, questions that follow up on ideas generated as you reconstruct your notes.
    If you delay going over your notes for even three or four hours, you will lose many crucial details. It's not too big a job. For now you

are not trying for a draft of your interview; all you're doing is going over your notes and adding more notes.

Using Partners or Small Groups to Help You Prepare for the Second Interview.   It will help you enormously to meet with a partner or small group and share what you have in your notes. Read back the main things your subject told you and all your observations, reflections, and questions. Then you can ask them to give you *their* observations, reflections, and questions about your notes. Outside eyes will invariably help you see implications that you didn't see earlier. You need to figure out some conclusions of your own, and others can give you a lot of help.

Step Five: Your Second Interview

Your second interview will follow comfortably and interestingly from your first one. You can start off by just summarizing for your subject the main things you learned from her, asking her to make corrections and additions. Almost always, your observations will spark other things in her mind. Afterward, you can ask her the questions you have worked out on the basis of the first interview, things you want to know more about. Here are a few topics for further questions:

- *Kinds.* Try to cover all the possibilities. For example, if your interviewee is a reporter and if she says she writes nothing but news stories, probe for other writing in her life. And even ask her to explore differences between *kinds* of news stories.
- *Processes.* Try for lots of details here: What happens in your interviewee's mind before she does any writing—during the hours or days before she puts a word on paper? What are her first words on paper? Notes? an outline? or just random jottings? Or does she go right to written-out drafts or perhaps even directly to final drafts? What are her feelings throughout the whole process? What about the role of other people? What kinds of feedback help her? And don't settle for a "general story of how I *always* or *usually* write." Probe for differences and exceptions.
- *Audience.* If your first interview didn't touch on this, ask her about her important readers, past and present: former teachers, present friends, supervisors. Get her to talk about what makes an audience helpful or not helpful for her. (Audience is a complicated issue because often, especially on the job, there is more than one audience. The news story may be for people who buy the paper, but the editor sees it first and has to like it; the memo may be for the clients or buyers, but it has to work for the writer's immediate supervisor too.) Does she think a lot or not so much

about audience when writing? At which points in the writing process does she think about audience most?

- *Changes.* What important changes have occurred in how she writes and feels about writing? Does she see other changes in the future? Does she have writing goals she hasn't yet met? What are her hopes about these?

- *Functions.* If your interviewee says that the function of her writing is just to inform or just to make money, ask her to think about subsidiary functions—perhaps different functions for different pieces, for example to persuade, to give orders, to help her understand her life, to give personal satisfaction. Ask her to think about function in connection with audience.

Step Six: From Interview to Interview Essay

Make sure to set aside time soon after your second interview to flesh out your sketchy notes and to write out some of your own reflections and conclusions. Again, see if you can enlist the help of your partner or small group in responding to your notes.

One way to move toward an essay is to create a collage: Simply choose the most interesting points and quotations from your subject—*and* your own most interesting observations, reflections, and conclusions—and then arrange them as separate fragments into a pleasing or intuitive sequence. Perhaps your teacher will even invite a collage instead of an essay. (See Workshop 4 for more about the collage form.)

But probably you will need to produce an interview essay. This is an interesting amalgam. It needs to contain lots of mere *summary* of what your subject told you (using quotations as much as you can). Yet the overall essay will reflect your slant and needs to contain much of your explicit thinking. You have to figure out what observations and conclusions you want to draw from all the material.

There is no single proper way to organize such an essay. In effect, you are writing an analysis-of-data essay. The simplest organization is obvious: First, here's my data; then here are my reflections and conclusions. But there are plenty of other ways to organize an analysis of data. You can start with *your* main point and then try to explain and demonstrate it with data. Or you can present a bit of data, then some of your thinking, then more data, then more of your thinking, and so on—in effect, telling the story of your thinking.

It will be crucial to get feedback from your partner or small group on a draft of this essay before making your final revision. See "Sharing and Responding" in this workshop.

About Accuracy in Quotation.   If you used a tape recorder, you can note somewhere that you did so and that you are quoting the actual words spoken by your subject. Even so, it is customary when transcribing someone's casual speech to do minor cleaning up: leaving out "um's" and "er's" and digressive phrases, and fixing grammar and the like. If you didn't use a tape recorder, do your best to find and reconstruct some actual words, phrases, and sentences and put them in quotation marks. Actual quotations pump lifeblood into an interview essay. But acknowledge that you were working from notes and therefore might not have gotten some of the words exactly right.

Suggestions for Collaboration

This is a particularly good workshop for collaborative writing. You can interview with one or more partners and then write up the interview and your conclusions collaboratively. Another approach is to interview different people and then write a collaborative paper that compares and contrasts your interviewees and draws some conclusions that all of you arrive at collaboratively.

If you have selected or been assigned to write a collaborative comparison essay, do 5 or 10 minutes of focused freewriting about what you see as the conclusions you can draw about your writer on the basis of your interview. Then get together with your partner(s) and trade freewritings as a way to get started on your collaborative analysis. Or you might write an extended dialogue with your partner(s). Either way, you may want to extend this written conversation through several interchanges as you did in Workshop 4.

If you are studying different writers, here are some questions to consider:

- How alike or different are the kinds of writing our interviewees do?
- In what ways are our interviewees' writing habits alike or different?
- What can we say about each of our interviewees' attitudes toward writing? What effects do these attitudes seem to have?
- How does the writing our interviewees do relate to the writing they did while in school? to the writing we do in school?
- What conclusions can we draw from each of the interviews? Are these conclusions consistent, or do we seem to draw very different conclusions from each of the interviews? If so, what does this suggest?
- What can we learn about our own writing processes from studying these interviews?

Once you and your partner(s) have discussed or written about these and other issues, you can begin to draft your collaborative essay. (You might want to look back at Workshop 4 for guidelines for collaborative writing.) Keep in mind that you and your partner don't have to agree on every statement you make. Disagreements can be thought-provoking for readers. The more significant the disagreement, the more urgent it is to present it to others.

Sharing and Responding

The most important person to share your essay with is the person you are writing about. It is only fair to let that person read a draft of what you have written. Even if your interviewee is so busy that she doesn't care about seeing a draft or the final product, it's important to make the offer. Give her a fairly coherent draft so that it is not a chore to read, but be sure it's not a final draft because you need to invite your subject to tell you where she disagrees with something you've written.

If she disagrees with your record of *what she said,* you have an obligation to revise according to her feedback. Accept her correction. Even if she actually *said* X, she now has the right to take it back and give you a corrected statement. If she disagrees with *your own*

Writing as Play   Capturing the Music of the Voice

Pick a sentence or two quoted directly from your interview: the actual words as the person said them. Use your *ear* to choose the passage. That is, pick a passage that "sounds like this person"—a passage where the *sound* of the speaking somehow captures what this person is like. Say the words over and over to yourself (or play them if you recorded the interview) till you can feel the "tune" or "music" of the words.

Then write down the words on a sheet of paper so they slide upward and downward—so as to capture the tune of the voice. We did this with one of Joseph's sentences near the end of Linda Cleary's profile of him (printed at the end of this workshop). You'll notice that we've drawn a curving line under the words to match the contour. This line helps illustrate more vividly the tune of the words. We had to use guesswork since we never actually heard Joseph speak. (It's also interesting to illustrate the different tunes that are possible with the same sentence.)

reflections or conclusions or thoughts, you don't have an absolute obligation to go along with her views. But try seeing things the way she does—try playing the believing game. See if that process leads you to change your mind.

Sharing with Members of Your Class.   If you are doing this workshop early in the semester, the main benefit from readers will come from the early forms of feedback we describe in the "Sharing and Responding" section of this book: "Sharing: No Response"; "Pointing and Center of Gravity"; "Summary and Sayback"; and "What Is Almost Said?" You might also ask readers whether they feel you have fulfilled the three criteria for an interview essay that we mentioned at the start of the workshop:

- Giving rich information about what and how your interviewee writes and how she thinks and feels about writing.
- Giving a feeling for what the person is like.
- Giving your own thinking as you make sense of all your data: a conclusion of your own.

You could also ask readers what lessons about their own writing they learned from reading your interview.

A Note about Publication.   It is common for local newspapers and magazines to publish interviews, including interviews with writers. A campus newspaper is a natural place for an interview with a faculty member, administrator, or staff member—focusing on the writing they do and how they go about it. Hometown newspapers are good places for interviews with people who live there. You might choose this essay to revise further (perhaps in a revising workshop) and send it off to see if you can get it published.

Process Journal and Cover Letter

You won't need the questions that follow if you can easily write about moments from this workshop when things went well or badly or surprisingly. What was going on for you in your thinking and feeling? How did words behave for you? But here are some questions to jog your memory:

- How did your note taking go? What was it like reconstructing your notes?
- When did your conclusion or main point come to you? Was it a struggle to find one, or did it just seem to appear? Finding the point in a great mass of messy data is one of the main cognitive skills involved in learning. On the basis of this workshop's assignment, give yourself advice on ways to develop this skill in the future.

- Compare the goals or functions your interviewee was trying to achieve in her writings and the goals or functions you try to achieve in the various writings you do. How often do you actually think about what your writing is trying to *do* to readers (other than fulfill an assignment)?

For your cover letter, it's good to include some or all of your process writing. But don't forget to answer some cover letter questions. Here are the main ones: What is your main point and what effect are you trying to have on readers? What do you feel works best in your paper and where are you unsatisfied? What changes did you make on the basis of any feedback? And most important: What feedback do you want now from a reader? But your teacher may ask you particular cover letter questions that pertain to this assignment.

A Sample Published Interview

The Social Consequences of Voicelessness   *Linda Miller Cleary*

Linda Miller Cleary has written extensively on issues of composition, literacy, and education, in articles and in such books as From the Other Side of the Desk: Students Speak Out about Writing *(1991). This interview is from that book. She is in the English Department at the University of Minnesota—Duluth. Notice how Cleary uses a simple but effective method for the dual task of an interview: giving lots of attention to Joseph's words yet also conveying her own thinking. She uses her opening and closing paragraphs to present her own thinking directly and bluntly, and then she uses* nothing but *Joseph's words for the rest of her essay. Thus she brings Joseph alive by giving us the sense that he's talking to us.*

A PROFILE OF JOSEPH

There's a logical consequence to the heavy "please-the-teacher" mentality that pervaded the experience of the successful students [I interviewed for my book]. Some students who felt disconnected from the writing they had to do did that work with a touch of anger; a loss occurred for them when the secondary school writing straitjacket was applied. Still other students, however, scared me because they accepted "pleasing the teacher" without perceiving it as a sellout, without seeing it as a loss of personal integrity. They learned to distance themselves from their writing, to please the audience, to be untrue to themselves. Furthermore, they became good at it. Joseph had mastered the art of pleasing his high school teachers.

◦✑

The Social Consequences of Voicelessness *continued*

In fifth and sixth grade, I got the urge to write a story once in a while. I remember writing about my dog. I guess I don't write for fun anymore. It's just writing for like a teacher or a judge. Most of the writing I do now can go back to learning from sixth-grade composition, like topic sentences of paragraphs and things like that. I guess the past set a good foundation for my writing now, about 50 percent of it, and then I think the rest of the 50 percent came recently, organized it, perfected it, made it easier.

In seventh grade our teacher was tougher, and we did have to do reports every once in a while. Before that we were learning grammar and stuff. We had a textbook with certain stories and interpretation of the stories, and I did really poorly. I didn't know exactly what kind of answers the teachers wanted to particular questions. I didn't really know how you're supposed to go about telling somebody about a story. I started telling the story, and my teacher stopped me and said, "Just tell what mainly happened; go to the end or something." It wasn't that hard to learn once you got the hang of it. You know what the teacher wants, and that would be a good summary. I didn't like literature. I guess I haven't liked it until recently because I didn't do too well. I didn't like spelling until I started doing well in it. I guess I didn't know exactly what was a good answer and what wasn't, and how specific to get. Our teacher was pretty hard.

In eighth grade we did start learning how to write formally, more formally, with the introduction and summary and topic sentences. The first essay that we did for him [was] just a regular article about science. I wrote it, and he brought it up in front of class and said, "This is an example of a good essay." So I guess that was my first. After a while it was actually pretty nice because I liked it better when I wrote better.

We wrote reports, essays, and things like that in ninth grade—more practice and learning new ways of writing. I did have a speech class, and we'd do a lot of writing there: essay, informative, and persuasive. But the first day I can remember in that class, we all stood up and said our names and a hobby that we had, and the next day we had to write an essay on that hobby. I had a friend who had two three-wheelers. That was really fun for me; I liked what I wrote about. That's probably the first time I started speaking in front of a class. It's pretty scary the first time. I always read what I was saying, but we were supposed to ad-lib a little bit. I got A's in the class; maybe she wasn't that strict.

I really have had to worry about what I was gonna write, always worrying if the audience will like it or not. It's been hard because I didn't know what my classmates would accept. The popular ones were really relaxed; I wasn't. I had to worry what I was gonna read in front of class. I'd worry about sounding awkward. I tried to stay away from jokes, I didn't know what kind of joke would work, and I'd get embarrassed if they didn't laugh. I usually tried to stay in the middle of acceptable. I wanted to be creative, but the worst fear was getting too creative. I wasn't writing it for something that I would like. It was more something that they would like. I remember

The Social Consequences of Voicelessness *continued*

when we had to write an advertisement about a certain product. You had to get creative and that worried me. What if you tried to be funny, and it wasn't funny? I remember in the end I just took a song, and I spoke with the song in an excited way. It was an airline vacation to Europe. They kinda liked it because of the song. It was an acceptable attention getter.

In debate we have to be persuasive and we have to be understandable, make a point that the judges will accept. In an essay it's just writing about something and the teacher grades it, and you are arguing basically. That's what debate is about. We use a lot of analogies, and I've used some of them in writing in English class, for ideas and organization. It's kind of a game. It takes a while to find out how or what exactly the audience is going to believe. In English I usually stay neutral. I used to not like literature, interpreting literature, because I didn't know what the teacher would want. But once you debate in speech you know what or which arguments will basically be accepted. When I start writing a speech, I feel strongly for that particular side, and so when I switch over to the opposite thinking, I start believing that side. I wouldn't say that I have any major opinions. A lot of it is presenting arguments that aren't really true. It's just whether or not the other debater can take it apart, or whether the judge will like it or not.

I don't really write for myself. I can't think of any time . . . Oh, okay, I did a voice of democracy thing once. They have a contest at each school where they gave us a topic, and they took the top three people from each school, and the first person got $100, the second got $75, and the third got $50. They'd send the speeches over to judges. And it was called The Challenge of American Citizenship. It was a really tough topic—a lot of ways you could interpret it. There was really no way you could tell what would be a good speech. I was thinking the normal ones would be voting and public service and all that. Voting is so obviously American citizenship that I decided to do something about citizenship and world peace, racism. It was the one time when I didn't do what I thought the judges would like. I did what I thought would be a good speech. I liked it, and I didn't win. People who did win did things like voting. I wish I had won the $100. I thought next time though I wouldn't be so original. I decided to do what would win. School writing is the same basically; I need to get the grade.

I guess with my English teacher it would be better to be original 'cause she'd be looking for that type of thing. When I gave the Voice of Democracy speech, they would be more likely to look at what they would want to hear, while if I was doing it for my teacher, she would take a look at it more objectively, and, "Okay, this is more original." If too many people in the class were going one way, I chose differently. I just wrote this paper on "To Build a Fire." We were supposed to pick a topic sentence from seven that she gave you, and then just write an introduction and conclusion with a couple of paragraphs to support it. The first thing I did was to look at the topics; 90 percent of the class was doing the same topics. I decided to look for other topic sentences and put them together. I've never rebelled about

The Social Consequences of Voicelessness   *continued*

what the teacher wanted us to write about. If the teacher chose something to write about, she usually gives us choices on how to approach it. A lot of kids in the class get mad because the teacher says you have the wrong opinion. I guess I haven't really had any problems with that, I just try to write what the teacher wants. I have my own decision to do it whichever way I want to do it, but still I do it in the general way that she wants.

I don't know, I guess it's nice being a good student. I have friends in debate and in a class like Enriched English, A.P. History. I have other friends, I have to change my line of speaking, and I guess that's a burden. I just have to be easy to understand. I guess respect is pretty important for me. It's important to fit in, to fit into some kind of crowd. I have a best friend, but he doesn't do that well, so I guess I need a group of friends that I can identify with. When I'm in a class that is intellectually oriented, it's really fun to be around that type of environment. In debate for example, I'm getting trophies, winning. The main thing that it does is get respect. When you win, when I bring home a trophy, sometimes I just forget to show it to my parents. I guess it's just respect of fellow debaters.

When Joseph finished his last interview, I felt a sense of discomfort that went beyond being sick to my stomach; the irony in his words made me sick at heart. At that moment I would gladly have handed over $100 to him if I thought it would have given him back his own voice. He had gone beyond the endeavor of considering what would be compelling to an audience in order to convince them of his opinion. Joseph was an earnest young man who was just coming into his own, in his own eyes and in the eyes of his fellow students. I could see him being a future senator in our Congress. Ralph Waldo Emerson said, "Nothing is at last sacred but the integrity of your own mind. Absolve you to yourself, and you shall have the suffrage of the world . . . I am ashamed to think how easily we capitulate to badges and names, to large societies and dead institutions." Joseph had capitulated, and I'm not sure that our democracy can withstand an educational system that rewards capitulation anymore. Has its demise started with the power of grades? Or does it start with the conformity that is permitted to rage rampant in the adolescent years? The forty students in the study did not sense tolerance for their differences, for their diversity and interests. They sought to discover what was "acceptable." If students aren't encouraged to develop their own opinions and to articulate them, I fear for what we call our democracy.

Essential Premises

Research is an integration of what one already knows (through observation and reading and conversation) and what one learns from additional sources.

The kind of research one undertakes depends entirely on one's purpose and the availability of sources.

Main Assignment Preview

Research results from the desire to know something. What that something is determines the kind of research the researcher undertakes and the sources he or she uses. Sometimes research questions lead you to seek information mainly from print sources: books, periodicals, and newspapers. At other times, research questions mainly lead you to observe, interview, and examine your past experience more closely. And, increasingly, research may lead you to the Internet and the World Wide Web. Quite often, researchers need data and information from a variety of sources. In this workshop, our goal is to get you to undertake several kinds of research. We hope you'll begin to believe as we do that individual research (observation, surveys, and interviewing*) and textual research (print, library, Internet) are equally valid; which to use depends on what you want to know.

Your main assignment for this workshop will be

1. To develop a research topic out of a previous piece of writing you've done for this class.

2. To design a research plan that calls for individual research (interviewing, surveying, and observing), library or print research, and—if resources are available—Internet research.

---

* When a researcher observes intently (often over a period of time) a particular environment and then writes a fully detailed description of it and what happens there, this is called ethnographic research. It relies on close observation, careful reporting, and rich, "thick" descriptions rather than on a survey of large numbers of examples.

3. To write a research paper that combines this information. Your final paper will need to include appropriate documentation.

4. To attach a 75-word abstract to your finished paper.

We're trying to get away from the old research paper mentality that makes you say, "Let's see, this is a research paper. Therefore, none of my own thinking belongs here. My job is to find a topic that lets me quote and summarize from the assigned number of books and articles. This is library work: filling out cards, making outlines, pasting it all together, and getting footnotes right." We're asking for a paper that grows out of your own thinking but that joins your thinking, not only to the thinking of others but also to what you can learn from observation and interviewing. In a sense your job is to create and carry forward a conversation: You'll bring the thinking you've already done together with the thinking and observations of others and get all this material talking together.

Alternative Assignment: The I-Search

Instead of actually producing a research paper, your teacher may give you the option of producing an "I-Search" paper. Essentially, this is a paper detailing why you chose your topic, how you went about finding information about it, and what you found out from each task you did. We'll say more about this alternative toward the end of this workshop. Here you just need to remember that if you choose this path, you'll need to keep good notes about the whole process of researching.

MAIN ASSIGNMENT
Writing a Research Paper

Step One: Deciding on a Topic

Mainly, in the assignments we've given you so far, we've asked you to write material out of your own head with input from your teacher and classmates in your writing class and in other classes. We think it highly likely that you found—while writing on some of these topics—that you wished you knew more about them. This is your chance to revise an earlier report on the basis of research: interviewing, observing, reading.

Set aside some time for looking back over all the pieces you've done for this writing course. (We hope that, in itself, will prove to be valuable.) As you read, jot down a list of possibilities for research.

Perhaps you wrote a narrative about the neighborhood, town, or city where you grew up. Maybe you wrote a persuasive or argumentative piece on college athletics. We've read quite a few persuasive and argumentative papers on the subjects of college food plans, campus security, and the pros and cons of ungraded courses. And we've read many, many analyses of newspaper editorials, advertisements, and all varieties of literature: poems, plays, novels, and so forth. All of these subjects can be developed into research topics.

To arrive at a topic, try setting up a question for yourself. For example, the student who wrote the argument paper on the college food plan (see pages 248–249 in Workshop 9) might have asked, "What kinds of food plans are provided by college campuses, and what are the benefits and problems of each?" A student who has written a persuasive or agumentative paper about the need for understanding across cultural boundaries might ask, "What kinds of cultural differences actually exist on my campus (or in my home neighborhood)?" The student who wrote "Devoured: Eating Disorders" (the sample piece at the end of this workshop) was anxious to explore the ways young women's false body images lead to self-destructive eating disorders.

Many students find it helpful at this stage to come up with more than one possible topic. Perhaps you'll find even three or four seeds in the writing you've already done. If so, spend about 10 minutes doing some writing on each topic and see which one stirs up your interest the most or seems to offer rich possibilities for research. Your teacher may give you some time in class to talk about topics also— preferably in small groups—so you'll get a feel for each one and can make a decision. But even if there is no in-class time for talking this way, you can talk to others outside class or at home and see what topic promises to keep you interested.

Step Two: First Round of Freewriting

Once you've selected a topic and framed a question for your research to answer, reread what you've already said about the topic and do some focused freewriting or clustering about what else you'd like to know. Share this freewriting with others in and outside the class.

Push yourself as much as you can to get down on paper what you already know and what your opinions on the subject are. Don't worry about whether what you write is right or not. The point is to make clear to yourself exactly where you're starting from. You may be surprised to discover that you actually know more than you think you do and have more opinions about your subject than you're aware of—or, not so positively, you may find out that you have strong opinions and nothing to back them up.

For instance, our meal-plan writer surely knows college regulations, the costs of various plans, the restrictions and privileges of each, his own experience with the food and the experiences of his friends, and his observations of others in the cafeteria. But he may discover that although he thinks the food and the service are awful, when he tries to find specific examples of that, he comes up short.

As you do this freewriting, interject questions as they come up: "Have the prices gone up recently? How much?" "What kinds of plans do other schools have?" "What provisions are made for those on special diets?" "Is there a profit? Who gets it?" "What are the students really complaining about?" Later you can reread and highlight these questions.

If you find yourself running dry—that is, if your topic simply doesn't seem to be working out for you or not holding your interest— look back at other possible topics you wrote on previously.

Step Three: Designing a Research Plan

For the purposes of this workshop, we ask you to design a research plan that requires you to do several kinds of research: library, individual, and possibly electronic. This may seem arbitrary to you (it is), but we want you to get some sense of the full range of research strategies and the ways these strategies complement one another. And perhaps it's not as arbitrary as it might seem at first, since most subjects can probably be profitably researched in all three ways.

To get started on a plan, make a list of questions you've thought up, starting with your major research question. If you have a chance to share your freewriting and your list, others will probably come up with additional questions. Decide which can best be answered by library research, which by observation and interviews, and which by electronic resources. Since we're asking you to do all of these activities, make sure you have questions in all categories.

As an example, a student who wishes to focus on cultural differences might list the following questions:

Questions for Interviewing

1. Do you see yourself as a minority of any kind? because of your race? your ethnic group? your gender? your religion? your physical appearance? your intellectual or social interests? your age? your status as a full-time or part-time student? as a commuting student? as a parent?

2. Do you tend to associate mainly with those who are part of this same minority?

3. In what other ways do you see yourself as different from students here?

4. Do you feel the same difference in your home neighborhood? in your job?

5. Do you think others (students, teachers, staff, colleagues at work, neighbors) treat you differently from the way they treat others? Why?

6. Does your sense of being different in some way affect how you behave? How?

Questions for a Survey*

1. In terms of ethnicity, how would you describe yourself?

2. Do you see yourself as a minority on campus?

3. Do you associate in your free time mainly with those whose ethnicity is similar to yours?

4. Do you think that you are discriminated against on campus?
   a. Often
   b. Sometimes
   c. Rarely

5. In your home environment, do you see yourself as a minority?

6. In your home environment, do you associate mainly with those whose ethnicity is similar to yours?

7. In your home environment, do you think that you are discriminated against?
   a. Often
   b. Sometimes
   c. Rarely

8. Where are you most likely to associate with those who are not of your ethnic group? For example, at home, in the classroom, in a place of religious worship, at places of entertainment (movies, dance halls, concerts, sporting events, and so forth)?

---

*Most of the questions you might ask during an interview can also be put on a survey that would solicit responses from a larger number of people. Information acquired as the result of a survey is usually, however, less rich because—unlike in an interview—you cannot usually follow up on interesting points that emerge as you talk to an interviewee.

Note: Surveys need to be clear and easy on the eyes. Try out several formats before deciding on one you can use.

Questions for Observation

1. What sort of differences are visible on your campus? in your neighborhood? at your job?

2. In each of these settings, do people spend most time with those who seem to be most like themselves? In which of these settings is that most true? least true?

3. Do people behave differently depending on whether they're interacting with those most or least like themselves?

4. How do students group themselves in your classes?

5. Do your teachers interact with all students the same way? Do you notice any differences?

Questions for the Library

1. Are statistics available about the makeup of the student body on your campus? on campuses across the country?

2. What information can I find about changes in the makeup of college students over the past 100 or so years?

3. Are there books written by people who describe what it's like being a member of a minority group? For example, what's it like to be handicapped in some way? What's it like to go back to college when you're 45? What's it like to be a woman in a mostly male setting? or vice versa?

4. Are there articles about the ways colleges (or businesses or neighborhoods) deal with human differences among their members? What seems to work? not work?

Questions for the Internet

1. What can I find out about the makeup at particular colleges by seeking out their home pages?

2. Are there special sites for students who see themselves as belonging to minority groups? sites for blind students? for older students?

3. Is there a government site that has information about current college students? a breakdown by ethnic group? by age? by gender?

4. Is there some site I can use to disseminate some of my interview questions and thus get input from students on other college campuses?

Once you have this bare-bones list of questions, you'll profit from talking them over with others. Get them to help you devise more questions and refine those you already have. And most important, get them to help you with questions for interviewing and observing. Then you're ready to decide more specifically how to go about your research: what to do first, next, and last.

All topics are not alike; some may require that you do a particular kind of research first. The main thing for you in this workshop is to learn to have comfortable traffic back and forth between your own thinking and observing and the thinking and information that others have published. In most workshops we emphasize collaboration with fellow students. Here we want you to understand that you can also collaborate with people you know only through their published works, through interviewing them, or through the words they post on the Internet. What you'll probably realize as you work through this assignment is that you'll need to move back and forth between all these varieties of research.

Before you actually begin to do the research you've laid out for yourself, we suggest that you write a brief list of some of the things you suspect your research will uncover. This may seem odd to you, but it often makes your research more exciting if you've already got some possible conclusions in mind. This list can be very sketchy—just fantasize that you already know all there is to know about your topic.

A note of caution: Students often think that research papers have to prove something. One of the lessons we stressed in Workshop 9 is that we can seldom prove things: All we can do is get people to listen. Except in rare cases, you're not going to get a final answer to whatever question you pose for yourself. The best you can do is gather data that give you insight into a possible answer, one that will be valid within the limits you set for yourself. You can't come to any conclusions about what American college students think about campus food, but you can reach some conclusions about what undergraduates (or perhaps only freshmen or just male freshmen) on your particular campus think about campus food in particular cafeterias right now.

You can't claim anything beyond what your research shows, but that doesn't mean you can't make suggestions or hypothesize about larger issues. It means you have to acknowledge what your data and information apply to and what they don't.

Step Four: Doing Research

Interviewing and Observing

Observing and interviewing are skills; you'll want to make sure you're doing them as well as possible. Before you begin your research through observing, map out where to observe and what sorts of activities to look for. The questions you draw up to further your research will be mainly questions to yourself while you're observing.

After a practice run, you may need to alter those questions. Most researchers build a practice run directly into their research plans, knowing that they can't always decide what to look for until they've started looking.

If you're going to design a questionnaire, make sure you try it out on friends or classmates first to uncover whatever glitches it may have. Researchers in the social sciences almost always do this. When you plan your interviewing, it's important to prepare a set list of questions if you're going to draw valid conclusions. You can also do these activities in tandem: First ask your informants to respond to a written questionnaire and follow that up by interviewing a random sample of those who responded. This is also an established research practice, performed, for example, by the U.S. Census Bureau. Also, before you start on your interviews, you may want to look at some of the advice in Workshop 10.

Strategies for research are as varied as the questions that can be asked. But you should be able to lay out a plan of action for yourself with the help of your teacher and your classmates. The important thing is to keep your task manageable, to make it into something you can handle within the time you have.

Surveying

It's a good idea to distribute your survey to your classmates first so you have some basis on which to judge how well you've constructed it. You can talk over the classroom results with your peers and do some revision of the survey form itself before you distribute it widely. Where to distribute it then becomes the issue. Perhaps your classmates will be willing to hand it out in their other classes or in their dormitories. One of us was even asked to fill out a survey on a train on the way home from the campus. You might try lunchrooms or other places where students congregate too. Meetings of campus activity groups are another possibility.

Using the Library

If you're not familiar with your campus library, you'll want to set aside some time to become comfortable finding your way around it.

Few people who use libraries ever master them. Realize that it's legitimate to ask librarians for help—and don't be afraid to ask dumb questions. Most are happy to help as long as you treat your own questions as occasions for learning, not as requests for them to do the work for you. Libraries are ideal places for wandering and browsing; people who like libraries let themselves pause and glance at books or documents that they are passing. Read a few titles, pick up a book, look at the table of contents, and read a page. Libraries are good for serendipitous finds. Don't give in to the feeling that many people have: "I don't belong here if I don't know where to find what I want." Here are some of the most promising places to look for information in a library:

- General encyclopedias (e.g., *Encyclopedia Americana* or *Encyclopedia Britannica*).
- Specialized encyclopedias (e.g., *McGraw-Hill Encyclopedia of Science and Technology, International Encyclopedia of Higher Education,* or *The New Grove Dictionary of Music and Musicians*). There are specialized encyclopedias in many areas. Ask the librarian about encyclopedias in your field of interest.
- Almanacs (e.g., *Universal Almanac* or *Facts on File*).
- Biographical dictionaries (e.g., *Dictionary of American Biography* or *International Who's Who*).
- General periodical indexes (e.g., *Readers' Guide to Periodical Literature* or *Book Review Digest*). Periodical indexes allow you to search for articles by subject, author, or title.
- Specialized periodical indexes (e.g., *Education Index* or *United States Government Publications*). There are many such specialized indexes.
- Abstracts (e.g., *Psychological Abstracts*). An abstract is a summary. Reference rooms in libraries offer online, CD-ROM, or print volumes in various subject areas that include abstracts of articles.

Exploring the Writing Process
On Researching to Inform

I decided to write my essay as an informative piece on AIDS, because I feel that the AIDS crisis is a very serious issue that has to be exhausted until everyone begins to care and take precautions. The Magic Johnson tragedy really shocked me and instilled a fear in me that made me want to find out more about AIDS, and maybe allow others to learn from my essay. My main goal of this essay is education; to educate myself and others about AIDS.

I took the time to thoroughly read pamphlets and magazines on AIDS. Once I was knowledgeable about the subject I then conducted surveys on some Stony Brook students. I asked them one question: "How is AIDS transmitted?" Only the least knowledgeable (ignorant) students' responses were placed in my essay.

Student

Abstracts can save you time by pinpointing which articles would help your research and which would not.

- Book catalogs. Online Public Access Catalogs (OPACs) are computerized catalogs that have replaced or are replacing card catalogs at most libraries. Almost all are easy to use, and printed instructions are usually available. If not, ask for help from a librarian. Many libraries' online catalogs also provide access to other libraries' holdings, as well as to online reference databases and digital text collections.
- CD-ROM and online searches. Most libraries are now equipped with an array of electronic resources ranging from *The Oxford English Dictionary* or *Newspaper Abstracts* on CD-ROM to dedicated computer terminals providing access to the Internet. (Many of the print resources just listed are now available online or on CD-ROM, and will in some cases be available *only* in this form in the future.) For more on electronic searches, see "Finding Sources Online" later in this section.

Our list of reference sources is, of course, only illustrative. There are far too many to list here. (A full writing handbook or a textbook devoted to research papers will give more.) To see what more specific resources might be available in your area—and you will often find a reference book that is just what you need—consult a guide like Eugene P. Sheehy's *A Guide to Reference Books* or ask the help of a librarian. The value of reference books is that they give you an overview of your topic and a range of books and articles you can track down.*

There's another trick for researching worth mentioning: Once you've located a book on the shelves, spend some time looking at other books on the same shelves. After all, books *are* arranged by subject. In this way, you will almost surely locate some books you may never have found through the library's catalog. Warning: As you use such books (and indeed any books or articles), check publication dates. If you are working on some topic in a rapidly developing field, materials can get outdated quickly.

The essential skill for doing library research is to learn a *different relationship to the printed (or electronic) word*. We tend to feel we have to *read* articles and books, but in research you need to learn to *glance, browse,* and *leaf* through material. You have learned the main thing if you can tell in a few seconds from a title or an abstract

---

* You might want to look at Pat Belanoff, Betsy Rohrschach, and Mia Oberlink's *The Right Handbook*, which presents a process for working through a research paper that fits well with this workshop.

whether something is worth tracking down, then tell in a minute or two whether an article or website is worth reading, and in two or three minutes whether a book is worth spending an hour trying to mine (not necessarily read).

Of course you have to do some *careful* reading too. Think of it this way: You don't have much time for this research assignment, so you'll want to end up having browsed and dipped into a number of books, articles, and online sources, and having found 50 to 100 pages worth reading carefully for the light they throw on your topic. The main task is to *find* the best 50 to 100 pages to read carefully—and not waste time reading the *wrong* 50 to 100 pages. Inevitably, however, you will do some reading you won't use. This procedure should make you more skilled and comfortable when you have something you want to investigate further.

Remember too that you cannot say *everything* about any topic. You always need to limit what you say in some way. Your research is always more convincing and valid to the degree that you realize—and show your reader that you realize—that you are not claiming to have read everything on the subject. This means that you can feel fine about acknowledging what you haven't done. One of the most interesting parts of a research paper can be a section that talks about questions or material you would pursue if you were able to carry on with more research or your suggestions for others who might want to do so. Good researchers almost always do this.

Using the Internet

This section assumes that you have access to a computer with a connection to the Internet and that you have used a browser such as Netscape Communicator or Internet Explorer. If you have never used a browser, ask your teacher about computer labs at your school. Ask the staff there (or a friendly, knowledgeable amateur) for help getting started.

With some practice, you should be at home on the Web in no time. Indeed, the Web's merit lies in the simplicity of its navigation and design: Not only can anyone learn to cruise the Web fairly quickly, but practically anyone can learn to make a webpage. This easy access does, however, create problems for the researcher. Because anyone can make a webpage cheaply and with relatively little labor, academically suspect information often masquerades as authoritative research. When researching on the Web, you have to spend more time discriminating between what is useful and what is useless. See "Evaluating Online Sources" (page 285) for advice on how to separate the wheat from the chaff.

Finding Sources Online

Start by finding your library's home page and looking for a list of online resources available. You may be able to search a number of reference databases online; some of these may even allow you to download the full texts of journal, magazine, and newspaper articles. Table 1 provides a *sampling* of the research databases one mid-sized college library offers online:

Table 1 Research Databases

Research Database	Description
EbscoHost	Several subject databases with over 2,500 periodicals in full text. Subject areas include humanities, social sciences, cultural studies, general sciences, education, business, and health.
Encyclopedia Britannica	Contains the full text of the 32-volume *Encyclopedia Britannica*.
ERIC	Citations and abstracts of international journals and report literature in education and related fields.
Lexis-Nexis	Approximately 5,000 legal, news, reference, and business sources, most full text.
Literature Resource Center	Information on literary figures from all time periods writing in such genres as fiction, nonfiction, poetry, drama, history, journalism, and more.
Medline	Source for clinical medical information covering all aspects of biomedicine, including the allied health fields; biological and physical sciences; and humanities and information science as they relate to medicine and health care.
MLA Bibliography	Indexes 3,000 English language and foreign periodicals as well as books, book chapters, and dissertations. Its subject matter includes critical works on literature, language, linguistics, and folklore.

Table 1 Research Databases—continued

Research Database	Description
ProQuest	PA Research II: The *New York Times, The Wall Street Journal, USA TODAY,* and *Barron's.*
	ABI/INFORM Global: Provides full-text articles from more than 600 journals on management techniques, corporate strategies, trends, and business conditions.
	American Medical Association: Publications of the American Medical Association including *JAMA, American Medical News,* and the Archives.
	Newspapers: Articles from 41 national newspapers, including *The Wall Street Journal,* The *New York Times* (current 90 days only), *Barron's,* and the *Washington Post.*
PsycINFO Direct	1.4 million bibliographic records of journal articles, books, and technical reports in the field of psychology.
Public Affairs Information Service (PAIS)	Covers public policy, social policy, and the social sciences.
Social Work Abstracts	More than 35,000 records from journals concerning social work and other related subjects.
Wilson Web	46,000 biographical essays on individuals past, present, living, and dead, representing all occupations and fields of endeavor.

Assuming you have a home computer, a connection to your school's network, and the appropriate passwords, you will be able to do much of your preliminary research from the comfort of your own home.

It is also possible, of course, to do research online through institutions other than your school (for example, a public library such as the Library of Congress at www.loc.gov), and to do research directly on the Internet. Be prepared, however, to invest some time in learning how to refine your online searches, ferret out relevant websites, and determine their relative usefulness.

If you've ever used an Internet search engine before, you probably have experienced the frustration of retrieving a huge number of URLs (Uniform Resource Locators, which are websites' addresses) with little or no relevance to your topic. (See Table 2 for a few commonly used search engines.) Instead of paging through thousands of links, you need to learn how to supply the search engine with more precise information about your topic.

Table 2

Search Tool	Description
AltaVista www.altavista.com	Comprehensive full-text search engine. Retrieves large number of results (not always relevant). Use when doing a specific search for obscure information.
Yahoo www.yahoo.com	Subject directory to selected resources, rather than a full-text search engine. Use when browsing, and for subject categories and overviews of your topic.
Google www.google.com	Full-text search engine *and* web directory. Uses newer software and hardware technology that makes many searches faster. So far receiving high praise from industry insiders.
MetaCrawler www.metacrawler.com	Metasearch engine. Searches multiple engines at one time (currently AltaVista, Excite, Google, GoTo, LookSmart, Lycos, MetaCatalog, and WebCrawler, among others).

Most engines allow you to use symbols that help you limit your search. (*All* will have instructions on how to conduct searches using that engine and specifically on how to limit search results. On the home page of the search engine, look for links that say "advanced searches," "refining your search," or "help.") Here are some of the most commonly used symbols:

- Quotation marks ("") designate *phrases* that must appear in the search results. If you type in *deviant behavior,* the search results will include all documents that contain the word *deviant* and all those that contain *behavior*. If, however, you type in the phrase *"deviant behavior"* (in quotes), you will receive only those documents containing both words, in the prescribed order.

- A plus sign (+) before a word (e.g., +*gun* +*laws*) indicates words that *must* appear in the search results, though not necessarily in any order.
- A minus sign (–) before a word (e.g., –*stock "car racing"*) indicates that you wish to exclude results containing that word. The example in parentheses would return results for *car racing* but would exclude sites concerning *stock car racing.*
- An asterisk (*) or wildcard allows you to search for words with various endings. For instance, the search term *bibl** will return any pages with *bible, bibles, biblia, biblical,* but also *bibliography, bibliophile,* and so on.

In addition, most search engines support Boolean operators, such as the following:

- AND returns all documents containing the words separated by AND (i.e., *Chinese* AND *checkers* AND *rules*).
- OR returns all documents containing either the word or phrase preceding or the word/phrase following OR (e.g., *"Louis XIV"* OR *"Sun King"*).
- NOT returns all documents containing the first word and excluding the second word (*butter* NOT *margarine*). For some search engines, you will have to type "AND NOT" rather than "NOT" to perform this function.
- Parentheses allow you to group together search terms in order to perform more complicated searches—such as *"Pope John Paul"* AND (*abortion* OR *contraception*).

Once you have learned how to refine your search, you will begin to return a more reasonable number of results. If you are still unable to find anything relevant to your source after refining your search in several ways, try another search engine. No two search engines will return the same results. If one search engine proves to be unhelpful, chances are that another one will point you in the right direction.

Evaluating Online Sources

To determine the potential usefulness of each source you've uncovered, read through it and ask yourself the following questions:

1. Is the source authoritative? If you don't see an author named, pursue links toward the home page of the site until you find information about where the article comes from. You must determine the reliability of the organization responsible for publishing the article and consider how carefully it screens its submissions. If you feel an article is more authoritative than the publication information suggests, don't be afraid to e-mail the person who maintains the site and ask for clarification.

Once you have gathered information about authorship and publication, you can move on to other questions: Does the article cite other relevant articles for the information it provides? Has it been published in a printed journal or magazine? Has it been read and approved by other scholars in the field (a process called peer review)? Is the author a recognized authority in the field? You may not find answers to all of these questions, but you can be much more confident of sources for which the answer is yes.

2. How impartial is the source? You should not rule out a source just because it takes a strong stand on a controversial issue, but writers of opinionated pieces often have not taken the time to research all sides of an issue. Once again, finding out information about who publishes the page is essential. In general, web addresses with an .edu (educational) or .gov (government) suffix tend to be more neutral and therefore more reliable. Commercial (.com) and not-for-profit organizations (.org) are more likely to have a vested interest in your topic.

3. Is the source presented in a professional manner? First and foremost, look for an indication of the time a page was last updated (usually at the bottom of a site's home page). If it has not been modified in the last six months, then you should question its reliability. Consider these issues as well:

- Are there links in the site that don't work?
- If there are images on the page, do any of them fail to load up in your window?
- Is the text hard to read because of the background color, or because it is cut off by images?
- Does the visual presentation of the page distract you from the text of the article?

The more that you answer yes to these questions, the less likely it is that this source—or the website that publishes it—will be around tomorrow.

4. Is it useful? Ultimately, questions about a source's reliability are not nearly as important as the question of usefulness: What aspect of your topic interested you in the first place, and what does this online source contribute to your own position? The sources that are the most persuasive and informative often cause us the most trouble since we are inclined to repeat their ideas rather than articulate our own. When you find such a source, it is a good idea to ask yourself how relevant this information is to your main point.

If one of your searches turns up an insightful discussion in a page with no academic credentials or institutional affiliation, the lack of formal authority for this discussion should not preclude you from using it. Many search engines, for instance, will return results that were originally posted in newsgroups.* You may want to e-mail the person who posted the message to find out how she learned so much about the topic and where you might find these sources. This person may be willing to be interviewed. If you are worried about whether an informal interview or newsgroup posting is sufficiently reliable, then ask your teacher. Most teachers recognize that a source that stirs your interest and reminds you of why you chose to write about a topic is far more *useful* than one that confuses, bores, or leads you astray.

Two Short Exercises on Evaluating Online Sources

Learning to assess the value of online sources is a difficult process. Nevertheless, if you fail to evaluate your online sources carefully before using them in your paper, the results can be disastrous. The following two exercises are intended to develop your critical skills.

Exercise One: Evaluating a Web Source

1. Open up your Internet browser and a word processing program. You will use the word processing window to compose the evaluation of your potential source.

2. Using your browser, locate a search engine (see Table 2) and find an online source that is relevant to your topic. Once you have found one, use the information on the page to create a proper bibliographic entry at the top of your word processing window. When you are done, save your document.

3. Read through the source with an eye to the evaluative questions listed earlier. While you are reading, note any features that suggest the relative authority of this page:
   - Who is the author?
   - When was it last updated?
   - What organization is responsible for publishing it?
   - What does the text of the article tell you about the author's competence in this field? Remember that you will have to visit other neighboring pages to find out more about your source.

4. Spend some time with each of the other three concerns:
   - How impartial is this source?
   - How professional is its presentation?
   - And most important, how potentially useful is it to your own project?
   - As you record your notes in the word processing window, remember to save before returning to your browser.

---

* Newsgroups work very much like a bulletin board: Anyone can visit a newsgroup and post messages to it. Since each newsgroup usually focuses on a narrow topic, there are often very informative messages posted.

5. Once you have considered all of the evaluative criteria, return to your word processing window, review your notes, and come to some conclusion about the usefulness of this source. With this conclusion as your thesis, organize your notes into points of support. Don't be afraid to conclude that this source won't be very useful for you: We don't expect you to find the perfect source today! A sober description of this source and its relation to your own research project is much more important. When you finish, save your work and find out what your teacher wants you to do with the document. (If your class will be continuing with the next collaborative exercise, then you can skip the first three steps.)

Exercise Two: Collaborative Feedback
Each group should contain three to four students.

1. In a word processing window, type your name and describe your research project in a sentence or two. After you have saved this description, leave the word processing window open. Launch a Web browser of your choice and use a search engine to find a source relevant to your topic.

2. Now switch back to your word processing window. Below your description, type in a bibliographic entry for this source (see "Documenting Your Work" on pages 290–298). Save this document and leave it and the browsing window open.

3. Now swap seats with someone else in your group. Read through the description of his or her project. Click over to the Web browser and read through the other student's source. While you are reading, note in the word processing window any features that suggest the value of this page as a source—that is, is it authoritative, impartial, professional, useful? Note these beneath the other student's bibliographic entry and leave at least two blank spaces between your comments and the bibliographic entry. Since you will have to do this for every group member, try not to spend more than 10 minutes on this.

4. When you have finished, proceed to another student's computer and follow the same steps. When you have responded to every student in your group, return to your own station and print out a description of your project, along with everyone else's comments.

5. Assemble with other group members and discuss which student had the most useful source. If there is time, present your group's conclusion to the rest of the class. What made this student's source superior to those of other group members? What were the weaknesses of this source?

Step Five: Writing an Exploratory Draft

Once you've done whatever tasks you set for yourself for the first segment of your research (observing/interviewing, library study, or doing
research online), you're ready to write an exploratory draft. Before
beginning, we recommend that you lay out all the notes and writing
you've done so far and read through everything. After this perusal, do
some freewriting to record what you've learned and how you react to
seeing all the material. Think particularly about whether you've discovered any patterns or recurrent themes in your writing and notes.

You may discover at this point that you're interested not in your
original question any more, but in some other question that has arisen
as you worked on this project. If this were a rigid assignment, you'd
have to continue with your original questions, but we're not being
rigid here. If you have come up with a more interesting question
or discovered something more thought provoking than what you
started out to discover, we hope you'll change your project to follow
up on it. In truth, such change of direction happens quite often in
real-world research. (And we suggest that if in other classes you come
up with something slightly different from the assignment, ask your
teacher whether you can adjust the assignment to what you've discovered. The worst your teacher can say is no. Many teachers will
say yes.)

As you write this draft or after you've finished it, jot down questions for yourself to use as the basis of your next round of research,
which may include a return to what you've already done to refine it
or a move to another form of research—either in or out of the library.

One of the fallacies about research is that researchers always use
everything they find and all research notes they write up. This is simply not true.

Step Six: Outlining, and Moving toward a Final Draft

Whenever you decide you have done as much research as necessary,
you are ready to write a full draft of your paper. Because the research
process gives you lots of notes and rough writing, you may lose direction or perspective. Thus, you may want to make an outline before you start your full draft. Or you may decide instead to make an
outline *after* you've written your draft. You don't need to spend a lot
of time on an outline. It can be as simple as this:

> I'll start by stating why I was interested in my subject and what
> my original thinking was, move to how I went about doing the re-
> search, lay out some of what I found, and end with my conclusions.

Or you may want something as detailed as this:

1. Statement of question.
2. Statement of methods of research.
3. Recounting of observations.
   a. Engineers.
   b. Classrooms.
4. Recounting of interviews.
   a. Engineers.
   b. Undergraduates.
5. Recounting of information gleaned from books and magazines.
6. Reflections on the ways the interviews, observations, and printed sources confirm one another, if at all.
   a. Similarities.
   b. Differences.
7. Conclusions.
8. Possible explanations of conclusions.
9. What I learned and what it means to me.
10. What I'd still like to know.

An important thing to remember about outlines—whether generalized or specific—is that they're only outlines: You need not follow them like a robot. As you begin to write, you may discover some better structure. That may cause you to go back and revise your outline, although you needn't do this if you feel that the structure you're working with is satisfactory.

You can get help from others at this stage. Read or describe your bits of information and data to them and ask them for suggestions about what they see as central and organizing. There are no right answers as to how a paper should be organized; it's a question of what works best for readers.* You may want to try out two or three organizations.

Step Seven: Documenting Your Work

You'll need to make sure that you know how to document the information you've used in your paper. Your teacher will tell you what

---

* There are some important exceptions here. If you write a research paper for a particular discipline such as chemistry or sociology, there are some conventions guiding how it should be put together, just as there is a standard form for scientific articles in certain fields.

Exploring the Writing Process
On Writing and Patience

The paper I recently sent off to the journal represents the most demanding and most satisfying work of my writing life so far. . . .

The project began two years ago, when for the sake of my own sanity I decided to focus on an interdisciplinary project—the interface of ecology and philosophy. I had been drowning in philosophy, condemned to be free. I had no moorings or orientation within philosophy, so I turned to my own experience and concerns to give me a foothold in reality. That allowed me the freedom to explore diverse aspects of philosophy without losing a basic sense of direction and purpose.

Slowly, I began to pull the ideas together. . . . Once in a while, I would try to draw my thoughts together into a self-definition, usually a short written statement. What am I doing? How? Why? Invariably my thought would break through that inadequate statement almost before my inadequate word processor was done printing it. I kept reading and thinking and talking, biding my time.

Last January, I began a period of more focused research, with a paper topic in mind. I don't know when I finally settled on a title, but the topic *was* the title: "How Ecological Is Ecophilosophy?" I read intensively, and scribbled down notes as my thought developed.

At last the time was ripe to begin writing. It was March, almost April. Drawing it all together, making it *fit* was more difficult than I had ever imagined. I was dealing with a lot of material and thought: *patience* became my chief tool. On paper, or on my WP, I worked it through, forcing the thoughts into words, forcing the words into structured forms, on the paper.

Inspiration would strike at odd times. I had to keep pencil and paper handy, just in case I had a flash. . . .

During the summer, I ignored it. I told people that I'd buried it in the backyard for the earthworms to edit. When autumn came, the time was ripe once more. Exhumed and reconsidered, with more and more feedback, the paper changed again and again, passing through successive stages of order and disorder. It would arrive at equilibrium, but my thought would break through it, breaking it apart, and it would demand reintegration. . . .

A few weeks ago, I was satisfied with my paper: it was good enough to submit for consideration. All I had to do was polish it up. So I read it over and found a dozen things to revise; they were minor points really, but

Exploring the Writing Process
On Writing and Patience   *continued*

important enough. So I "fixed" them, and read it over again. I found a dozen things to revise. Again and again.

I foresaw no end to it but the slow demise of my paper. If I picked at it ad infinitum it would come apart again, and I doubted I had the energy or the time to rebuild it. My thought was already moving beyond it, to new things. The moment was propitious: I mailed it to the journal.

Bob Kirkman

style of documentation she wishes you to use. She may also want to go over some of that technical information in class. If you've used a survey, you should include it plus a tabulation of the answers. If you used the Internet, you'll also need to document that as a source.

Documentation of sources is particularly important in research papers—just as important for personal research as for library research. None of us has the right to claim credit for the ideas and words of others regardless of whether we read them or heard them in an interview. And, from a pragmatic point of view, documentation lends authority to your research paper. If people know that you feel safe in revealing your sources, thus giving readers the opportunity to check their validity, they're far more likely to give your words credit.

Styles and conventions of documenting and acknowledging indebtedness to the ideas of others vary widely across disciplines. (Even concepts of authorship can vary from discipline to discipline.) When doing research in other classes, be sure you take time to become familiar with the conventions of that particular discipline. If in doubt, *ask.* We've heard of too many cases where students were accused of plagiarizing but were actually victims of their own lack of knowledge about how to document.

Quotations

It is possible to do a considerable amount of research and learn from the information and opinions of interviewees and published works— and write a terrific paper of your own without a single quotation or footnote. (Joyce has no footnotes in *Ulysses* for all the details he checked up on.) But for this assignment we are asking for some quotations and footnotes. Your reader should feel he is in a large room with a number of people—other voices—involved in the issue. Quotations that allow these voices to come through to your readers will give them a feel for the texture of research on your issue.

Footnotes Aren't Footnotes Anymore

"Footnote" is the word that probably springs to mind when you think of how to document your sources: a *note* at the *foot* of the page. But we are following the recent Modern Language Association (MLA) guidelines for citing sources *without* footnotes. The new MLA citation system makes life easier for both writers and readers and is now standard for academic writing in most of the humanities. (You can still use footnotes for an aside to the reader, but try not to use too many since they can make a reader feel bumped around.)

The citation system that fits the social or natural sciences is the American Psychological Association (APA) system. At the end of our listing of examples in the MLA style, we'll list the major differences between MLA and APA. But always be aware of our advice about methods of documentation in various disciplines.

Documentation procedure has two elements: the *parenthetical citation* in your text as you go along, and the *list of works cited* at the end. When you want to document a source—that is, to tell readers what article, book, or interviewee you are referring to—add a small parenthetical citation. Parentheses show readers where to look for the full information about the article or book in the final list of works cited.

Parenthetical Citations

In parentheses place only the information that readers need for finding the article or book in your list of works cited. Thus:

- Give *only* the page number(s) in your parentheses if you mention the author in your text. For example, your text might read as follows:

  Hammond writes that early jazz recordings contain little if any improvisation (87).

  Note that the closing parenthesis is *inside* the sentence's punctuation.

- If the author's name is not in your sentence, then add the name to the parentheses. For example:

  At least one music historian has noted that early jazz recordings contain little if any improvisation (Hammond 87).

  Note that there's no comma between the author's name and the page number. The last name alone is sufficient unless you are using two authors with the same name.

- If you cite more than one work by Hammond in your essay, add the title (or shortened title) to your parentheses—for example, (Hammond, *An Experience* 87). But you can skip the title if you mention it in your text. Note the comma after the author's name but not after the title.

Other conventions:

- Titles of articles or chapters are in quotation marks; book titles are italicized or underlined with no quotation marks.*
- If the work has more than one volume, specify which one you are citing, followed by a colon and the page number—for example, (1:179).
- If citing a passage from a poem, give line numbers. If citing a passage from a play, give act, scene, and lines—for example, (4.5.11–14).
- If there are two or three authors, list them; for more than three, cite only the first author and add "et al."

In APA style, always give the date of the work, but don't give page numbers unless it's a direct quotation. Thus our first example above, if changed to APA, would be simply (1970). The second example would be (Hammond, 1970). Note the comma before the date.

Works Cited

This is a list of outside sources you cite in your paper. Place it at the end of your research paper on a separate sheet. Here are examples of the most common kinds of citations:

> *Print and other traditional sources.*   The items are alphabetized by author and follow this general sequence: author, title, publisher. Here's the order in more detail:
>
> - Author (last name first).
> - Full title of the work you're citing. If this is part of a larger work, the title will be in quotation marks.
> - The title of any larger work, magazine, or journal—if the work you're citing is part of a larger work. This title will be underlined or italicized.
> - Name of the editor or translator, if any (first name first).
> - Edition.
> - Volume number. For example, if the work consists of five volumes, and you used only volumes 2 and 3, you need to make that clear.

---

* Most word processing programs allow you to italicize titles. Nevertheless, some teachers might prefer that you continue to underline them. Check with your teacher before submitting final copy. Probably the most important thing is that you are consistent in your citation style.

- City of publication.
- Publisher.
- Year of publication.
- Page numbers (if the work you're citing is only a portion of the larger publication).

Note: If the work you cite is unsigned (e.g., an article in an encyclopedia or newspaper), begin with the title.

Book

Cameron, Julia. *The Right to Write: An Invitation and Initiation into the Writing Life.* New York: Putnam-Penguin, 1999.

Note: If Cameron had been the editor rather than the author, her name would be followed by a comma and "ed."

Article in a periodical: newspaper

Campbell, Paula Walker. "Controversial Proposal on Public Access to Research Data Draws 10,000 Comments." *Chronicle of Higher Education* 16 Apr. 1999: A42.

Article in a periodical: monthly magazine

Gardner, Howard. "Who Owns Intelligence?" *Atlantic Monthly* Feb. 1999: 67–76.

Article in a periodical: scholarly journal

Gillette, Mary Ann, and Carol Videon. "Seeking Quality on the Internet: A Case Study of Composition Students' Works Cited." *Teaching English in the Two-Year College* 26 (1998): 189–95.

Note two things: (1) The second author's name is not reversed. (2) Because the pages of this journal are continuously numbered throughout the year, we have "26 (1998): 189–95." If it were a journal where each issue started with page 1, the note would read "26.2 (1998): 189–95." (The "2" here means the second issue of that year.)

Article or other work in an anthology

Gioia, Dana. "My Confessional Sestina." *Rebel Angels: 25 Poets of the New Formalism.* Ed. Mark Jarman and David Mason. Brownsville, OR: Story Line, 1996. 48–9.

Hammond, John. "An Experience in Jazz History." *Black Music in Our Culture: Curricular Ideas on the Subjects, Materials, and Problems.* Ed. Dominique-René de Lerma. Kent: Kent State UP, 1970. 42–53. Rpt. in *Keeping Time: Readings in Jazz History.* Ed. Robert Walser. New York: Oxford UP, 1999. 86–96.

Note: The second source listed here is a scholarly essay
reprinted in a current anthology. The facts of the original
publication *must* be provided for scholarly articles
subsequently reprinted: note the abbreviation "rpt." (reprint),
which clarifies the relation between the two sources.

Letter or personal interview

Fontaine, Sheryl. Letter to the authors [or "Telephone interview"
or "Personal communication"]. 14 Apr. 1999.

Review

O'Neill, Peggy. Rev. of *Reflection in the Writing Classroom,* by
Kathleen Blake Yancey. *Teaching English in the Two-Year
College* 26 (1998): 202–204.

Electronic sources. The documentation of electronic sources,
like these sources themselves, is in a state of constant flux.
The general principles mirror those governing the
documentation of print sources, but the information itself is
necessarily somewhat different. One key difference is the
requirement in many cases to include the *date you accessed* a
particular site. The general pattern for online sources runs as
follows (with each piece of information required only *if
applicable and available*):

- Author(s).
- Title of the work you're citing, underlined or italicized. (If the
  piece you're citing is part of a larger work, then the title
  would be in quotation marks.)
- Name of editor(s), compiler(s), or translator(s).
- Publication information for any print version of the source.
- Title of any larger work (scholarly project, database, or peri-
  odical) in which the cited work appears.
- Name of the editor of the scholarly project or database.
- Version number of the source or, for an electronic journal, the
  volume number, issue number, or other identifying number.
- Date of electronic publication or of the latest update.
- Name of any sponsoring institution or organization, such as
  a museum or university.
- Date of access and network address.

For a professional or personal site, the information is less
complicated. This is the general pattern:

- Author(s).
- Title of site—if there is no title, use a generic term such as
  "Home page" (without underlining or quotes). If the page has

an official title (for example, *Italo Calvino Page*), it would be underlined or italicized.
* Name of sponsoring organization, if any.
* Date of access and network address.

CD-ROM, magnetic tape, and diskettes. These sources are handled somewhat differently; they are closer to traditional print sources in format:
* Author(s).
* Title of publication.
* Name of editor, compiler, or translator.
* Publication medium (CD-ROM, diskette, or magnetic tape).
* Edition, release, or version.
* Place of publication.
* Name of publisher.
* Date of publication.

Examples of some of the most common entries follow:

Online database, scholarly project, or personal or professional website

Novosel, Tony. *The Great War.* 27 Apr. 1999 <http://www.pitt.edu/~pugachev/greatwar/ww1.html>.*

THOMAS: Legislative Information on the Internet. 9 Apr. 1999. Lib. of Congress, Washington. 25 Apr. 1999 <http://thomas.loc.gov/>.

Voice of the Shuttle: Web Page for Humanities Research. Ed. Alan Liu. 22 Apr. 1999. English Dept., Univ. of CA, Santa Barbara. 28 Apr. 1999 <http://humanitas.ucsb.edu/>.

Material from an online database or scholarly project

Bimber, Bruce. "The Death of an Agency: Office of Technology Assessment & Budget Politics in the 104th Congress." *Voice of the Shuttle: Web Page for Humanities Research.* Ed. Alan Liu. 22 Apr. 1999. English Dept., Univ. of CA, Santa Barbara. 28 Apr. 1999 <http://humanitas.ucsb.edu/liu/bimber.html>.

Article in an online periodical

Herbert, Bob. "The Other America." *New York Times on the Web* 9 Apr. 1999. 25 Apr. 1999 <http://www.nytimes.com/library/opinion/herbert/ 040899herbert.html>.

---

* The angled marks (< >) used in citations of electronic sources are part of the citation style, not part of the URLs. Type in only what's between them when searching for the sites online.

Material from a CD-ROM.

Whiting, R.M., and Ignace J. Gelb. "Writing." *Microsoft Encarta 98 Encyclopedia Deluxe Edition.* CD-ROM. 1998 ed. Redmond, WA: Microsoft, 1997.

Note how citations have "hung margins"; that is, the first line of each citation is flush left (all the way to the left margin of type on the page), and succeeding lines of each citation are indented one-half inch—as we have shown them. Our examples are single-spaced as they would be in published or printed matter. Teachers will probably want you to double-space your citations.

APA Style

If you are using APA style, you will call the list of sources "References" rather than "Works Cited." The chief differences in style are that initials rather than first names are used, the date of the work appears immediately after the author's name, only the first word of the source is capitalized (although journal titles are capitalized in the conventional manner), and no quotation marks are used for journal articles. Thus, you would have the following:

Cameron, J. 1999. *The right to write: an invitation and initiation into the writing life.* New York: Putnam-Penguin.

Gillett, M.A., and C. Videon. 1998. Seeking quality on the Internet: a case study of composition students' works cited. *Teaching English in the Two-Year College,* 26: 189–95.

You'll also notice some minor differences in punctuation.

We have shown here only the most common kinds of citations. You will need to consult a good handbook for more complicated ones, especially for works from unusual sources (such as a television advertisement, record jacket, or map). A particularly good source for documentation styles in the humanities is the Modern Language Association's website: http://www.mla.org. From this home page, click on "MLA Style Manual." Chapters 6 and 7 will probably be the most useful.

Step Eight: Writing an Abstract

You may have noticed while doing your research that quite a few of the articles you read in periodicals were preceded by a paragraph or so that summarized the content of the articles. This is an abstract. Abstracts are enormously helpful because they can keep a researcher from reading articles that are not helpful for her research and point her directly to articles that might be helpful. Basically, an abstract is a summary (often about 100 words—though your teacher may specify a length for you) of your subject, the process of your research, what you uncovered, and what you conclude.

It's best to write your abstract right before you do a final revision. Producing a summary such as this can pull together what you've done and create a focus for you as well as for the reader. If you discover, while working on your abstract, that you are having difficulty summarizing, it may be because you haven't been focused enough. Thus, trying to write an abstract can lead you to revise effectively.

Once you have revised your paper into final form, you may need to make some adjustments to your abstract. But don't forget that the abstract is an important part of the argument and needs to be attached to your paper when you submit it to your teacher or to peer readers.

ALTERNATIVE TO THE MAIN ASSIGNMENT
The I-Search

You can think of this paper as a narrative of the steps you took to collect information for your research paper. Now, though, instead of writing the actual research paper, you will be writing a paper that sets forth clearly the steps of your research. It should include, at a minimum, the reasons you chose your topic, what you hoped or expected to discover, and what you did discover. For each step (interviewing, searching the Internet, using the library, observing), state why you chose that particular method for getting information, what you actually uncovered, and how this information led you to your next step. Be sure to record both your successes and your failures; you may have undertaken some task that yielded no information at all, or you may have ended up collecting lots of information that you later discarded. All researchers experience such setbacks. Finally, sum up what you learned about doing research, and what you would do differently next time (including any new topic you've learned about that you'd like at some point to investigate further). The basic difference between the I-search paper and a more traditional research paper is that the former is a record of the *process* of your research and the latter is a record of the *product* of your research.

Writing as Play | Changing Fonts, Colors, and Typefaces

We think the I-search paper is fun, but perhaps you'd like to try something different. Here's another suggestion: Go through your finished, word processed paper and play with type size and font. Pick the most important idea and make it boldface, enlarge the font, or use a fancy typeface of some kind. Select the sentences that present supporting points and change their typefaces in some way that differentiates them from your main idea. Then look at your paper for other commonalities: You might want to put all specific examples in a common font; you might want to put various connectives (such as *so, but, and, therefore*) in special sizes and fonts. If you have a color printer, you can play with color also. You can put quoted material in a different font—and all citations in some other font. You could use boldface for and enlarge the names of all those whose works you've cited.

What we've described does not exhaust the possibilities. We're sure you can think of other ways to play with fonts, colors, and typefaces and inject them into your piece.

When you're done, consider whether highlighting the various parts of your paper affects the way you read it. If so, how? Ask a friend to read both versions. How does the altered look of the paper affect her reading of it?

Suggestions for Collaboration

Most researchers know they need to pool their work in order to begin to think about definitive answers. You and another student or even your whole group may decide to focus on one topic, which you can research together. You can then integrate what you've done and turn this workshop into a collaborative writing task. This sort of project will give you a feel for the kinds of collaborative work so prevalent in the scientific and business world today.

If you decide to make this into a major collaborative project, you may want to go back and read over the sections on collaborative writing in Workshop 4.

Sharing and Responding

For your early exploratory freewriting, you might use "Summary and Sayback" (Section 3 in "Sharing and Responding"). This sort of feedback will help you figure out where you are going or want to go. Ask listeners to concentrate particularly on what they see as the implications of what you've written. In addition to "Summary and Sayback," you may find the following questions helpful:

- What do you think I'm primarily interested in finding out?
- Do you think that the task I'm setting for myself is feasible? And if not, how can I alter it?
- How do you think I can go about answering my question or finding out what I want to know?

For later drafts, you'll find "Summary and Sayback" valuable again. But you might also ask your readers to do "Skeleton Feedback and Descriptive Outline" in Section 10 of "Sharing and Responding."

We suggest that you also write out some questions for which you specifically want listeners and readers to give you feedback. Here are some general questions you may find helpful at this stage of your project:

- Have I accomplished what I led you to expect I was going to accomplish?
- Have I given you sufficient evidence to justify whatever conclusions I've drawn?
- Does my organization work? Does my paper seem to be a unified whole?
- What do you hear as my position or point of view or bias in this paper? Do you see me openly showing it or keeping it hidden? Whatever my approach, how does it work for you? How do you react to the relationship between my opinion or feelings here and the information I present?
- Have I made clear the limits of my subject?

Process Journal and Cover Letter

What did you notice about and what can you learn from
- How you went about choosing a topic?
- Your first efforts in the library, especially if you had not used a library much before?
- Your first efforts on the Internet, especially if you had not used the Internet in this way before? Using the Internet can be overwhelming because it appears to make so much information accessible—more than one person can hope to master.
- Your success (or difficulties) with integrating your thinking and the thinking or information of others? Did your thinking change much or not at all on the basis of your personal research? your library work?

What advice can you give yourself for doing future research projects and papers?

For your cover letter, it's good to include some or all of your process writing. But don't forget to answer some cover letter questions.

Here are the main ones: What is your main point and what effect are you trying to have on readers? What do you feel works best in your paper and where are you unsatisfied? What changes did you make on the basis of any feedback? And most important: What feedback do you want now from a reader? But your teacher may ask you particular cover letter questions that pertain to this assignment.

RUMINATIONS AND THEORY
The Ongoing Conversation

> Imagine that you enter a parlor. You come late. When you arrive, others have long preceded you, and they are engaged in a heated discussion, a discussion too heated for them to pause and tell you exactly what it is about. In fact, the discussion had already begun long before any of them got there, so that no one present is qualified to retrace for you all the steps that had gone before. You listen for a while, until you decide that you have caught the tenor of the argument; then you put in your oar. Someone answers; you answer him; another comes to your defense; another aligns himself against you, to either the embarrassment or gratification of your opponent, depending upon the quality of your ally's assistance. However, the discussion is interminable. The hour grows late, you must depart. And you do depart, with the discussion still vigorously in progress.
>
> Kenneth Burke, *Rhetoric of Motives*

The usual thing we do when we need to know something is to ask questions. Often what we need to know is very simple: What time is it? How do I get to the zoo? In these cases, we ask someone and that's usually the end of our research. (That we may get the wrong answer is irrelevant since we won't realize that until later.) But once we've gotten an answer, we're in the position of passing it along to others. We can now direct someone else to the zoo—and that person can direct another, and on and on. And perhaps the person who gave us directions originally got them from someone else. So we're in the midst of a conversation whose beginning we were not present for and whose ending we're unlikely to be present for either.

But just as often what we need to know may be more complex. How have digital watches affected people's sense of time? Why do people go to the zoo? What do we get out of looking at animals? To get answers to these questions, we need to do more than ask one question of one person. We need to figure out how to ask questions, observe reactions, and draw conclusions. And often what we want to know may require us to seek out information in books and periodicals.

Just as often, though, we can't state precisely what we want or need to know. So, we have to do a fair amount of thinking, talking, writing, and reflecting in order to pinpoint and focus our purpose. In effect, we put ourselves into conversation with ourselves and with others. In a sense, this too is research. More than one philosopher has noted that asking the right questions is often more meaningful than getting the right answers.

However we come to decide what our research will be and how best to do it, when we finally do report it to others, we continue the conversation we had joined when we began our research. In fact, whenever we use language, written or oral, we are joining an ongoing conversation—either with ourselves or with others.

When you do print-based research in a library, you are entering into a conversation with those who wrote centuries ago or thousands of miles away. But, to situate yourself within that conversation and to make valid contributions to it, you need to know what has been said in it. This is the basic purpose of most education: to help you find your place in the ongoing flow of history. Unless you show your familiarity with this conversation, most people will not give much weight to your contribution to it. In truth, they probably won't even listen to you. If, for example, you want to write about the role of economics in society, you should probably be familiar with canonical works on the subject: Malthus and Marx and others whom your economics teachers will identify for you. You'll also need to become familiar with what is currently being written on the subject. This knowledge will enable you to make valuable contributions to this particular ongoing conversation. And, if you want to make some permanent impact on that conversation, you'll write your words down so they'll be available for future study. Writing thus allows all of us to talk to the past and the future as well as to the present.

But you can also have an ongoing conversation with yourself. That conversation will obviously draw part of its substance from what you've read and what you've heard from others. A large part of its substance will come from interaction with what you've previously thought and said. This conversation may concern the same subjects as the historical conversations: the meaning of life, human relationships, and so forth. For instance, you probably find yourself saying something like, "I used to think X about the difference between Republicans and Democrats, but I now think Y." Or, "I used to want to be an engineer, but now I think I'd rather be a teacher."

What we say to ourselves changes as we experience more of the world around us and as that world changes. For most of us, the conversation with ourselves is unrecorded. One of our aims in this book is to push you to record some of this personal conversation in your freewriting and exploratory writing. If you've done this, you've discovered how often such personal conversation can be interesting to others as well as to yourself. So often we've had students who moan that they have nothing to say. They believe this because they haven't yet realized that their personal ruminations can be engrossing for others.

Why are we writing about this in a workshop on researching? Because we believe that research is a way of integrating our personal conversations with ourselves into our conversations with others across history and geography. Most research begins simply, but all research is a combination of personal insights and an awareness of what others have contributed. This is what makes it a conversation. And similar qualities make most writing a conversation with others and with yourself about matters you and they wish to talk about.

Two Sample Student Research Papers.

Devoured: Eating Disorders   *Concetta Acunzo*

"Mirror, mirror on the wall, who's the fairest of them all?" This is the question the Queen, in the classic Brothers Grimm fairy tale *Snow White,* asks as she gazes into her mirror. Invariably telling her what she wants to hear, that she is indeed the most beautiful woman in the land, the mirror's answer one day suddenly changes: the Queen no longer is the "fairest of them all"; instead, her beauty has been surpassed by the younger and lovelier Snow White. The Queen is unwilling to accept the new and unwelcome response; she will go to any lengths to once again attain the original reply. The Queen's scenario is not all that different than the predicament of someone suffering from an eating disorder. She too is not receiving the answer she wishes to hear. She too will utilize all measures to transform herself into the greatest—or thinnest—possible beauty. She too is reaching for an unattainable goal.

Beauty is the defining characteristic of American women. The overwhelming pressure to be beautiful is most intense during early adolescence. Girls worry about their clothes, makeup, and hair, but, most of all, they agonize over their weight. Adolescent girls are taught that obesity equates failure. People are so terrified of becoming fat that a recent study found that 11 percent of Americans would abort a fetus if they were told it had a tendency toward obesity (Pipher, *Reviving Ophelia* 184). Ironically, eating is probably our most ancient form of social activity (Pipher, *Hunger Pains* 17). Food, however, is the cause of much anxiety, particularly among women who have been culturally conditioned to hate their bodies. Eating disorders, resulting from excessive preoccupation with thinness, societal pressures, and various other factors, run rampant in America. The eating disorders anorexia nervosa (*anorexia* is from the Greek for "loss of ap-

Devoured: Eating Disorders   *continued*

petite") and bulimia nervosa (*bulimia* is from the Greek for "ox appetite") are characterized by an implacable and distorted attitude toward weight, eating, and fatness (Hsu 1). Anorexia is self-starvation; bulimia involves a binge-purge cycle. Anorexia and bulimia are not merely consequences of food abuse; they are part of an emotional system that affects every aspect of the sufferer's life (Farrell, Ch. 1).

Each year, over 10 million people are diagnosed with eating disorders in America. Approximately 90 percent of those affected are female, while only 10 percent are male (Felker). The fact that men are more realistic about their appearance and women generally distort their body images is responsible for the disproportion of this statistic. Studies show that 90 percent of all women overestimate their own body size (Pipher, *Hunger Pains* 10); only 25 percent of anorectics and 40 percent of bulimics are actually overweight before the onset of the illness (Hsu 14). In recent years, this size overestimation has been developing in younger girls. Children are growing increasingly preoccupied with weight and appearance. By age five, children select pictures of thin people when asked to identify good-looking others (Pipher, *Reviving Ophelia* 185). Surveys indicate that 50 percent of nine-year-old girls diet. Girls as young as 10 years old are developing eating disorders. Why are children reading nutritional information labels when they should be playing hopscotch or catch?

Society and cultural biases are largely responsible for the escalating obsession with thinness and the stigma attached to obesity. The omnipresent media consistently portrays desirable women as excessively thin—unattainably skinny. (It says something about our society when one of the most popular shows on television is *Baywatch,* where the actors and actresses wear nothing more than skimpy bathing suits.) Watching these women on the television or seeing them in magazines causes real women to loathe their own bodies. Thomas Cash, a professor of psychology at Old Dominion University in Virginia, reports that in 1972, 23 percent of United States women said they were dissatisfied with their overall appearance; today, that figure has more than doubled to 52 percent (Schneider 67). The ever-changing society plays a primary role in this alteration of female thought. In the past 30 years, the voluptuous size 12 image of Marilyn Monroe has been transformed into size 2 models like Kate Moss. Since 1979, Miss America contestants have become so skinny that the majority are at least 15 percent below the recommended body weight, which is also the same percentage to be considered a symptom of anorexia nervosa (Schneider 67). Today, the average model is 5'10" and 110 pounds; the average American woman is 5'4" and 145 pounds. As real women grow heavier, models have become slimmer. When unnatural thinness becomes attractive, girls do unnatural things to be slight.

As a traditionally Western civilization problem, anorexia nervosa, to quote Peter Rowen, is a question of "being thirsty in the rain" (Pipher, *Reviving Ophelia* 174). Anorectics are starving while there is food all around

Devoured: Eating Disorders *continued*

them. Anorexia is a disease of control, and suppressing one's appetite or consumption when surrounded by food signifies the ultimate success. Though the word anorexia implies absence of hunger, anorectics, in actuality, are constantly hungry. They are obsessed with food, but, ironically, are starving themselves.

Typical anorectics are the brightest and best young women; it is the good girls, the dutiful daughters, and the overachievers who are at the greatest risk for anorexia (Pipher, *Reviving Ophelia* 174). Anorexia often begins during early adolescence with ordinary teenage dieting; the disease frequently starts with cutting out a certain food or eliminating fat from the diet. From there, anorexia develops into an extreme restriction of caloric intake and often excessive exercising. Instead of concluding the diet when she reaches her target weight, the perfectionist young woman continues on a path to weight obsession and rigidity concerning food.

The anorectic is commonly referred to as looking like "the victim of a concentration camp" (Bruch vii). Anorectics have both the physical and psychological characteristics of starvation. Their abdomens are distended, their hair dull, their nails brittle; amenorrhea—or the absence of menstruation—occurs; they are weak, and prone to infections. Anorexia slows or prevents growth and halts puberty. Emotionally, anorectics are depressed, irritable, pessimistic, apathetic, and entirely preoccupied with food. Anorexia nervosa, or self-starvation, is both physically and psychologically debilitating.

Bulimia is the most common eating disorder in young women. The disease begins as a method of controlling weight, but it evolves into a life-threatening obsession. For bulimics, life revolves around eating, purging, and weight. Like all addictions, bulimia is a compulsive, obsessive, self-destructive, and progressive disorder. Bingeing and purging are the addictive behaviors; food is the drug of choice (Pipher, *Reviving Ophelia* 169).

While anorexia traditionally begins during junior high school, bulimia tends to develop during later adolescence. It is commonly referred to as the "college girl's" disease because the estimates of incidence run as high as one-fourth of all college-age women (Pipher, *Reviving Ophelia* 170). Like anorectics, bulimics are oversocialized to the feminine role (Pipher, *Reviving Ophelia* 170). They are the ultimate people-pleasers; bulimics are generally attractive, with remarkable social skills. Often they are the cheerleaders and homecoming queens, the straight-A students and prides of their families (Pipher, *Reviving Ophelia* 170).

Frequently, the patient enters the bulimic cycle of fasting, bingeing, and purging. The majority, over 80 percent, develop the cycle by first giving in to the increasing desire to eat and thereafter self-inducing vomiting either because the fullness is intolerable or because they want to get rid of the calories (Hsu 15). After a binge, a bulimic is likely to be overtaken by feelings of panic. Though she may have consumed anywhere between 5,000 and 50,000 calories, her preoccupation is with losing weight. She is

Devoured: Eating Disorders *continued*

overwhelmed by guilt and forces herself to purge. About two-thirds of bulimics regularly use vomiting to control their weight, while one-third predominantly abuse laxatives. Many, of course, combine both methods. About 40 percent of bulimics also misuse diet pills. Lastly, many bulimics also take to exercising in an attempt to rid themselves of surplus calories.

Extensive bingeing and purging places young women at risk of serious health problems. Often they have dental problems, esophageal tears, gastrointestinal problems, and sometimes dangerous electrolytic imbalances that can trigger heart attacks. The mortality rates are estimated to be about 3 percent (Buckroyd 24). Psychological alterations are also the result of bulimia. Bulimics experience personality changes as they learn to accept bingeing as the main staple of their existence. Driven by another binge, they become obsessed, extremely secretive, and guilty about their habit. Bulimics have lost their main objective in life: control. As a result, they are typically depressed, irritable, and withdrawn.

Bulimic young women have lost their true selves in a toilet. The "telltale" mark, the line that exists on the index finger after repeated episodes of self-induced vomiting, is not the only scar bulimics carry with them. They also possess the knowledge, buried deep within them, that their identities have been devoured by a deadly disease. In their eagerness to please, they have developed an addiction that destroys their central core (Pipher, *Reviving Ophelia* 170); the road to recovery is a long and meandering one.

Margaret Mead defined an ideal culture as one in which there was a place for every human gift (Pipher, *Hunger Pains* 121). This ideal culture would allow its members to grow to their fullest potential. Regrettably, Mead's philosophy has gotten lost in this society where thinness equals success. After all, according to American ideology, "one can never be too rich or too thin." Consequently, women are dominated by a fear of becoming fat which frequently leads to the development of eating disorders. Anorexia, self-starvation, and bulimia, the binge-purge cycle, are rampant. Like *Snow White*'s Queen, desperate measures can be taken but, in reality, the end does not justify the means. Just as the mirror will never tell the Queen what she wants to hear, the numbers on the scale will never show the victim of an eating disorder the weight she wants to see.

Works Cited

Bruch, Hilde. *The Golden Cage: The Enigma of Anorexia Nervosa.* Cambridge: Harvard UP, 1978.

Buckroyd, Julia. *Anorexia and Bulimia: Your Questions Answered.* New York: Element Books, 1996.

Farrell, Em. *Lost for Words: The Psychoanalysis of Anorexia and Bulimia.* London: Process Press, 1995. 30 Apr. 1999 <http://human-nature.com/farrell/contents. html>.

Felker, Kenneth R. and Cathie Stivers. "The Relationship of Gender and Family Environment to Eating Disorder Risk in Adolescents." *Adolescence* 29 (1994):

Devoured: Eating Disorders   *continued*

821–35. *Infotrac Academic ASAP.* 30 Apr. 1999 <http://rdas.mmm.edu/bin/ rdas._dll/RDAS_SVR=web2.searchbank.com/itw/session/234/538/13014136 w5/8!xrn_1_1__A16477233>.

Hsu, L. K. George. *Eating Disorders.* New York: Guilford, 1990.

Pipher, Mary Bray. *Hunger Pains: The Modern Woman's Tragic Quest for Thinness.* Rpt. ed. New York: Ballantine-Random, 1997.

———. *Reviving Ophelia: Saving the Selves of Adolescent Girls.* New York: Putnam-Penguin, 1994.

Schneider, Linda H., Steven J. Cooper and Katherine A. Halmi, eds. *The Psychobiology of Human Eating Disorders: Preclinical and Clinical Perspectives.* Annals of New York Academy of Sciences 575. New York: New York Academy of Sciences, 1989.

A SAMPLE STUDENT RESEARCH PAPER*

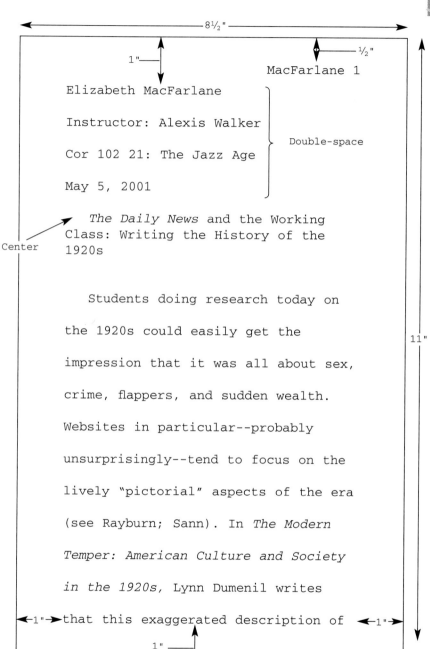

8½"

1"

½"

MacFarlane 1

Elizabeth MacFarlane

Instructor: Alexis Walker

Cor 102 21: The Jazz Age

May 5, 2001

Double-space

Center

The Daily News and the Working Class: Writing the History of the 1920s

11"

Students doing research today on the 1920s could easily get the impression that it was all about sex, crime, flappers, and sudden wealth. Websites in particular--probably unsurprisingly--tend to focus on the lively "pictorial" aspects of the era (see Rayburn; Sann). In *The Modern Temper: American Culture and Society in the 1920s,* Lynn Dumenil writes

1" that this exaggerated description of 1" 1"

* Note: This page shows the standard format for a college research paper. The page size has been reduced to match the trim of this book.

MacFarlane 2

the era was formed slowly over the years by historians fascinated by the decade's drama, and by students' "romantic visions of the twenties filtered through the lens of *The Great Gatsby*" (4). In fact, the "romantic visions" of the decade can be traced back not only to later readings of the era's fiction or historians' illusions, but to its tabloid journalism, and the masses for whom it was written. In New York, at least, the *Daily News* fed its readers an image of the era even more fantastic than that afforded by *The Great Gatsby*--and with nearly as large a debt to the imagination.

McGivena points out in his book about the *Daily News* that newspapers played a large role in the lives of the people in the twenties (22). Since there was no television and radios were not very common until the end of the decade, newpapers were the main source of information for many working-class people. When the tabloid *News* was first published in 1919, the *New York Times*

MacFarlane 3

had the greatest circulation (341,5559) in the

city. The *Times* had always prided itself on being

"the epitome of conservatism" and did not at first

see the *News* as competition (Chapman 10). Within

2 years, however, the *News* had a circulation of

400,000, while the *Times* had dropped to only

336,000.

In part because of the growth of tabloids in

the era, the 1920s were known as the decade of

"Jazz Journalism." The term "tabloid" (derived

from Tabloid™, a pharmaceutical term for a drug

in condensed form) originally referred to the

small size of the paper used for printing

("Tabloid"). It quickly acquired an association

with sensationalism, thanks to the tabloids' tone

and content. Sensationalism in newspapers had

been around in England at least since the 1840s

(Mott 666). What distinguished tabloid journalism

of the 1920s from that of other eras, aside from

the smaller format, was the low cost of the

newspapers and the extensive use of photography

MacFarlane 4

(Emery 553). These were key factors in the success of the *Daily News*.

Joseph M. Patterson, founder of the paper, was described by journalist Jack Alexander in the August 6, 1938, issue of *The New Yorker* as a member of the wealthy class who did not fit in (10). He was considered a socialist thinker because he had written two books protesting social injustice and economic oppression. His idea was to start a tabloid newspaper that would reach out to immigrants and the poorly educated. It pleased him that his "circulation potential was not among the readers of the *New York Times*" (Chapman 47). He tried to pass for a regular guy on the street, often wearing wrinkled, dirty clothes and lounging by newsstands to see people's reactions when they saw his newspaper. The fact that he agreed to a series of interviews by Alexander that portrayed him as a legend in his own time, however, suggests that he was also a very good businessman trying to sell his newspaper to a previously untapped audience in an innovative way.

World War I influenced the way that both journalists and readers saw newspapers. Earlier, major newspapers were subsidized by political parties, and writers were influenced by the men who owned them. If a reporter were to write something not to his editor's liking, he could expect to be fired. During the war, however, newspapers were subject to censorship of a different kind: for the first time, they were subject to the restrictions imposed by the government's newly formed Censorship Committee (Schudson 141). Journalists became disillusioned because they were threatened with imprisonment for reporting things the way they happened. News of lost battles was not reported. Around the same time, President Wilson created the Committee of Public Information, which was essentially an ad agency whose aim was to help raise money for the war, the Red Cross, and the Salvation Army

MacFarlane 6

(Schudson 142).

It is not surprising that ex-war correspondents later believed that facts themselves could not be trusted. The public became aware of the situation after the war was over. The censorship ended, but this knowledge probably made them more willing to buy a newspaper that frankly called itself the "Best Fiction in New York" (the *News*) instead of one described as "All the News That's Fit to Print" (the *Times*).

From the beginning, there were many differences between the *Daily News* and the more "respectable" newspapers such as the *New York Times*. Most notable was the use of photography. The use of halftone technology was developed in New York and allowed pictures to be reproduced next to print. The *Daily News* was the first newspaper to use this technique with a rotary press, which allowed them to print a very cheap "picture newspaper" (Rogers 1). Earlier attempts

MacFarlane 7

at combining sensational text with photography were not as successful in attracting large audiences because of those papers' high cost (Mott 518). Patterson, on the other hand, was able to use photos as a means to reach his intended audience of the poor, the less educated, and immigrants.

In a 1927 magazine article, one sociologist attributed the success of tabloids to the "see and believe theory," which held that people knew that "exaggerations could be found in print but [believed] that pictures did not lie" (Tenenbaum 4). In the beginning, at least, there was "no-holds-barred" competition among photographers for getting photos that would sell. The most famous example was the execution picture of Ruth Snyder. As Frederick Lewis Allen stated in his book *Only Yesterday: an Informal History of the 1920s*, that trial got "more play in the press than the sinking of the Titanic" (164). In an effort to outdo the other newspapers, the *News*

sent a reporter into the death chamber with a
small camera taped to his leg. The result was a
full-page front cover photo with the caption
"DEAD" over it. It sold more copies than any
other issue to this day (Rogers 4).

On September 20, 1920, a *News* photographer
just happened to be on Wall Street when a bomb
went off, killing several people. He was the only
one there before police sealed the area off for
investigation. In that instance, history shaped
the sensationalism of the newspaper by providing
shocking and gory images, but the pictures added
to history by providing something that would not
otherwise have existed--a lasting image of the
event. A written account would have provided the
facts, but pictures have a more immediate impact
and thus are more likely to be remembered by a
mass audience.

Writing in *The Nation* in 1926, journalist
Silas Bent argued that "picture-features are a
throwback to a time before the alphabet was

invented" (32). Though the comment sounds
disparaging, it was this that made news
accessible to illiterates and to immigrants who
hadn't learned to read English. Patterson
arranged to have it sold at foreign language
newsstands, among other venues--and it sold.
Using graphic images, the *Daily News* was able to
embed the images of the era in the minds of its
readers.

For those who could read, but not necessarily
very well, the *Daily News*, unlike the *Times*, was
written in short sentences that were easy to
understand. The era's newly crowded cities meant
more unskilled, less educated people riding in
mass transit (Dumenil 8). These commuters were
attracted to the convenience of the *Daily News*'s
small size and short, easy-to-follow stories. The
brevity of the stories was fitting for the faster
pace of the new era of cars and (later) the
airplane.

The focus of what the two papers chose to

MacFarlane 10

print was also different. On the first day that
the *News* was printed, the *Times* had less than
half of one column on movies and only 3 inches on
theatre, whereas the *News* devoted a full page to
them. Unlike the *Times*, it featured contests,
games, and comics. Usually, only one out of eight
stories on the front cover of the *Times* got any
coverage at all in the *Daily News* (Bessie 93).
The *Daily News* sought to amuse and distract the
population--and it appeared to work, if sales are
any indication. Most people simply preferred
murders and sex scandals over world affairs on
the front page.

On March 1, 1920, for example, the *Times*
featured troubles in Europe and labor problems in
America; the *News* featured a series of detective
stories and a report on its own beauty contest.
The big stories of the day in the *Daily News* were
the Hall-Mills murder (involving a love
triangle), the Ruth Snyder trial, Lindbergh's
solo flight across the Atlantic, Hollywood

MacFarlane 11

scandals involving Fatty Arbuckle, Clara Bow, and
Rudolph Valentino, and sports. In 1924, the
Teapot Dome coverage was cut short in favor of a
story about a man named Floyd Collins who was
stuck in a cave. The *News* sent a reporter down to
photograph his dead body. Soon afterward, several
people died in a mining accident, but they
received only minimal coverage because people
wouldn't buy another story about a cave (McGivena
113). Very little notice was paid to the ongoing
Senate battle regarding the League of Nations,
and the downward economic trend.

The *News* further appealed to the interests of
the "common man" by printing the names of its
columnists and the first names and addresses of
the people in their articles. The idea was to
give the readers a sense of living in a small
town--offering many of them the feeling of
camaraderie that they may have missed by moving
to the big city. At the same time, many of the
tabloids throughout the United States printed

similar content (such as comics and gossip columns), thanks to the founding of the Associated Press after WWI: People reading the *News* in New York knew that on the same day someone "back home" could be reading the same advice column.

No matter what else they claim to be, newspapers are a business, and their existence depends on their pleasing the public. The *Times* and other newspapers accordingly started imitating certain aspects of the *Daily News*. Three of the major newspapers of the era--*The World*, *The Tribune*, and the *Times*--began racing to build a Sunday section with the most pictures. The *Times* started to use pictures on every page, and it added columns on books, art, theatre, music, dance, Hollywood gossip, and movies. In 1920 the *Times* actually bought advertising space in the *News* in order to tell people that their Sunday edition contained a picture section (McGivena 259).

Perhaps the biggest evidence of change in this direction can be seen in the coverage of sports. In 1926, four hundred reporters covered the prizefight between Jack Dempsey and Gene Tunney. Even though Dempsey lost the fight, he became the hero of the people because of the glowing terms used by reporters to describe him. The fight was transformed into a battle between the pretentious Easterner and the primitive, innocent Westerner. (It bears comparison to another fiction of its time--*The Great Gatsby*--in which the innocent Westerner (Gatsby) falls prey to the evils of the East.) Surprisingly, the paper that gave the fight the most coverage was the *Times*. They had an exclusive interview with Dempsey, which they advertised in a headline the same size as the one they had used when the Armistice was signed.

Contrary to Dumenil's idea that the "roaring twenties" were the product of later eras, social critics and journalists of the 1920s such as Walter Lippman and Silas Bent were already concerned about the effects that 1920s-era journalism would have on the public. In "Blazing Publicity," Lippman worried that the public mind--"addled by the vivid power of the sensational publicity machine--would not be capable of participating in the difficult work of democracy" (1). He was particularly upset when the tabloids focused on the Snyder trial, while a great flood in Mississippi that had killed hundreds received no coverage. He feared that the era's most important events would be forgotten by posterity; his fear seems to have come true, at least in part.

He compared the media to a light that is directed by newspapermen on arbitrary events that leaves everything else in darkness. He called the media a "machine without morals or taste" (1). In a sense, he was right--but of couse, the media was merely responding to the public's desire to escape the reality of government, labor, and educational problems. Bent was so against

tabloids that he said they could never call
themselves newspapers. In his view, any news that
mattered was "beyond the reach of the camera"
(1). The majority of the people, however, weren't
interested in these intellectuals' concerns.

Death and tragedy have always fascinated
people, but in the 1920s they became part of a
daily diet accessible to almost anyone, in the
form of the *Daily News*. Since sensationalism
engaged the emotions of the audience, the
intellectuals' claim that it perverted moral
judgment might have some basis in reality. If
people were constantly bombarded by stories about
sex and crime, they might have come to see them
as the norm, or at least "normal." It could also
be said that the public dictated what was printed
in the tabloids, if indirectly. If this is the
case, then newspapers could be considered the
literary expression of the people. Even though
the average factory worker wasn't a bootlegging
gangster or an aviator flying solo across the

ocean, those things were part of the shared experience of the 1920s and represented the feeling of the time.

So while Dumenil was correct in suggesting that sloppy historians and readers of works of the Lost Generation are partially responsible for our hedonistic vision of the roaring twenties, one should also acknowledge the role of the working class and their influence on the tabloids that helped to create this image. One thing future historians could legitimately learn about the era from the *Daily News* is the public's desire to believe what they saw rather than what they were told, as well as their desire for distraction and entertainment.

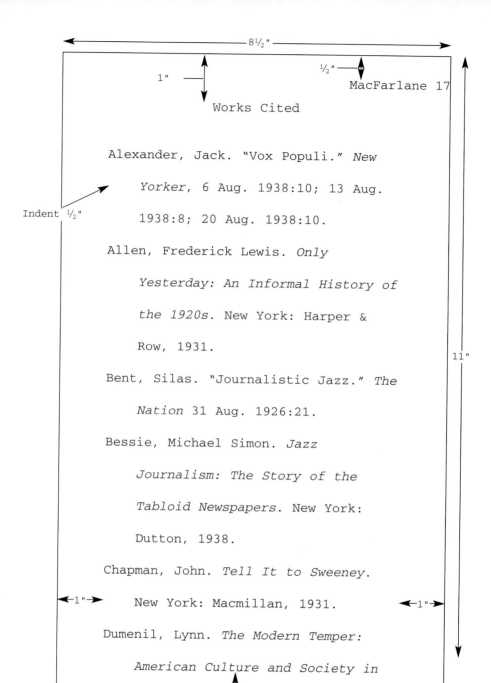

Works Cited

Alexander, Jack. "Vox Populi." *New Yorker*, 6 Aug. 1938:10; 13 Aug. 1938:8; 20 Aug. 1938:10.

Allen, Frederick Lewis. *Only Yesterday: An Informal History of the 1920s*. New York: Harper & Row, 1931.

Bent, Silas. "Journalistic Jazz." *The Nation* 31 Aug. 1926:21.

Bessie, Michael Simon. *Jazz Journalism: The Story of the Tabloid Newspapers*. New York: Dutton, 1938.

Chapman, John. *Tell It to Sweeney*. New York: Macmillan, 1931.

Dumenil, Lynn. *The Modern Temper: American Culture and Society in*

Note: The page size has been reduced to match the trim of this book.

the 1920s. New York: Hill & Wang, 1995.

Emery, Edwin. *The Press and America: An Interpretative History of the Mass Media.* 3rd ed. Saddlebrook, NJ: Prentice, 1972.

Lippman, Walter. "Blazing Publicity." *Vanity Fair* 1920. 6 Mar. 2001 <http:home.earthlink.net/~srduncombe/sense.htm>.

McGivena, Leo E. *The News: The First Fifty Years of New York's Picture Newspaper.* New York: News Syndicate, 1969.

Mott, Frank Luther. *American Journalism: A History of Newspapers in the United States.* New York: Macmillan, 1941.

Rayburn, Kevin. *The 1920s.* 2000. 30 Apr. 2001 <http://www.louisville.edu/~kprayb01/1920s.html>.

Rogers, Madeline. "The Picture Snatchers." *American Heritage* October 1994: 66–71.

Sann, Paul. *The Lawless Decade: A Pictorial History of a Great American Transition.* Sept. 1, 1999; 28 Apr. 2001 <http://www.paulsann.

MacFarlane 3

org/thelawlessdecade/index.html>.

Schudson, Michael. *Discovering the News: A Social
History of American Newspapers*. New York:
Basic, 1978.

"Tabloid." *The American Heritage Dictionary of
the English Language*. 4th ed. Boston:
Houghton Mifflin, 2000; New York:
Bartleby.com, 2000. Bartleby.com. 3 May 2001
<http://www.bartleby.com/61/>.

Tenenbaum, James. "The Camera Learns to Lie." *The
Nation* 8 June 1927:30-2.

Reflecting on Your Writing
Portfolios

Essential Premises

Examining one's writings and the processes that went into composing them is a valuable learning activity that can lead to improved writing and thinking.

Writing is not just a school activity; it has a role to play in private and public life outside the classroom.

MAIN ASSIGNMENT
Creating a Portfolio

Our experience has taught us that writers learn the most by becoming students of their own writing processes. Thus, our major aim here is to get you to learn something about yourself and your writing process that will be useful when you are doing future writing tasks in school. But we also hope the activities that follow will help you see some role for writing in your life outside of school assignments. Along the way you may discover for yourself that writing leads to learning.

Your main assignment will be to create a portfolio of the work you've done during this school term and add to it an autobiography of yourself as a writer. And since you will be using the writing you've done throughout the semester as a basis for your autobiography, this assignment will encourage you to look back on the term and assess honestly what happened to you and your writing.

This assignment will help you solidify and benefit from what you have been learning all this term. Some of what you've learned you've been explicitly aware you were learning; but you have learned many other things in an intuitive, unconscious way. This autobiography will help you see and consolidate all you have learned. It needn't be too much work, yet you can discover much about your own learning and how it has affected the way you write.

The theme of your autobiography is the theme of the course: *the writing process.* The autobiography will help you see the writing process in detail and empirically, not just settle for generalizations. The *facts* about what you actually do when you write are probably somewhat different from what you *think* you do. Discovering these facts almost always makes your writing easier and better.

Step One: Gathering Your Materials

Your teacher may have asked you at the beginning of the term to start a portfolio and keep everything you write in it. Or she may have asked you to put only certain things in it. Perhaps she has looked at it—even evaluated it—once or twice already. In our classes we like our students to put a wide variety of kinds of writing in their portfolios: some journal pieces, freewriting, exploratory writing, responses

Exploring the Writing Process
On Workplace Writing

Since graduation, I have been working administratively. When I began the job, I feared that I would unwillingly convert to a bureaucrat, and begin to write as one. I may be wrong, but I think the office work has actually improved my writing skills, particularly in correspondence. My writing is now more direct, clear, and assertive. I regularly write to people asking for things, and I ask in a specific, shameless, and brief manner. Sometimes I feel bossy while I do it, but nobody seems to mind, so I keep doing it.

In my office, it is common for an important letter written by either me or a co-worker to be proofread by at least six sets of eyes. This has made criticism and evaluation less painful for me. I have come to learn that it's the page, not the writer that is important, that people have more important things to think about than what a piece of writing has to say about me. Before this job, I was much more apprehensive about showing my writing to other people. As an undergraduate, for instance, I would wince and apologize excessively when handing papers in. Now I am less embarrassed by mistakes and I do not try to explain them.

Donna Whicher

to readings, drafts, peer responses, and process writing, as well as finished pieces. We also like students to put into their portfolios other pieces of writing we haven't asked for that they may be particularly proud of: pieces written for other classes and even pieces written for pleasure.

Your teacher will tell you what she would like you to include in your portfolio. Chances are that if she is going to use the portfolio to help decide your grade for the term, she won't want everything in there and will ask you to make some selections either with or without help from her and your classmates. These pieces will serve as a basis for your autobiography, which in turn will serve as a kind of cover sheet for your portfolio.

Once you have your material together, read back over it and do some freewriting about what you see there.

Possible Issues or Themes for Your Autobiography

Here is a list of topics that will help you figure out the main issues or themes for your autobiography. Read back through your portfolio and your process journal and see what they tell you about these topics. Then try to do a bit of freewriting about each one. For now, the important thing to remember is that you're not trying to draw conclusions; you're still in the data collection stage.

Moments What important incidents do you remember from past writing experiences?

Stages Intuitively divide your life as a writer into a few stages or periods; then ask yourself what characterizes each of those stages.

Kinds What kinds of writing have you done in the past and what kinds do you do now? Remember that there are many more kinds of writing than those you've done in school. Making lists is writing; so are graffiti. What is different about your experience with different kinds of writing?

In-school versus out-of-school writing Do you go about both of these the same way? differently? Do you feel the same way about both? Why or why not?

Audience Who are the important people you have written for? (Not just teachers.) What effects have these different audiences had? on your feelings? on your writing? Which audiences helped you the most or held you back? How often do you feel yourself to be the only audience of what you are writing? (Don't forget "ghost audiences" or audiences we carry around in our heads and unconsciously try to please—usually left over from experiences with past audiences.) Many people remember bad audiences more than good ones. Is that true of you? Why?

Physical   Where do you write? When? How quickly or slowly? What are the effects of using pen, pencil, typewriter, or word processor? How do you hold and move your body? Do you feel tense or relaxed after a session of writing? Tell everything that could be figured out from a video recording of your writing from start to finish.

Process   Try to isolate specific steps in your writing process— for example, generating words and responses, copywriting, publishing. Nonwriting counts too: sitting and thinking, talking to people. Which of these give you the most trouble? the least? the most satisfaction? the least? Why?

Intervention   In what ways have others intervened in your writing? ("Here, let me show you!" "Do it this way." "You must start by making an outline." "You must start by freewriting.") How has intervention affected your writing?

Response and feedback   What kinds of response and feedback have you gotten—and not just from teachers? What effects did this feedback have on you? (Don't forget no response and nonverbal response—silence and laughter.)

Writing for other classes versus writing for this class   If you've written papers for other classes this term, what's different about how you went about it? Did you do any freewriting, produce a draft that your teacher responded to either verbally or in writing, revise one or more times, copyedit? Compare the total effort involved in that project and the total effort involved in writing a piece for this class. Pay attention to any differences in feelings or attitudes toward the two pieces of writing. If you did not use the techniques we've been stressing in this book, do you think you could have or should have? Why or why not?

Problems   Stuck points and breakthroughs. What's hardest for you or what gets in the way most? How have you made or not made progress? Where have you made the greatest progress?

Myths   What are some of the feelings or ideas that you've had about your writing (or that most people seem to have) that you now see are *false?* Where did these myths come from? What purposes did they serve and what effect have they had on you? What follows from abandoning them?

The word "writer"   Whom do you think of as a writer? What are the characteristics of a writer? Can you think of yourself as a writer? If not, why not?

Temperament or character   Do you see any relation between your writing process and your temperament, character, or feelings? Does your writing process show you to be loose or tight, vulnerable or confident? In general, do you think that someone's writing process reflects his or her character?

Step Two: Making a Draft of Your Autobiography

You should now have much raw material—some developed, some just bits. Read through all of this and all your process writing from the term. (You probably have more than you realize; some of your assignments have been process writing or include bits of it. You'll find other bits here and there. Some will be in notebooks for other subjects.) Mark the bits that are interesting and useful. You can probably use some of this process writing as part of your paper if you choose and cut well.

Next, consider what all this process writing is telling you. Do some freewriting, outlining, or note jotting to figure out what your autobiography might focus on.

Two additional things we consider particularly important in any writer's autobiography. One is a mini-study or close look at a single specific piece of writing. The second is an analysis of how your present writing process differs from the way you used to write. We could have included both of these in our earlier list, but we wanted to give them special emphasis.

Exploring the Writing Process
On Writing while Shaving

Each man has his own way. After all, most writing is done away from the typewriter, away from the desk. I'd say it occurs in the quiet, silent moments, while you're walking or shaving or playing a game or whatever, or even talking to someone you're not vitally interested in. You're working, your mind is working, on this problem in the back of your head. So, when you get to the machine it's a mere matter of transfer.

Henry Miller

1. For your mini-study, choose something that you wrote this term. Choose the piece that—as the psychologists say—you "cathect" most, the piece you have the strongest feelings about or feel the strongest connection with. You can learn most from looking honestly and in detail at such a piece. You might also, however, simply pick the piece for which you have the most process writing— the most evidence about what actually was going on as you wrote. Evidence maximizes learning. Spend some time reconstructing how you wrote this piece from beginning to end in as much detail as possible; look at the writing itself, the various drafts, and see what they tell you. Select specific passages that you can quote and comment on. Do some freewriting, outlining, and jotting about what you figure out as you study this piece.

2. Think back on the writing you did before this course. (Some of your process writing will be about that too. You might have included it in the collage you did early in the term about your writing history.) What does that early writing tell you? Many of you have probably saved papers written in high school. Some of you may have written (or still be writing) materials on your job. You might want to look at these and see how much you can remember about writing them. This should lead you to some conclusions about the similarities and differences between how you used to write and how you write now. This, in turn, should make clearer the effects of this term's work on your writing.

Now you have the ingredients for producing a draft. You can do some cutting and pasting and arranging, but make sure to let this draft-making be a process of *new discovery,* not merely an assembling of what you already have. Look at all this material that you now suspect belongs in your draft. What does it mean? What does it add up to? What emphasis, claim, focus, shape, approach, spirit do you want your autobiography to have? If you keep these questions in mind, you will find new answers as you write and paste.

In making your draft, you are finally ready to ask the practical question: What useful advice or suggestions can you give yourself for future writing? What are the dangers for you as a writer? What do you wish someone would whisper in your ear as you undertake writing tasks in the future?

A good writer's autobiography can be structured like a story or like an essay. That is, you can build it around either of the two major structural impulses for writing:

- *Narrative, temporal.* ("And then, and then, and then . . ."—with scattered "so whats" that tell the point of the story.)
- *Expository, conceptual.* ("Here's my first point and what it means

and why it's important; here's my second point . . . , and here's my third point . . ." and so on.)

If you choose the story mode, make sure there is enough "so what." Don't let it be just a story. If you are clever, you can make some of the "so what"—the significance—be implied or unstated. But some of it has to be explicit. Of course, there's nothing wrong with "just a story"—*as* a story—but this assignment asks you to spell out some of the meaning or significance. If you choose the essay or expository mode, don't let it get too dry, abstract, or generalized. Keep the life in it by using specific examples, telling mini-stories, and incorporating descriptions, including particulars and quotations from writing you did, feedback you got, and so forth.

Try to emphasize for yourself that this task can be fun, not just work. Remember:

- You are the authority on you.
- You've done lots of writing and thinking this term about yourself as a writer. What has been the most interesting and useful to *you?*
- Your audience is not only your teacher but also yourself. What you can figure out for yourself is really more important than what you can figure out for your teacher. Your classmates are an additional audience. Your teacher will probably give you a chance to share your autobiography, but if not, find a way. Autobiographies are almost always a treat to read and hear.

Exploring the Writing Process
On the Heaven in Poetry

In general, my writing has always been considered horrible by others. I have never received praise from anyone. Yet I remember my preteen years being filled with poetry. I would write about everything that I could. There was a poem hiding behind everything. It was like heaven. Just being able to pick up a pen and have those wonderful words flow, as if by magic, onto my paper. I never read them (my poems) out loud, for fear that I would not be able to truly express the feeling of each. Each word, phrase, and sentence had a special aura about it. I could never be able to give them their due. Those words from my hands were like heaven.

Ngozi Allick

Minimal Guidelines for Your Autobiography

Make certain your autobiography includes *at least* the following. Undoubtedly you'll want to do more; this is just a foundation for you to check your draft against.

1. Examination of your writing both *before* taking this course and *during* this course. That is, the autobiography should function somewhat as a way of talking about how this course affected or did not affect how you write.

2. Examination of one piece or episode of writing in some detail. Indeed, you could center the whole autobiography around your examination of one piece of writing, bringing in the other parts of your autobiography in relation to this piece.

3. Quotations from your writing. Show how these examples of words on the page illustrate (or do not illustrate) what you are saying about your writing process. That is, explain the relationship between your process and your product—between *what's* on the page and *how* it got there.

4. Examination of comments or feedback by others. Comments can be from teachers, friends, or classmates, from this course or other courses.

5. A bit of advice for yourself: On the basis of all this exploration, what suggestions can you give yourself to make your writing go better in the future? Give your autobiography a *practical* dimension. Make it something that you will find useful to read over in the future when you are engaged in writing.

Writing as Play   Your Choice

Include in your portfolio a piece you've written outside, on your own, without a school assignment. Perhaps it's a poem or a short story or a letter to someone that you do not mind others seeing. Instead of a piece of writing, draw a picture of yourself that pertains in some way to yourself as a writer; you can create a computer-generated image also if you wish. If you're one of the many who today have a Web page, you can print a copy of it and put it in. Perhaps you write songs; if so, you could include a tape of the song. Or perhaps you play a musical instrument; you can then include a tape of yourself playing.

Remember that one of the strengths of a portfolio is that it gives a reader a fuller picture of you as a writer. The "fun" thing you include can give a reader a still fuller picture by presenting some aspect of yourself that may not be evident through your writing.

Exploring the Writing Process
On Reading—Understanding—Feedback

From *A Case Study of Myself*

The funny thing about the feedback that I received in this course is that I don't think I ever immediately understood what it was saying. The typed feedback letters were immensely helpful. But, I've realized after reading back through them all that what I read and what you wrote in the first place are two different things entirely!

For example, there are sentences which I swear I never read before, suddenly appearing on the page when I go back two weeks later to read it. Also, it seems that what I took your point to be—what you were trying to emphasize—when I first read the feedback and what I understand your points to be now are not the same, either.

I think that I have come up with an explanation for this phenomenon. It seems to me that a piece is very important to me when I write it, when I hand it in, when I get feedback on it, and for about one week afterward, because a piece of writing in this class is sort of representative of just where I am in the class right then—how I'm feeling.

The feedback is sort of like an affirmation that what I wrote was valid or "good." I guess that I've been trained this way. And even though I know that your feedback doesn't aim to say "yes" or "no," "good" or "bad," I still can't help reading it that way. So the feedback sheet comes to me and I say, "Did he like it?" instead of just taking in what you've said.

Because of this, when I get a sheet back and interpret what you've written, I almost end up changing your intention. The words on the page get translated through my own agenda (read: did he like it?) and I lose (or even fail to see!) what you're actually saying. Going back and reading through the sheets, it seems that many things that I took to be negative weren't. They just weren't worded in that "yes, this is an A or this is very good" way that I was expecting.

This, to me is shocking. I've always thought of myself as a person who takes constructive feedback of any sort exceptionally well. But now I realize that I don't take *any* type of feedback well, except for the sort of polar feedback that grades or extreme "yes" or "no's" produce. I used to think that I was an open-minded student, evidenced by the fact that I enjoy getting specific, negative feedback almost more than I enjoy positive feedback. I was proud of this.

Exploring the Writing Process
On Reading—Understanding—Feedback   *continued*

But now I realize that I *like* that feedback because when I get it, it's spelled out for me—"what I did wrong." I don't have to evaluate myself or question my writing at all. I just have to take the expert's word for it. And this is easy.

I used to think, being a prospective teacher (sort of), that giving meaningful feedback would be simple: just be specific. But now, having evaluated my own responses to feedback, I wonder: Will being specific with feedback and asking for revisions make for a better writer, or just make for a better paper? And which is more important?

Victoria Malzone

Sharing and Responding

The most useful feedback is probably what's produced by using the techniques in Section 2, "Pointing and Center of Gravity," and Section 3, "Summary and Sayback," in the "Sharing and Responding" part of this book. But you may also want to get some comments on how your structure is coming across, especially when you've gotten to the final draft. To get some feedback on this, you can use the "Sharing and Responding" sections grouped under structural responses.

Here are some more specific questions to use, but the important thing is for you to ask for the kind of feedback *you* feel most useful.

- What changes do you see in me as a writer? What do you think I've learned during this term? What do you think I need to work on most? What do I seem most confident about? least confident about?
- Do you think some of what I've recorded contradicts any conclusions I've drawn? Do you feel gaps, something missing that would make the picture of me as a writer more complete?
- What do you find the most surprising or unique about my autobiography?
- What did you find helpful for yourself as a writer from my autobiography? What did you learn from me that you find the most valuable?

Process Journal and Cover Letter

As always, these are merely suggestions. You may want the last segment of your autobiography to consist of comment on and analysis of what it was like writing it.

- How did you feel about this assignment before you started it? Did you think you would enjoy doing it? find it a bore? feel unable to come up with enough material? What were your feelings when you were finished?
- Were you able to come up with genuine advice for yourself—advice that you think will be truly useful?
- If you had a chance to hear or read the autobiographies of others, what were your reactions? Did you sense mainly similarities or differences between theirs and yours?
- Do you think *how* you write makes a difference? Why or why not?
- Do you think writing is or will be important to you? What evidence do you have for your answer?

For your cover letter, it's good to include some or all of your process writing. But don't forget to answer some cover letter questions. Here are the main ones: What is your main point and what effect are you trying to have on readers? What do you feel works best in your paper and where are you unsatisfied? What changes did you make on the basis of any feedback? And most important: What feedback do you want now from a reader? But your teacher may ask you particular cover letter questions that pertain to this assignment.

RUMINATIONS AND THEORY
Autobiography and Metacognition

Writing autobiography is a form of metacognition. Perhaps you've seen the word *metacognition* before you started this course—maybe in a psychology or education class. *Meta* is a prefix that comes from Greek; one of its meanings is "going beyond" or "higher." Thus metacognition literally means going beyond cognition or knowing; metacognitive theories, then, are those that consider our ability to know what we know.

Kenneth Burke, a modern rhetorician (we used some of his words to start the "Ruminations and Theory" section in Workshop 11, "Researching"), writes in *Permanence and Change* of the trout who, having escaped once from a hook embedded in bait, is afterward warier. The trout may miss out on some genuine food because something about it looks like what almost caught him. And the trout may also fall for bait offered in some other way. No matter: The trout's behavior has changed.

Human beings, Burke goes on to say, can go one step further than a trout, for we "can greatly extend the scope of the critical process"; we are the only species "possessing an equipment for going beyond the criticism of experience to a criticism of criticism . . . we may also interpret our interpretations." The "equipment" that allows us to criticize our criticism and interpret our interpretations is language. And writing, we add, allows us to physically see that criticism and those interpretations. It allows us to observe our observations.

Research suggests that our unconscious mind is both cognitive and emotional. Events we have not perceived can affect how we behave. In extreme cases, they may lead to psychosis that can be eradicated only if the patient becomes aware of the unconscious roots of the psychosis. We don't want to suggest that writing is psychosis, but we do believe that our unconscious affects how we write. No one teaches any of us how to put the words "round," "big," "box," and "green" in the right order, but as native speakers we are going to come up with "big round green box" unless we're deliberately seeking a particular effect. (And even that proves our point, because we wouldn't get that particular effect if readers didn't automatically "know" the usual order.) Our unconscious mind stores much complex knowledge we don't quite understand but can learn to tap. But our unconscious mind can also lay traps for us that we may not understand. Analyzing our own writing behavior and actual pieces of our own writing can help us understand the ways that our unconscious helps and hinders. This, too, is a way of knowing what we know.

Metacognition is not only valuable for mental activities. Athletes and their coaches are well aware of the power of metacognition, of studying and analyzing physical behavior. Football teams watch videos of prior games as a way to improve performance. Often when teams have had a particularly disastrous day, a coach will sit them down immediately after the game—even before they take showers—and insist that they replay crucial moments while they're still fresh in their minds. The coach does this to show them not just what they did wrong but how they can do better the next time. Video technology has developed to the point where gymnasts' movements can be digitalized on a screen so that athletes and their coaches can analyze them minutely. Ballet dancers practice before mirrors so that they can see themselves. Exercise therapists even tell us that exercise is more effective when the person exercising thinks about what she is doing—thinks about the movements of the muscles and limbs. When you write, you're exercising a kind of muscle. We believe that a muscle becomes stronger if you look at its actual movements on a regular basis.

Students sometimes become bored with process writing. They've told us so; their teachers have told us so. But we are not dissuaded. We continue to believe that if you can learn what process writing really is—not just mechanically going through the questions in every workshop, but actually probing the steps of your own writing—your writing will improve. The Russian psychologist and learning theorist Lev Vygotsky concluded after years of observing children's learning behavior that human beings are far more likely to move to higher learning if they understand what they've already learned—that is, if they know what they know.

Thus we think that you can best come to conclusions about ways to improve your writing process by studying your writing process— by collecting as much information as you can about it and drawing conclusions about it *only* as a result of discovering patterns in it. This is the philosophy that lies behind the assignment here. We use our students' autobiographies as guides to help us design our courses and assignments. Obviously we cannot design a course for one individual, so we seek common elements in the autobiographies we read. In other words, we generalize in an effort to come to conclusions that are valid for many student writers. Despite this, however, we recognize that each student's writing process is slightly different. We recognize the importance of specific data even as we make attempts at generalizations. But your task (at least right now) is different from ours. Your concern is to improve your writing. Thus your autobiography needs to focus solely on you and to draw conclusions solely from your personal experiences and specific interactions with others in a variety of writing environments.

We'll conclude with a quotation from the *Notebooks* of Samuel Taylor Coleridge, who has much to say about imagination and creativity:

Consciousness . . . mind, life, will, body, organ (as compared with machine), nature, spirit, sin, habit, sense, understanding, reason: here are fourteen words. Have you ever reflectively and quietly asked yourself the meaning of any one of these, and asked yourself to return the answer in *distinct* terms, not applicable to any of the other words? Or have you contented yourself with the vague floating meaning that will just save you from absurdity in the use of the word, just as the clown's botany would do, who knew that potatoes were roots, and cabbages greens? Or, if you have the gift of wit, shelter yourself under Augustine's equivocation, "I know it perfectly well till I am asked." Know? Ay, as an oyster knows its life. *But do you know your knowledge?*

Three Sample Autobiographies

A Case Study of Myself as a Writer   *Leah K. Clarkson*

The first thing I realized about writing was that it had to be done quickly and well. I understood, as a child, that writing and reading were indispensable, and that the sooner one mastered both, the easier life would be. I also understood that one needed to be good at these things to be considered "smart." With this knowledge firmly instilled in my subconscious, I set out to become the fastest, cleanest writer I could be. I knew that spelling was important, and topic sentences, and I knew that tone stood for a lot. I knew that writing for school was not like speaking, and that scribbling a letter or yet another diary entry was not the same as constructing an essay for class. I took incorrect spelling personally. My writing had all of the trappings of goodness. It was clean and clear, and generally precise, although in college I did go through a period of convoluted verbosity as I struggled to meet the minimum page requirements for papers.

I have to say, then, that my early experiences with writing were not traumatizing in the least. I was fortunate enough to have very good teachers who encouraged me to write. I can recall no nightmarish writing episodes in which an evil professor destroyed the spirit of joy in my writing by humiliatingly pointing out my shoddy grammar or sloppy presentation. The only mildly interesting event I can recall occurred when I was in the third grade. I got a C in penmanship because I had transferred from a French school to an American school, and I couldn't write in the Palmer method of handwriting, although my alternate, eurocursive was actually quite nice. I knew that this was unfair and my parents agreed, so, again, I incurred no lasting trauma. I do remember always feeling a little as though I was getting away with something because I could get praise simply by stringing together a coherent sentence. All of this changed when I got to college.

In college I began to get scared when I saw the labor that was going on all around me. Friends of mine would suffer and get extensions and then stay up all night and suffer some more just to turn out eight to ten pages about something they would probably never study again. I began to worry because my system, where I sat down with a pad for a few hours, wrote out my paper, then retyped and revised in an hour or two, seemed too easy. And it was. It was too easy. It was as though my brain would abandon me, and my common sense, during the few hours that I spent cobbling together my papers. I would spend far more time making pretty sentences and paragraphs, putting punctuation in all the right places, figuring out good words to use, than I would actually trying to communicate my point. I've realized, now, that this system emerged not simply out of laziness, but out of fear. The fear that if I paid attention to my writing I would find it to be substandard. The fear that if I began to work on my prose I would be so overwhelmed that I wouldn't finish the paper on time. The fear that if it came down to the last minute before the deadline and I absolutely had to com-

A Case Study of Myself as a Writer *continued*

plete my paper I might miss the opportunity to do something more fun. I wrote my papers chronically early and woefully speedily. And I pretty much continued to get away with it, although now I had many more misgivings to repress.

I should state here that for most of my life I considered myself an actor. I lived to ape and pretend and mimic and mock and entertain. I loved it because I knew that a good actor can safely cloak himself and still have power. The shell of the actor performs while his essence sits back and delivers ironic commentary on the action. My last year of college I decided to give up being an actor for many reasons too banal to go into. I decided to write a creative BA thesis, and then the focus of my writing shifted entirely. I became a "fiction writer" with a whole host of issues separate from those that dictate grammar, punctuation, main point. All of a sudden, it didn't matter so much that I knew how to say something—what mattered was that I thought that I had something to say. But the acting wasn't easy to let go of—and it's difficult now for me to write fiction without considering all of the ways in which being an actor has affected the way that I write.

When I think about my writing now, I realize how much of my development of a writing "style" involved the simultaneous emergence of a non-style. Even though I knew how to say things well, I thought that I had very little to say. I was afraid of taking up space, which is one of the reasons that I quit acting in my third year of college. I quit acting because I was tired of being on display, and I thought that writing fiction would be a more subtle way of making my presence known to the world. Unfortunately my distaste for expansiveness led to a major problem in my fiction writing—essentially, that I take up too little space. My writing is tight and constrained. Everything correctly spelled and commas in all of the right places, but not enough on the page. Too few flights of fancy.

Since beginning the MFA program a month ago, I've also been thinking a lot about voice. I've kept a journal for most of my life, since the fourth grade, and I can look back through them and know exactly what I was reading at the time. There's the Anne of Green Gables period where everything is written flowery and sugary-sweet with lots of italics, there's the Diary of Anne Frank period which is very earnest with a lot of sweeping generalizations about the state of the world and what it means to be a young girl in it (I think I even embarrassingly called my diary Kitty for a while, but later went back and crossed it out because I realized what a cheesy rip-off that was by the time I was in Junior High.) Anyway, the list goes on. Unfortunately, the same thing happens to me now. I read a short story and if the voice clicks with me, I'm in it, and I can't get out for a few weeks. I can't read Salinger at all—it's a death-knell for my writing, and Amis and Waugh throw me into paroxysms of imitation that also take months to work out. This seems to be a leftover from my acting days, and the realization that I do this leads me to another observation: Writing fiction means writing yourself onto the page.

A Case Study of Myself as a Writer   *continued*

This is incredibly frightening.

I took my first fiction writing class during my second year of college. The professor was Richard Stern, a notoriously crusty professor and writer at the University of Chicago. We had to turn in a writing sample before the first meeting and, during the first class, Stern read aloud the names of people who had NOT made the cut. They had to get up, one at a time, and leave the room. The silence was excruciating. Finally, it came down to thirteen people, all of us sitting holding our breath as though we were in some sort of academic beauty pageant. We waited for the final three names to be called. Stern called out two more names, and two more flushed students shoved their filofaxes into their backpacks and slunk out the door. One more name to be called. "Clarkson." he said. I prepared to leave. "Can I see you out in the hallway?"

Once in the hallway Stern told me that he thought I could take the class, but that I was very young, and so might want to consider waiting another year. Somehow, in the face of his very frightening professorial demeanor, to this man who reeked of Bellow, to this staple of Chicago fiction, I found the guts to say "I think I can do it. I want to do it." And he let me in. And the first piece I got back from him was almost illegible because he had put so many red marks on it. Some of my favorite comments were "Learn how to write." and "Enough with this semipoetic drivel." But I appreciated it. I liked it because I felt as though I'd been caught out, finally, as though it was a relief that someone finally knew that I was only pretending to know how to write well. I think that class was what made me decide definitely to quit acting, although I wouldn't do so for another year. Because acting was easy. And writing fiction was hard. I was really grateful to Stern for being a tyrant. And believe me, nothing anyone says about my writing now hurts my feelings. They can't be harder on it than Stern was, and Stern taught me to be hard on myself.

Being hard on myself has been a problem, though. Because I'll know that something isn't working but my only solution is to scrap the whole thing or remain stalled because it seems that what's frequently wrong isn't just a sentence or a paragraph or a segue but the whole voice of a piece. Even writing this right now I'm annoyed by the tone I feel I've assumed, a tone appropriate to a piece titled "A Case Study of Myself as a Writer."

Often in my fiction I feel like I sound cutesy and preachy and like I'm writing a kiddy novel, which maybe I am, because I read quite a bit as a child and I worry that the years of reading all of those books over and over and over have basically ruined me as a writer. And I'm scared to death that I'll wake up one morning and find myself writing children's fiction the same way I woke up and found myself teaching drama to Junior High kids in a Catholic school in downtown Chicago with people shouting "Miss Clarkson, Miss Clarkson" all the livelong day. I DON'T WANT TO BE JUDY BLUME. I DON'T WANT TO WRITE FOR KIDS.

If I don't want to do this, though, I have to let the real me out onto the

🖋️A Case Study of Myself as a Writer   *continued*

page. I have to stop self-editing, I have to stop stopping myself before I've even started. I have to learn again how to take up space, and yell for attention. I have to kill that little voice in my head that insists on broadcasting an ironic play-by-play whenever I sit in front of the computer writing fiction.

It's hard to know how to conclude this paper, because I'm more aware than ever now that my writing, and myself, are experiencing mysterious permutations with every passing day. I have to resist the urge to boringly sum up the points that I have stated in the last few pages (often repetitively). Perhaps I'll end on a less formal note, and include this e-mail that I wrote recently to a friend of mine. I think it expresses my current frustrations pretty well, and it expresses them in something a little closer to my true "voice." Please excuse the expletives:

> Dear Melissa,
>
> I've plopped down into a crisis of sorts, my first big writing debacle here at UMASS. It all started—well, it all started a long time ago, which is what I'm discovering. But basically here I was, writing along like gangbusters, busted out three stories and then turned around to find out that what I had in my hands was a pile of utter crap. And that's no lie.
>
> Now. Don't get me wrong. I'm not whining about how I can't trick out a pretty phrase or cobble together a pleasing stream of witty prose. This I can do. But to what end? To no end. I write stories about nuns and hookers and lepers and have no idea what I'm talking about. I feel like my stuff stinks and I sound like a goddamn Judy Blume novel and I can't bear the thought of becoming just another Elizabeth Wortzel writing about depression and eating disorders and the guy who hurt me and etc. The world just don't need another one of those. So I'm discussing this with a friend and he says, "Why don't you just give me something to read?"
>
> So I hi my ass home and spend four hours finishing the nun story. I go back and change all of this stuff and feel like "Hmm. This story still reeks but at least I realized I was going the wrong way and now I'm going the right way & etc." I even feel kind of proud because, you know, even if it's crap it's 15 pages Times 11 font 1.5 spaced crap. And the commas are all in the right places.
>
> Well, he pointed out that my writing was incredibly anal (my words, not his, I think he said "tight") and he said he couldn't believe it was a first draft because there should be a lot to excise in such a thing but there wasn't anything. I realized that for the last few years I've been praying just like good old Dottie Parker "Please, GOD let me write like a man" and it ain't happening. I'm all bound up about what people will think of me because unless you're a grade-A primo genius writing is you. It's you, baby, splayed out on the table and that-scares-the-shit out of me. Acting my God, acting was so easy. And I was better at it. I was a maestro at that. So what am I doing? I think it all has to do with being a girl. With being a stupid girl, you know? It's so unfair that that's the case, that somewhere along the line I got it into my little blondish head that if I

A Case Study of Myself as a Writer   *continued*

wasn't a stud rock star at something that I'd better just run in the other direction or if I decided to give it a go anyway I'd better be as ironic about it as possible.

So I had a bit of a breakthrough this morning. I was lying in bed, still thinking all of this over (thank God I was on the sauce last night or I wouldn't have slept a wink) and I was thinking: What should I write? What can I write that's honest? And everything I thought of, I realized, I simultaneously brought the hammer down on, smashing its soft little skull into oblivion. Feeling ugly NO being crushed-out NO what to wear on a date NO how it feels to be rejected NO the time I went to XYZ NO. And I've got to stop that. I just have to. I have to make that leap.

Jesus, I'm sorry, Melee. What a rant.

Love,
Leah

Autobiography*   *Mitchell Shack*

I hate to start out on a negative comment, but I feel I must say that I don't like to think of this as a case study. It makes me feel as if I am preparing a report for a doctor or psychiatrist. Actually I would like to think of it as simply an expression of my feelings about my accomplishments and struggles of being a writer.

In order to write such a paper, I must remember not only works I have written this semester, but also ones that I have written in the past years. Remembering the latter bunch is not such an easy task; not just because of the time difference between now and when they were written, but because I would rather not remember some of the papers. The papers were not actually bad, but I have bad memories of my writings in those days. What I mean is that those papers were written because I was forced to write them; not because I wanted to write them. The papers accomplished the task that they were supposed to do, but they did little more. They were quite boring and uninspired works. Actually the word "works" is an accurate description of those writings because that's exactly what I thought of them—as doing work.

Most of my writings—correction—all of my writings, were assignments in high school, usually English essays. These papers were usually about a book we read in class, or an essay on a test. My style of writing was simple. I just stated the facts, one right after another, and somehow linked all these facts together to form an essay. There was little creativity at all and it was amazing that the teacher didn't doze off before reaching my closing paragraph.

Well, that's how I stood coming into this class, and I anticipated little change in my attitude upon completion of this class. As a matter of fact, I

* Mitchell Shack's "Image of an Ice-Cream Man" can be found on pp. 36–37.

Autobiography   *continued*

thought that I was going to hate writing even more than I already did, if that was even possible. Much to my surprise my attitude took a complete reversal during the span of this course. "What brought about that change?" you may ask. I think it is because I began to write about things that I wanted to write, not things that other people wanted me to write. I began to even enjoy my writing; something that was previously all too painful just to think about. My writings have drastically improved because of this change in attitude. My papers have become more creative and not just a list of facts anymore. My style of writing has become more natural. It has become smoother and I have "opened up" more so that I can get what I'm thinking in my head down on the paper. That may not seem like a big task to some people, but it would have seemed almost impossible to me just a few months ago. My papers have changed from simply stating what happened to explaining how I felt when it happened. I have also learned new techniques and methods of writing which I will pick up on later.

So far I have been telling you about changes that have come as a result of taking this course, so I think I should give some examples of these changes to prove my point. The paper that I like the best was a descriptive narrative about my favorite person of my childhood, the ice-cream man, so I think it's only fair to talk about that piece. I enjoyed this piece because I was able to open up and explain how I felt and what I was thinking at that time and not just give a plot summary. For example one line from the story says, "The truck from far away looked like an old bread truck, but it would not have mattered one bit if it looked like a garbage truck, just as long as it sold ice cream." The same line written before this class would have probably looked more like "The truck was white and looked like a bread truck." I changed from just putting down facts to putting down feelings along with those facts. This brightens up my papers greatly, gives a more personal feel to it, and makes it much more interesting and entertaining to read. I accomplished this task in an "Image of an Ice-Cream Man," and that is why I feel this paper is a representative of not only one of my better papers, but also of my improvements in writing over previous years.

There are many techniques that I learned which I can attribute to my change in writing. One such thing is the use of freewriting. I have never before used freewriting, and early in the semester I just thought it was a waste of time. In looking back over my papers and some of the freewriting I did that led to those papers I realized I was mistaken. Many of my ideas came as a result of freewriting; some of which I may not have thought of if I just sat down and wrote the paper. I used freewriting in the "Image of an Ice-Cream Man," and the paper benefited from its use. For example, I wrote, "I watched him as he was making it, and my mouth watered just looking at all the ice cream, lollipops, bubble gum, chocolate bars, Italian ices, and other candy I saw inside the truck." This line and many of the others were taken right out of my freewriting. The freewriting allowed me to open up and "look back" in my mind and remember things that I have forgotten over the years.

Autobiography   *continued*

In the line above, using freewriting allowed me to remember in my mind exactly what the truck looked like and what I saw when I looked in it. Another thing that I like about freewriting is that I am not restricted to a topic or an idea. I can let my mind wander and go where it wants to go. I don't even have to worry about punctuation, grammar, or anything else that can inhibit my thinking. The result is usually writing that "flows" and seems natural, and this type of writing can enhance any paper.

Another useful technique which I learned is the loop writing process. I only used this process for one paper, and I must admit that what resulted was one of my weakest papers. This was not because of the loop writing process, but it's because of what I did in actually writing the paper after using the loop writing process. To tell you the truth, the loop writing process worked too well. The process consisted of using all different ways of thinking about a topic to get ideas on that topic. This included my first thoughts, prejudices, dialogues, lies, stories, and portraits about the topic. I used this process in writing "How Death Motivates Us in Life," and my problem was that I came up with too many ideas about the topic. The loop writing process allowed me to think of so many different aspects of the topic and for each aspect come up with several ideas pertaining to it. The problem came when I tried to write an essay which incorporated all these ideas in them. I mentioned all these ideas, but because of the great number of them, I didn't go into any single one in great detail. This resulted in a lot of superficial ideas, but no depth to my paper. What I should have done was pick out the ideas that proved my point the best and go into depth with those items. What I am trying to get across is that the loop writing process is very helpful, especially with topics that you seem short on ideas to pursue. But I have to be careful and not get carried away with myself and try to fit every single idea that I come up with into my paper.

So far I have been talking about methods I learned which aided me in my writings, but I haven't really talked about how I go about using these methods in actually creating a piece. Believe it or not, my favorite way of writing is to compose my paper directly on my computer. This may seem odd or difficult to some people, but to me it works fine. Actually I usually start by freewriting on the topic, or using the loop writing technique if I'm short on ideas. Next I usually make a rough outline of what I am going to say. I try to think about how I want my paper organized and in what order each point should go, and then I create the basic form of an outline. I then go back and jot down a few examples under each argument to prove it. I don't write in sentence form; I just scribble down a few key words and later on when I actually write my paper I look over these key words and then write about them.

This is the part when my computer comes into play. I load up my word processor, set my margins, and start writing. I like using the computer rather than a typewriter or pen and paper because I can edit directly as I go along. I can switch sentences around, delete words, add phrases, and do many

Autobiography *continued*

other operations immediately. The words look on screen as they will on paper so I can see the structure forming and know how the finished product will look. I can go back and change my paper three weeks or three months later without having to retype it since it is saved on disk. Also my word processing program contains a spelling checker which I find very useful since I am far from being the world champion in spelling bees, and it contains a thesaurus so I can have some place to turn to if I get stuck [. . .].

One thing that I haven't already mentioned and I feel is a major reason why I enjoyed taking this course is that I was actually able to tell a story. I was able to relate an experience that over the years didn't seem important enough to tell anybody. This year I got the chance and just being able to do that has made this course worthwhile for me.

A Look Inside: Myself as a Writer   *Greg Teets*

Mind-Before

When he finished he looked
and saw that it was not
pleasing to his eyes.

New System

Process Journal

"The piece moved and grew like it was alive.
"I'm beginning to think that nothing is ever
finished . . . unless it's written down.
"The 'felt sense' clicked and it became easy to
express my emotions on paper and I wasn't ashamed
or afraid.
"The 'invisible' writing makes me focus on
what is popping up in my head, not what's
happening around me.
"Now, I find writing fun and relaxing.
"[I]t seems like there is a lot of
garbage in my head. I can write it
down and it goes away.
"I've discovered that I am a
very spontaneous thinker. The
momentary ideas are usually
the best.
"For days I've been
trying to think of a
narrative, but nothing satisfied me.

A Look Inside: Myself as a Writer *continued*

Finally, boom, big revelation,
bingo!
  "Now, I am able
to release my thoughts.
Instead of trying to
structure them and
then write them down
I do the reverse.
The 'Doty'* system
works much better
than my old system."
      And God saw that it was good.
        It was very good.

*Eugene Doty was this student's teacher.

Sharing & Responding

Cover Letter

Summary of Kinds of Responses

Procedures for Giving and Receiving Responses

Full Explanations of Kinds of Responses—with Samples

1. Sharing: No Response or Responses from the Self
2. Pointing and Center of Gravity
3. Summary and Sayback
4. What Is Almost Said? What Do You Want to Hear More About?
5. Reply
6. Voice
7. Movies of the Reader's Mind
8. Metaphorical Descriptions
9. Believing and Doubting
10. Skeleton Feedback and Descriptive Outline
11. Criterion-Based Feedback

Final Word: Taking Charge of the Feedback Process by Choosing Among These Techniques

Sample Essays

Cover Letter

Dear Students and Teachers,

In this guide we present a variety of methods for sharing your writing and getting helpful responses. First we'll give a brief overview of the methods; then we'll explain them in more detail and illustrate their use on two sample essays.

Our goal is to help you become comfortable and skilled at asking for feedback and giving it. We think this may well be the most valuable part of our book, the part you are most likely to use after the course is over.

Suggestions for Using "Sharing and Responding"

There are more techniques here than you can use on any one occasion. But we want you to *try* them all in order to learn the wide range of options you have for feedback. Then *you* will be in a position to ask for the kind of feedback that is right for you—depending on your preferences or temperament, the kind of piece you're working on, and the stage it's at. Many people don't like getting feedback on their writing because they feel they are on the chopping block. They don't realize how many options they could ask for, and so they end up helplessly putting themselves in the hands of readers. "Sharing and Responding" will help you take charge of the process of getting responses.

We also urge you to try out these techniques in order. They go from easier to harder, from safer to riskier, and from quicker to more time-consuming. This progression builds a feedback situation of support and trust. Don't assume, though, that the later kinds of responding are better: Some of the earliest ones remain the most useful despite being quick and easy.

Our Underlying Premises and Convictions

We find that most students are instinctively reluctant to judge or evaluate each other's writing and give advice about how to improve it. We think their instincts are wise. Evaluation and advice are not what writers need most. What writers need most (and fortunately it's what is easiest to provide) is an *audience:* a thoughtful, interested audience rather than evaluators or editors or advice-givers. In the long run, you will learn the most about writing from feeling the *presence of interested readers*—like feeling the weight of a fish at the end of the line. You can't trust evaluations or advice. Even experts on writing usually disagree with each other. And even when they agree about what is weak, they often disagree about how to fix it.

Therefore we urge you to follow a crucial principle for feedback: Don't let anyone give you evaluation or advice unless they also give you the perceptions and reactions it is based on—that is, unless they describe *what they see* and *how they are reacting*. For example, if a reader says, "The organization is confusing in your piece," make sure she goes back and describes the sequence of parts in your piece as she sees them or the sequence of her reactions as she was reading: When did she first start feeling confused, and what kind of confusion was it? What was going on in her mind and feelings at different points? Otherwise, you don't know what her comment really means.

Many students have seldom written except in school, seldom given their writing to anyone but a teacher, and always gotten some kind of evaluative response. But it's hard for writers to prosper unless they give their work to a variety of readers, not just teachers, and get a variety of responses: no response, non-evaluative responses, and evaluative responses. The suggestions here will give you the variety of audience relationships you need to develop a more productive sense of audience.

You will improve your writing much faster if you let us and your teacher help you build a community in your classroom: a place where people hear clearly even what is mumbled, understand what is badly written, and look for the validity even in what they disagree with. Eventually you will learn to write to the enemy—to write surrounded by sharks. But you will learn that necessary skill better if, for a while, you practice writing to allies and listening to friends.

Two Paradoxes of Responding

First paradox: the *reader* is always right; yet the *writer* is always right. That is, readers get to decide what's true about their reactions—about what they see or think or feel. It's senseless to quarrel with readers about their experience of what's happening to them (though you can ask them to explain their experience more fully).

Nevertheless, you as the writer get to decide what to do about any of this feedback from readers, what changes to make, if any. You don't have to follow their advice. Just listen openly and swallow it all. You can do that better if you realize that you get to take your time and make up your own mind.

Second paradox: the writer must be in charge; yet the writer must sit quietly and do nothing. As writer, you must be in control. It's your writing. Don't be passive or helpless. You get to decide what kind of feedback, if any, you need. Are you trying to improve this particular piece? Or perhaps you don't care so much about working on this piece any more but just want feedback on it to learn about your writing in general. Or perhaps you don't want to work on anything but just enjoy sharing this piece and hearing what others have to say. Don't let readers make these decisions for you. Ask for what you want and don't be afraid to stop them if they give you the wrong thing. For example, sometimes it's important to insist, "I'm still very tender about this piece. I just want to hear what it sounds like for now and not get any feedback at all." Or, "Just tell me about sentences or transitions that are unclear, and help me with copyediting. I don't want to hear any of your reactions to my ideas."

Nevertheless, you mostly have to sit back and just listen. If you are talking a lot, you are probably blocking good feedback. For example, don't argue if they misunderstand what you wrote. Their misunderstanding is valuable, and you need to understand it in order to see how your words function. If they want to give you feedback you didn't ask for—or not give you what you asked for—they may have good reasons. If you aren't getting honest, serious, or caring feedback, don't blame your readers. You may not have convinced them that you really want it.

How We Wrote "Sharing and Responding"

In our first drafts of the *Community of Writers,* we put all our sharing and responding suggestions in the workshops themselves. But then we ran into a dilemma. We realized that we wanted to give students and teachers lots of choice of which workshops to use and what order to use them in. Yet we *didn't* want to give that much choice about which feedback techniques to use and which order to use them in. For it's crucial to us that you go through a progression of feedback techniques that gives the best learning and builds the most trust. Because of this dilemma, we hit on the plan of having a separate "Sharing and Responding" guide (though we have also kept a few suggestions in each workshop).

Also, this part in the first edition of our textbook was too complicated: Too many kinds of response were arranged in groupings that were too complex. We realize now that as we worked out this book for the first time, we built too much of our background thinking into the structure itself. Writers often speak of "scaffolding": structures put up in order to help construct the building in the first place—but that can be taken down after the building is done. We had too much scaffolding in the first edition. You'll find the same thing sometimes happens to you. You'll write something and it comes out complicated; but once you've got it written, you finally understand it better and you can then revise to make it simpler.

We'd like to get your responses to "Sharing and Responding." Like you, we can profit from readers' responses. (You can write to us at the publisher's address.)

Peter Elbow
Pat Belanoff

Summary of Kinds of Responses

Here is an overview of 11 different and valuable ways of responding to writing, and a few thoughts about when each kind is valuable. We will explain them more fully later and illustrate their use on sample essays. After you have tried them out, you can glance back over this summary when you want to decide which kind of feedback to request.

1. Sharing: No Response

Read your piece aloud to listeners and ask, "Would you please just listen and enjoy?" You can also give them your text to read silently, though you don't usually learn as much this way. Simple sharing is also a way to listen better to your own responses to your own piece, without having to think about how others respond. You learn an enormous amount from hearing yourself read your own words or from reading them over when you know that someone else is also reading them.

Plain sharing or no response is valuable in many situations—when you don't have much time, at very early stages when you just want to try something out or feel very tentative, or when you are completely finished and don't plan to make any changes at all—as a form of simple communication or celebration. Sharing gives you an unpressured setting for getting comfortable reading your words out loud and listening to the writing of others.

2. Pointing and Center of Gravity

Pointing: "Which words or phrases or passages somehow strike you? stick in mind? get through?" Center of gravity: "Which sections somehow seem important or resonant or generative?" You are not asking necessarily for the main points but for sections or passages that seem to resonate or linger in mind. Sometimes a seemingly minor detail or example—even an aside or a digression—can be a center of gravity.

These quick, easy, interesting forms of response are good for timid or inexperienced responders, or for early drafts. They help you establish a sense of contact with readers. Center of gravity response is particularly interesting for showing you rich and interesting parts of your piece that you might have neglected but that might be worth exploring and developing. Center of gravity can help you see your piece in a different light and suggest ways to make major revisions.

3. Summary and Sayback

Summary: "Please summarize what you have heard. Tell me what you hear as the main thing and the almost-main things." (Variations: "Give me a phrase as title and a one-word title—first using my words and then using your words.") Sayback: "Please say back to me in your own words what you hear me getting at in my piece. But say it in a slightly questioning or tentative way—as an invitation for me to reply with my own restatement of what I'm getting at."

These are both useful at any stage in the writing process to see whether readers got the points you are trying to give. But sayback is particularly useful at early stages when you are still groping and haven't yet been able to find what you really want to say. You can read a collection of exploratory passages for sayback response. When readers say back to you what they hear—and invite you to reply—it often leads you to find exactly the words or thoughts or emphasis you were looking for.

4. What Is Almost Said? What Do You Want to Hear More About?

Just ask readers those very questions.

This kind of response is particularly useful when you need to *develop* or enrich your piece—when you sense there is more here but you haven't been able to get your finger on it yet. This kind of question gives you concrete substantive help because it leads your readers to give you some of *their ideas* to add to yours. Remember this too: What you imply but don't say in your writing is often very loud to readers but unheard by you and has an enormous effect on how they respond.

Extreme variation: "Make a guess about what was on my mind that I didn't write about."

5. Reply

Simply ask, "What are *your* thoughts about my topic? Now that you've heard what I've had to say, what do *you* have to say?"

This kind of response is useful at any point, but it is particularly useful at early stages when you haven't worked out your thinking. Indeed, you can ask for this kind of response even before you've written a draft; perhaps you jotted down some notes. You can say, "I'm thinking about saying X, Y, and Z. How would you reply? What are your thoughts about this topic?" This is actually the most natural and common response to any human discourse. You are inviting a small discussion of the topic.

6. Voice

(a) "How much voice do you hear in my writing? Is my language alive and human? Or is it dead, no-one-home, unsayable?" (b) "What kind of voice(s) do you hear in my writing? Timid? Confident? Sarcastic? Pleading?" Or "What kind of person does my writing sound like? What side(s) of me come through in my writing?" Most of all, "Do you trust the voice or person you hear in my writing?"

This kind of feedback can be useful at any stage. When people describe the voice they hear in writing, they often get right to the heart of subtle but important matters of language and approach. They don't have to be able to talk in technical terms ("You seem to use lots of passive verbs and nominalized phrases"); they can say, "You sound kind of bureaucratic and pompous and I wonder if you actually believe what you are saying."

7. Movies of the Reader's Mind

Ask readers to tell you honestly and in detail what is going on in their minds as they read your words. There are three powerful ways to help readers give you this kind of response: (a) Interrupt their reading a few times and find out what's happening at that moment. (b) Get them to tell you their reactions in the form of a *story* that takes place in time. (c) If they make it-statements ("It was confusing"), make them translate these into I-statements ("I felt confused starting here about . . .").

Movies of the reader's mind make the most sense when you have a fairly developed draft and you want to know how it works on readers, rather than when you're still trying to develop your ideas. Movies are the richest and most valuable form of response, but they require that you feel some confidence in yourself and support from your reader, because when readers tell you honestly what is happening while they are reading your piece, they may tell you they don't like it or even get mad at it.

8. Metaphorical Descriptions

Ask readers to describe your writing in terms of clothing (e.g., jeans, tuxedo, lycra running suit), weather (e.g., foggy, stormy, sunny, humid), animals, colors, shapes.

This kind of response is helpful at any point. It gives you a new view, a new lens; it's particularly helpful when you feel stale on a piece, perhaps because you have worked so long on it. Sometimes young or inexperienced readers are good at giving you this kind of response when they are unskilled at other kinds.

9. Believing and Doubting

Believing: "Try to believe everything I have written, even if you disagree or find it crazy. At least *pretend* to believe it. Looking at things from my point of view, tell me what else you see. Be my friend and ally and give me more evidence, arguments, and ideas to help me make my case better." *Doubting:* "Try to doubt everything I have written, even if you love it. Take on the role of enemy and find all the arguments that can be made against me. Pretend to be someone who hates my writing. What would he or she notice?"

These forms of feedback are particularly useful for persuasive essays or arguments, though the believing game can help you flesh out and enrich the world of a story or poem. Believing is good when you are struggling and want help. It's a way to get readers to give you new ideas and arguments and to improve your piece in all sorts of ways. Doubting is good after you've gotten a piece as strong as you can get it and you want to send it out or hand it in—but first find out how hostile readers will fight you.

10. Skeleton Feedback and Descriptive Outline

Skeleton feedback: "Please help me work out my reasoning: my main point, my subpoints, my supporting evidence, and my assumptions about my topic and about my audience." *Descriptive outline:* "Please write *says* and *does* sentences for my whole paper and then for each paragraph or section." A *says* sentence summarizes the meaning or message, and a *does* sentence describes the function.

These are the most useful for essays. They are feasible only if the reader has the text in hand and can take a good deal of time and care—and perhaps write out responses. Because they give you the most distance and perspective on what you have written, they are uniquely useful for giving *yourself* feedback. Both kinds of feedback help you on late drafts when you want to test out your reasoning and organization. But skeleton feedback is particularly useful on early drafts when you are still trying to figure out what to say or emphasize and how to organize your thoughts.

A Voyage Through The Feedback Islands

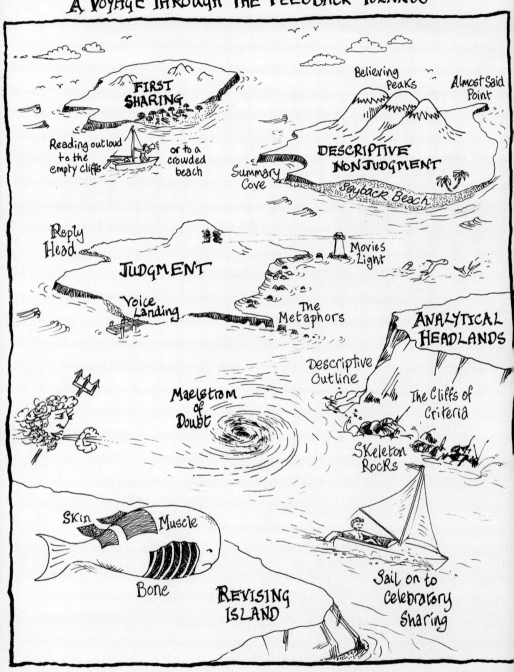

11. Criterion-Based Feedback

Ask readers to give you their thoughts about specific criteria that you are wondering about or struggling with: "Does this sound too technical?" "Is this section too long?" "Do my jokes work for you?" "Do you feel I've addressed the objections of people who disagree?" "Please find mistakes in spelling and grammar and typing." You can also ask readers to address what they think are the important criteria for your piece. You can ask too about traditional criteria for essays: focus on the assignment or task, content (ideas, reasoning, support, originality), organization, clarity of language, and voice.

You ask for criterion-based feedback when you have questions about specific aspects of your piece. You can also ask for it when you need a quick overview of strengths and weaknesses. This kind of feedback depends on skilled and experienced readers. (But even with them you should still take it with a grain of salt, for if someone says your piece is boring, other readers might well disagree. Movies of the reader's mind are more trustworthy because they give you a better picture of the personal reactions *behind* these judgments.)

Sharing & Responding

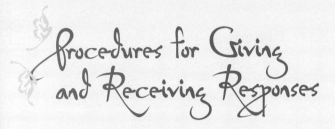

Procedures for Giving and Receiving Responses

We've briefly summarized your choices among *kinds of response*. Now we want to emphasize your choices among *procedures for getting responses*. It's important to test these out, too—to see which ones are the most helpful for you in different situations.

Early or Late Drafts?

Responses are helpful on both early and late drafts; indeed, it's a big help to discuss your thinking even before you have written at all. The following response modes are particularly helpful for very early drafts: pointing, center of gravity, summary, sayback, almost said, and reply. At the other extreme, it can be helpful and interesting to get feedback even on *final drafts* that you don't plan to revise any more: You will learn more about how your writing works on readers and how readers read. When poets and fiction writers give readings, the goal is pleasure and celebration, not feedback. (Keep your eye out for notices of readings by poets and writers in local schools, libraries, and bookstores. They give pleasure and learning too.)

Pairs or Groups?

On the one hand, the more readers the better. Readers are different, and reading is a subjective act so you don't know much if you only know how one reader reacts. On the other hand, hearing from more readers takes more time, and you can learn a lot from one reader if she is a good one—if she can really tell you in detail about what she sees and what goes on in her head as she reads your words. Also, it's easier to build an honest relationship of trust and support between just two people. (If you know you are working on something important and will want to get feedback at various stages, you can use your trusted readers one or two at a time.) You can have it both ways too—getting brief feedback from a group and then dividing into pairs for fuller responses (or vice versa).

New Faces or the Same Old Faces?

If you change readers, you get variety and new perspectives. But good sharing and responding depend on a climate of safety and trust. Certain things can't occur until reader and writer have built up trust, and that takes longer than you might think. Most writers find one or two trusted readers or editors, and rely on them over and over.

Share Out Loud or Give Readers Copies on Paper?

The process of reading out loud brings important learning: You can feel strengths and weaknesses physically—in your mouth as you pronounce your words and in your ear as you hear them. And you can tell about the effects of your words by watching your listeners. Reading out loud is more alive. But if your piece is long or time is short, it will be best to give paper copies. Paper texts give readers more time to read closely and reflect on your writing, especially if the material is complex. Remember, however, that if listeners can't follow the main train of thought in even a complex essay as you read it out loud, it is probably not clear enough.

Probably the best method is to combine the two modalities by reading your paper out loud while giving listeners a copy to follow.

Writers have always used the mail to share writing with readers and get responses, but electronic mail and fax machines have encouraged many more people to "meet" across hundreds and thousands of miles. Some people use these media not just for transmitting pieces of writing and responses but even for real-time conversation about the writing.

About Reading Out Loud When Listeners Don't Have a Paper Copy

You need to read your piece twice. Otherwise listeners can't hear it well enough to give helpful responses. But if you don't want to read it twice in a row (which can feel embarrassing), there is a good solution. Have each person read once for no response; hear all the papers; then have each person read again for response. Listeners need a bit of silence after each reading to collect their thoughts and jot down a few notes; this way no one will be too influenced later by hearing the responses of others.

Also, it can be interesting and useful to have the second reading given by someone other than the writer. This way listeners get to hear two different versions of the words. When someone reads a piece of writing out loud, that in itself constitutes feedback: it reveals a great deal about what the reader sees as the meaning, emphasis, implications, and voice or tone of the piece. Some critics and writers say that a set of words is not realized or complete until read out loud—that words on the page are like a play script or musical notes on a page, mere ingredients for the creation of the real thing, which is a performance.

Some writers get others to give both readings, but we think that's sad because you learn so much from reading your own words. If you feel very shy or even afraid to read your writing, that means it's even more important to do so.

Responding Out Loud or on Paper?

Both modes are valuable. Spoken responses are easier to give, more casual and social. And it's interesting for responders to hear the responses of the others. Written responses can be more careful and considered, and the writer gets to take them home and ponder them while revising.

Spoken and written responses can be combined in two interesting ways. (1) Participants meet in a group, each person reads (with or without paper copies), and everyone gives spoken responses—perhaps somewhat briefly. Then each participant takes one person's paper home and writes out a fuller and more considered response. The responder might try to summarize or comment on some of the earlier spoken responses.

(2) This is a kind of reverse sequence. All group members give copies of their paper to everyone else. Then members go home and read all the papers and take a few notes about their responses to each one. But each member has responsibility for giving a careful written response to only one paper. When the group meets for sharing responses, the person who wrote out the feedback starts by reading what he wrote (and hands his written feedback to the writer), but then the others chime in and add responses on the basis of their reading and notes. This method is particularly useful if there isn't much time for group work or if the pieces of writing are somewhat long.

How Much Response to Get?

At one extreme, you'll benefit from no response at all—that is, from private writing where you get to ignore readers for a while, and from mere sharing where you get to connect with readers and feel their presence but not get any responses.

At the other extreme, it's crucial sometimes to take the time for extended and careful response—perhaps in writing—from at least one or two readers. We urge you to create some occasions where you ask a reader or two to take your paper home and write out at least two or three pages that provide (a) a description of what they see (skeleton or descriptive outline, description of voice, and so forth); (b) a description of how they reacted (movies of their minds—what the words *do* to them); (c) what they see as strengths and weaknesses of your paper and suggestions for improving it. If your teacher asks for this extensive approach to feedback, she will probably ask you to write out your reactions to those responses, in particular whether you think their evaluation and advice make sense or not, and why.

A middle course is to get three to five minutes of response from each reader. This won't give you the complete story of the readers' perceptions or reactions, but it will give you the most powerful thing of all: the leverage you need to imagine what your piece of writing looks like through someone else's eyes. Sometimes just one tiny remark is all you need to help you suddenly stop seeing your words *only* from your own point of view and start experiencing how differently they sound to someone else.

Ways to Help Response Pairs or Groups Work Better

There are no magic right methods, but there are some helpful rules of thumb.

Make sure that someone agrees to watch the time so that people at the end don't get cheated.

Remember that even though you may feel naked or vulnerable in sharing your writing, especially if it is an early draft, readers will be just as naked and vulnerable if they give you good feedback. To give accurate movies of the mind is a generous gift: honest responders are willing to be guinea pigs and let you see inside their heads. And this kind of honesty goes against many habits and customs of student life. Classmates won't give you this gift unless you treat them with great respect *and* are very assertive about insisting that you really want good feedback. (As teachers, we used to shake our fingers at students who weren't giving much feedback and try to cajole them into being "more responsible responders." But that never seemed to help. We discovered we could get better results by turning back to the *writer* and saying: "Are *you* willing to put up with not getting feedback? *We* can't make them do it. Only you can.")

Try to avoid arguments—between responders or between writer and responder. Arguments waste time, and they make responders less willing to be honest. But most of all, you usually benefit from having different and unreconciled responses to your text. Don't look for a right answer but for how your writing looks through different sets of eyes. And when readers disagree, that brings home the central principle here: *You* get to make up your own mind about how to interpret the feedback, how seriously to take it, and what changes to make, if any.

Spend some time talking about how the feedback process is working. Try taking a few moments now and then to write out informal answers to these questions.

- What works best in your group?
- What is not working well?
- Do you wish members were more critical of your work? less critical?
- Which has been the most helpful to you, oral or written responses?
- Does your group work best with detailed instructions? with little guidance?
- Is there someone who always seems to take charge? or who doesn't participate much? How do you feel about this?

You can share these responses yourselves and identify problems and discuss ways to make things work better. You can make these comments anonymous if you wish by giving them to another group to read to you. Your teacher may ask for these responses and use them as a basis for full-class discussion.

Final Note

Does this seem too complicated? There is, in fact, a lot to learn if you want to get useful responses and give them. But after you and your friends have *tried out* all these techniques and built up a relationship of trust, then you can make the whole feedback process simple. You don't have to decide on any particular kind of feedback to ask for; you can just say, "Tell me about your responses" or "Just write me a letter." You can trust them to give you what is most valuable. But if you leave it wide open this way *before* readers have practiced all these responding techniques, you often get very little—or even get something hurtful. It won't take you too long to try out the 11 kinds of feedback, especially since you can sometimes use more than one in one session.

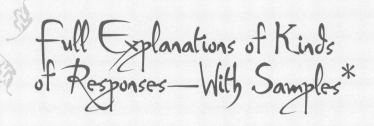

Full Explanations of Kinds of Responses—With Samples*

1. Sharing: No Response or Responses Only from the Self

If you've never done freewriting before—writing without stopping and not showing your words to anyone at all—it can feel peculiar. But most people quickly find it comfortable and helpful. Similarly, if you've never done sharing before—reading your words to someone without getting any response at all—that too can feel peculiar. When you read your words aloud (or give people a copy of your writing), you probably have an urge to ask them how they *liked* it—whether they thought it was any good. Because all school writing is evaluated, we sometimes assume that the *point* of writing is to be evaluated. But when we speak to someone, do we immediately ask them how good our words were? No. We want a reply, not an evaluation. We speak because we are trying to communicate and connect.

With sharing we're emphasizing writing as communicating and connecting, rather than performing for a judgment. You'll find that it's a relief to give your writing to others (aloud or on paper) just to communicate, just for the fun of it—just so they can hear what you have to say and learn from you. It's a relief to say (on some occasions, anyway), "The hell with whether they liked it or agree with it. I just want them to *hear* it." If you practice sharing in the right spirit, you will soon find it as natural and helpful as freewriting.

And what is the right spirit? In sharing, the goal is for writers to *give* and for listeners to *receive*. Writing is gift giving. When you give someone a gift, you don't want her to criticize; you want her to use it and enjoy it. If you happen to give someone a gift he doesn't like, do you want him to complain? No, you want him to thank you all the same.

We stress reading your words aloud here, especially at first, because you learn so much by using your mouth and ears. And there is a special psychological benefit from learning to say your words aloud:

---

*For sample peer responses, we are indebted to Alexander Jackson, Arun Jacob Rao, Christine Schnaitter, and others.

You get over the fear of making a noise with your written words. But it is also useful to share silently, by giving readers a copy of what you've written. Many teachers periodically create a class magazine. Sometimes they set this up officially with a lab fee to cover costs; sometimes they just ask everyone to bring in multiple copies of a piece. If you single-space your piece, you can often fit it on one sheet, back-to-back. Also, you'll find it a pleasure to make a little magazine at the end of the course of your favorite three or four pieces of your own writing (with a nice cover), and give copies to a handful of friends and family.

We suggested earlier that as you try out different kinds of feedback, you might try out more than one kind in one session. But don't combine sharing with feedback (not at first, anyway). The whole point of sharing is to get *no* response. Even if it feels odd at first, try to notice the benefits of it.

Guidelines for the Writer Who Is Sharing Aloud

- Take a moment to look at your listeners, relax, and take a deep breath. Say a few introductory words if that helps.
- Read slowly, clearly. *Own* your writing; read it with authority even if you are not satisfied with it. Concentrate on the meaning of what you're reading. Don't worry about whether listeners like it.
- Take a pause between paragraphs. Let people interrupt to ask you to repeat or go slower, but don't let them give you any feedback. After you're finished, just go on to the next person.

Exploring the Writing Process

I felt good about reading my piece of writing to the response group yesterday. It was good for me to be in control, by being able to specify what kind of response I wanted to receive. One thing that frightens me as a writer reading my stuff, is that once it's out there, I'm terribly vulnerable. It is often like sharing a secret part of myself. Or like giving birth. As long as the idea stays within me, it is protected, but once it is "born," it is vulnerable. I think of getting my Shakespeare paper back from M. with the B+ and the marks all over it. I had a very hard time starting the next paper. I didn't trust my ability. I felt the unseen censor's heavy presence. I know that his intentions were to help me to improve my writing, but my problem was to get past the roadblock of my damaged ego [. . .]. I can't change how the world deals with my writing, so maybe the key is in working on my own attitude toward the criticism I get.

Jo Ferrell

Guidelines for Listeners

- Your job is to receive without response. Say "Thank you," but give no feedback of any kind.
- If the writer is racing or mumbling so you can't understand, interrupt him appreciatively but firmly, and ask him to read more slowly and clearly.
- When the writer has finished reading, thank her and go on to the next person. If there is time after everyone has read, you might want to hear the pieces again—especially the more complex ones. Or you might agree to discuss the *topics,* but don't let the discussion turn into feedback on each other's writing.

2. Pointing and Center of Gravity

These two kinds of feedback fit well with two readings of your piece. After the first reading, listeners can point to the words and phrases that struck them or seemed most memorable. This is a way of letting a writer know which bits of his writing got through or made the strongest impression.

Then after each person's second reading, listeners can tell where they sense any *centers of gravity:* spots they sense as generative centers or sources of energy in the text. They might not be main points. Sometimes an image, phrase, detail, or digression seems to have special life or weight in the piece.

When you read, don't rush, even though you might feel nervous. Allow a bit of silence after each reading. Give listeners time to collect their impressions.

Why Would Anyone Want Nonjudgmental, Noncritical Feedback?

This and the next two kinds of response ("Summary and Sayback" and "What Is Almost Said?") ask for nonjudgmental and mostly descriptive response. If this feels odd, consider the following reasons:

- We benefit most from feedback on *early* drafts, but it doesn't make sense to evaluate an early draft. When we put off feedback until after we've slaved over something, it's hard to revise because we've invested too much sweat and blood. Nonjudgmental feedback gives us early feedback and new ideas and simply ignores the fact that, of course, there are obvious problems in our early draft. It makes readers into allies rather than adversaries while they help us see our still evolving text better and give us new insights.
- Perhaps we're trying out a new kind of writing or an approach that we're weak at: We're trying to break out of the rut of what we can already do well. Or we're working on something so difficult but important that we don't want criticism yet. We just need

Sharing & Responding

some *perspective* on our piece. We need a reader to trust us, to trust that we can see faults ourselves and work through them. And frankly we also need some encouragement and support in seeing what's right or strong in the piece.

- We may want feedback from someone who is a good reader but who can only criticize. It's her only gear. We need her perceptions but not her knife. Asking for descriptive responses is a way to nudge her out of her judgmental rut.

- We often need to give feedback to a weak or inexperienced writer or to a writer in a rut. Often we sense that criticism and "helpful advice" are not what he needs. Sure, his writing has serious problems, but what he needs is encouragement and confidence. We often sense that the very thing that's been undermining his writing is too much criticism: He's been clenching too hard; he's been criticizing and rewriting every phrase as he writes it until all the energy and clarity are gone from his writing. He'll write better when he trusts himself better. Nonjudgmental feedback will help.

SAMPLES OF FEEDBACK: POINTING AND CENTER OF GRAVITY

The sample essays will be found on pages 400–404.

Pointing for "What's Wrong with Black English?" One Reader

- Big saggy pants and knit caps.
- America is cool.
- Blacks of America and their culture have the power of attracting people.
- Banning Black English and forcing them to learn Standard English only hurts the children's identity because it means to the children that their language and culture are rejected in the public place.
- "Children have the right to their own language." This is a quote used in the paper, but it is strong and direct and stands out.
- Feelings of public separateness do not come from the language only.
- The advocates of nonbilingual education may believe that the only culture in this country should be the one of the dominant white middle class.

Another Reader

- Black children should be taught both in Black English (Ebonics) and the Standard English.
- Forcing them to learn Standard English only hurts the children's identity.
- Their language and culture are rejected.
- Children have the right to their own language.

- Language is a culture.
- If you lose your language, you lose the way of expressing yourself.
- Standard English . . . white middle-class rules and codes are necessary tools for success.
- Like it or not, they [the white middle class] mark the place where "power" currently exists.
- The reason people love America is its diversity.
- Melting pot of many ethnic groups.
- Coming from the racially homogenous country like Japan, I see the standardization of America as a great loss to today's diversified world.

Pointing for "The Power of Sprinkles"
One Reader

- I don't want to do this.
- Our GPA will suffer.
- E-mail isn't the same.
- If you can write for that then why can't you write for this?

Another Reader

- I don 't want to do this I don't want to do this I don't want to do this!
- We have to do this.
- I hate writing!
- You argue all the time.
- Stupid messages aren't just stupid—they're fun!
- And what about the diary?
- It doesn't count.
- Well, if you can write for that, why can't you write for this?
- Because this is assigned!
- Minimum length is good. It tells us how much detail we're supposed to go into and how much we should say about something.
- Adding more would make it worse. It's hard putting in bull _ _ _ _.
- We never do things my way.
- We don't always have to do things the way we're supposed to. Sometimes it works much better if we do our own thing, and just make it look like what it's supposed to be.
- As soon as it's over, we can get a Smurf sundae.
- With sprinkles?
- Of course.
- It's a deal. Let's get started.

Centers of Gravity for "What's Wrong with Black English?"
One Reader

- The image of Japanese kids with baggy sagging pants and girls braiding their hair with beads and huge crowds dancing to rap music.
- Vicious circle of uneducated, poor, single mothers and lives depending on the welfare.

- Destroying a language is destroying people.
- In the nineteenth century, many people came to the New World because they saw this country as a melting pot of many ethnic groups, and they thought there would be room for them to live their lives.

Another Reader

- When the bilingually educated blacks are the majority of the black population of America, it will again change white people's ways of thinking and the history of the country.
- Advocates of nonbilingual education may believe that the only culture in this country should be the one of the dominant white middle class.
- The reason people love America is its diversity.

***Centers of Gravity* for "The Power of Sprinkles"**
One Reader

- Examples the writer gives to demonstrate the necessity for communication in life.
- Reasons why students get marked down on papers.
- Reasons why writing for an assignment is not fun.

Another Reader

- The fact that essays don't have to be long and boring. You can use your imagination to have fun while writing essays.
- Sprinkles.

3. Summary and Sayback

Try these two variations and see which one feels more useful to you (or perhaps work out some combination of the two). If your piece is not too long or complex, you can get summary feedback after the first reading and sayback after the second. (If your piece is long or complex, you need two readings even for summary feedback.)

Summary is a way to find out how readers understand your words—whether your message got through. Many needless misunderstandings come about because readers are arguing about the strengths or weaknesses of someone's ideas without realizing they have different interpretations of what those ideas *are*. The procedure is simple: Ask readers for a one-sentence summary, a one-phrase summary, and a one-word summary. (You can even ask for two versions of these summaries: one version that uses words from your writing and one where listeners must use their own language.) Another way to ask: "Give me a couple of titles for this piece."

Sayback (or active listening) is a simple but subtle variation. The author reads and the listener says back what she hears the writer getting at. But she says it back in a slightly open, questioning fashion in order to invite the writer to restate what she means. In effect the listener is saying, "Do you mean. . . ?" so that the writer can say, "No, not quite. What I mean is. . . ." Or "Yes, but let me put it this way. . . ." Or even—and this is pay dirt—"Yes, I *was* saying that, but *now* I want to say. . . ." Sayback helped her move past her original thinking.

In short, sayback is an invitation to the writer to find new words and thoughts—to *move* in her thinking. Sayback helps the writing continue to cook, bubble, percolate. It helps the writer think about what she hasn't yet said or even thought of.

Thus, though sayback is useful any time, it is particularly useful at an early stage in your writing when you have written only in an exploratory way and things haven't jelled yet.

Here's an important variation: *Sayback to help you figure out what you are doing.* Get your listener to tell what he senses as your *goals* (the effects you want your writing to have) and your *strategies* (how you want to achieve those effects with language). Use his guesses as a springboard to help you talk out your goals and strategies for this piece. The best thing for revising is to get clearer in your mind what you're trying to accomplish and what language strategies you want to use. Take plenty of time to talk and take notes.*

To the Listener Giving Sayback

- Don't worry about whether you like or don't like something: That's irrelevant here. Listen and get engaged with what you hear.
- After listening, try to sum up in a sentence or two what you feel the writer is getting at. For sayback, say your response in a mildly questioning tone that invites the writer to respond. Think of yourself as inviting the writer to restate and thereby get closer to what she really wants to say.

To the Writer Asking for Sayback

- Listen openly to the listener's sayback. If the listener seems to misunderstand what you have written, don't fight it. Use this misunderstanding as a spur to find new words for what you are really trying to say. The process of listening to a misunderstanding and then saying what you really mean often helps you find new

---

*We are grateful to have learned about the use of sayback responding from Sondra Perl and Elaine Avidon of the New York City Writing Project.

key words and phrases that get right to the heart of the matter and prevent future misunderstanding.

- Don't feel stuck with what you've already written; don't defend it. Keep your mind open and receptive: think of this as help in shifting, adjusting, refining your thinking.

SAMPLES OF FEEDBACK: SUMMARY AND SAYBACK

Summary for "What's Wrong with Black English?"
One Reader

- Black English is very important and it should also be taught to black children together with standard English.

Another Reader

- You admonish whites and society for saying that Black English is bad. It is useful and is part of the cultural identity of a portion of the people; thus it should be taught in schools. This is a part of the cultural diversity that makes America great.

Summary for "The Power of Sprinkles"
One Reader

- The statement behind this essay is that sometimes it is hard to write, especially when you are told to. You may feel like you want to put it off or not bother. But it serves a purpose. A good way to write is to say what you know and feel, and then mold that into what is required. You may have to bribe yourself, but if that is what it takes to get you started, then do it.

Exploring the Writing Process

Group work is really interesting now. I never liked sharing before I took this class but now I even look forward to it. English was always not one of my better subjects, especially writing anything other than letters to my friends or opinion papers. I never wanted to share my writing because I felt stupid and like I wasn't a good writer. It's really easy to share my work now and I met great people in the class. Sharing and working together is a way to get to know people better and gives you a group of people that you can feel comfortable with and even become close friends with.

A Student

Another Reader

- The writer talks the problem out in detail with herself, comes to a solution, and then moves on.

Sayback for "What's Wrong with Black English?"
One Reader

- I hear you saying that Black English is very popular because some people in Japan like it? You are saying that it is going to be easy for black children to learn both kinds of English?

Another Reader

- I understood the writer to be arguing in support of Ebonics in the classroom. The writer assumes Ebonics to be a language of black Americans, and she asserts that although Ebonics is considered a lower class language, children should be taught it in schools so the children may gain confidence of their culture. The writer was stating that when the language of blacks is rejected by society, it is a rejection of their culture in the American society. In the middle of the paper, the writer essentially argues that blacks cannot communicate or express themselves through the English language, so they should be taught in Ebonics in order to gain cultural confidence. She concludes that bilingual education should be implemented in schools so Black culture can remain alive and strong and continue to add diversity to America.

Sayback for "The Power of Sprinkles"
One Reader

- Writing can be a struggle. I hear you giving a picture of the opposing forces in all of us that promote procrastination, especially when we don't exactly want to do the work. Sometimes it is necessary to reason with ourselves to do something. A bribe may be necessary, but it is a small price to pay for the reward we get from a job well done. I wonder if you are implying that it may not work this way for everyone.

Another Reader

- You are having an ongoing conversation with yourself, an internal dialogue complaining to yourself about why you hate to write. Your inner voice reminds you of the positive aspects of writing, how you write on an everyday basis, how writing skills are essential for communication in life. You agree with your inner voice but say that such daily writing is fun because you are free to say what you want; you wonder why teachers ask for extended "bull_ _ _." You talk about not being able to express your true opinions for fear of getting your grade docked by a disagreeing teacher. Toward the end, the two voices agree that you can be unique and dare to add creativity; sometimes when you do

that, the finished product is much better because you invested yourself; you can add humor and silliness and the quality only improves.

4. What Is Almost Said? What Do You Want to Hear More About?

This response technique moves slightly away from what's in the text.
No text can ever tell readers everything they need for understanding
it; all texts assume that readers already know some of what the writer
knows. Literary theorists speak of what's not there as "gaps." When
readers respond to a piece of writing by telling you what's almost
said or implied, they are telling you how they are filling in your gaps:
what they feel hovering around the edges, what they feel you have
assumed.

A helpful and playful variation is to ask readers to guess what was
on your mind that you *didn't* write about. This kind of feedback often
gets at an undercurrent or mood or atmosphere that is only faintly
present in your writing but that has an important subliminal effect on
your readers. Naturally, it is highly subjective and tells you more
about the reader's mind than about your text—yet what it *does* tell
you about your text is often extremely valuable.

*SAMPLES OF FEEDBACK: WHAT IS ALMOST SAID? WHAT
DO YOU WANT TO HEAR MORE ABOUT?*

What Is Almost Said? for "What's Wrong with Black English?"
One Reader

- Opponents of bilingual education are cultural suppressors who are striving to keep underclass blacks underclass.
- Teaching Black English in schools is the only way to help blacks feel important in society.
- Standard English is white.
- Language keeps culture alive.

Another Reader

- Communication and unity in the U.S. won't be harmed if Black English is taught.
- Japan and other countries don't have much diversity.
- You like to hear Black English.

What Is Almost Said? for "The Power of Sprinkles"
One Reader

- Teachers like to make writing tedious, uncreative, boring.
- Restriction of creativity is oppression.
- Bribery works—even on yourself.

- A lot of students do an awful lot of writing other than what is assigned in school.
- To do anything well, you have to break the rules.
- To do anything well, you have to bribe and compromise.
- To do anything well, you have to get the different parts of yourself to work together cooperatively.

Another Reader

- Writing essays can be like doing other common everyday things we do without thinking.
- Everyone consists of at least two people—a "we." You never need to be lonely.
- The voice that says you need to write is the real you.
- The voice that doesn't want to write is the real you.
- e. e. cummings has made a great literary impact and his poetry is limited by nothing.
- In life you don't just have to learn to get along with other people, you have to learn to get along with yourself.

What Do You Want to Hear More About? for "What's Wrong with Black English?"
One Reader

- How many schools are presently doing that? teaching bilingually?
- What is the dropout rate for black students compared to white students?
- I assume Black English is a slang or loose form of regular English. You imply it's a whole language. Is this true? I'd like to hear more about this.
- I'd like to know the story of some particular students. What was it like when they couldn't use their own language? What was it like when they were invited to use their own language?

Another Reader

- I'm interested in what you say in the second paragraph: "When the bilingually educated blacks consist of the majority of the black population of America, it will again change the white people's ways of thinking and the history of this country." I want to hear how you think it will change people's thinking. How will the emergence of a middle-class black population influence others?
- What do you mean in the fifth paragraph when you say, "an understanding of white middle class rules and codes are necessary tools for social success"? What rules and codes are you referring to specifically?

What Do You Want to Hear More About? for "The Power of Sprinkles"
One Reader

- What sort of essays do you write with "silly stuff"? How about using pictures for writing essays?

- What are some tricks for getting teachers to accept creative and silly and fun writing?
- It sounds like you basically enjoy writing—if the conditions are OK. Is that true? How did you manage that?

Another Reader

- Do you often write dialogues in your head?
- Do you really have these dialogues silently in your head—or was this just a way to write something? Do you ever talk out loud to yourself?
- Which voice is most you? Or are they both equal?
- Can you use this technique about other difficulties, like whether to go out with someone?
- Which voice wins the most battles?

5. Reply

When you ask readers to reply to what you have written, you are asking for the most human and natural kind of response. And you are also asking readers to treat your writing in the most serious way: to *engage* with it at the level of substance. In effect, you are saying, "Please take my writing and my thinking seriously enough to reply to what I have said instead of ignoring or side-stepping my ideas and just talking about how well I have presented them. Reply to my text as a human, not as a helper, teacher, evaluator, or coach." When you ask for a reply, you are really inviting your listeners to enter into a discussion with you about the topic. You are thus also inviting them to leave your writing behind as they get involved in the issues themselves. Nevertheless, such a discussion can be one of the most helpful things of all for your writing. Since you are inviting a discussion, you should feel free to jump in and take full part. For this kind of feedback, you don't need to hold back and mostly listen.

SAMPLES OF FEEDBACK: REPLY

Reply for "What's Wrong with Black English?"
One Reader

Dear Yoko,

Although I liked reading your essay, I want to argue against it. I have always considered Ebonics a type of slang, but now I'm not sure. Is it a real language? Does it follow a specific set of rules? Also, how is society hurting children's identity by not teaching Ebonics in schools? I agree with you that "children have the right to their own language," but it can be spoken at home, with friends, and in the neighborhood. The language will not die if it isn't taught in class. The arguments against bilingual education you use in the essay seem rather extreme to me. I feel like you have limited your options by so forcefully arguing for bilingual education. Perhaps your argument would be even stronger if you could mention more opposing arguments to bilingual education. This way, I would know you have at least considered them and then rejected them.

Another Reader

All through my schooling, teachers corrected my mistakes in language. Especially in writing, but sometimes even in speaking. I'm white so they weren't "black" mistakes. They were just mistakes. I've never thought that maybe I have a right to my mistakes. It sounds crazy, but it's fun to think about. I never thought about all these corrections as hurting my cultural confidence, but they sure hurt my writing confidence. I grew up feeling dumb and feeling I could never have a job that required writing. I think I could have done better if teachers had respected my language more and not considered me dumb because I made so many mistakes.

Reply for "The Power of Sprinkles"
One Reader

Dear Gabrielle,

I love your essay. I often talk out problems to myself also. I could relate to your confused feelings about writing. I can remember writing essays in high-school English classes and wondering if I should express my full opinions or be safe and write what I knew would receive an A. I have noticed since I've been at college, however, that professors encourage freedom in writing and creativity. This makes me think further about what high-school teachers want students to learn. By restricting students to follow a format, teachers are oppressing students' abilities. I really enjoyed the outcome of the dialogue when both of your voices agreed to challenge the teacher's expectations and write a creative essay.

Another Reader

It looked as though you were having fun with this. I enjoy reading it, but I'm jealous and actually it makes me mad. People like you could always get better grades with your creative tricks. I can't find ways to worm out of the actual assignment as it is spelled out. I do what I'm supposed to do, I work harder than you, and I always get a worse grade.

Exploring the Writing Process

I spent a long time writing a good draft of a memo to teachers in the writing program. I was making suggestions for an evaluation process I wanted them to use. (I wanted them to write reflectively about their teaching and visit each other's classes.) I worked out a plan very carefully and at the end I really *wanted* them to do this—realizing of course that some would not want to. The more I thought about it, the more I felt I was right. I ended up putting it very strongly: They *have* to do it.

I read my draft out loud in a staff meeting to Pat, Bruce, Jeff, Aaron, and Cindy. Wanted feedback. People were slow to bring up that final bit (that they *have* to do it), but finally Cindy brought it up bluntly as a problem. Some disagreed and said, in effect, "Yes, we've got to insist." But Bruce and Jeff thought the way I wrote it went too far—would get readers' backs up unnecessarily. ("I don't want to be inflammatory," I said, and Aaron replied, "But you seem to want to make a flame.")

I wanted to defend what I wrote, but I held back; but the impulse to defend kept recurring. Finally I saw that I *could* make my point more mildly—and it would get my point across *more*

effectively. I could see it was better the milder way. Finally, I ended up feeling, "That's what I *wanted* to say."

I tell the story—it came to me this morning as I woke up early—as a paradigm of how feedback can and should work, of writing as a potentially collaborative social process. That is, it now strikes me that I *needed* to write those things; I needed to punch it to them. But by having the chance to read it out loud to this surrogate audience rather than the real one—an audience of peers with whom I felt safe—I could "get it said." And then listen; and finally hear.

By the end, I felt comfortable and grateful at the outcome—even though of course some little part of me still experienced it as having to "back down" and "accept criticism." Yet by the end, it didn't feel like backing down and "doing it their way." By the end it was what *I* wanted to say.

In short, the process of reading a draft to a safe audience and getting feedback wasn't just a way to "fix" my draft. The main thing was that *it allowed my mind to change.* My intention ended up being different from what it had been.

Peter Elbow

6. Voice

Voice is a large, rich concept that you can explore more fully in the workshop we devoted to it in Workshop 7. But to get feedback about voice you can ask two questions that get at two dimensions of voice in writing: (a) "How much voice do you hear in my writing? Is my language alive, human, resonant? Or is it dead, no-one-thing, silent, unsayable?" (b) "What kind of voice or voices do you hear in my writing? Timid? Confident? Sarcastic? Whispering? Shouting? Pleading?" There are some interesting variations on the second question: "What kind of person does my writing sound like?" Or "What kind of person do I become in my writing?" Or "What side of me does my writing bring out?" Keep in mind that there are often *several voices* intertwined in a piece of writing. If you listen closely, you may hear someone move back and forth between confidence and uncertainty, between sincerity and sarcasm. The writing may draw out the various sides of the writer. Multiple voices need not be a problem; we all have multiple voices. The issue is whether they work well together or get in each other's way. In the case of essays, it's important to ask, "Do you trust the voice or person you hear in my writing?"

Responses about the voice or voices in a piece of writing are remarkably interesting and useful. They go to the heart of what makes writing work for readers, since our response to writing is often shaped by our sense of what kind of voice we are hearing. And voice gets to the heart of how we as writers come up with words, because we often write best when we feel we are "giving voice" to our thoughts; and we often revise best when we sense that the voice doesn't sound right and change it to get closer to the voice we want. In short, our *ear* may be the most powerful organ we have for both reading and writing. But some readers need a bit of practice in learning to hear and describe the voices in writing.

Make sure, as always, that everyone's piece gets two readings—perhaps by having one straight read-through and then a second reading for response.

Feedback about voice lends itself particularly to what is one of the most useful forms of feedback: rendering or enacting your words. You might get a listener to do your second reading, or even two listeners to do both readings. Or get listeners to read short bits where they hear a voice. It's interesting and fun to ask readers to bring out the voice or voices as they read. They'll have an easier time if you are willing to invite them to exaggerate or play around a bit: to read it as if they were whining or arrogant or depressed, or whatever the voice suggests to them. This can lead to some parody and silliness, so you mustn't take offense. The goal is to help you hear the various voices and potential voices in your words. If you are willing to invite this kind of performance, it will become the most lively and enjoyable of all forms of feedback.

SAMPLES OF FEEDBACK: VOICE

Voice for "What's Wrong with Black English?" One Reader

Your voice starts out relaxed, friendly, and casual and then gets more authoritative as you start arguing by giving citations and examples to support your claims. This makes it sound like a research essay written for a tough class. Then at the end your voice gets back to the more relaxed tone it had in the beginning.

Another Reader

The tone of the voice in your paper is strong, assured, and confident. It seems it would be impossible to sway you in any other direction—you seem absolutely convinced about your argument. It almost comes across as stubborn. Your voice is sincere and even passionate about the topic—almost devoted to proving to your audience that you are right. I don't hear any trace of wondering or doubt in your voice.

Voice for "The Power of Sprinkles" One Reader

The whole essay is in quotes and uses a lot of "I." It's all in an out-loud voice—like speaking more than like writing. The writer is frustrated and annoyed toward writing essays and is arguing with herself. The voice is very strong and challenging as the author is arguing.

Another Reader

The voice that doesn't want to write the essay is always changing: whining, arguing, thinking of clever points, being angry, making jokes. The voice that says you have to write the essay always has an answer; in the end it's a little smarter or a little better at handling the troublemaker voice. It's like the mommy who knows how to handle the quick-thinking rebellious child. It's just like a mommy to avoid an all-out fight and to use ice-cream as a bribe.

7. Movies of the Reader's Mind

What we need most as writers is not evaluation of the quality of our writing or advice about how to fix it, but an accurate account of what goes on inside readers' heads as they read our words. We need to learn to *feel* those readers on the other end of our line. When are they with us? When are they resisting? What kind of resistance is it—disagreement or annoyance? When are their minds wandering?

Movies of the reader's mind are the form of response that really underlies all other forms—the foundation of all feedback. After all, everything anyone might say about a text grows out of some reaction. Suppose, for example, that someone reads your essay and says she doesn't really agree with your main point or doesn't like your voice in this piece. You need to ask her to back up and give you the movies of her mind that led to this conclusion: What did she understand your main point or your voice to be? Her movies may reveal to you that she doesn't disagree with you or dislike the voice; she *misunderstood* them. Therefore the cure (if you decide you want to adjust the piece for this reader) might not be to change your point or your voice but to make them stronger so that they are not misunderstood.

It's not so easy to give good movies of the mind. For example, a reader might tell you he feels your tone is too aggressive and wants you to soften it. But what were his *reactions*—the movies of his mind—that led to this reaction? Perhaps at first he can't tell you. ("I don't know. I was just bothered; that's all.") But if you ask him to ferret out those too-quick-to-notice reactions behind that conclusion, he might tell you that he felt irritated by what he thought were some sly digs you were making about people you disagree with. Once you learn what was actually happening in this reader, you can draw your own conclusions instead of having to buy or resist his. After getting back to his reactions, you may decide that the problem was not the digs themselves but the slyness. You might well decide that the solution you need is not to remove or soften what he felt as sly digs but to make your disagreement with others much more frank and blunt.

Movies of a reader's mind can be confusing until you are used to them. They consist of nothing but facts or raw data, not conclusions; and the same piece of writing causes different things to happen in different minds. What you get is messy. But movies gradually help you develop your sensitivity to what your words are likely to do inside readers' minds.

Movies do not require experts. Indeed, sometimes you get wonderfully clear and helpful movies from children or very naive readers. Sometimes sophisticated readers have a hard time getting behind their judgments and conclusions to the feelings and reactions that led to them. You need honesty and trust.

Here are some ways to help readers learn to notice and describe their reactions while reading:

- *Serialize or interrupt your text.* Read your writing to listeners one section at a time (or hand them your text one section at a time). At each interruption, get them to tell you what's going on in their heads right at that moment. These "stop-frame movies" are particularly important near the beginning of your piece so that you can find out how your opening affects readers. In particular, you need to know whether your opening has made them resist you or go along with you. That is, readers' reactions to the rest of your piece often depend on whether they became friendly or unfriendly during the first few paragraphs. For the rest of your piece, either they are pedaling with you and helping you along or they are dragging their heels and seeing every possible problem. If you give them a written version of your piece to read at home, persuade them to interrupt their reading at least two or three times and take a few notes of what's actually happening in their minds at the time of each interruption. This technique helps them capture their reactions on the fly.

- *Get their responses in story form.*   Get readers to tell you their responses in a form like this: "First I felt this, then I thought that," and so on. The story form prevents them from falling into useless global generalities like "I enjoyed it" or "It was exciting" or "I was bored."

- *Get I-statements.*   If a reader says, "You should change this word or move that paragraph," you don't know what was happening to him: Was he bored, confused, or in disagreement? Get readers to tell their reactions in sentences starting with "I." Did that word annoy him or just feel wrong? Did the paragraph actually confuse him or just feel inelegant?

We have held off movies of the reader's mind until now—until you've tried other kinds of feedback and, we hope, developed trust in yourself and a relationship of trust and support with your readers—because movies are not always easy to listen to. If readers tell you honestly what went on as they were reading your words, you may well hear something like, "I was getting madder and madder because I felt lost—starting in the first paragraph. And I felt your voice was arrogant too, and so I wanted to quarrel with everything, even when I agreed with your actual points." It's hard to benefit from responses like that unless you feel them coming from a friend or ally.

When a reader gives you movies of reactions that are very critical, remember that she is not trying to be fair or impartial (as in "evaluating by criteria," which comes later in our sequence). She is just trying to tell you accurately what was *occurring* in her. She is not pretending to be God making a fair or objective judgment. These are simply her subjective reactions, and they might be different from those of most other readers.

Here are some other suggestions for getting movies of readers' minds:

- Don't make apologies or explanations of your writing before they hear or read it and respond, because these will heavily influence how they react.
- Don't quarrel with what a reader says, even if he's utterly misunderstanding what you wrote. You're not trying to educate readers about your text; you're trying to get *them* to educate *you* about your text.
- Invite exaggeration or parody. This can be scary, but also a big help if your readers are having trouble telling you what's happening as they read or if they seem to be beating around the bush. For example, readers might feel vaguely bothered by something in your writing but be unable to explain what they feel. "It's OK," they'll say. "I pretty much liked what you wrote." But you can feel some hesitation or reservation. If you feel brave enough to invite them to exaggerate their reaction, they will often find words for what's going on and say something like this: "If I were to exaggerate, I'd say you are beating me over the head here." You need to feel fairly secure before you ask for exaggeration because it may lead to a strong statement. But an element of play or humor can keep things from getting too sticky. For example, another helpful question is this: "What would a *parody* of my paper look like?" They might then reply, "Well, I guess it would be a three-page soapbox rant that's all one breathless sentence." You can reassure them that you know this is not an accurate or fair picture of your piece, but this distorted picture captures a *tendency* in your piece.
- Movies of the mind require honesty from readers and reveal as much about them as about your writing. If you aren't getting honesty, perhaps you haven't convinced your readers that you really want it.

SAMPLES OF FEEDBACK: MOVIES OF THE READER'S MIND

Movies of the Reader's Mind for "What's Wrong with Black English?" One Reader

- When she said that some Japanese liked the fashion of blacks, it reminded me of my friend in Singapore who liked rap music so much that he was willing to pay high prices for it.
- Isn't "African-American" more acceptable than "black"?
- I could not see the link between music and English when she was talking about blacks attracting people and then suddenly moved to the debate about language among educators.

- I felt that the tone was authoritative when she said that black children "should" be taught in both Black English and Standard English. But I didn't quite agree with the point, as it is not easy to master two kinds of English simultaneously.
- I could see images of minds of confused and disappointed black children when they are told that their culture is not accepted in the public.
- I felt the quotation made a very good point—that the schools have to change, not the children.
- I felt that the statement, "You cannot abandon language just because it is spoken by poor people," has a lot of meaning. It brought the title of the essay back into my mind.
- I completely agree that language is culture. It reminded me of another class I'm taking (about the interpretation of meaning) where that was exactly what I have argued.
- I definitely agree that in today's society, power exists in Standard English, and I can see the importance for black children of learning Standard English as well.
- At the end I get reminded of the introduction as she addresses the Japanese liking of American culture because of its diversity. But in my mind I actually doubted that.

Another Reader

- The first paragraph grabbed my attention immediately. The writer talks about African-American cultural influence in Japan. The writer, being Japanese herself, gives an insider's view, and she goes on talking about personal observations which intrigued me even more. I wanted to hear more about American black culture and how other cultures imitate it. I wondered how else "blacks of America and their culture have the power of attracting people." I am eager to hear more.
- In the second paragraph, I am beginning to disagree with the writer when she says that banning Black English only hurts children's identity and is a public rejection of their culture and language. Because this is my first disagreement, I notice myself doubting the writer more.
- As I read the third paragraph, I become confused. I don't understand the author's reasoning. How can public separation be brought about by a culture feeling shame because of their poverty? The writer argues that instilling pride in the next generation of blacks (teaching them Ebonics in school) will help them climb the socioeconomic ladder. Now I am lost again when the writer says America will view blacks differently when the majority of them become middle class—and the way they become middle class is through learning Ebonics. Why will it change the view of blacks in America? How will it change the view?
- As I read the fourth paragraph, I feel offended when I get to the point that "Standard English and an understanding of white middle-class rules and codes are necessary tools for social success." This upset

me. I never realized that middle-class rules and codes set by the middle class ensure success. However, I suppose I felt offended because I am white and middle class. I think I would have felt better if she broadened her view by at least bringing in arguments criticizing bilingual education. She can still reject them, but I would have felt more place for my views and feelings.

- As a read back over it all, I feel unsettled. I still resist but I see I have to think more and find out more. It wasn't till I read back over it more carefully that I realized that she said clearly that she was arguing for also teaching Standard English to black students.

Yet Another Reader

The first time I read "What's Wrong with Black English?" was by accident. I was flipping through the 1997–1998 Writing Program anthology and just happened upon it. The title caught my eye instantly. Then I read it. It felt racy and I liked how it expressed racial issues bluntly; I'd never heard anything like this before. Most of this piece was admonishing whites and teachers for believing Black English was incorrect. I was raised to believe that was true. I liked that Ms. Koga used opposing view points in her argument; it shows the other side of this issue.

Movies of a Reader's Mind for "The Power of Sprinkles"
One Reader

- What is going on? was my first reaction, and then it all became very clear.
- I felt that the repetition of "I don't want to do this" conveyed a strong force of feelings.
- I could picture the two sides of a person's mind debating over what should be done.
- I could relate to almost everything the author talks about, as these are all common, everyday things that all college students do.
- I felt that there is little chance of disagreement with the essay since both sides of everything mentioned is presented almost immediately.
- I found the essay fun to read as I was getting involved by taking one side of the author's mind and trying to see if my arguments are being countered. I felt as though I were arguing with my own mind.
- When the author said "because this is assigned!" I was saying to myself, Exactly! and thus I agree that something we are told to do by a specific deadline is different than deciding to do something by ourself.
- I got a little bored at the part about "making an essay longer or shorter"—since I don't feel problems about that.
- The "green eggs and ham" things reminded me of the fiction essay I wrote, and I agree that it was fun.
- The ending made me smile and reflect back to the title. Till then I didn't think about the title. I suddenly felt that the author thought of the title only after completing the essay.

Exploring the Writing Process

Explanatory note: Our normal method of collaborating on the first edition was for one of us to start a unit—do a very rough draft—and give it to the other to work on. The second person would just take it over—make it his or hers, make extensive changes—especially because the first version was often still quite unformed. Then what the second person produced would go back to the first person for more revision. All this usually on disks rather than on paper.

In this way we often lost track of who started something and who "owned" a section or an idea. We pretty much drifted or fell into this method: we were in a hurry, we knew we had a lot to write, and we didn't have time or energy to "protect" everything we wrote. Most of all we trusted each other. It worked remarkably well.

But for this particular unit we proceeded differently. Peter had worked out a fairly full outline, and I took on the job of writing a draft from that outline. Then, instead of Peter taking it over from there—as we normally did—he wrote marginal feedback and gave it back to me to revise. Thus we drifted into a problematic arrangement for this unit: I was writing a unit that felt like Peter's— and getting feedback from him about how to revise what I'd written.

I'm revising according to feedback and angry. Why doesn't he write the damn thing himself if he knows so surely what he wants? It's insulting—giving it back to me to do *his* way. I can't do it. I feel as though I'm not into it, not into the ideas—just into superficial stuff, trying to make it what someone else wants it to be. I'd like to just give it back to him and say that: "Here, you have such a sure idea about what this should be, why give it to me to do? I'm not a typist." Does he think I'm inept? stupid? Maybe he's right. Maybe I'm no good at this and he's saying these things so he won't have to say that. He doesn't think "Life is unfair" is good. But I like it and I'll keep it. He wants this to be mainly a paper handed in to a professor in some other class, not an explanation for the self of something difficult. But I prefer the latter. So I kept trying to make the unit into what he wanted, while still thinking my idea was good.

But somehow (because he's a nice guy I guess) I kept on working with the suggestions. And as I wrote, I got caught up in thinking about getting students to see something two different ways: for themselves and for others. An interesting problem presented itself to me for solution. Could I make it work out that way? I began to explore, and suddenly it

Another Reader

As I read the first part of the paper, I automatically associate myself with the writer since she is addressing an issue I deal with as well (as a student). Therefore I automatically have trust in the writer and am interested in reading the rest of the essay. As I read and the two voices continue to fight about writing the assigment, I begin to hear the argument in my head and I notice myself emphasizing the words. When there is an exclamation point, I read the sentence with energy and emphasis.

As I read further into the paper, I only become more involved and more supportive of voice one. The voices converse with each other about teachers who attach so many limitations on writing that it isn't fun. While reading, bad memories came to my mind of high-school days when I had to conform to the writing teacher's requirements. I, too, would get

Exploring the Writing Process   *continued*

was *my* idea; although it wasn't suddenly—just my realization of what had happened seemed sudden. Apparently I was writing according to the feedback, and the idea became mine. I saw an interesting way to develop it, potential for the unit I hadn't seen before, ideas I had never written before. I got excited about it because it was good. Then I could write again without anger or resistance.

The feedback was gone; I really didn't look at any more of the marginal comments because they no longer mattered. I had my own way to go. I just forgot the way it had been done. When I finished up and polished it a bit, I looked back and who'd believe it! I had, on my own, come to saying almost exactly the same thing he said later on in the part of the

feedback I hadn't even read. That's eerie! This must be an instance of authentically situated voice—somehow using the words and ideas of others and forging them in the furnace of my own word hoard. The ideas I got caught up with seemed to begin to write themselves out. But they also produced an interesting intellectual challenge to me. And there was something very satisfying about discovering that the two of us had been on the same wavelength—or close anyhow. His good ideas had fertilized my good ideas, and we ended up with something that was undoubtedly better than anything either of us could have done alone. It has been worth working through the anger.

Pat Belanoff

back essays that I labored over saying it didn't meet the length requirement, and the score would drop one letter grade. I can relate to the frustrations of voice one. I was proud of the voices at the end of the essay
when they decided to write how and what they wanted. The voices valued
freedom in writing more than following rules. I felt really positive when I finished reading the essay. I thought to myself, She's right, you can beat the
system if you're clever!

8. Metaphorical Descriptions

It turns out that you can usually see a faint star better out of the corner of your eye than when you look at it directly. The same thing
happens in the middle of the night when you try to see the faint luminous dial of the bedside clock: a squint from the corner of your eye
usually shows you more. So too, we can often capture more of what
we know about something if we talk *indirectly*—through metaphor—
than if we try to say directly what we see. For metaphorical feedback,
get readers to describe what you have written in some of the following terms:

Weather(s). What is the weather of the writing? sunny?
drizzling? foggy? Try noticing different weathers in different
parts of the writing.

Clothing. How has the writer "dressed" what he has to say? in
faded denims? in formal dinner wear? in a carefully chosen
torn T-shirt?

Shape. Picture the shape of the piece—perhaps even in a
drawing.

Color(s). If the writing were a color, what would it be?
Different colors at different spots?

Animal(s). Ditto.

Writer-to-reader relationship. Draw a picture or tell a story
with the writer and the reader in it. See what kind of
relationship seems to get implied between writer and reader.

To give metaphorical feedback, you must enter into the game.
Don't strain or struggle for answers: just relax and say the answers
that come to mind, even if you don't understand them or know why
they come to mind. Some of the answers may seem off the wall, even
if they are valuable and insightful. Just give answers and trust the connections your mind comes up with.

The writer, too, must listen in the same spirit of play: listen and
accept and not struggle to figure out what these answers mean. The

writer, like the responder, needs to trust that there is useful material in there, even if it's mixed with things that aren't so useful. An owl swallows a mouse whole and trusts her innards to sort out what is useful and what's not. You too can eat like an owl: Listen in an attitude of trust that your mind will use what makes sense and ignore what does not.

There's a side benefit to this kind of feedback. It highlights an important truth for almost all feedback: that we are not looking for "right answers." We're looking for individual perceptions—ways of seeing. And it all works best if there is a spirit of play and trust.

SAMPLES OF FEEDBACK: METAPHORICAL DESCRIPTIONS

Metaphorical Descriptions for "What's Wrong with Black English?" One Reader

- This essay reminds me of a fast moving thunderstorm. It starts off as dark clouds on the horizon. Then the patter of rain begins. Suddenly the wind picks up and lightning splits the sky. The soft sound of rain is transformed into hard pellets as it punishes the earth, slamming into the ground. But just as quickly as it came, the storm passes. The roiling clouds move on to reveal the sun glinting off the newly wetted earth.
- Shape. Polygon.
- Animal. Squirrel.

Another Reader

- If the essay were an item of clothing, it would be a brand new pair of jeans that don't quite fit right and that have a few holes that weren't apparent at the department store when the jeans were bought.
- If the essay were a type of weather, it would begin as a sunny day which then turns into fog with scattered rain showers.
- If the essay were an animal, it would be a mischievous cat.
- If the essay were a shape, it would be a hexagon.

Metaphorical Descriptions for "The Power of Sprinkles" One Reader

- If the essay were an item of clothing, it would be a reversible, warm, colorful down coat with lots of hidden pockets for gum and Chapstick.
- If the essay were weather, it would be a refreshing cool sprinkle on a hot, sticky, humid day.
- If the essay were an animal, it would be a monkey.
- If the essay were a color, it would be chartreuse.
- If the essay were a shape, it would be a diamond.

Sharing & Responding

Another Reader

- Weather. It's like thunder and lightning at the beginning during the argument and it calms down to the smooth waves of the sea at the end.
- Clothing. Plain T-shirt and shorts.
- Shape. Triangle.
- Color. Light green.
- Animal. Mongoose.
- Picture of the writer-to-reader relationship. It's as if the author is constantly talking to me, but actually ignoring me because she is arguing with herself.

Exploring the Writing Process

Why can't I deal with this? The feedback from both of them is enormously useful, but it makes me uncomfortable and mad. I'm all stirred up. It leaves me upset and unable to sleep or relax. I think the crucial factor is that it doesn't feel like it's coming from an ally. I feel I have to fight. That's the main response: Wanting to fight them. Energized for fight. Aggression. Unable to relax. Unable to put it aside. Caught.

I guess you could call that useful. It certainly triggers a piece of my character that is strong. I'm a fighter. My intellectual life is, in a way, a fight. (Perhaps I should talk about this in the Believing essay. I'm in combat.) But it's so exhausting always to be in combat. Yes, it is energizing; it keeps one going. But is it really the best way to go? I wonder if it brings out the *best* thinking. Thinking with my dukes up too much?

Compare the effect of this feedback with the effect of the feedback I got from Paul on the same draft. It was so energizing and comforting. But not sleepy comforting. It made me go back to my thoughts and ideas. It got me *unstuck* from the adversarial defensive mode where I'm trying to beat these guys. It sent me back into my thoughts and simply had me explore what I had to say.

The comparison casts an interesting light on the public and private dimensions of writing. Feedback from _____ and _____ keeps me fixated on *them*—on audience. I want to beat them. Paul's feedback sends me back into myself and my thinking and helps me forget about audience.

Peter Elbow

9. Believing and Doubting

This kind of response zeros in on the content or ideas in your writing. It invariably gives you more ideas, more material. The obvious place to use it is on essays, but if you ask readers to play the believing and doubting game with your stories, you'll get interesting feedback too.

Believing

Simply ask readers to believe everything you have written, and then tell you what they notice as a result of believing. Even if they disagree strongly with what you have written, their job is to *pretend* to agree. In this way, they will act as your ally: They can give you more reasons or evidence for what you have written; they can give you different and better ways of thinking about your topic.

Doubting

Now ask readers to pretend that everything you've written is wrong—to find as many reasons as they can why you are wrong in what you say (or why your story doesn't make sense).

Here are some techniques that help with doubting and believing:
- *Role-play.* Instead of being yourself, pretend to be someone else who *does* believe or doubt the piece, and think of the things this person would see and say. It's a game; just pretend.
- Imagine a different world where everything that the piece says is true (or false): Enter into that make-believe world and tell what you see. Or tell the story of what a world would be like where everything that the piece says is true (or false).

Usually it makes the most sense to start with the believing game. So first, ask your readers to find all the possibilities and richness in what you have written: Build it up before tearing it down. But if readers have trouble believing, they might need to start with the doubting game. This can get the doubting out of their system or satisfy that skeptical itch, and afterward they might find themselves freer to enter into a way of thinking that is foreign to them.

You don't necessarily need to get both kinds of feedback. If you are working on an early draft—or if you feel very fragile about something you have written—it can be very useful to get *only* believing responses. This is a way to ask people frankly to support and help you in making your case or imagining the world you are trying to describe. Conversely, if you have a late draft that you feel confident about and are trying to prepare for a tough audience, you might ask only for doubting.

Sharing & Responding

Readers will benefit from a spirit of play in giving this kind of response, and you will, too, as a writer, especially when you are listening to the doubting response. People can get carried away with the skeptical wet-blanket game. (School trains us to doubt, not to believe.) You might hear lots of reasons why what you wrote is wrong. But, taken as a game, doubting needn't bother you. What's more, this play dimension helps you take all feedback in the right spirit. For feedback is nothing but help in trying to see what you have written through various lenses—to see what you can't see with *your* lens.

SAMPLES OF FEEDBACK: BELIEVING AND DOUBTING

Believing for "What's Wrong with Black English?"
One Reader

Children should be proud of their own language. They can't be expected to speak a different language in the school and a different language at home while thinking that the latter is inferior. Schools should see that Black English is popular not only in the U.S. but also in other countries and should teach it. Students can't use language well if they are ashamed of their real language. Teachers would be more successful in helping all students have confidence and enjoy reading and writing if they learned to honor Black English.

Another Reader

- A predominantly white middle class is oppressing the cultures of the poor, or anyone different. The white middle class is afraid of the coming of values from a different culture, they persecute it; they don't want a shift in power.
- Language is culture. All should be taught in our public schools. The country will be stronger when we can benefit from all citizens and all cultures.
- The English language is actually already a mixture of all kinds of different languages, slangs, and dialects. That's what makes it a rich language. Honoring Black English will eventually make Standard English more vibrant.
- Some of the best contributions to U.S. music have come from black culture, especially jazz and much popular music. The same thing can happen with language. Black language is turning up in literature.
- We'll see that the concept of "standard language" is a problem and just talk instead about "good and effective language."
- Black students will be able to help white students understand language better because they'll have two languages and be good at switching, especially when this switching happens as part of school, not as a hidden process.

Believing for "The Power of Sprinkles"
One Reader

- There is a sense of nobleness in challenging people's expectations of you.
- Writing is fun. We can make jokes even with what is unpleasant.
- If you avoid the straightforward path, things will be easier and more fun.

Another Reader

- We all argue with ourselves like this.
- There is no "I"—only a "we." We are nothing but a collection of shifting voices.
- Writing is usually a struggle, but there are always ways around the struggle. If we really talk to ourselves honestly, we can find a way to handle things.
- Life is essentially a playful game.

Doubting for "What's Wrong with Black English?"
One Reader

- Black students will benefit more from having to use Standard English in schools. Teachers can help black students use Standard English and still not put them down or make them feel that there is something wrong with them or their language. And black students can still use their own language at home and with friends.
- Another language in our crappy school system would overtax our resources.
- Standard English will be enriched better by Black English if black students have to use it.

Another Reader

- Well, when you speak of Japan, how many people in Japan enjoy Black English? And that has nothing to do with the schools in the U.S. not teaching Black English. How is it possible to teach both forms of English in one school when there are white students also in the classes? And even if they did teach both forms of English, how would it be fair for black children to have to learn both the languages and still cope with their other schoolwork while the white students have less burden?
- A single unifying language is necessary for any country to be whole. America was based on the idea of a ruling middle class. It just happens that a significant portion of the middle class is white. I know many African-American middle-class people, and most of them do not use Black English. Your assumption that Standard English is white is incorrect. Standard English is just middle class in accordance with the values that our society holds.

Doubting for "The Power of Sprinkles"
One Reader

- You can't just write anything silly and claim that you have written an essay. An essay should spell out your thoughts, and they must be carefully crafted and properly refined in order to make a good essay.
- Why do you have to wait till the last minute to do your homework—until when your friends are watching a movie? How can you concentrate on the essay this way?

Another Reader

- Not everyone has problems writing.
- Are you schizophrenic?
- Planning time to do your homework might help; it makes things easier.

10. Skeleton Feedback and Descriptive Outline

In literature classes we tend to *describe* what is going on in a story, poem, or novel rather than judge it or find mistakes. Inherent in such an approach is *respect for the text,* and the response is a way to see the text better, allowing the text to speak on its own. You will benefit from asking for the same kind of respect for your writing and from showing that kind of respect to the writing of others. We suggest here two ways for describing a text.

Skeleton Feedback

A good way to analyze the reasoning and the structure in almost any essay is to get readers to answer the following questions:

- What do you see as the main point/claim/assertion of the whole paper?
- What are the main reasons or subsidiary points? It's fine to list them as they come—in any order.
- Taking each reason in turn, what support or evidence or examples are given—or could be given—for it?
- What assumptions does the paper seem to make about the topic or issue? That is, what does the essay take for granted?
- What assumptions does the paper seem to make about the audience? Who or what kinds of readers does the writer seem to be talking to (and how are they most likely to react to the ideas in the paper)? How does the writer seem to treat the readers? as enemies? friends? children? In short, what is the writer's stance toward the audience?

- Finally, what suggestions do you have? about the order or organization? about things to add or drop or change?

It probably makes the most sense for readers to answer these questions in writing and at leisure—with the text in hand. However, you could get this kind of feedback orally from one listener, or by getting a small group to cooperate in working out shared answers to the questions.

Use the skeleton process for help with early, exploratory, rough, fragmentary writing. The skeleton process is ideal for helping you build an essay out of very rough early writing. Perhaps you have nothing but fragments that you've written at various times on a difficult and confusing topic where you cannot even figure out your thinking. (We hope you realize that this fragmentary approach is a great way to start writing about hard topics.) But in this situation you need to add a couple of introductory steps before proceeding with the skeleton process as we have described it.

Start by reading through your rough fragmentary draft material or freewriting, and as you do so, simply write down a one-sentence summary of every *idea* or *point* or *example* you come to that seems at all pertinent. Write them down in whatever order you come to them—not worrying at all about what's major and what's minor.

This process gives you something surprisingly helpful: a random, pre-outline list of "points." Once you've made this list—not having to try to get your mind around what's logical or what your main point is—*now* you can read it over and finally see the lay of the land. Now you can get conceptual perspective and figure out your main point. First just ask yourself: *Which* point, among all those points on your list, *is* most important? When you choose it, you may realize that it's only your "most important point *so far*"—so now you can figure out what you *really want to say* that you haven't yet been able to say so far.

Having gotten this far, now you are ready to go to the first step of the skeleton feedback process—as just described. (When you are at this early stage of still trying to write your first genuine draft, you can skip the last two points in the skeleton sequence.)

By the way, you don't have to do this all alone. You can get *other* people to help you figure out your thinking by using this same process on your early rough writing.

Descriptive Outline

This procedure (developed by Kenneth Bruffee) involves a sustained process of analyzing the *meaning* and *function* of discourse. You can't really do a descriptive outline unless you have the text in hand and take plenty of time. And this feedback needs to be written.

The procedure is to write a *says* sentence and a *does* sentence for each paragraph or section, and then for the whole essay. A *says* sentence summarizes the meaning or message. A *does* sentence describes the function—what the paragraph or piece is trying to do or accomplish with readers (for example, "This paragraph introduces the topic of the essay by means of a humorous anecdote" or "This paragraph brings up an objection that some readers might feel, and then tries to answer that objection").

The key to writing *does* sentences is to keep them different from the *says* sentences. Keep them from even mentioning the content of the paragraph. Thus, you shouldn't be able to tell from a *does* sentence whether the paragraph is talking about cars or ice cream. Here is a *does* sentence that slides into being a *says* sentence: "This paragraph gives an example of how women's liberation has affected men more than it has women." To make it a real *does* sentence, remove any mention of the ideas or content and talk only about function: "This paragraph gives an example" would do. Or better, "This paragraph gives an example designed to surprise the reader."

The power in both skeleton feedback and descriptive outlines comes from the distance and detachment they provide. Thus, they are useful for *giving yourself* feedback—particularly when you feel all tangled or caught up in your piece from having worked long and closely on it.

SAMPLES OF FEEDBACK: SKELETON FEEDBACK AND DESCRIPTIVE OUTLINE

Skeleton Feedback for "What's Wrong with Black English?" One Reader

Main point:
- Allowing black children to be taught in Black English will give them cultural confidence which will in turn help them rise in society.

Other points and support:
- Blacks of America are influential worldwide.
  —Writer's experience in Japan.
- Forcing black children to learn in English is hurting their identity.
  —They see their culture is rejected in public.
  —Also, the quotation from Delpit.
- Speaking a language felt as lower class makes people feel ashamed of themselves and causes public separation of groups.
  —Supported by a quotation from Rodriguez.
  —But the writer doesn't agree with this point.
- Language keeps culture alive.

—Appeal to common sense. I don't see others supporting this point.
- White middle-class rules and codes are necessary for success.
—Appeal to common sense. I don't see others supporting this point.
- The United States is admired for its diversity.
—Appeal to history and national pride.

Assumptions:
- Ebonics is a language.
- Public separation is due to cultural groups feeling inadequate.
- When the majority of blacks become middle class, America's whole way of thinking will change.
- Opponents of bilingual teaching trying to put blacks down.
- The audience is knowledgeable about Ebonics.

Assumptions about audience:
- The writer seems to treat us in a friendly open way. She is strongly sincere in her argument, but she seems to assume that we will agree with her when she gives her reasons. She's using reason and quiet emotion. Even though she's making an argument, I feel she would be surprised that I am still resisting her.

Suggestions:
- Spend more time understanding and dealing with resisting arguments. I'm confused at her wording in her use of the first quotation. Give me some examples or stories of how this is actually needed or would actually work.

Skeleton Feedback for "The Power of Sprinkles"
One Reader

Main point:
- Writing doesn't need guidelines and it doesn't have to be formal to be a good, solid, effective piece of work.

Other points:
- Teachers discourage writers from expressing sincere opinions by forcing them to write about topics that they hold no interest in.
- Teachers discourage freedom in writing by setting length limits and maximums.
- The writer only enjoys writing when on a daily basis for fun and writing for a class should not be different.
- Personal satisfaction is much greater when one is allowed to write creatively, the way she wants.

Assumptions about audience:
- The writer assumes we can get along without any explanations of what's happening. She assumes we'll go along with the playfulness and not worry that we don't know till the end what the title means.

Suggestions:
- I can't think of any suggestions. It works so well.

Another Reader

Main point:
* We can get this paper written if we learn to talk to each other, listen to each other, and work together.

Other points:
* I don't want to write.
* There are positive aspects of writing. You write every day. Writing skills are essential for communication in life (e-mail, memos, lists, directions, notes, letters, journals, etc.).
* Yes, but such daily writing rituals are fun because I am free to say what I want and at whatever length I want. Why do teachers ask us to add more to papers, when they are only asking for extended "bull_ _ _ _." I'm not free to express my true opinions due to fear of getting my grade docked by a disagreeing teacher.
* Sometimes I can be unique and creative even on school assignments. Sometimes when I do what I want instead of what I am told, the finished product is better. I can add humor and silliness to papers and the quality improves.
* Let's work together and do it just this once—and give ourselves a treat for a reward.

Descriptive Outline for "What's Wrong with Black English?" One Reader

* Says, essay as a whole: Black English is necessary in the classroom in order for poor blacks to improve their position in society.
* Does, essay as a whole: Does present an argument.
* Says, first paragraph: Blacks are admired worldwide; their culture will die or suffer if their "language" is not used in school.
* Does, first paragraph: Gives an observation or example from a great distance—and doesn't even bring up the issue of the essay.
* Says, second paragraph: Schools need to foster black pride in African-American children.
* Does, second paragraph: Moves to U.S. and brings up main topic; summarizes and argues her position; adds quotation for support.
* Says, third paragraph: Some people think that children who don't speak Standard English will be helped by being made to use it in school, but that isn't the way to help them.
* Does, third paragraph: Gives an opposing argument and answers it.
* Says, fourth paragraph: Black children need to be taught Standard English too in order to be successful in society.
* Does, fourth paragraph: Emphasizes that the writer is not arguing an either/or position but a both/and position.
* Says, final paragraph: The strength and spirit of America have come from its acceptance of many cultures.
* Does, fifth paragraph: Summarizes and concludes by appealing to history and national pride.

Note: A descriptive outline isn't appropriate for a playful and indirect dialogue like "The Power of Sprinkles."

11. Criterion-Based Feedback

You may well have been getting a bit of this kind of feedback all along. No matter what kind of response you are asking for, it's hard not to ask your readers a few questions about aspects of your writing you feel uncertain about. "I've been trying to get this complicated piece clearly organized and easy to follow. Have I succeeded for you?" "I've done a lot of cutting. Does it feel too choppy?" "I want this to be fun to read, not a chore."

The piece of writing itself will suggest certain of its own criteria— usually depending on function. For example, the main job might be to *convey information*. Or, as the writer, you can specify the criteria you consider most important—for example, tone or voice.

Criteria for Nonfiction Writing

The criteria traditionally applied to essays or nonfiction or expository writing are these:
- *Focus on task.* If the piece is written in response to an assignment, question, or task, does it squarely *address* it?
- *Content.* Are there good ideas, interesting or original insights? Are the ideas supported with reasons, evidence, examples?
- *Organization.* It's important to realize that even unconventional organization can be successful. The *real* questions about organization are always these: Does the *beginning* serve as a good way to bring readers in? Do the *middle parts* lead readers successfully where they need to go? Does the *ending* give a satisfying sense of completion or closure? Notice, for example, that many successful essays begin with an anecdote or example such that readers don't even know what the essay will be about, much less what it will be saying. Such an opening is successful if the anecdote works to get readers involved—so that they don't mind not knowing where they are going.
- *Coherence among sentences.* Do sentences seem to follow satisfactorily from each other?
- *Clarity of language.*
- *Voice.* What is the voice or persona and the stance toward the reader, and do they work well?
- *Mechanics.* Spelling, grammar, punctuation; proofreading.

Criteria for Fiction Writing

The criteria that are traditionally applied to imaginative writing, such as fiction or narrative, are these:

- *Plot.* Is it a believable, interesting, or meaningful story?
- *Character.* Do we find characters real or interesting?
- *Description, vividness of details.* Do we experience what's there?
- *Language.* Not just "Is it clear?" but "Is it alive and resonant with meaning—perhaps through imagery and metaphor?"
- *Meaning; "So what?"* Is there a meaning or impact that makes the piece seem important or resonant?

Specifying Criteria Helps in Giving Feedback to Yourself

Criteria give you a kind of leverage or perspective and help focus your attention on things you might otherwise miss when you read over what you've written. Before reading over a draft, you can pause and consciously ask yourself, "What criteria are the most important for this piece of writing?" or "What features of writing do I especially need to be careful about?" This will help you see more.

To Readers

You can make your criterion-based responses more valuable in two ways:

- *Be specific.* Point to particular passages and words that lead you to the judgments you make.
- *Be honest* and try to give the writer the movies of your mind that lie behind these judgments. That is, what *reactions in you* led to these judgments? For example, if you felt the organization was poor, were you actually feeling lost as you read, or just somewhat distracted or merely disapproving?

SAMPLES OF FEEDBACK: CRITERION-BASED FEEDBACK

Criterion-Based Feedback for "What's Wrong with Black English?" One Reader

- Clarity of sentences and ideas: I found it smooth to read, easy to follow. But I felt a bit confused in her use of the quotation at the end of the second paragraph.
- Voice: I found it ambitious, honest, quietly strong, confident.
- Ability to convince: For me, more explanations were needed and the original ideas need to be expanded.
- Techniques for arguing: a lot.
  - She used a novel approach by coming at a U.S. debate from a Japanese point of view.

- She acknowledged an opposing argument, but only one.
- She used quotations from published authors on both sides of the issue.
- She appealed to history and national pride.
- She tried to show how her position is not really one-sided.

Criterion-Based Feedback for "The Power of Sprinkles"
One Reader

- Style: Very creative.
- Clarity: The argument was easy to understand.
- Voice: Informal language used, but it is a personal conversation and would only be appropriate in such context.
- Tone: Sincere and yet also ironic and witty.
- Ability to convince: The voices gave good arguments and examples.
- Ability to throw light on the psychology of writing and dealing with assignment: Hearing two voices got at the complexity of inner struggle.

Sharing & Responding

Final Word: Taking Charge of the Feedback Process by Choosing Among These Techniques

We want to end by emphasizing the main point here: As a writer, you need to take charge of the process of getting responses to your work. We've created what could be called an artificial anatomy of *kinds* of feedback in order to help you take charge. For if you simply ask people to give you responses to what you've written and don't give any help or direction, they will probably just imitate the responses they remember getting from teachers. With the best will in the world, they will probably try to find things that are wrong or weak and then try to tell you how to fix them. Yet they are likely to do this badly. They may be correct in feeling that there's something wrong with your piece, but they may well misidentify the problem and suggest a revision that doesn't actually improve your piece. And even if they see the real problem and suggest a workable revision, this may not be the kind of response that will help you most given your temperament and where you are with this piece.

Now that you've tried out these kinds of feedback—both getting them and giving them—you will be better at knowing what kind of feedback would help you most, and better at helping someone give it to you. And if you want feedback from someone outside your class who hasn't practiced these techniques, you can explain what you want or even show them samples in this book, and they will get a pretty clear idea of what you are asking for.

When you have a trusted reader or you feel pretty solid about the draft in hand, you might want to invite the reader to give whatever kind of feedback he or she most wants to give. And sometimes a writer will invite you to give whatever feedback you want. In such a situation, obviously you can give a kind of blend. We will end with an example of such a blending for each of the essays we've been dealing with.

We put this blend in the form of a letter since that's the form we use most often for giving feedback to our friends, colleagues, and students. And it's the form we usually ask our students to use with each other. The letter is a friendly and flexible form.

Dear Yoko,

I was impressed by your essay but it made me struggle too. I learned a lot from it and it made me think—think hard—but as I was reading I often wanted to argue against you. Now that I've read your essay a couple of times and thought about it, I don't resist you so much, but I still resist some. I don't feel as though I'm finished reacting and digesting your essay. Here are some responses at this point. As I read your essay, I hear you arguing for the importance and value of Black English, arguing that it should be used and taught, and criticizing people who want to prevent that from happening.

Up till now, I've always considered Ebonics a type of slang; I've always been taught that it is simply "loose" or "bad" English—that the places where it differs from Standard English are "mistakes." But now you are making me think again. Is it a real language that follows a full set of rules? If so, I need to rethink my resistance, especially since my experience has come as a white person brought up in white neighborhoods and schools.

Despite any resistance, I had no trouble seeing lots of strong points in your essay. You'll see on your paper where I've put straight lines underneath words and phrases or alongside passages that I felt as especially strong or clear or striking. I used some wiggly lines at points where something didn't work so well for me.

Here are other strengths I felt:

It's clear, strong, sincere writing throughout. Impassioned but not shouting.

You come at this issue from an outside angle. It's powerful to open with an image of kids in Japan and close by talking about the U.S. being valued by others for its diversity.

I guess it's your outside point of view that helps you sidestep the either/or fight and stand up for both sides of the argument. That is, even though you are arguing for teaching Black English and inviting it to be used, still you are also saying that black children should be taught to be good at using Standard English. But maybe you could make this approach even clearer. For throughout my first reading, I thought you were only on the Black English side of the fight. I didn't quite figure out your middle position or double position till my second reading.

Here are some of the questions I had as I was reading:

Can you say more about how society is hurting children's identity by not teaching Ebonics in schools? I agree with you that "children have the right to their own language," but can't they speak their language at home, with friends, and in the neighborhood? Will the language die if it isn't taught in class? Or do you think it will?

Can you explain what you mean when you say, "When the bilingually educated blacks consist of the majority of the black population of America, it will again change the white people's ways of thinking and the history of this country?"

Can you pay a bit more attention to arguments against bilingual education? This would have been helpful for me and might have helped other resistant readers.

Thanks for making me think so hard and making me open up an issue I thought was closed.

Dear Gabrielle,

It was a treat to read your essay. I never would have thought of fulfilling an essay assignment by writing something like this. I don't even know what to call it. My overall feeling is that *you* could get away with it, but *I* never could. But maybe your example will make me try to experiment. But I have a feeling I never could do it like you do.

I drew straight lines for words and passages that felt strong or hit home. Lots of them. Only one or two wiggly lines where I was confused.

When I started reading your piece, I said to myself, What is going on? But soon it all became very clear. You describe a struggle I often feel. I get sucked right in and it makes me want to read the rest. As I read on and the two voices continue to fight about writing the assignment, I begin to hear the words out loud in my head.

Actually everything about the essay seems strong to me. But I kept thinking about whether the teacher would accept this if the assignment was for an "essay." Really, my main question is, What happened when you turned this in?

I thought the voice that didn't want to write was the strongest, the loudest. It's so true about not being able to write what you want to write for teachers. And yet the other voice was more clever. In a way I was reluctant for that voice to trick the other one into writing. I wanted the other one to hold out and not give in.

As I tried to analyze your piece, my first thought was that it really does the job of an essay because it analyzes so well all the struggles and factors involved in writing for teachers. But then I thought that in a way it's really about something else: how the mind works—how we deal with difficulties. I wondered whether I actually talk to myself this way. I don't think I do. And yet your conversation somehow felt familiar to me.

What seemed particularly clever to me, after thinking about it for a while, was how this essay itself was a kind of example of what it's about. Just like the one part of you has to trick the other part into doing what she doesn't want to do, so this essay has to trick the teacher into accepting something that's different from a regular essay. You are trying to win the teacher over. I like how the essay is about trickery, creativity, and breaking the rules.

Sample Essays

What's Wrong with Black English?   *Yoko Koga*

"Isn't America a diversified country?" When I learned that there were people who had to abandon their culture and language to be an American, I could not but ask this question. Then I asked, "What does it mean to be an American?" These questions had never come to a Japanese girl whose country consists of only one race and only one language.

Over the past five years or so, many fashionable streets in Tokyo have been flooded with young people wearing big sagging pants and knit caps. It was a fad for a while for girls to braid their hair with beads. They say that the fashion of blacks in the inner cities in America is cool. So they imitate them. Not only the fashion, they also love rap music, reggae, soul music, and Caribbean music. When a famous rap musician came to Budokan, the biggest concert hall in Tokyo, twenty thousand fans rushed to fill it. Every Sunday, Yoyogi Park, the central park of Tokyo, is filled with groups of young people dancing to rap music. They perform so wonderfully that many people stop and watch them. Huge crowds along the street enjoy these performances. Because of the revival of the 60s, films of Martin Luther King, Jr., and Malcolm X were big hits. Blacks of America and their culture have the power of attracting people, especially younger generations.

When I learned that there is a debate among educators whether they should educate black children in Black English or in Standard English, I was surprised. Why should they not educate their children in the children's own language? I thought it was everyone's basic right. Black children should be taught both in Black English (or Ebonics) and Standard English, the language of their own and the language of the country they live in. This bilingual approach helps build poor children's self-esteem immensely. Banning Black English and forcing them to learn Standard English only hurts the children's identity because it means to the children that their language and culture are rejected in the public place. Instead of banning the students' natural English, educators in the black population should teach how powerful Black English and culture are. They should encourage their students by teaching how black culture has influenced American history, has changed people's way of thinking, and attracts people like those in my country, Japan. The insight that originally inspired Lisa D. Delpit to write her seminal article, "Skills and Other Dilemmas" (1987), expresses the point of this issue very well. Although Delpit came to disagree with this formulation later, she stated it succinctly in her 1988 piece, "The Silenced Dialogue":

What's Wrong with Black English? *continued*

> Children have the right to their own language, their own culture. We must fight cultural hegemony and fight the system by insisting that children be allowed to express themselves in their own language style. It is not they, the children, who must change, but the schools. To push children to do anything else is repressive and reactionary. (280)

I think this statement represents the core idea of bilingual education and any argument should start from the belief that "children have the right to their own language."

There are some people who oppose the idea of bilingual education. They argue that the children whose native languages are not Standard English should be corrected at the beginning of their public education because those languages indicate that one is from the lower class of America, and that jeopardizes children's future success in this society. Richard Rodriguez opposes bilingual education in *Hunger of Memory:*

> I have heard "radical" linguists make the point that Black English is a complex and intricate version of English. And I do not doubt it. But neither do I think that Black English should be a language of public instruction. What makes Black English inappropriate in classrooms is not something in the language. It is rather what lower-class speakers make of it. Just as Spanish would have been a dangerous language to use in the schooling of teenagers for whom it reinforces feelings of public separateness. (101)

He claims that speaking the language of lower classes is the cause of public separation. I think, however, the feelings of public separateness do not come from the language only. The feeling arises in minority people, including African Americans, because they cannot be proud of themselves. It is because they know they are economically poor. If you could educate your next generation to be proud of their culture, they could get out of the vicious circle of "uneducated, poor, single mothers depending on welfare." You cannot abandon a language just because it is spoken by poor people. The language is used because there are people who need the language to express their feelings and to hand down their culture to the next generation. In a way, a language is a culture. Destroying a language is destroying people, because if you lose your language, you lose the way of expressing yourself. When the bilingually educated blacks consist of the majority of the black population of America, it will again change the white people's ways of thinking and the history of this country.

The argument that teaching Standard English to black children is important is understandable since Standard English and an understanding of white middle class rules and codes are necessary tools for social success. Children from the poor area should be taught these rules because, like it or not, they mark the place where "power" currently exists, and the children must get into there eventually. However, the children's own "English"

What's Wrong with Black English? *continued*

should still be the public language in the classroom. Ideally the students should be taught by "bilingual" teachers who speak and understand the values and problems of both cultures, white middle class and black. As Delpit suggested in "The Silenced Dialogue":

> Appropriate education for poor children and children of color can only be devised in consultation with adults who share their culture. Black parents, teachers of color, and members of poor communities must be allowed to participate fully in the discussion of what kind of instruction is in their children's best interest. Good liberal intentions are not enough. (282)

The advocates of nonbilingual education may believe that the only culture in this country should be the one of the dominant white middle class. Hence everybody should speak "their" English, the so-called Standard English. However, the cultures of America which people of other countries admire are not only the whites'. When many Japanese say they love America, they mention the "cultures" of America. The reason people love America is its diversity. And they are amazed at the generosity this country shows to its diverse population. America's capacity for holding so many different people and cultures has been one of the major attractions that draws so many people to this country. In the nineteenth century, many people came to the New World because they saw this country as a melting pot of many ethnic groups, and they thought there would be a room for them to live their lives. I think this is still the main reason for people coming to this country. If America starts denying its diversity by unifying its languages, it means it denies its history and the spirit of the country. To hold the richness of its culture, America should keep education of its next generation in various languages. Coming from the racially homogeneous country like Japan, I see the standardization of America as a great loss to today's diversified world.

Works Cited

Delpit, Lisa D. "The Silenced Dialogue: Power and Pedagogy in Educating Other People's Children." *Harvard Educational Review* 58.3 (1988): 280–98.

Rodriguez, Richard. *Hunger of Memory: The Education of Richard Rodriguez.* Boston: D. R. Godine, 1982.

The Power of Sprinkles *Gabrielle Radik*

"I don't want to do this! I'm bored, and I'm tired, and this thing doesn't make any sense, and everyone's watching the movie in the other room, and I want to watch too, and I don't want to do this I don't want to do this I don't want to do this!"

The Power of Sprinkles *continued*

"We have to do this. It's important. If we don't turn in the essays then we don't do well in the class and we won't be able to participate in the discussion and our grade will go down and our GPA will suffer and we'll lose some of our scholarships."

"But you know I hate writing! Especially this kind, because we have to say things the way the teacher wants to hear them, and as often as not we have to do research and work it into the paper somewhere. Sometimes they make us argue a point, and I just don't like doing that."

"You're arguing a point right now. You argue all the time. And we've done writing before—we write to make lists, and give directions. Every now and again we take notes."

"When was the last time we took notes, I'd like to know? If we've taken notes recently, then I had nothing to do with it!"

"OK, never mind about the notes. Forget the notes. We write memos to the roommate, and we write stupid messages on the door."

"Yeah . . . but . . . but those don't take very long, and if we don't write the lists, then we forget things. And if we don't write directions, then no one can find us. And if we don't write the memos, then the roommate gets annoyed. And stupid messages aren't just stupid—they're fun!"

"We write e-mail. That takes a long time. We spend time every day writing e-mail."

"E-mail isn't the same! The messages are fun, like all those forwards we send. Besides, we're in a contest with the friend about how many e-mail forwards we can send each other! You know that! And when we write to the other friends it's because we can't talk to them because the phone is too expensive. You know I like people."

"Sometimes it isn't e-mail though. We've written letters to the friends. Those are always long. And what about the diary?"

"We only write to the friends when we can't talk to them or when there's a problem and we want them to listen to everything we have to say. And how often do we add to the diary? I'll tell you when. Only when we have stuff to argue about or when we've done something we don't want to forget. It only has five entries. It doesn't count."

"Well, if you can write for that, why can't you write for this?"

"Because this is assigned! It's something we were told we had to do; there's a certain way that we're supposed to do it. If we do it my way, it doesn't count. We have to finish it by a certain time, and anything I have to do by a certain time isn't fun. It's duty. And we have to make it a certain length; I can't just say what I want to say. We have to make sure we're saying enough or it'll look like we didn't put any work into it because it isn't long enough."

"Sometimes a minimum length is good. It tells us how much detail we're supposed to go into and how much we should say about something."

"Yeah, well, sort of. But then there's what happens when we've finished everything we want to say and we think it's good and it makes sense

The Power of Sprinkles　*continued*

the way we have it and adding more would make it worse. But it isn't long enough! If we pass it in the way it is, we get marked down because we didn't do enough work. So we have to add stuff somewhere in the end, or somewhere in the thing, that really isn't important, just to make it longer. It's hard putting in bull_ _ _ _ without making it look like bull_ _ _ _. Or when we come to as long as it's supposed to be, and we still have more to say."

"All right, you have a point there. But the teacher-person has to penalize students for that sort of thing, or the stupid people would get away with too much."

"Yeah, I suppose."

"We've been writing them for years. Book reports, essays, research papers, thesis papers, lots of stuff."

"And I hated every minute of them. Remember, I put up a fight every time."

"You mean you whined every time."

"Hey! It's only because we never do things my way."

"We don't always have to do things the way we're supposed to. Sometimes it works much better if we do our own thing, and just make it look like what it's supposed to be. We've written those Green Eggs & Ham things. Those were sort of like essays. You enjoyed those."

"We didn't have to make those look like anything. They were just because we wanted to, and they were silly and random. I like random silly stuff. Like tapeworms and pickles and plungers and iguanas and anything beginning with J and . . ."

"OK, OK, I get the picture. How about we just do this assignment, and then we can go watch the movie. I want to see it, too, you know. We'll just make this one random somehow. Yeah, we'll put in something silly, just as long as the whole thing makes sense so that the teacher-person is happy. And as soon as it's over, we can get a Smurf sundae . . ."

"With sprinkles?"

"Of course."

"It's a deal. Let's get started . . ."

Writing under Pressure
Exams and Situations of Stress

There are two situations that often make writing difficult: (1) writing when you have a time limit, such as when you are taking an exam, and (2) writing when you can't think straight because you are anxious or confused.

Writing When You Have a Time Limit

In this textbook we stress writing as a complex process of thinking something through: Start with exploratory writing and gradually work your way to an understanding of what you want to say. Invite chaos and then work gradually toward coherence. Clarity of mind is not what you start out with but what you end up with. This is indeed the best way to get to new thinking and to your best thinking, and to produce writing that is the most intellectually alive.

But this long and messy process is a luxury you can't afford when you have only 30 or 60 minutes for writing an essay on an exam. If you have a longer essay exam of two or three hours, you can invite a little of this process, but not much. If you can write your exam on a computer, you can do more revising than if you have to write by hand.

When time is short, and especially if you are writing by hand, you need to try for clarity of mind at the beginning. We suggest the following steps:

Step One: Read the Question Carefully. Slowly. Repeatedly.

The most common cause of low grades on exams and other assignments is neglecting or misunderstanding the question. Unless the exam question is extremely simple and straightforward, you need to take yourself in hand and force yourself to think hard about exactly what it's asking. Jot things down for a couple of minutes. As you think about the question, try to avoid these two common problems:

(a) *Neglecting the question.* Students sometimes have a lot to say that is *related* to the question and *could* function as an excellent answer. But when they write down all this good material, they forget to link it clearly enough to the question. So the grader (often reading late at night and sleepy) says, "Didn't answer the question!" and grades it way down.

(b) *Not digging deep enough.* Students sometimes "stick to the question" so carefully that they restrict themselves and run out of things to say after only a few moments. Ask yourself questions like these: "What is the question *really* asking?" "What questions lie behind the question?" "What does the question assume or imply?" If the question asks about "better solutions," ask yourself about "better for whom or for what purposes?" If the question asks about "causes," ask yourself about the different ways in which things are caused. But when you go behind or beyond the question in these ways, make sure you show how you *are* dealing with the question.

Step Two: Make an Outline

If you now have a pretty good sense of what you want to say in your essay, you don't need the process we're calling a "pre-outline grab bag" and can go right to making the outline itself. But if the exam question is difficult and you still feel confused about how to answer the question, start by making:

A pre-outline grab bag. Simply write down every idea or point or example you can think of that somehow feels relevant to this question; write them down in whatever order they pop into your mind. This random, pre-outline list—where you don't have to worry about what your main point is—will help you do what you have to do next: Decide on a main point. This puts you in a position to make:

The outline itself. Now you can put down your points in a good order—in an order that leads readers on a clear path from the question to your answer. It helps to remember that this is not a matter of finding the *single* answer to a problem in logic or the *perfect* train of thought; there are always *various* interesting and valid paths you could take from the question to your answer. You aren't so much trying to solve a problem in geometry as trying to find a good story to tell—a story of your thinking.

Try to make sure your outline focuses on one main overarching point. But a main point doesn't have to be a simple point. For example, your main point could be that there are *three* different causes of something or that *two* different arguments or points of view are valid even though most people think they conflict with each other. Also the *path* to your single main point doesn't have to be simple; you can treat a couple of subissues or side controversies in order to support your single main point.

As you are taking that path toward your main point, give your readers plenty of hints about the main point. Don't let them feel lost. In short, most teachers are looking for what most good thinkers are looking for: *both* simplicity and complexity. They'll mark you down if it's merely simple, and they'll mark you down if it's complex but confusing.

Harnessing the best leverage of an outline. Given the time limits of an exam, perhaps you should settle for the quickest and easiest kind of outline: just single words or phrases. Here's an example for part of an essay about speech and writing:

- speech/writing
    - audience
        - speech audience
        - writing audience
    - effects

This is fine if you are pretty confident about your line of thinking. But if your topic is complicated and difficult, this kind of outline lacks leverage because it contains only single words and short phrases. It doesn't *spell out* your thinking and therefore can lead you into tangles.

Therefore, if your topic is hard, try for a more explicit outline by forcing yourself to write actual sentences rather than just single words or short phrases. Simple sentences are fine, better, really, and it's OK to skip some words. But make each sentence *say* something or do work—not just *point* in a direction. Your goal is not an abstract, static structure, but a *story of thinking*—thinking that *moves* your reader on a path from the question to your conclusions. Notice how the following outline will help your thinking and writing better than the previous one:

- I'll compare speech and writing.
- Audience is a big factor.
- In speaking, audience is live in front of us (usually).
- In writing, audience is usually absent.
- Therefore in speaking we usually feel the audience more. We usually fit words to them better.
- In writing we often don't feel the audience and don't fit words to them or forget about their point of view.

Some people don't think you can have an outline unless there is hierarchical indenting. But the point here is to make your list of sentences tell a story of thinking that works *without* the aid of indenting.

Sentences help you *feel* the logic and movement of your train of thought.

By the way, as you write any outline, leave a bit of space between items—so that you can add points later as you find the need.

Step Three: Writing out Your Essay

If you are writing by hand, write on every other line so that you can come back and make additions or corrections. Don't worry about using up a lot of paper. Writing on alternate lines is also easier for teachers to read—which is an important factor.

Even though this is more or less one-draft writing and you can't freewrite garbage, don't agonize over small details of wording. The best method is to get yourself to *talk* onto the page rather than trying to *construct* grammatical sentences. This talking will lead to some informality in your wording, but that's perfectly acceptable on exams. And don't spend much time thinking about spelling either. Just make sure you save some time at the end to go back over what you've written and make a few corrections in mechanics.

Follow your outline and make sure to give your readers lots of signposts to identify your structure. (Here are some examples of the kinds of sentences or phrases that help save readers from getting lost: "In this essay I will be making one main argument, but to back it up, I need to consider two side issues." "My first point is this." "My last point might seem surprising but it is as follows." "I want to show a conflict between two ideas that many people think are in agreement.") Don't run away from blunt, even clumsy phrasings that spell out what you are doing. ("First I will. . . . Now I will. . . . My main point is. . . ." Try to help readers feel the logic of your train of thinking with signpost words like "in addition," "moreover," "however," "on the other hand," and "you might think so-and-so, but really, it's thus-and-such."

Writing When You Can't Think Straight

We often have to write a paper even though something in our life has derailed us: Someone we care about is ill or has jilted us; we are seething with hurt or anger. There are many situations that can short-circuit our brain.

The most obvious solution is to put the writing task aside for a while and let the circuits reestablish themselves—to allow the mind to heal. Take a hike and let a day or two pass. But if there's not much time, the most curative activity is to get a trusted friend to listen while we talk about everything that has upset us. Make it clear that his or her job is to listen supportively and just remember that deep down we are smart and strong—and *not* to try to think of answers or cures for our problem. If we speak and our friend listens supportively, we can usually find the perspective we need to put aside our upset for a while. Indeed, if someone listens to us well, we can often see how to deal with what's upsetting us. If such a friend is not available, we can *create* a friend out of blank paper. We can simply freewrite about what has upset us. Spill our feelings on paper. This too will usually help us to clear our minds and feelings and to feel fresh again. (Don't be surprised if tears come. They help.)

But what if the paper is due tomorrow morning and it's 1:30 A.M. now and no friends are awake to listen to you spout off and you've tried freewriting for two 15-minute sessions—and you still can't think straight? The problem is that your upset is causing your mind to lose its normal ability to hold on to more than one thought at a time. When you try to think two thoughts or think about a connection between two or three ideas—especially if you try to create a train of thought—your mind shuts down. This happens to all of us. See if it helps to follow these steps:

1. The best help for writing under these conditions comes from the two-step outline. Start with the "pre-outline grab bag" process (see p. A-2) and write down every point that you can think of that pertains to your topic. Don't write them on a piece of paper. Instead get a pile of cards (or cut up regular paper into card-size slips) and write each point on a separate card or slip of paper. Write them as they come to you—in any order. That way, you only have to think one thought at a time. But try to make each one a little sentence, not just a word or phrase.

2. After you've written out this pile of thoughts, lay out the slips around you and begin to group them together according to your feeling of which ones sort of go together. In effect, you are now moving gradually into the second step of creating an outline.

3. Next, choose one clump of cards or slips of paper—perhaps the clump that appeals to you most—and gradually coax your mind into figuring out why this group goes together. In effect, you are now trying to feel the larger idea in each clump. Write it out (if you have not already done so) on one of the cards. Do this for all your clumps.

4. Next, try to work toward a sequence. Try to feel which clumps or main ideas go before or after the others. Again, remember you aren't doing geometry or algebra, you are trying to tell a story— a story of thinking.

5. As you are working out a sequence and a story, figure out your main, overall point. Make sure to write that out too on a slip or card. Once you've written out a one-sentence main point, look back at your sequence or story and make sure it fits your main point. You may make changes in the sequence of your cards or slips of paper, but remember: *You're not aiming for perfection.* Given your fragile state of mind, you are trying to *get by* with something acceptable or decent.

Notice the process you have been using. You are upset and your mind cannot hold onto more than one idea at a time or think about relationships among ideas. Therefore, you give your mind a break by using a simple calculating machine that consists of movable slips of paper. Throughout the process, your mind never has to deal with more than one thought.

Now you know pretty much what you are going to say and pretty much the order for saying it. You are in a position to start writing your draft. See if you can take some time away from your paper at this point to clear your head before you try to write out a draft. Even a half hour can help.

Writing out a Draft.   Even though you are probably feeling much better now, you may well find it difficult to write clear, well-constructed sentences. Give yourself permission to write ugly, ungainly, absurd, broken *non*-sentences. The goal is to get your thoughts into *sort-of-prose.* It's fine to use sentences like these: "I'm not sure, but it seems like. . . ." "Here's something that I want to say: . . . ," "The thing of it is. . . ." Try to *talk* your thinking onto paper; the more you can talk it, the easier time you'll have.

As you are writing, don't get stopped or tangled trying to fix sentences or stymied by fussing over a grammar or usage problem. Keep slogging forward. Keep following your outline and writing out your thinking. It will probably get better.

Again, clear your head with a short break that will distance you a bit from your language and help you examine it with more perspective. After you have a draft of the whole thing, you'll be surprised how easy it is to go back through it to clarify and clean up the language. Your best tool is your voice, using your actual mouth and throat. Force yourself to speak every phrase and sentence aloud. As you do so, you'll find it easy and natural to change words and phrases so that they fit more comfortably in your mouth. Keep in mind that there is usually no need for complete rephrasing or rewriting: The sentence often becomes strong and comfortable if you just omit many of the words you used earlier as you were fighting to produce sort-of-prose.

You might find it helpful to take another tiny break so you can come back and check the spelling, punctuation, and grammar with fresher eyes.

Exercise: Practice Now for Future Struggle

You'll find it easier to use these techniques under exam conditions or when you are upset and anxious if you try them out now under safer conditions. You need to get the feel of them. Try following the steps we have proposed, but if it helps you to make some adjustments, that's fine. Your goal should be to mold *our* processes to *your* needs.

Set yourself a deadline of a half hour or one hour to write a practice essay exam. Choose a topic where you'll have to struggle a bit to figure out what you want to say. That is, choose a topic that forces you to use the two-step outine process. See if you can find a topic that is both meaty and difficult for you—choose a topic about which you don't yet know your thinking so that you will have to fight your way to a new train of thought. Perhaps your textbook lists questions at the ends of units. Here are a few topics we can suggest:

- Think of two or three different courses, subjects, or disciplines that interest you. Perhaps they are possible majors for you. Compare and contrast the ways of thinking, the assumptions, and the values in these fields.
- Discuss the advantages and disadvantages of traditional gender-role upbringing for men and women doing careers in science.
- Describe an opinion, attitude, or point of view that seems highly valued in our culture—and one about which you have divided feelings. You see the value in it, yet it bothers you. Write an essay in which you try to clarify your thinking on this matter.
- In comparing humans to (other) animals, what is more important—the ways they differ or the ways they are the same or similar?

Index